# Foreword

The revised edition of the Outboard Motors and Boating brings up-to-date the many details important to safe and enjoyable boating including motor construction, operation, maintenance and basic safety factors. Other important features include rules and regulations while on the water.

The recreational and practical boatman as well as the mechanic and serviceman will find that careful consideration has been given to all engine adjustments and service operations including maintenance and repairs essential to successful outboard boating.

Day-to-day, do-it-yourself maintenance will help keep your outboard motor operating year after year. This consists merely of making sure the motor is getting the correct fuel/oil mixture, keeping the engine clean, and pulling weeds off the propeller. Every once in a while it's a good idea to clean the fuel filter, check the spark plugs, and make sure the propeller is not too chipped or bent. The more complex service problems are explained step-by-step.

Throughout the book, functions of the various engine parts and auxiliaries, such as carburetor, ignition, cooling system, etc., are explained and illustrated in order to give a better understanding as to why and when certain repairs and servicing must be made.

The service chapters give the mechanic and serviceman full information on the proper procedure in making major repairs of all kinds. A glossary of nautical terms is also included, presenting the reader with a set of new terms and phrases to back up his practical knowledge gained by the reading of the book.

# Contents

# Chapter 1

# Outboard Motor Installation

Ideal outboard motor boat performance depends primarily on an evenly matched boat and motor. So often the motor itself is blamed for inefficient operation when actually it is the boat or installation of the motor on the boat. If the motor is too small for the boat, the speed will be slow and sluggish. If the motor is too large, the boat will be overpowered, hard to handle, and prone to swamp and upset. Boat manufacturers specify the maximum horsepower that is safe for a particular boat.

There are several ways which horsepower versus boat size may be calculated. In general, however, boat manufacturers follow the *Outboard Boating Club of America* recommendation. These recommendations taken from their Standards Manual (1961 Edition) are as follows:

## DETERMINING MAXIMUM HORSEPOWER

*Step 1.* Multiply overall boat length by overall stern width. (Overall stern width is defined as the widest part of the stern. Overall boat length is defined as hull length in feet and inches as measured from the stem face to transom output, the highest point on a straight line parallel to the keel, excluding any extending structures such as outboard brackets, fins, etc.)

*Step 2.* On the horizontal axis of the Boat Horsepower Curve, Fig. 1, locate the point that corresponds to the product arrived

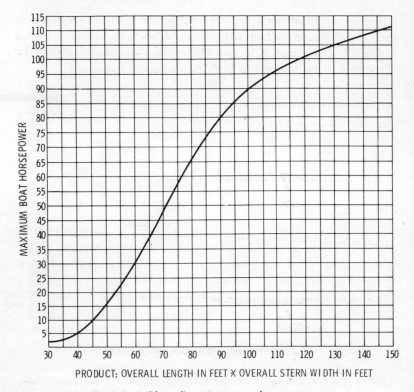

**Fig. 1. Typical boat dimensions *versus* horsepower curve.**

at in Step. 1. Follow the vertical line up to where it meets the curve. Read across the vertical axis to find the equivalent point on the axis. Then take the printed number immediately above this point as the maximum horsepower for the boat. Example: If the point on the vertical axis is 32, the printed number immediately above is 35.

As mentioned before, poor performance, although thought to be caused by the motor, has actually been traced to the boat, hence, it is advisable to first check the boat for the following conditions:

*Condition of hull*—Straight line boat bottoms are the fastest and most efficient. Numerous boats are not perfectly true but have a built-in curve or hook just forward of the transom. A curve in the hull will cause the boat to plow, and a hook, or rocker as shown in Fig. 2. will cause it to porpoise. These conditions should be eliminated if the motor and boat are to function properly.

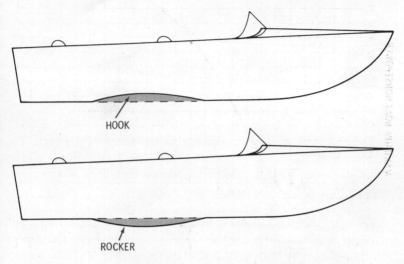

HOOK

ROCKER

**Fig. 2. Deformations that cause poor performance.**

*Hull finish*—A rough hull finish will create excessive drag resulting in loss of speed and power. For best performance the hull should be smooth. Moss, barnacles, or other surface irregularities that increase skin friction of the boat bottom will cause considerable loss of boat speed.

*Keel*—For best performance the boat keel should be tapered slightly, bringing each side back to a feather edge, starting approximately 12 to 18 inches from the stern. This keel construction avoids possible turbulence. Also, to eliminate undesirable rooster tails, the stern of the keel should be cut off at an angle of 15 degrees as indicated in Fig. 3.

*Weight distribution*—Some boats are so sensitive to weight distribution that with motors of medium power, a weight must be shifted forward to make the boat plane on top of the water; in others, weight must be shifted aft.

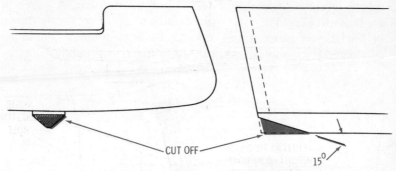

**Fig. 3. Method of keel trimming for best performance.**

The center of gravity location affects the speed of the boat. For maximum speed, move weight back until the boat propoises or is about to propoise. This reduces the wetted surface to a minimum, only the rear half of the boat bottom being wet.

*Transom heights*—Proper transom height is important. The transom height is taken as the vertical distance from the top of the transom to the bottom or keel of the boat (Fig. 4). The correct recommended transom height in most instances is 15 inches from the transom on which the motor is mounted to the bottom of the stern boat keel. A 20-inch transom is required for motors of large horsepower ratings. Fig. 5 illustrates the recommended transom heights for cruiser and runabout installation.

A greater transom height will increase boat speed but will make cavitation, or hollow pocketing. The effect of transom height on speed is slight at low speeds (15-20 mph) but important at speeds of 30-35 mph and above. If the transom is too low, it may be possible to build it up to the proper height. If it is too high, it may be desirable to notch in the top of the transom to the depth necessary to accommodate the motor. Turbulent water caused by a square end keel may also cause cavitation and should be taken into consideration when mounting the engine.

*Transom angle*—The transom or tilt angle should be such that, when operating the boat, the engine is vertical with the water surface. When this condition is obtained, the line of propeller thrust

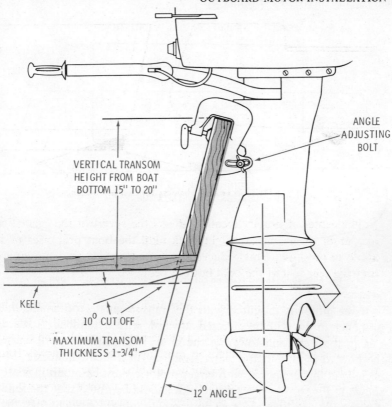

ANGLE
ADJUSTING
BOLT

VERTICAL TRANSOM
HEIGHT FROM BOAT
BOTTOM 15" TO 20"

KEEL

10° CUT OFF

MAXIMUM TRANSOM
THICKNESS 1-3/4"

12° ANGLE

**Fig. 4. Typical outboard motor installation giving approximate transom dimensions and other data.**

will be parallel to the boat line of travel. Outboard motors are generally provided with a special tilt-pin and adjustable clamp bracket which will permit adjustment of the tilt angle in relation to the boat transom.

The average boat transom angle is approximately 12 degrees. Greater transom angle can be compensated for by adjusting the clamp bracket. A boat with a straight transom or a motor mounted with too great an angle between stern and motor will result in a downward thrust of the propeller causing the stern of the boat to dig in and the *bow* to *rear up*. This condition will result in squatting of the boat, pushing the water before it, rather than gliding over the water surface.

13

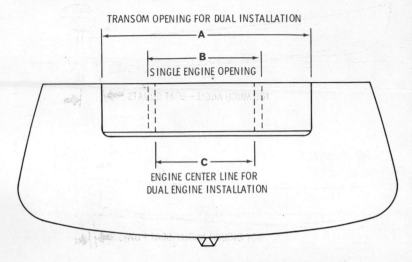

**Fig. 5. Recommended transom for cruiser and runabout installation.**

If the motor is mounted with the transom angle too small, the propeller thrust will be directed upward, with a tendency toward raising the stern and lowering the bow. This condition will cause the bow to plow into the water, resulting in difficult handling, especially at higher speeds with larger motors. Various mountings are shown in Fig. 6. In this connection it should be noted that the load distribution (passengers and equipment) must be such that the boat will remain properly trimmed, and the angle of the motor adjusted for best performance.

*Mounting motor on boat*—Installation of the motor on the transom should be given very careful attention. The clamp bracket must not only support the weight of the motor, but is also subject to thrust loads, shock loads, and steering stresses. These forces are applied directly to the transom through the clamp-bracket assembly.

To avoid damage to the transom and to prevent the motor from working loose due to vibration, it is important that the clamp screws are securely and evenly tightened. During operation, the clamp screws should be checked occasionally for tightness. The transom thickness may vary according to the size of the motor and

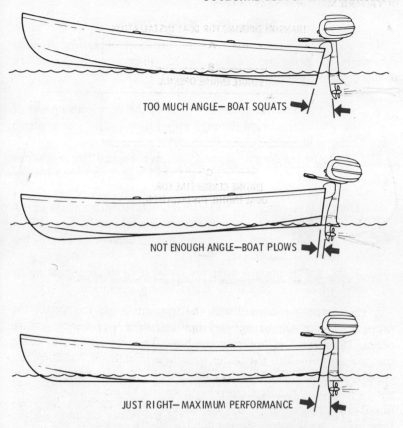

TOO MUCH ANGLE—BOAT SQUATS

NOT ENOUGH ANGLE—BOAT PLOWS

JUST RIGHT—MAXIMUM PERFORMANCE

**Fig. 6. Showing effect of transom or tilt angle.**

hull. In some cases, the transom may be too thick to accommodate the motor clamp. This condition will require notching out to suit the clamp.

## SAFETY CHAIN

For additional security in outboard boating, a safety cable or chain (usually furnished with the motor) should be connected between the boat and clamp bracket or safety clip to prevent the loss of the motor if the motor clamp should accidentally work loose during operation.

15

## BREAKING IN MOTOR

To break-in a new motor is not a difficult operation. Special consideration during the break-in period will prevent the possibility of motor damage. Observe the following:

1.  Never operate the motor dry or with the gear housing out of the water, or severe damage may result in the water pump and power head.
2.  After the motor is started, do not exceed three-quarter throttle for one hour, and avoid sustained high speed for the next four hours.
3.  Do not use more than the recommended proportion of oil in the fuel mixture, because too much oil can be harmful.
4.  Do not add "break-in" compounds to the fuel mixture, because these too can be harmful.
5.  If the engine should suddenly show signs of over-heating or loss of power, check the water pump operation.

## REMOVING MOTOR FROM BOAT

When removing the motor, it is necessary to first disconnect the fuel line and run the motor in neutral gear at idle speed until the excess fuel is removed from the carburetor. Disconnect the remote control, electrical cable, and safety chain from the motor. Loosen the thumbscrews and tilt the motor to drain off the water, then lift the motor vertically from the transom of the boat.

The drain-holes provided in the lower unit will allow water to drain out of the motor when it is held for a few minutes in a vertical position. When laying the motor down, always make sure that the cylinders are higher than the lower unit to prevent any possibility of water seeping into the cylinder-block assembly.

## MOTOR STORAGE

Motors which are to be stored must be serviced to prevent damage from moisture and dust. If the motor has been operating in salt water, the cooling system should be thoroughly flushed with fresh water.

All fuel should be drained from the tank and carburetor. Remove each spark plug and put two teaspoonfuls of oil (same as used in the fuel mixture) into the cylinder. Remove the flywheel and spray oil over the cylinder walls. If the spark plugs are cracked, broken, or badly burned, they should be replaced.

Drain the gear housing and refill with the proper type of lubricant. Wipe the entire exterior of the motor with a cloth saturated with oil to form an exterior oil film. Upon completion of the foregoing operations, completely wrap the motor in a piece of canvas or heavy waterproof paper and store in an upright position in a dry place. The preferable way of storing motors is to set them on wooden racks with the hand clamps tightened sufficiently to prevent movement.

## PREPARING MOTOR FOR SERVICE

To prepare a motor for service after storage, clean all oil accumulation from the outside and wipe the engine clean with a dry rag. Remove the motor covers and inspect carefully. Check the gears, propeller shaft, and bearings to see that they are all in good condition. Check the gear housing and refill, if necessary, with an approved lubricant.

Remove the flywheel cover plate and clean and adjust the magneto contact points. Clean the fuel filter. Clean out the fuel tank, fuel feed-line, and carburetor. Particular attention should again be paid to the spark plugs for chipped or broken porcelain. Check spark-plug gap and reset to .025 in. clearance. Carefully check all parts of the motor for damage or loose parts. Replace or tighten as required.

## CARE OF SUBMERGED MOTORS

A motor that has been submerged must be serviced immediately in order to prevent damage. To prevent submergence, or loss of motor, always use a safety-chain between boat and motor.

To get the motor in operating condition, it is necessary to drain and clean the fuel tank. The carburetor, fuel lines, and spark plugs should be removed and thoroughly cleaned.

To remove water from the cylinders and crankcase, revolve the flywheel slowly, with the carburetor open and crankcase down. The spark may be checked by grounding one wire from the magneto to some part of motor, then holding the remaining wire about 1/8 of an inch from the cylinder, pull the flywheel over rapidly with the starter handle. Continue the foregoing procedure until all wires have been checked.

If, when testing for spark according to the foregoing, no spark or only a weak spark is obtained, it is an indication that the magneto armature and other parts are water soaked. Remove the magneto and thoroughly clean and dry. Clean and adjust the breaker points. If, after further tests, no spark is obtained, the magneto should be removed to a service shop for part replacement if necessary. With the spark plugs removed, pour a small amount of oil into each cylinder, and turn the crankshaft several times to obtain complete distribution. After replacement of all parts that were removed, and a check for loose parts, fill the gas tank with a new fuel mixture and proceed to start the motor.

## COLD WEATHER CARE

When operating outboards during cold weather seasons, extra care of the motor is necessary. If, during freezing weather, water is permitted to freeze in the motor, it usually results in cracked cylinders and water jackets.

There is no danger to the motor during operation, but when the motor is stored away during cold weather, all water must be removed from it by setting the motor in an upright position while removing the water flush plug. Put the speed control at stop and pull the starter cord several times to pump out all remaining water. If there is any indication of water in the gear case, drain and refill with an approved lubricant.

## SALT WATER OPERATION

Operation in salt water results in the accumulation of salt or mineral deposits in the cooling system water passages and around the cylinder water jackets.

Unless removed regularly, deposits will build up to the extent that the cooling water circulation will be restricted or cut off entirely. These deposits, in addition, act as a heat insulator which will reduce the transfer of heat from the motor cylinders to the cooling water, resulting in overheating and inefficiency, which, if not checked, may result in serious motor damage.

In this connection it should be noted that, while most motors are treated by the manufacturers to resist salt-water corrosion, there always remains a possibility of salt and silt deposits buildup which can be eliminated by occasional fresh-water flushing.

When operating in salt water, therefore, do not allow the motor to stand in water when not in use. Thoroughly flush the motor externally with fresh water to remove salt deposits. Flush the cooling system by operating the motor for a couple of minutes in a barrel of fresh water, being careful not to race the motor while in the barrel or tank.

The motor may also be flushed out by using a flushing nozzle as shown in Fig. 7. This will effectively remove accumulated deposits in the cooling system. After the foregoing operations, wipe off the motor with a slightly oily rag. The lower gear case should be checked after each day's use to ascertain that it is filled with grease and does not contain any salt water. Electric starting engines should have their negative battery terminal disconnected when in dock or storage for any considerable length of time to prevent damage by electrolysis.

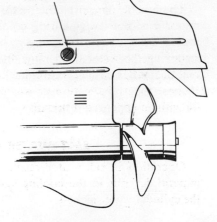

FLUSH PLUG

Fig. 7. A plug in the gear housing is removed to allow insertion of the spray nozzle.

## Fouling

A smooth surfaced boat bottom is necessary in order to prevent overworking the outboard or inboard-outboard motor. This is not an easy task when the boat sits in salt water for any period of time. There are certain organisms which attach themselves to the bottom surfaces of a boat. They are located mostly in warmer waters with high salt content. These organisms are called a number of names—barnacles, weed, grass, shipworms, gribbles, putty bugs, etc.

Probably the most unpopular type of fouling is the barnacle. When it attaches to the hull of a boat, its hard, conical shell disrupts the streamlining to such an extent that a fairly large attachment can greatly increase the fuel consumption and reduce the maximum speed far below its normal rate.

When barnacles and other fouling animals are first born they are called larvae. Barnacle larvae go through two development stages before becoming adults. During this time they are able to swim for short distances, and do so for several days, toward the end of which time they search for suitable surfaces on which to land.

When a young barnacle finds a good surface, it crawls around over a small area for about ten minutes, searching for a choice location. It then anchors firmly, using a cement on its two front "legs," and slowly begins to form its familiar conical shell. Fig. 8A, B, and C.

The barnacle is most susceptible to the poisons in antifouling paints during the short period just before it anchors to the surface, because it is then still able to detach itself and swim away to find a better surface. Once it has firmly attached and begins to build its shell, the barnacle can no longer swim and *has* to stay attached to the surface.

Algae is usually referred to as "grass" or weed. Algae is as troublesome as barnacles in some areas. Their long leaves, strands or filaments resist the flow of water past the hull. The seeds of algae are called spores. They drift through the water with the currents in much the same manner as land plant seeds are carried by the wind. Some kinds of spore, however, have "tails" which

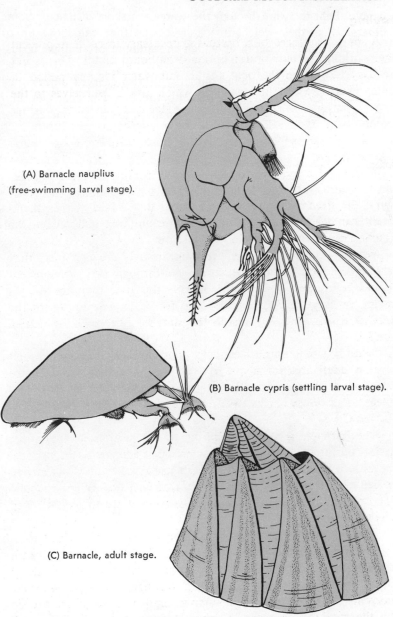

(A) Barnacle nauplius
(free-swimming larval stage).

(B) Barnacle cypris (settling larval stage).

(C) Barnacle, adult stage.

**Fig. 8. Various stages of barnacles.**

enable them to swim through the water for short distances. Some others adjust their weight in water so that they can move up or down and find the depth at which the amount of sunlight is just right for them.

When the spores come in contact with a submerged object, they adhere to the surface and grow into the familiar fronds or filaments. Many of the algae need small amounts of metals like

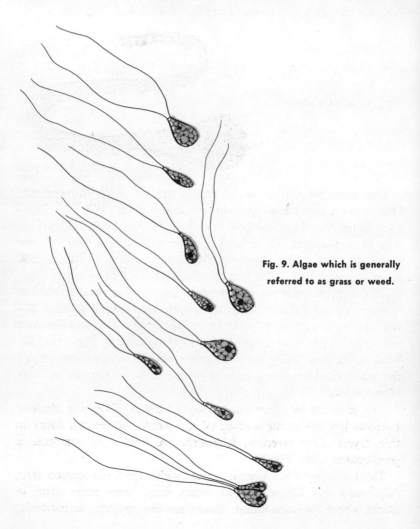

Fig. 9. Algae which is generally referred to as grass or weed.

copper to help them grow. In order to kill algae it is necessary to feed them large quantities of copper, for very small amounts may even cause them to flourish. Fig. 9.

Other types of fouling organisms are bryozoans, which are thin encrustations or small tufts of animal life, oysters, annelids (tube-worms) and hydroids. These foul a boat bottom by much the same means as a barnacle, settling as larvae and growing into the irregular shapes which cause increased hull friction. Fig. 10.

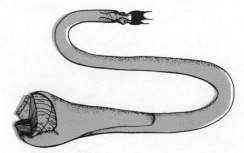

Fig. 10. An adult shipworm.

The principal marine wood borers are teredids (shipworms). Others are Limnoria. Shipworm larvae are about .001″ in diameter. When they begin to bore, the hole they make in the surface is only a pinpoint. Once they get beneath the surface of the wood, however, they grow rapidly and dig burrows which may be as much as half an inch in diameter and a foot or more long. In this way, the interior structure of the wood is weakened, but damage is very difficult to detect on the surface. Shipworm larvae cannot penetrate a good paint film, but can gain entrance where paint has been scraped or has sloughed off. They are difficult to destroy. They are sometimes able to survive even when the wood they are living in is kept out of the water for as long as two weeks.

The presence of Limnoria is easy to detect. They dig shallow burrows just below the surface of the wood and wear it away in thin layers. Like teredids, Limnoria are unable to penetrate a good coat of paint. Fig. 11.

There are two other marine borers which are less common than shipworms and Limnoria, but which cause even more grief in places where they are found. These are the pholads, or martesia,

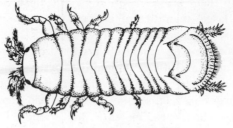

Fig. 11. The Lunnaria or Gribble.

and Sphaeroma, or the putty bug. Martesia look a little like a small clam. The hole it can put in your boat will usually look as if it were done with a drill. The putty bug gets its common name from the fact that it usually finds its way into the boat bottom through the paint cracks over the seams. Once it eats its way through the soft (and sometimes even nutritious) seam compound, it has no trouble entering the planking through the unpainted portions under the seams. Fig. 12.

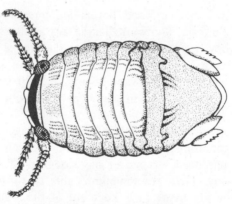

Fig. 12. The Sphaeroma or Putty Bug.

## Preventing Fouling

Paints have been developed for the prevention of fouling. Most of them contain copper which is leached at a given rate. Even fibreglass boats must be painted to prevent fouling. The thickness of the film of paint determines how long it will last. The paint lasts about 10 months for every 1 mil (.001″) of thickness. Some

## Table 1. Guide to Fouling on East and West Coasts

Compiled from charts in "Marine Fouling and Its Prevention" by Woods Hole Institute (1952) by Stanley Glass-Mary Stewart-Marine Lab. University of Miami

| Location | Jan. | Feb. | March | April | May | June | July | Aug. | Sept. | Oct. | Nov. | Dec. |
|---|---|---|---|---|---|---|---|---|---|---|---|---|
| Lamoine, MAINE | | | | | hyd<br>½ barn<br>½ gr. al | hyd<br>e. b<br>BARN<br>gr. al<br>t. w | hyd<br>e. b<br>mus<br>BARN<br>½ gr. al<br>t. w | hyd<br>e. b<br>mus<br>BARN<br>T. W | hyd<br>e. b<br>mus<br>½ barn<br>t. w | hyd.<br>e. b | | |
| Woods Hole, MASSACHUSETTS | al<br>bryo | bryo<br>barn | BRY<br>barn | BRY<br>barn | bry<br>½ bar<br>½ tun | al<br>bry<br>½ bar<br>tun<br>bug | al<br>bry<br>BARN<br>tun<br>bug | al<br>bry<br>barn<br>tun<br>bug | al<br>bry<br>barn<br>tun<br>bug | barn<br>tun<br>bug | ½ bug | |
| Norfolk, VIRGINIA | barn | | | barn | barn<br>al | barn<br>al<br>tun<br>t. w | barn<br>tun<br>t. w | barn<br>al<br>tun<br>t. w<br>hyd | barn<br>tun<br>t. w | barn<br>tun<br>t. w | barn | |
| Beaufort, NORTH CAROLINA | hyd<br>tun<br>barn | tun<br>barn | | hyd<br>½ bug<br>barn | hyd<br>BUG<br>BRY<br>tun<br>barn | hyd<br>SP<br>BUG<br>BRY<br>tun<br>oy<br>BARN | HYD<br>½ SP<br>BUG<br>bry<br>tun<br>oy<br>BARN | HYD<br>½ sp<br>BUG<br>bry<br>tun<br>oy<br>BARN | hyd<br>sp<br>BUG<br>BRY<br>tun<br>oy<br>barn | hyd<br>bug<br>BRY<br>tun<br>oy<br>barn | HYD<br>bug<br>bry<br>tun<br>barn | HYD<br>bug<br>tun<br>½ barn |
| Kure Beach, NORTH CAROLINA | | barn | tun<br>barn | tun<br>barn | tun<br>barn<br>hyd | tun<br>BARN<br>hyd<br>bug | TUN<br>BARN<br>hyd<br>BUG | tun<br>BARN<br>HYD<br>BUG<br>an | tun<br>BARN<br>hyd<br>bug<br>an | barn<br>hyd<br>bug<br>an | barn<br>hyd<br>bug | barn<br>hyd |

## Table 1. Guide to Fouling on East and West Coasts (Cont'd)

Compiled from charts in "Marine Fouling and Its Prevention" by Woods Hole Institute (1952) by Stanley Glass-Mary Stewart-Marine Lab. University of Miami

| Location | Jan. | Feb. | March | April | May | June | July | Aug. | Sept. | Oct. | Nov. | Dec. |
|---|---|---|---|---|---|---|---|---|---|---|---|---|
| Daytona, FLORIDA | al<br>hyd<br>mol<br>barn | al<br>hyd<br>barn | al<br>hyd<br>barn<br>bry<br>tun<br>t.w | al<br>hyd<br>mol<br>barn<br>BRY<br>tun | al<br>hyd<br>MOL<br>barn<br>BRY<br>T.W | al<br>mol<br>barn<br>BRY<br>T.W | ½ al<br>hyd<br>barn<br>BRY<br>T.W | barn<br>BRY<br>T.W | al<br>hyd<br>barn<br>BRY<br>T.W | al<br>hyd<br>barn<br>BRY | al<br>hyd<br>barn<br>BRY | al<br>hyd<br>barn<br>BRY<br>t.w |
| Miami, FLORIDA | al<br>hyd<br>BUG<br>E.B<br>tun<br>t.w<br>barn | al<br>hyd<br>BUG<br>E.B.<br>tun<br>BARN | al<br>hyd<br>BUG<br>E.B<br>tun<br>t.w<br>BARN | AL<br>hyd<br>BUG<br>E.B<br>tun<br>T.W<br>BARN | AL<br>HYD<br>BUG<br>e.b<br>TUN<br>T.W<br>barn<br>an | AL<br>HYD<br>e.b<br>TUN<br>t.w<br>barn | HYD<br>TUN<br>t.w<br>barn | HYD<br>TUN<br>t.w<br>barn | HYD<br>e.b<br>TUN<br>t.w<br>BARN | HYD<br>e.b<br>tun<br>t.w<br>BARN | HYD<br>BUG<br>e.b<br>tun<br>T.W<br>barn<br>an | hyd<br>BUG<br>E.B<br>tun<br>t.w<br>barn |
| Pensacola, FLORIDA | bug<br>barn | barn | | barn | bug<br>barn<br>bry | bug<br>barn<br>bry | bug<br>barn<br>bry<br>al | barn<br>bry<br>al | barn<br>bry | barn<br>bry | bug<br>barn<br>bry | buug<br>barn<br>bry |
| Friday Harbor, PUGET SOUND, WASHINGTON | bry<br><br>t.w | bry<br><br>t.w | bry<br><br>t.w | t.w | barn<br>t.w | bry<br>barn<br>T.W | bry<br>BARN<br>bug<br>T.W | bry<br>BARN<br>BUG<br>t.w | bry<br>BARN<br>BUG<br>mol<br>hyd<br>t.w | mol<br>hyd<br>t.w | hyd<br>t.w | hyd<br>bry<br>t.w |

## Table 1. Guide to Fouling on East and West Coasts (Cont'd)

Compiled from charts in "Marine Fouling and Its Prevention" by Woods Hole Institute (1952) by Stanley Glass-Mary Stewart-Marine Lab. University of Miami

| Location | Jan. | Feb. | March | April | May | June | July | Aug. | Sept. | Oct. | Nov. | Dec. |
|---|---|---|---|---|---|---|---|---|---|---|---|---|
| Oakland, CALIFORNIA | al | al | al | al | al | al | al | al | al | al | al | al |
| | | | t.w | t.w | t.w | T.W | T.W | t.w | t.w | t.w | t.w | |
| | | | mus | mus | mus | | | | | | | |
| | | | barn | barn | BARN | | | | | | | |
| La Jolla, CALIFORNIA | al | al | al | al | al | al | al | al | al | al | al | al |
| | HYD | hyd | hyd | HYD | HYD | hyd | hyd | hyd | hyd | HYD | HYD | HYD |
| | barn | | | barn | barn | barn | BARN | BARN | BARN | barn | barn | barn |
| | | | | bug | bug | bug | bug | bug | bug | bug | bug | bug |
| | | | | | oy | oy | oy | oy | oy | oy | oy | oy |
| | | | | | T.W | t.w | t.w | t.w | t.w | t.w | t.w | t.w |
| San Diego, CALIFORNIA | BR. AL | BR. AL | BR. AL | BR. AL | BR. AL | br. al | br. al | br. al | br. al | | br. al | br. al |
| | T.W | T.W | T.W | T.W | t.w | t.w | t.w | t.w | t.w | T.W | T.W | T.W |
| | bug | bug | BUG | BUG | BUG | BUG | BUG | BUG | bug | bug | bug | bug |
| | tun | tun | tun | tun | tun | TUN | TUN | TUN | tun | tun | TUN | tun |
| | barn | barn | BARN | BARN | BARN | BARN | BARN | barn | barn | barn | barn | barn |

### KEY TO ABBREVIATIONS

| | | | |
|---|---|---|---|
| 1/2 —One half month | br —brown | gr —green | oy —oysters |
| al —algae | bry —bryozoans | hyd —hydroids | s. p —sponges |
| an —Anomia | bug —bugula | mol —mollusks | t. w —tubeworms |
| barn —barnacles | e. b —encrusting bryozoans | mus —mussels | tun —tunicates |

CAPITAL LETTERS INDICATE PEAK PERIODS — MONTHS OF HEAVIEST FOULING.

(Courtesy of Dolphin Paint and Chemical Company)

of the paints are 2 mils thick when applied and others are 1 mil thick.

To give you protection from fouling, a paint film should be established at about 3 to 4 mils. This can be maintained by applying only the amount of paint that will be used up between haul outs. Further control of application thickness and working properties can be obtained by mixing paints at suggested ratios. The paint will dry in the water so it can be launched wet, or it can be applied to a boat going into dry storage and will be effective when the boat is launched at the owner convenience.

In order to see what type of fouling occurs, and where, Table 1. *Guide to Fouling on East and West Coasts* will help determine what your problems may be when using your boat in salt water.

Today's outboard motor is a complicated and precision piece of machinery. The days of the simple "only six movable parts" type of outboard are past. The present outboard motor is designed to serve a more knowledgeable, more demanding, a more boating-oriented public. Like any fine piece of machinery, your outboard motor requires servicing from time to time.

Courtesy Johnson Motors, Div. of Outboard Marine Corp.

The most powerful outboard motor, the 200 horsepower V-6, was recently introduced. The *little brother* of the 200 is the 175. The engine has a 149.4 cubic-inch
90-degree V-block powerhead. It has tuned exhaust, dual fuel pumps, three two-
barrel carburetors and *MagFlash* electronic ignition. It can be had in both 20 inch
or 25 inch shaft models.

Courtesy Johnson Motors, Div. of Outboard Marine Corp.

# Chapter 2

# Outboard Motor
# Starting and Operation

One of the disadvantages in the use of internal combustion engines is that an outside source of power must be supplied for cranking the engine in starting. Depending on the cranking arrangement, outboard motors may be started in one of the following ways:

1. Manually by pull-rope, or
2. Electrically from a push-button station.

Early starters for cranking outboard motors consisted of a simple pull-rope wound around a pulley on top of the motor. A quick pull on the rope cranked the engine several revolutions for starting.

## PREPARATION

Before an attempt at starting the motor is made, read the *operating instructions* usually supplied by the motor manufacturer. The following checks are common to most motors equipped for *manual starting:*

1. Check to be sure that the fuel tank is filled with a fresh clean mixture of oil and gasoline.
2. Check the starting controls, and be sure that the fuel shut-off valve is open, that the air vent screw is open, and that

the mixture setting is correct. The air vent must be *open* during operation and *closed* when the motor is not in use.

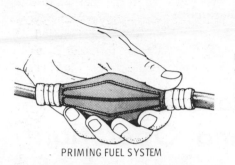

PRIMING FUEL SYSTEM

Fig. 1. The carburetor and fuel system are primed by squeezing the primer bulb on the fuel line. When fully primed, pressure will be felt on the primer bulb.

3. In motors equipped with a separate fuel tank, attach the hose to the motor and squeeze the primer tube bulb (shown in Fig. 1) several times, or until the primer becomes firm, to fill the carburetor.
4. Before starting, place the gearshift in neutral position, and the speed control at the start position (usually marked on the twist-grip handle shown in Fig. 2).

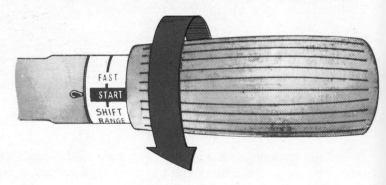

Fig. 2. The starting and speed control mechanism is usually regulated by a twist-grip handle.

5. Pull out the choke knob while starting. This should be done when the motor is hot as well as when it is cold.
6. To start the motor, pull the starter cord outward slowly until engagement of the ratchet mechanism is felt, then continue

outward with a vigorous full stroke. When the motor fires, release the choke knob and starter rewind mechanism shown in Fig. 3.

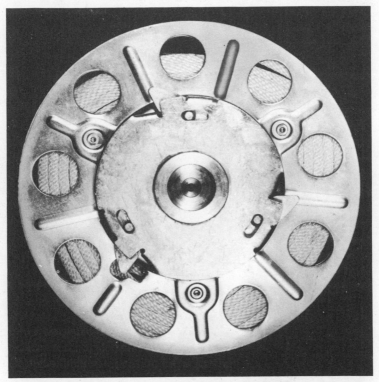

Courtesy Mercury Marine, Div. of Brunswick Corp.

**Fig. 3. The ratchet release mechanism is designed so that the starter cannot engage during rewind.**

7.  After the motor starts, allow it to warm up while in neutral. For a smooth running performance, it may be necessary to reset the carburetor knob slightly.

Motors equipped for electric starting are prepared for starting in the same way as are motors with the manual starting features, except that instead of pulling the starting cord, the choke and starting button are actuated simultaneously. For a full description of the electrical starting system, see Chapter 10.

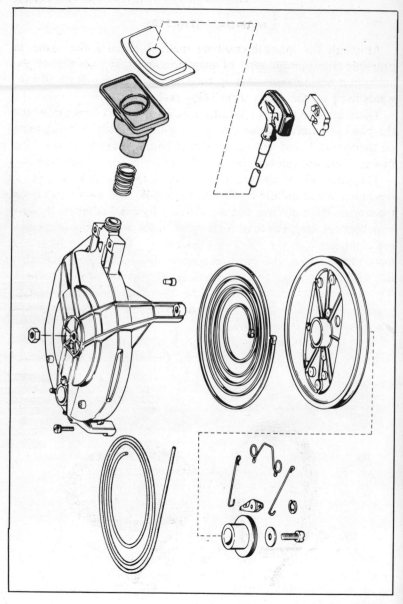

Courtesy Johnson Motors, Div. of Outboard Marine Corp.

**Fig. 4. Automatic rewind starter assembly.**

## MANUAL STARTERS

Although the manual cranking method remains the same in principle, the present type of manual starters are usually of the *automatic rewind type;* that is, the starting rope automatically rewinds itself on the pulley after being pulled.

There are two types of automatic rewind starters—one in which the pawl assembly is mounted on the pulley and the ratchet plate on the flywheel, and another in which the pawls are located on the flywheel and the ratchet plate on the pulley in the starter housing.

The principle of starting with either automatic rewind type is the same. When pulling on the starter handle, the starter pawls on the starter make positive contact with the flywheel adapter, thereby impelling the magneto to make a spark at the spark plug and causing combustion in the cylinder, thus starting the motor. After the motor has started, the pawls disengage the ratchet automatically due to the centrifugal force created by the rotation of the flywheel. The starter mechanism remains idle after the motor has started; thus, there is little wear on any of the parts and very little attention is required.

A typical outboard motor starter in which the starter pawl assembly is mounted on the pulley and the ratchet on the flywheel

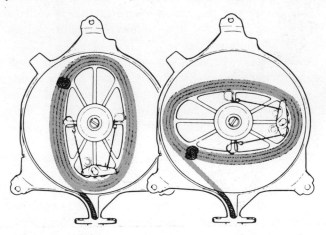

Fig. 5. Starting pulley arrangement design with an increased leverage obtained with an elliptically shaped pulley.

is shown in Fig. 4. As noted in the illustrations, the starter pawls are connected to the equalizer cup by springs. In operation, when the starting cord is pulled, the frictional drag on the cup will cause the pawls to extend, thus engaging the ratchet on the flywheel. When the motor has started, the ratchet teeth will slip past the spring-loaded pawls until the operator releases pressure on the starter cord, allowing the pawls to withdraw from the ratchet. When the cord is rewound on the pulley by spring action, the starter mechanism remains idle until another starting of the motor is required. The principle of operation for both types of starters is similar, the only difference being the location of the actuating assembly.

Another outboard motor starter operating on the same principles as the previously described automatic rewind type, but with provision for an extended leverage, is shown in Fig. 5. As noted, the starter pulley is oval in shape and is timed with the piston strokes so that during the compression stroke, less effort is needed to pull the motor through.

## MOTOR OPERATING PRINCIPLES

The basic operating principles of an outboard motor do not differ in any important respect from that of the conventional gasoline engine. Engines of this construction, alternately called motors, provide motive power for lawn mowers, tractors, chain saws, motorcycles, and automobiles.

In this connection it should be noted that gasoline engines, as a rule, are not interchangeable; that is, a lawn-mower engine would not be suitable to drive, for example, the propeller of an outboard installation. However, the method of operation and a majority of the component parts of each engine are similar, and may even be interchanged.

By definition, a gasoline engine is simply a heat-conversion machine in which the necessary pressure to produce motion of the mechanism results from the ignition or exploding of a fuel-air mixture within the engine cylinder. The fuel used in two-cycle outboard motors is normally unleaded gasoline intermixed with a small amount of oil. In a four-cycle engine, the lubricating oil is provided in the crankcase. This description makes a simple comparison between a two-cycle and a four-cycle gasoline engine to familiarize the individual who may not be acquainted with the principles of internal combustion engines.

There are two basic types of gasoline engines: (1) those operating on a four-stroke cycle (commonly known as a four-cycle engine), and, (2) those operating on a two-stroke cycle (commonly known as a two-cycle engine). The principal difference between the two types is that the four-cycle engine, even though only one cylinder, fires every other time the piston reaches the top of its travel or stroke (away from the center of the crankshaft). A four-cycle engine may be made up of more than one cylinder (generally 4, 6, or 8, as in automobiles). It also has individual inlet and exhaust valves for each cylinder.

## Two-Cycle Principle

By contrast, the piston in a two-cycle engine acts as both an inlet and exhaust valve, as shown in Fig. 6. In starting a two-cycle

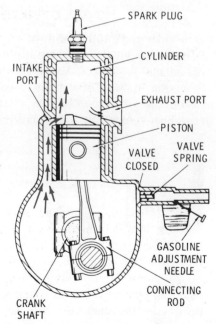

Fig. 6. Diagram illustrating the principal parts of a two-cycle gasoline engine.

37

engine, the crankshaft turns over and the piston rises, assuming that the cylinder is filled with a mixture of air and fuel which is compressed (squeezed into a small space). Then, at its high point of travel, BTDC (before top dead center), the compressed mixture is ignited by the spark from a spark plug.

The resulting explosion within the cylinder forces the piston down, exerting the working energy to the crankshaft. During its upward stroke, the piston has drawn a fresh charge of fuel and air through the intake valve (which is in the center main bearing) into the crankcase. This crankcase, which is airtight, contains the crankshaft and connecting rod. On the downward stroke, the charge of fuel and air previously drawn in is compressed and, when the piston reaches its maximum travel (bottom), an exhaust port is uncovered on the side of the cylinder wall through which the burned gases escape, and the pressure falls. An instant later, the momentum created uncovers an inlet port on the opposite side, and the fresh charge forces its way up from the crankcase and drives the remainder of the burned gases before it. A projection on the top of the piston, on the intake side, deflects the fresh charge and prevents it from passing directly across the cylinder and out the exhaust.

This heat-conversion engine is powered by a process based on a fundamental law of physics which states that gas will expand upon application of heat. If the gas is confined with no outlet for expansion, the pressure of the gas will increase when heat is applied. In this heat-conversion, or gasoline engine, this pressure acts against

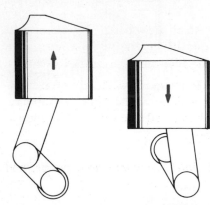

Fig. 7. Illustrating piston which converts straight line force into rotary motion through the action of a connecting rod.

the head of the piston, causing it to be pushed away from the combustion chamber. The piston is connected to a crankshaft by a connecting rod that converts this straight-line force into a rotary motion which supplies power to the crankshaft and propeller, as shown in Fig. 7.

A simple explanation of the physics of motion in an internal combustion engine may be had by observing the use of a brace and bit when drilling a hole. The arm and elbow move back and forth, but the hand goes around in circles. The elbow corresponds to the piston, the forearm would be the connecting rod, and the brace is like the throw of the crankshaft.

## The Charge

The air-fuel mixture introduced into the combustion chamber by the carburetor is admitted only intermittently, and the amount supplied is known as the *charge*. The combustion of each charge takes place under pressure attained by *compression* as a result of the upward movement of the piston after the charge is admitted and all valves closed.

## Effect of Ignition

The operation of igniting the gaseous mixture in the engine cylinder by means of a suitable device, such as a spark plug, is known as ignition. In order to complete combustion of the fuel mixture, heat is required, and this, although very small, is derived from the electric spark provided by the spark plug.

## The Cycle

The cycle is a series of events which are repeated in regular order and this constitutes the principle of internal-combustion engine operation. The cycle includes the following operational events:

1. The admission of a fuel-air charge into the cylinder.
2. Compression, followed by ignition of the explosive mixture.
3. Expansion of the ignited charge and absorption of its energy.
4. Expulsion of the burned gases.

These four events are called: *Intake, compression, power,* and *exhaust.*

39

In operation of a gasoline engine, the number of strokes required by the piston to complete the cycle varies with the type of engine. Thus, in a *two-stroke cycle engine,* the cycle of events are completed in two strokes of the piston. On such engines, each cylinder delivers a power stroke at every revolution of the crankshaft.

The *four-stroke cycle engine* differs from that of the *two-stroke cycle type,* mainly in that the cycle is extended through four strokes of the piston; that is, two upward and two downward. There is, therefore, only one power stroke for every other revolution of the crankshaft in the four-stroke cycle type. Another basic difference is that, while the four-stroke cycle engine carriers its lubricating oil in the crankcase and uses clear gasoline, the two-stroke cycle type uses oil mixed with gasoline for fuel and lubrication.

There are two types of two-stroke cycle outboard motors—the two-port and the three-port. It is generally understood that a two-port motor starts easier than a three-port, because the fuel-air mixture reaches the firing chamber faster. In the three-port motor, the crankcase compression is sealed and built up by means of the ports in the cylinders and pistons which coincide for intake at the top of the stroke and for the by-pass to the cylinder head at the bottom of the stroke.

### Two-Port (Two-Stroke Cycle)

The operating principles of a two-port motor for a complete operating cycle are as follows:

With reference to Fig. 8A, it will be noted that at this point the piston is on its upward stroke. A charge of fuel-air mixture is being pulled into the crankcase by the vacuum created during the upward movement of the piston. This in turn causes the check valve or the rotary disc valve to open. The mixture remains trapped in the crankcase because both the intake and exhaust ports are covered by the piston skirt. The fresh fuel and air charge is being compressed by the upward movement of the piston. The ignition timing mechanism causes the spark plug to fire when the piston reaches its highest point in the cylinder.

After the explosion, the piston moves down very rapidly as a result of the combustion pressure. As the piston reaches the lowest part of its power stroke (Fig. 8B), it has uncovered the

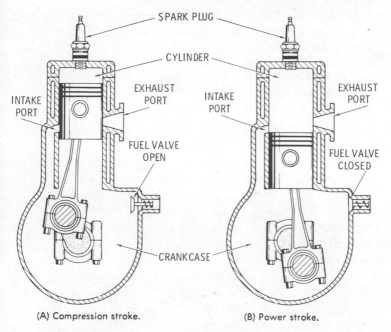

(A) Compression stroke.        (B) Power stroke.

Fig. 8. Diagrammatic view of a two-port, two-stroke cycle engine.

intake port which allows clean air-fuel mixture to rush into the head of the cylinder. As this fresh material speeds into the cylinder, it assists to expel the exploded material through the exhaust port.

The piston at this time immediately starts its upward movement, closing the intake and exhaust ports and, at the same time, drawing a new fuel charge into the crankcase. As the piston on its upward movement reaches the top of the cylinder, the spark plug will again ignite the air-fuel charge. The foregoing cycle must be repeated several times a second to maintain operation and to produce rotating power to the propeller.

## Three-Port (Two-Stroke Cycle)

The three-port motor differs from that of the two-port, mainly in the matter of fuel admission. Valves between the crankcase and carburetor (fuel admission valves) may be of the rotary, or the leaf (reed) type. Basically, a complete operating cycle is as follows:

With reference to Fig. 9A showing the operating features, it will be noted that at this point the piston is approaching the end of its upward stroke and the crankshaft throw is about to pass the center, which is the maximum upward travel of the piston.

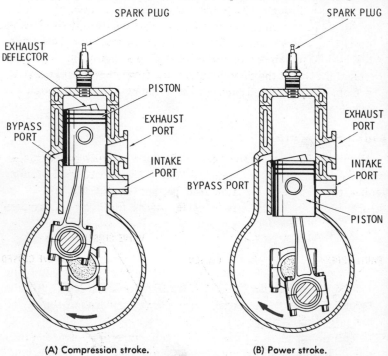

(A) Compression stroke.                    (B) Power stroke.

Fig. 9. Illustrating the principles of operation for a three-port, two-stroke cycle gasoline engine.

This *upward movement* of the piston is called the *compression stroke,* since it compresses the air-fuel mixture in preparation for ignition. Simultaneously, it creates a partial vacuum in the crankcase so that, as the intake port is uncovered, the fuel-air mixture for a new charge flows in from the carburetor. When the piston is at, or nearest, its highest point, the spark plug ignites the compress mixture.

In Fig. 9B, the piston is part-way down as a result of the combustion pressure. This stroke is called the *expansion* or *power* stroke, since it furnishes power to turn the propeller.

As the piston descends, it closes the intake port and compresses the air-fuel charge in the crankcase. When the piston approaches the end of its downward stroke, its motion uncovers the exhaust port through which the burned gases escape.

At about this time the piston has also uncovered the bypass port, and a fresh charge forces its way in from the crankcase, driving the remainder of the burned charge before it. A projection at the top of the piston deflects the fresh charge and prevents it from passing directly across the cylinder and out through the exhaust port.

## Four-Stroke Cycle

As previously noted, the basic difference between a two-stroke and a four-stroke cycle engine is that a two-stroke cycle engine ignites the charge every time the piston reaches the top of its stroke, while in a four-stroke cycle engine the charge is ignited

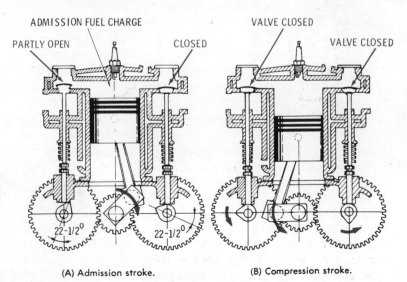

(A) Admission stroke.          (B) Compression stroke.

**Fig. 10. Cutaway view of a four-cycle motor showing position of piston and valves during the first two events of the cycle.**

only every other time the piston reaches the top of its stroke. Also, in a four-cycle engine, lubricating oil is carried in the crankcase and pure gasoline is used.

Another difference to be noted is that while in a two-cycle engine the piston acts as both inlet and exhaust valve, the operation of a four-cycle engine provides for an exhaust and intake valve in each cylinder to admit the fuel mixture and to permit the exhaust gases to be expelled.

With reference to Figs. 10 and 11, showing diagrammatically the four events of *intake, compression, power* and *exhaust* occurring during a cycle in a four-stroke cycle engine, the actions are principally as follows:

Prior to introduction of the events of the cycle, it should be noted that the cylinder head carries two valves—an intake and exhaust valve. Each of these valves are geared to the piston by means of camshafts in such a way that the camshaft makes one complete revolution while the crankshaft makes two revolutions. To complete the assembly, a spark plug is located in the top of the cylinder head.

The intake stroke, alternately termed suction or admission stroke, is shown in Fig. 10, and is the first step in the cycle. Here the piston is moving downward, and as a result, a slight vacuum is created in the cylinder above the piston. This vacuum assists in drawing the air-fuel mixture into the cylinder from the carburetor through the open fuel intake valve. When the piston reaches the bottom of its stroke, the fuel intake valve closes, sealing the fuel mixture in the cylinder.

The compression stroke is the next step in the cycle. As noted in Fig. 11, the piston is now being forced in an upward direction by the rotating inertia of the crankshaft. Both intake and exhaust valves are closed and will remain closed during the entire stroke. As the piston moves upward, the air-fuel charge is compressed to as little as one-tenth of its original volume in the combustion chamber above the piston. When the piston reaches the end of its upward stroke, the crankshaft has made one complete revolution. This completes the compression stroke.

The third step in the cycle is the power or expansion stroke, and is the only stroke in the cycle that contributes to the output

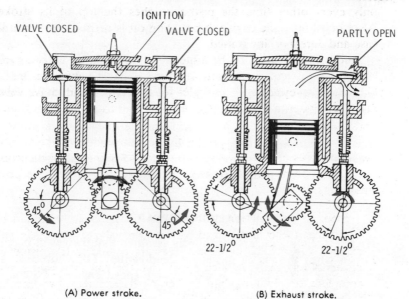

IGNITION

VALVE CLOSED        VALVE CLOSED            PARTLY OPEN

45°       45°

22-1/2°       22-1/2°

(A) Power stroke.           (B) Exhaust stroke.

**Fig. 11. Cutaway illustration of a four-cycle motor showing position of piston and valves during the last two events of the cycle.**

of the engine. As noted in Fig. 11, the piston is now at its top-most or dead-center position. The compressed fuel mixture at this time is ignited by an electric spark generated at the spark-plug gap. The heat of combustion causes the burning gases to expand, forcing the piston to move downward to produce mechanical energy and turn the crankshaft. In order to remove burned gases promptly, the exhaust valve opens when the crank is at an angle of about sixty degrees with the bottom dead center, so that the piston has almost twenty-five percent of its stroke to complete when the exhaust valve opens. When the piston reaches the bottom of the cylinder during its power stroke, the crankshaft has made one and one-half revolutions.

The final step in the cycle is termed the exhaust stroke, since it functions to exhaust the burned gases in preparation for the commencement of another cycle. Opening of the exhaust valve early permits the cylinder pressure to drop almost to that of the atmosphere by the time the crank passes the lower dead center

45

and starts to push the piston upward. It is in this way that a large portion of the burned gases are removed before the exhaust stroke begins. The remainder of the cylinder contents of burned gases is forced out through the open exhaust valve during the period the piston moves upward. When the piston reaches its maximum upward position, the cycle is completed and another cycle commences. As noted from the foregoing, the crankshaft at the completion of the cycle has made two complete revolutions, and the piston has completed four strokes—namely, two upward and two downward.

## VALVE OVERLAP

In the foregoing illustrations it was assumed that the valves begin to open when the piston passes its dead-center. This, however, is not the case in the highly developed high-speed engines. To compensate for the time required by the air or gas to flow through the manifold, the valves are timed to overlap a certain amount, the amount of overlap depending on the design and speed of the engine.

In theory, the admission valve should open at the exact time the piston starts down in the cylinder and should close at the instant the piston starts upward in the cylinder on the compression stroke. Both the admission and exhaust valves should remain closed during compression and expansion, and the exhaust valve would then open at the end of the power stroke and close at the end of the exhaust stroke. Such an arrangement may be satisfactory for a slow-speed engine, but with increased speed a certain amount of valve overlap is necessary to obtain better distribution of the charge.

## TWO-STROKE VERSUS FOUR-STROKE CYCLE ENGINES

Small outboard motors are nearly always of the two-stroke cycle type. This is mainly because of simplicity in design and operation, combined with lightweight and low cost. Two-stroke cycle engines, however, have certain disadvantages in that the fuel mixture must be preconditioned. A certain amount of oil must be mixed with the gasoline for proper lubrication of the engine parts.

It should be borne in mind, however, that the two-stroke cycle engine is less efficient with respect to fuel consumption than the four-stroke cycle type. This is primarily because of the latter's more effective valve system. Thus, where fuel economy is important, the four-stroke cycle is recommended.

## POWER OUTPUT

In our discussion of the fundamental principles of operation, it will be noted that the two-stroke cycle engine delivers twice as many power impulses per cycle to the crankshaft as the four-stroke cycle type. Theoretically, then, the two-stroke cycle engine would have twice the power output as a four-stroke cycle engine of the same size. This, however, is not true because of the waste in fuel and power when some of the incoming fuel mixture combines with the exhaust gases and goes out with them. The volumetric efficiency of the two-stroke cycle engine is thus reduced to a considerable extent.

As a general conclusion, it may be stated that for small light engines used in outboard service, and where economy is not of great importance, the two-stroke cycle engine is generally preferred.

Big water used to be the province of big boats. Not so today. Modern, rugged fiberglass boats of "deep vee" designs are capable of handling rough weather in safety. But the skill of the pilot must measure up to his equipment, warn the *Mercury* boating authorities. Don't go out on the ocean blue until you're an experienced and knowledgeable boatman.

Courtesy Mercury Marine, Div. of Brunswick Corp.

The latest phenomenon in boating circles is the bass boat, a marvel of speed and electronic gadgetry. Tournament bass fishing, where the right rig is almost as important as angling skills, is growing rapidly in the southern tier of states.

Courtesy Mercury Marine, Div. of Brunswick Corp.

Stern drive, or inboard-outboard power, continues to gain favor among recreational boaters. This *MerCruiser*-powered rig is one of about 70,000 stern drive craft which will be sold this year in the United States. As late as 1963, stern drive boat sales totaled only about 8,000 annually.

Courtesy Mercury Marine, Div. of Brunswick Corp.

People who have been boating awhile discover that their fellow men seem a little more relaxed and gregarious when they're out on the water. The lucky owners of this luxurious houseboat even underscored these traits by calling their craft "Friendship."

Courtesy Mercury Marine, Div. of Brunswick Corp.

A never-to-be-forgotten moment is caught in the making. Grandpa's next task will be to show the young fisherman how to prepare his catch.

Courtesy Mercury Marine, Div. of Brunswick Corp.

# Chapter 3

# Remote Control

The use of remote throttle-and-shift controls has moved the outboard motor pilot from a position beside the motor at the rear of the boat to a more comfortable post with a steering wheel at the approximate center of the boat (Fig. 1). The actuating source

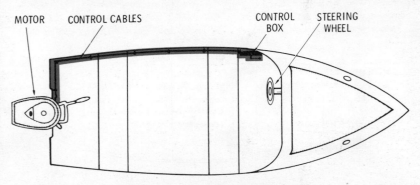

MOTOR     CONTROL CABLES                    CONTROL     STEERING
                                              BOX        WHEEL

Fig. 1. Typical remote control installation.

may be mechanical or electrical, as by hydraulic or relay action. Perhaps one of the simplest examples of remote control is that of rudder operation by means of special tiller ropes and pulleys; the ropes being attached to, and wound on, the steering-wheel drum.

Remote control, as associated with outboard motors, is used to perform any of the following functions:

1. Steering control.
2. Throttle control.
3. Gearshift control.

51

Combined with remote steering, throttle, and gearshift control, the outboard motor can be started, shifted, and fully controlled from any position in the boat.

## TILLER CONTROLS

By definition, the tiller is that lever of wood or metal attached to the rudder head and used for turning the rudder from side to side as required for steering the boat. Thus, the tiller is simply a

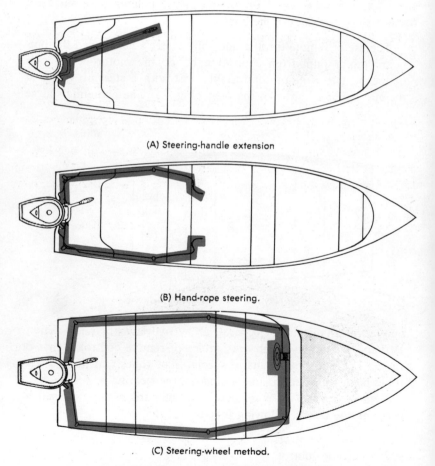

(A) Steering-handle extension

(B) Hand-rope steering.

(C) Steering-wheel method.

**Fig. 2. Illustrating various methods of tiller control.**

lever arm or other device employed to regulate the direction of the boat.

One of the simplest methods of steering the boat by remote action is to extend the steering handle by a suitable stick or rod as shown in Fig. 2, or by special attachment gears furnished by outboard motor manufacturers. Other methods of tiller control usually involve the use of tiller ropes and pulleys. Figs. 2B and 2C illustrate two methods in which the ropes are used for attachment to the tiller and then wired up by means of pulleys to eliminate friction along the sides of the boat.

Fig. 2C illustrates a common method of steering which differs from that shown in Fig. 2B, mainly in that positive tiller control is obtained by a centrally located steering wheel and drum attachment. As will be noted, the tiller ropes are wound around the drum in such a way that a turn on the steering wheel will cause the rudder to turn toward the right or left, thus causing the boat to change its direction accordingly.

Figs. 3 and 4 illustrate typical steering installations with steering cables located as shown. For best service, cable pulleys should be located as far outboard as possible. To prevent undue tension in

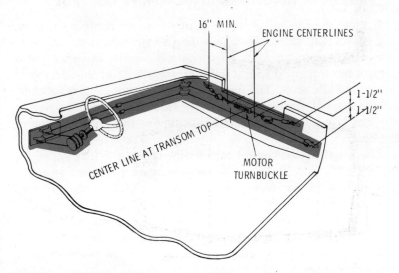

**Fig. 3. A typical single-side steering installation which shows the cable and pulley attachments.**

the cables as the motor is pivoted or tilted, attachment straps should be located with reference to the transom top as indicated.

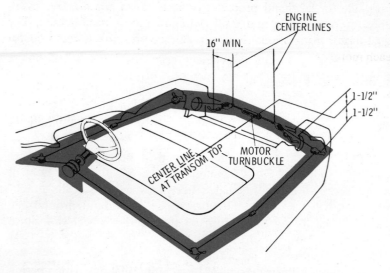

**Fig. 4. Steering-cable installation with cable occupying both sides of boat.**

## REMOTE THROTTLE AND GEARSHIFT CONTROL

Remote throttle and gearshift controls are available in kit form, and may easily be installed according to manufacturer's instructions. In its simplest form, such controls consist essentially of a control box equipped with a shift and throttle lever, in addition to sector and idle gears. The function of the control cable is to transfer the manual action of the operator from the normal position at the motor to a more comfortable position in the center portion of the boat.

The length of the control cables depends on the location of the control box. Since there are no reliable standards with respect to the location of the steering wheel and control box, the operator should choose the best possible location with maximum visibility and with due regard to trim and facility for movement.

In this connection, it should be noted that, in order to compensate for engine torque caused by the direction of propeller rotation, the steering wheel and control box should be located on the starboard side of the boat for right-hand propeller rotation and the port side for left-hand propeller rotation. Such controls are available for both single and dual outboard motor installations. For dual-motor installations, however, one control box is required for each motor.

## Installation Procedure

A typical two-lever throttle and shift-control box suitable for remote control is shown in Figs. 5 and 6. When assembling the cables to the control box, proceed as follows:

1. Disassemble control box and remove gear racks.
2. Insert control wire in gear rack, flush with end of gear rack.
3. Insert rack cables in control box. Trunnions on cables must fit in bosses on control box. Be sure last tooth of speed-control lever gear segment engages last tooth of rack (Fig. 5), and last tooth of shift-control lever gear segment engages last tooth of rack (Fig. 6).
4. Assemble control box and cables for either port or starboard installation. Tighten assembly screws securely.

Remote control kits are usually furnished with remote control box, cables, and fittings separate. Cables must first be installed in

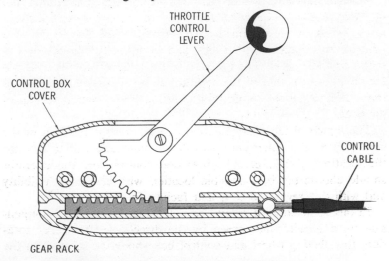

Fig. 5. Two-lever throttle remote-control box mechanism.

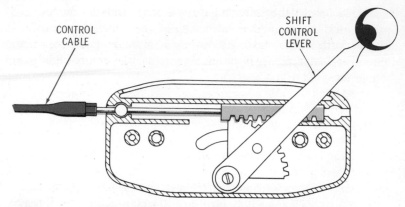

Fig. 6. Shift-control box suitable for remote control.

the control box, and the control box adjusted to the desired position of the boat. Cables should be secured to the boat with clamps provided in the kit and fittings attached to the cables at the motor end. It is important that the cable fittings at the motor end be attached last, since the relation of the length of the control wires and the casings may change due to various curves made in the cables when securing them to the boat and motor.

When assembling cables to the motor, proceed as follows:

1. On the motor ends of both cables, secure the anchor ball, jam nut, and clip. Be sure that the jam nut and end clip are tightened securely. Also, remember that when threading the end clips, do not use pliers to hold the cable as this may mar its surface.

2. At the motor end of the cables, grasp the cable sleeve with one hand and with the other push in on the cable until it makes contact with the clevis in the control box. Turn the end clip clockwise until the cable end is threaded all the way into the clevis. Repeat this operation for the other cable.

3. All the preceding steps can be accomplished with the cables and control box on the dock or shore. After both cables have been threaded into the clevis, the next step is to test for the correct adjustment of the control. To test the control-box adjustment, the motor ends of the cables must be at-

tached to the shift and throttle pins, and the anchor balls must be secured in place. Keep the cables as straight as possible when testing the adjustment. Should any adjustment be required, it will be much easier if the control box is not attached to the boat.

4.  After the cables have been attached to the motor, and the anchor balls are in place with the covers secured, proceed to test the control adjustment.

To test the throttle adjustment, proceed as follows:

1.  Hold the control box firmly and place the shift lever in forward gear and move the throttle lever all the way forward. Check to see that the advance stop screw on the motor is bottomed against the manifold.
2.  Move the throttle lever all the way back toward the *slow* position. Make sure that the idle stop screw on the motor is bottomed against the crankcase.
3.  If the advance and idle stop screws bottom out as indicated, no adjustments are required. However, if one does not bottom, the cable travel in this position needs to be increased. To regulate the cable travel, loosen the anchor cover. Thread the cable sleeve into the control box to increase the idle travel. Thread the cable sleeve out of the control box to increase the advance travel. Do this until both the idle and throttle stop screws bottom.

To test the shift adjustment, proceed as follows:

1.  Hold the control box firmly with the throttle in the *slow* position and move the shift lever all the way forward. (Note: It may be necessary to turn the propeller slightly in order to shift the control lever into forward and reverse gear.) With the shift-control lever in forward, go back to the motor and carefully detach the end clip. Note whether the motor is in full forward gear. Attach the end clip.
2.  At the control box, pull the lever all the way back. At the motor, carefully detach the end clip and note whether the motor is in full reverse gear. Attach the end clip.

3. If the motor shifts fully into forward and reverse gear, no adjustments are required. If the motor does not shift fully into one gear, the cable travel will need to be increased in this direction until the motor will shift equally into either gear. To regulate the travel into either forward or reverse, loosen the anchor cover. Thread the cable sleeve into the control box to increase the travel into reverse gear. Thread the sleeve out of the box to increase the travel into forward. With the control box properly adjusted, the shift-control lever will be nearly vertical to the box in neutral gear.

4. After the remote control has been properly adjusted, detach the end clips and anchor balls from the motor, being careful not to change the distance that the cable sleeves are threaded into the control box.

5. Route the cables along the gunwale of the boat, avoiding any sharp bends. Attach the cables to the motor, then proceed to mount the control box. Be sure to allow sufficient room for the control levers to swing through their complete arc.

6. After having mounted the control box, make a final test of its operation.

Store the oars and let's go waterskiing! The lightweight inflatable enables even a 7.5-hp outboard to pop a skier for a brisk ride above the waves.
Courtesy Mercury Marine, Div. of Brunswick Corp.

# Chapter 4

# Power Head Construction and Service

An outboard motor, because of its operational features, is designed with an upper enclosure or housing for the engine assembly, and a lower unit containing the propeller and associated parts. Because the upper part of the outboard motor assembly contains the prime mover, or power unit, it is generally termed the *power head*. The power head consists of:

1. Cylinder block and crankcase assembly.
3. Crankshaft and center main-bearing assembly.
4. Crankcase end caps.
5. Manifold covers.
   a. Intake and exhaust manifolds.
   b. Cylinder-block covers.

Other components forming a part of the power head are the carburetor, valves, magneto, and spark plugs. The design and arrangement of the cylinders determines the type of motor and is termed as:

1. Single cylinder.
3. Opposed twin cylinder.
3. Alternate twin cylinder.
4. Four cylinder.
5. Six cylinder.

The number of cylinders required in a particular engine usually depends on its size and application. Thus, the smaller outboard motors are frequently of the single-cylinder type, whereas motors of larger horsepower contain two or more cylinders.

## SINGLE CYLINDER TYPE

The basic parts of the power-head of a two-stroke cycle, single-cylinder engine are shown in Figs. 1 and 2. As noted in Fig. 1,

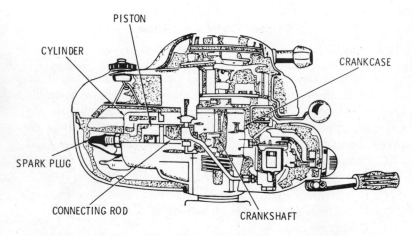

**Fig. 1. Power-head assembly for a single-cylinder, two-cycle motor.**

this compact assembly consists of the single cylinder and cylinder head with a water jacket surrounding the upper part of the cylinder. Other visible parts are the piston, connecting rod, crankshaft, and crankcase. The carburetor is attached directly to the crankcase, and the fuel mixture is controlled by means of a reed-type valve.

Early motors of this type usually had cylinders constructed of high quality cast iron. Customary practice had been to cast the

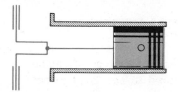

**Fig. 2. Piston and crankshaft arrangement in a single-cylinder, two-cycle motor.**

cylinder assembly, including the bore, water-jacket exhaust and intake ports, manifold, and cylinder head as one integral piece of gray iron.

The method now, however, is to die-cast the cylinder assemblies, with cast-iron cylinder bores, or steel sleeves, aluminum water jackets, bearing supports, bronze bearing inserts, and crankcase sections integral. This method of manufacture has not only reduced the weight per motor horsepower, but has improved the quality of the motor assembly as well.

## OPPOSED TWIN CYLINDER

This outboard motor construction method is shown in Figs. 3 and 4. There are two cylinders on opposite sides of the crankcase,

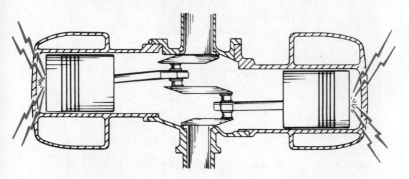

Fig. 3. Power-head assembly for an opposed twin-cylinder outboard motor.

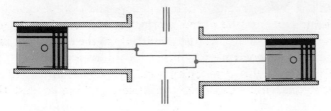

Fig. 4. Piston and crankshaft arrangement in a twin-cylinder opposed outboard motor.

and both cylinders are ignited simultaneously. This type of engine has its disadvantages and is not manufactured to any great extent

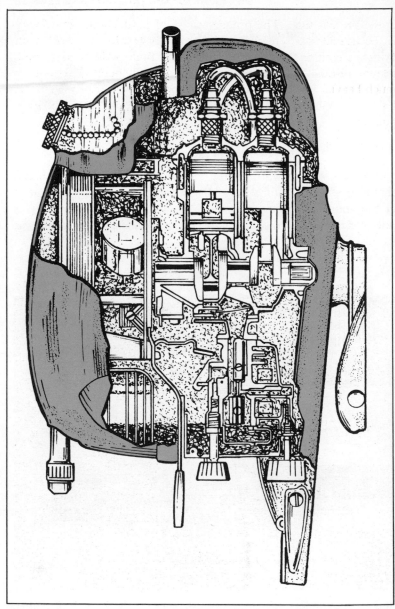

Fig. 5. Cutaway view of a power-head assembly for an alternate-firing, twin-cylinder motor.

at the present time. The primary cause of its declining popularity is the heavier parts required to withstand the pressure from both cylinders igniting their charges at the same time. Also, to carry both pistons through the compression stroke simultaneously requires a much heavier flywheel, adding to the cost and weight of the engine. Excessive vibration and starting difficulties are other trouble pointers.

## ALTERNATE TWIN CYLINDER

Alternate firing twin-cylinder motor have desirable functional characteristics for outboard use. They have gained wide popularity in the small and medium-class sizes. The cutaway view of the power head of a two-stroke cycle two-cylinder alternate firing motor is shown in Fig. 5.

As noted, the power head represents a well designed and compact assembly. The cylinder assemblies are die-cast with inserted

Courtesy Mercury Marine, Div. of Brunswick Corp.

Fig. 6. Cutaway view of the combustion chamber in an alternate-firing, twin-cylinder motor.

63

steel sleeves and aluminum water jackets. The friction type of bearing consists of a bushing, or cylindrical sleeve, of bronze machined to size.

As noted from the crankshaft in Figs. 6 and 7, the crank pins are located opposite one another. Thus, it follows that the pistons must move in opposite directions in the cylinders. When one piston is moving outward on the compression stroke, the other is moving inward on the expansion or power stroke. Each cylinder is designed to ignite its charge once every revolution, but alternately, resulting in two power impulses for each revolution of the crankshaft.

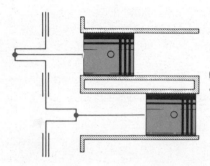

Fig. 7. Diagram showing the cylinder and crankshaft arrangement in a two-cylinder alternate-firing outboard motor.

The gravity-feed carburetor is attached directly to the crankcase by means of reed or rotary-type valves. The charge is usually ignited by a flywheel-type magneto, except in large motors where the electric system may incorporate an electric starting motor and an alternating-current generator, which together with a rectifier provides charging current for the battery. On such engines, the ignition is usually furnished by a separately mounted aircraft-type magneto driven by a pulley from the engine crankshaft.

## FOUR CYLINDER

The power heads of two-stroke cycle, four-cylinder outboard motors are normally designed in one of the following types:

    a.  Four cylinder V-type.
    b.  Four cylinder, opposed firing.
    c.  Four cylinder, in line.

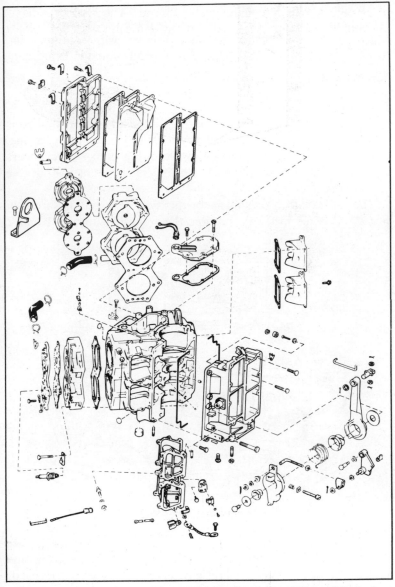

Fig. 8. Exploded view of a power-head assembly for a two-cycle, V-4 type outboard motor.

Any one of the foregoing designations refers to outboard motors of medium or large sizes. It is obvious that the power requirements will not have to be divided into four cylinders with accompanying increase in cost and materials when a small motor is being considered.

## Four Cylinder V-Type

The cylinder arrangement in this outboard motor design is similar to the popular, four-stroke cycle, V-type automotive engine. The V-type four-cylinder engine shown in Fig. 8 has the cylinders cast in a single die-cast block. The cylinders are set at a 90-degree angle to one another.

The crankshaft arrangement for this type of engine is shown in Fig. 9. As noted in the illustration, the crankshaft throws 1 and 2

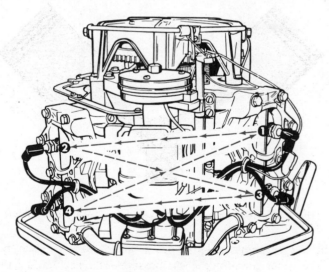

Fig. 9. View of a four-cylinder, two-cycle, V-type power head.

are 180 degrees from throws 3 and 4, because the cylinders are set 90 degrees apart, and since firing alternates between top and bottom cylinders, a power impulse is generated every 90 degrees, or at every one-fourth revolution of the crankshaft. Thus, all four cylinders will fire for each crankshaft revolution.

From the foregoing it will be noted that the V-4 design produces the same number of powered strokes as the V-8 automobile engine because two-stroke cycle operation produces a power stroke each time a piston passes over top center of the cylinder, as shown in Fig. 10. This design produces a smooth running engine with a minimum of vibration.

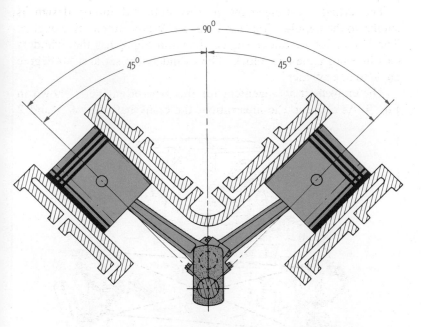

Fig. 10. Angular arrangement of the cylinders in a V-4 outboard motor.

The V-type crankcase provides a fuel passage to each cylinder from the intake manifold. These passages channel the fuel mixture into the cavity formed by the cylinder and crankcase, where it is compressed by the piston movement, then bypassed into the cylinder. The engine magneto is of the distributor type and is driven by the flywheel pulley. Engine cooling is thermostatically controlled, permitting the temperature to remain at a constant value regardless of the outside water temperature. The water pump is located in the lower unit, the impeller being operated by the engine driveshaft.

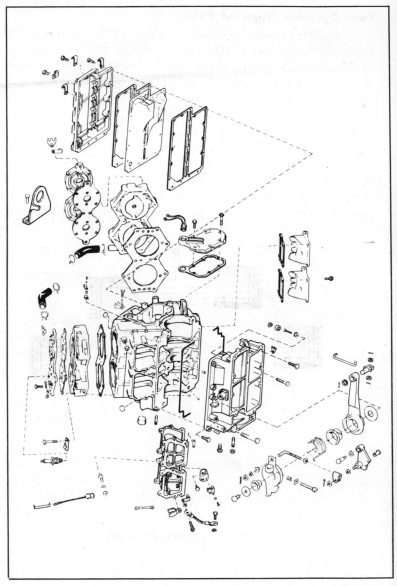

Courtesy Johnson Motors, Div. of Outboard Marine Corp.

**Fig. 11. Exploded view of a power-head in opposed firing of a four-cylinder outboard motor.**

## Four Cylinder Opposed Firing

In the four cylinder, opposed firing type of outboard motor, the upper and lower pair of cylinders fire alternately. Since each pair of cylinders are on the same stroke simultaneously, the power stroke delivered by each pair of cylinders occurs once for every 180-degree rotation of the crankshaft, or twice for each revolution.

A motor assembly of this type may be considered similar to two alternate firing twins mounted on the opposite side of a common crankcase, as noted in Fig. 11. The crankshaft is of the two-throw design with four crank pins and three bearings (top, center, and bottom). As noted in Fig. 12, the twin cylinders are attached to opposite sides of the crankcase, with the cylinder blocks offset

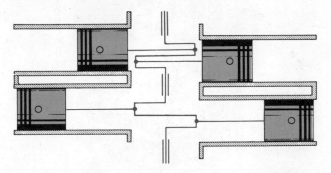

Fig. 12. Elementary diagram showing cylinder and crankshaft arrangement.

slightly from one another to facilitate connecting-rod and crank-shaft attachment. Fig. 13 illustrates the new *Thunderbolt* pointless ignition system. For a more detailed explanation see Chapter 10.

## SIX-CYLINDER IN-LINE

Three spark plugs of the *Mercury* six-cylinder engine are fired in three cylinders by one set of breaker points and the other three by another set of breaker points. As each set of breakers fires three plugs, a careful synchronization job is required. Improper dwell or phasing can result in rough engine performance, as three plugs could be firing early and three plugs late. Each set of points has an independent ignition source. The cam is three-lobed and each set of breaker points fires 120 degrees apart. The second set, however, must fire at 60-degree intervals from the first. One set of breaker points fires at 0, 120, and 240 degrees, and the second set of points fires at 60, 180, and 300 degrees. In other words, the *Mercury* six-cylinder engine fires at 60-degree intervals giving six

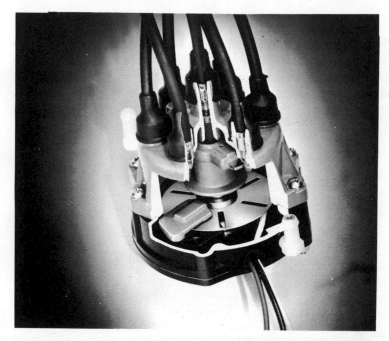

Courtesy Mercury Marine, Div. of Brunswick Corp.

**Fig. 13. The *Mercury Thunderbolt* ignition which does not require breaker points.**

equally-spaced power impulses for each revolution of the crankshaft.

## POWER HEAD DETAILS

The various moving and stationary parts in outboard motors are similar in their function and design, although the arrangement of the parts may differ considerably depending on the type of engine.

The moving parts which act to transform the energy contained in the incoming fuel mixture into useful power may be classed as:

1. Piston.
2. Connecting rod.
3. Crankshaft.
4. Flywheel.

The stationary parts are the cylinder(s) and crankcase.

## Pistons

The piston moving up and down in the cylinder is one of the most important working parts of the engine mechanism. For the outboard motor it consists essentially of a cylindrical casting,

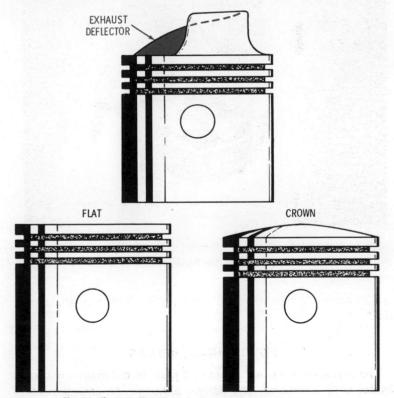

Fig. 14. Illustrating various shapes of piston heads.

Fig. 14, closed at the top and open at the bottom end. It is attached to a wrist pin and connecting rod which transmits the reciprocating movement of the piston into the rotary motion of the crankshaft. A piston (in a two-stroke cycle engine) performs the following functions:

1. It receives the force of combustion which is transferred by the connecting rod to the crankshaft in the form of power.
2. It controls the flow of fuel charge and exhaust gases as it covers and uncovers the ports in the cylinder during its movements.

As noted in Fig. 15, the head of the piston has a deflector cast integrally with the piston, the purpose of which is to direct the

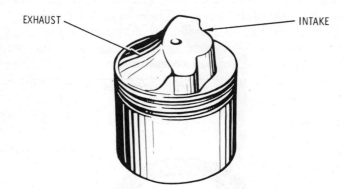

EXHAUST                                         INTAKE

Fig. 15. Typical piston-head construction for a two-cycle gasoline engine.

fresh fuel charge from the crankcase upward along one side of the cylinder. This assists in deflecting the exhaust gases out through the exhaust port.

The material presently employed in piston manufacture is aluminum alloy, although cast-iron pistons are also used. The reason for the popularity of aluminum pistons is their light weight, in addition to being a better conductor of heat, than the cast-iron type. Pistons employed in outboard motors are usually of the solid-skirt type, with the piston accurately ground to allow the necessary tolerance between the moving piston and the cylinder.

Modern outboard engines run at a high speed; the pistons have to travel up and down from a few hundred to thousands of times a minute. A weight moving up and down at such speed requires a very great force to stop it and a very great force to start it. This force, due to *inertia,* is transmitted by the connecting rod to the bearings and it is this force which pounds against the bearings and produces vibration. It is important that this force be reduced to a minimum, and that was the reason for the introduction of aluminum-alloy pistons, since aluminum is very light.

To reduce the weight of cast-iron pistons, they must be made very thin. While this might give the desired lightness, a thin piston offers so much resistance to heat flow that the piston would become unduly hot. Quicker acceleration is also possible with aluminum-alloy pistons because of the reduction in weight. Another advantage is that aluminum is a much better conductor of heat than iron, hence the temperature of the head of the piston is lower than when made of cast iron. A disadvantage is that aluminum alloy expands much more than cast iron with a rise of temperature. As a result, early aluminum-alloy pistons were made with

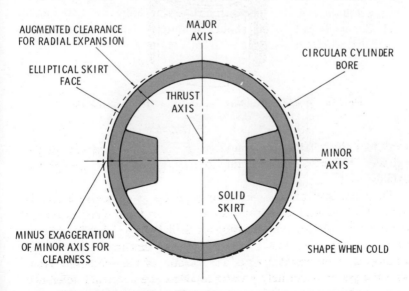

**Fig. 16. Bottom view of a piston illustrating elliptical or cam grinding.**

considerable clearance so that they would not be too large at the working temperature. This resulted in piston slap.

Many aluminum-alloy pistons are "cam" ground; that is, they are purposely machined with the skirts slightly oval. This oval shaping of the piston, commonly referred to as cam grinding, is intended to compensate for expansion. The reason for this is that the skirts will be slightly oval when cold in such a fashion that the thrust faces will have the greater diameter, but the skirt will become more nearly round when the piston expands at operating temperature. See Fig. 16.

*Piston Pins*—Piston pins, also known as wrist pins, serve as a connection between the upper end of the connecting rod and the piston. Piston pins are made of alloy steel with precision finish and are case-heardened and sometimes chromium plated to increase their wearing qualities. It forms a pivot connecting one end of the connecting rod to the piston which transforms lateral oscillating motion of the rod to reciprocating motion of the piston. To securely lock the piston pin in place, spring-lock rings are used.

*Piston Rings*—The function of piston rings is to provide a seal between the piston and cylinder, permitting the gases to be compressed in the cylinder. The piston rings, therefore, must contact the cylinder walls evenly and should fit snugly in the ring grooves to prevent the compressed gases from escaping.

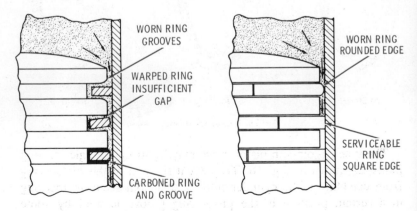

WORN RING GROOVES

WARPED RING INSUFFICIENT GAP

CARBONED RING AND GROOVE

WORN RING ROUNDED EDGE

SERVICEABLE RING SQUARE EDGE

**Fig. 17. Illustrating possible ring wear by excessive ring pressure.**

Excessive ring pressure will result in drag between the ring and the cylinder wall, creating high operating temperature, sluggish performance, and abnormal ring, ring groove, and cylinder wall wear. Insufficient ring pressure, on the other hand, will result in blow-by, loss of power, overheating, and carbon formation on the skirt of the piston, as illustrated in Fig. 17.

Piston rings of the type used in two-cycle engines are usually made of cast-iron alloy. The number of compression rings required are usually two or three depending on the size and compression ratio of the engine. The sealing effect of the ring is obtained by pre-establishing a slight strain in the original casting, or by other means in the process of manufacture; thus, after machining to the correct dimensions and cutting, the ends of the ring spring apart. The space created by this action is referred to as the ring gap.

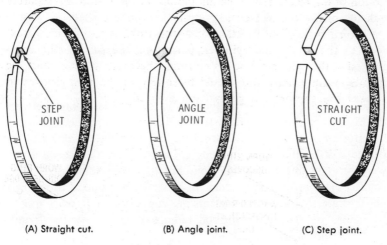

(A) Straight cut.      (B) Angle joint.      (C) Step joint.

**Fig. 18. Typical compression rings.**

The type of joints in piston rings may be straight, angle, or step joints, as shown in Fig. 18. To prevent the end of the piston ring from catching in the cylinder port, a small pin securing the ring in a certain position in the piston-ring groove is used by some manufacturers, as illustrated in Fig. 19.

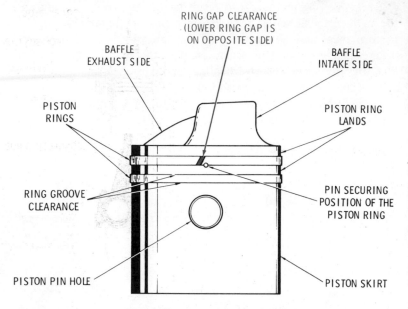

**Fig. 19. Illustrating piston-ring installation.**

## Connecting Rods

The purpose of the connecting rod is to provide linkage between the piston and the crankshaft. It serves to transform the reciprocating motion of the piston into rotary motion of the crankshaft. The pressure of combustion being applied to the piston head is a downward straight-line thrust and consequently cannot be used unless transformed into rotary motion. In order to be applied to the propeller shaft, the piston movements are converted into rotary motion by means of the connecting-rod linkage with the rotating crankshaft, as shown in Fig. 20.

Connecting rods must be light and yet strong enough to transmit the thrust of the piston. They are normally constructed of aluminum alloy with bronze bearing inserts at the top, or from steel forgings, depending on the type of bearing to be used and the size of the engine. They are usually made in the form of an I-beam for lightness and maximum strength. Wrist-pin bearings on the small end of the rod are usually of bronze, or bronze and steel, since the

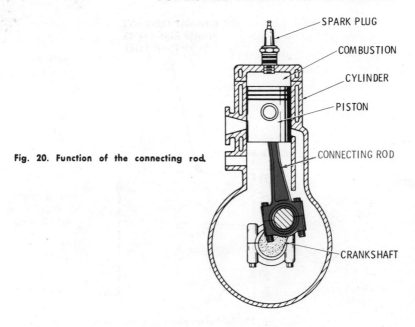

SPARK PLUG

COMBUSTION

CYLINDER

PISTON

CONNECTING ROD

CRANKSHAFT

Fig. 20. Function of the connecting rod.

degree of motion at this point is comparatively small, being governed by the angularity of the connecting rod.

Connecting rods may be straight or offset, depending on the cylinder and firing arrangement of the engine. Thus, offset rods (Fig. 21A) are usually provided for opposed twin motors where the cylinders are offset and not in line with one another. Straight rods (Fig. 21B) are furnished on all alternate firing twin-cylinder

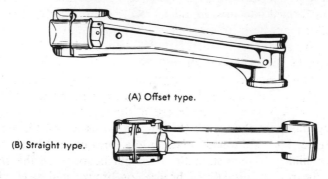

(A) Offset type.

(B) Straight type.

Fig. 21. Typical connecting rods.

motors. The lower part of the connecting rod is split to permit it to be clamped around the crankshaft. The bottom part, or cap, is made of the same material as the rod and is attached by two connecting-rod bolts.

Bearings to reduce the friction between the crankshaft and connecting rod are classified as *friction* and *nonfriction*. The friction type of bearing consists of a split bushing or cylindrical sleeve attached to the rod. The nonfriction type bearings may be of the *roller* or *needle* type, as illustrated in Fig. 22. The roller bearings

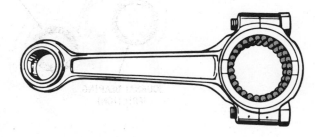

(A) Roller bearings.

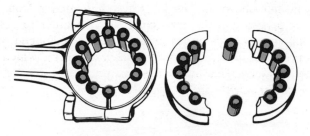

(B) Needle-type bearings.

**Fig. 22. Connecting-rod bearings.**

are of the conventional type, with the crank pin end of sufficient size to accommodate the necessary rollers.

To install, the rollers are generally set in a split-cage or retainer. Each half of the assembly is then placed on the crank pin. This is followed by installation of the connecting rod and shaft which, when bolted together, makes up a nonfriction bearing assembly, as shown in Fig. 23.

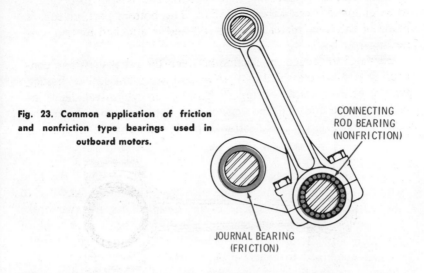

Fig. 23. Common application of friction and nonfriction type bearings used in outboard motors.

CONNECTING
ROD BEARING
(NONFRICTION)

JOURNAL BEARING
(FRICTION)

## Crankshafts

The crankshaft, shown in Fig. 24, receives its motion from the reciprocating pistons and the connecting rods. In order to obtain a nonfluctuating rotary motion, crankshafts are equipped with one or more offsets or throws (one for each cylinder), which together with counterweights and a flywheel provide power for the propeller. Counterweights are shown in Fig. 25.

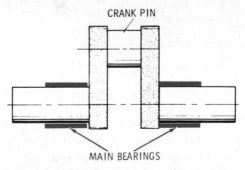

CRANK PIN

MAIN BEARINGS

Fig. 24. Elementary single-cylinder crankshaft showing construction.

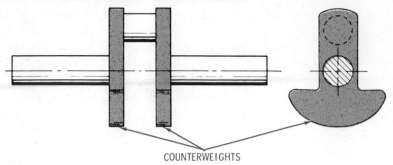

COUNTERWEIGHTS

**Fig. 25. Single-cylinder crankshaft with counterweights.**

Crankshafts must be correctly proportioned to carry the load while turning at high speed, and also to withstand shocks due to the nature of the gas-engine cycle. Crankshafts for two-stroke cycle motors are generally made of a drop-forging of alloy steel, or cast from an alloy of steel and nickel. The rough casting or forging is then machined to exact specifications.

Owing to the high rotative speed for which modern engines are designed, counterweights or counterbalances are necessary to avoid excessive vibration. These are usually forged integrally with the crankshaft.

The function of the counter balances are:

1. To balance the weights of the piston, connecting rod, crank arms, and crank pin, so that the assembly of moving parts

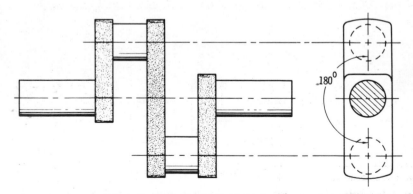

**Fig. 26. Elementary two-throw crankshaft used in two-cylinder engines.**

will be in static equilibrium for all points of the stroke. See Fig. 26.

2. To provide an opposing centrifugal force to counteract the oppositely directed centrifugal force due to the connecting rod, crank arms, and crank pin.

3. To counteract the inertia loads due to the moving parts during the accelerating and retarding portions of their travel, and in this way avoid a considerable amount of vibration which would otherwise occur.

*Crankshaft Bearings*—The function of the crankshaft bearing is to support the rotating crankshaft and to eliminate friction between the rotating parts. There are two general types of bearings—*friction* and *nonfriction*. The friction type consists of a bushing or

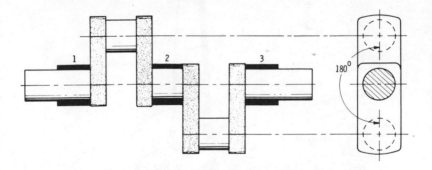

Fig. 27. Double-throw crankshaft with center bearing and two crank pins.

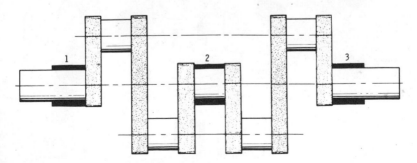

Fig. 28. Double-throw crankshaft with four crank pins.

cylindrical bronze sleeve machined to size, and may be of solid or split construction as shown in Figs. 27 and 28.

The nonfriction type of bearing may be of either the ball or roller type and consists normally of an inner and outer raceway with the balls or rollers held in place by a retaining unit. Although common practice is to provide friction-type bearings for the crankshaft journals and connecting rods, especially in the smaller outboard motor sizes, a combination of friction and nonfriction bearings is frequently employed on the larger motors, friction bearings on the crankshaft journals, and nonfriction bearings on the crankshafts. A crankshaft with center main bearings is shown in Fig. 29.

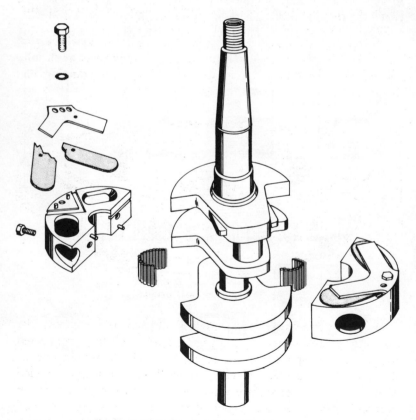

Fig. 29. Crankshaft and center main-bearing assembly.

On racing-type outboard motors, nonfriction bearings are used throughout the motor assembly. Thus, it is customary to employ ball or roller bearings on the crankshaft journals, rollers on the crankshaft, ball bearings on the drive or pinion shaft, with ball bearings or rollers on the propeller shaft. Wrist-pin bearings are most frequently of the friction type.

## Flywheels

The purpose of the flywheel in a two-stroke engine is to secure the momentum necessary to keep the crankshaft turning during the nonpower or compression part of the engine cycle. The flywheel will thus permit the engine to idle smoothly through that part of the cycle when power is not being produced, and to keep the engine turning at a nearly uniform rate of speed.

On engines equipped with starting motors, the flywheel rim carries a gear-teeth ring, either integral with the flywheel or shrunk on, which meshes with the starter driving gear for cranking the engine at starting, as shown in Fig. 30.

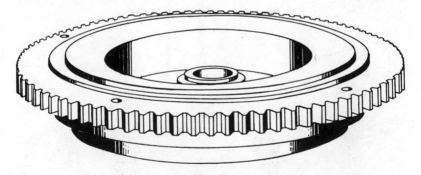

Fig. 30. Typical flywheel assembly.

On most two-stroke cycle engines the flywheel contains the magneto-ignition system. The flywheel-type magneto is connected to one or more spark plugs by means of special high-tension conductors. On air-cooled engines, the flywheel is usually provided with fins on its outer surface which act as a fan for air circulation over the cylinder surface. Flywheels employed on small two- and four-cycle engines are usually made of cast or forged aluminum alloy, the hub forming an integral part of the flywheel shell, or else a steel hub is attached to the wheel.

## ENGINE CYLINDERS

Engine cylinder blocks are usually made of aluminum, with cast-iron cylinder bores, or steel sleeves, aluminum water jackets, bronze bearing inserts, and crankcase section integral.

The cylinders must be round and straight to realize maximum power output, and their arrangement depends on the type of motor. Thus, single- and two-cylinder opposed-firing motors usually have individually cast cylinders, whereas alternate-firing and four-cylinder opposed engines have two cylinders cast in a single block. Larger engines, such as the V-type four and six, and all vertical in-line types, have cylinders cast in a single block.

A typical die-cast cylinder block is shown in Fig. 31. As will be noted in the illustration, the cylinder sleeves are fitted inside the

Courtesy Johnson Motors, Div. of Outboard Marine Corp.

**Fig. 31. A typical die-cast cylinder block.**

die-cast cylinder block, with water jackets a part of the complete assembly. The cylinders are provided with intake and exhaust ports to permit the fuel mixture from the crankcase to enter and to allow the burned gases to be expelled. These ports are located diametrically opposite one another.

## Crankcase

The crankcase, as the name implies, contains the crankshaft and is, in addition, a reservoir for the fuel mixture. The fuel mixture is admitted to the crankcase either through a port opening or through a passageway in the crankcase. In addition, the crankcase serves as a support for the cylinder block or blocks, as well as for the carburetor. Because the crankcase also serves as a compression chamber, it must be made leakproof.

Crankcases on outboard motors are usually cast of an aluminum alloy and made as compact as possible to insure lightness. They may be either of the single piece or split type. Some single-piece crankcases are made of aluminum-alloy casting, with a removable lower bearing; on other types the upper bearing may be replaceable. Late-model outboard motors have the upper bearing cast integrally with the casing and is therefore not replaceable.

In the split-type of crankcase, one half is usually cast integrally with the cylinder block, the crankcase being split along the centerline of the crankshaft journals. The number of bearings vary with the type of motor. Thus, single-cylinder engines have two main bearings, whereas engines with two or more cylinders have three main bearings.

*Crankcase Bleeder*—In a two-stroke cycle engine, the crankcase has a tendency to load up with unburned liquid fuel when operated continuously for an extended period of time at slow speed, with the result that it becomes "flooded" when an increase in speed is required. Flooding in this manner is evidenced by excessive smoking of the exhaust gases, faltering, and erratic operation until the accumulated fuel has been discharged. In extreme cases, the motor may stop because of spark-plug fouling.

To prevent the foregoing, numerous manufacturers of outboard motors have incorporated a special bleeder valve that functions automatically throughout the motor speed range. The arrangement consists essentially of a small hole or channel leading from a pocket in each crankcase chamber to an automatic check valve located at the bottom of the power head.

In operation, the fuel which settles out of the fuel mixture during periods of slow-speed running, accumulates in the pocket provided for this purpose and fills the channel down to the check valve, where it remains until the piston travels downward on its power stroke. The resultant crankcase compression now forces the leaf valve off its seat and will permit liquid fuel to escape through the outlet and on into the driveshaft casing where it is finally discharged with the exhaust gases.

In this connection, it should be noted that there are two check plates, one for each crankcase chamber. During the upward stroke of the piston there is no discharge, since during this time interval the low pressure or suction still exists in the crankcase, with the result that the check plate is held back on its seat (by spring pressure) to prevent air flow from the opposite direction.

Some outboard-motor manufacturers provide a special scavenger pump to carry off the accumulated liquid fuel from the crankcase. Pumps employed for this purpose are usually of the diaphragm type, operating automatically on pressure changes in the engine crankcase.

## POWER HEAD SERVICE

The power head consists of the cylinders, pistons, rods, crankshaft, and crankcase. Other components include the flywheel, magneto, carburetor, reed valves, spark plugs, etc. Although the power heads of all outboard motors are similar in a great many respects in regard to the disassembly, assembly, and inspection of the various components, there is a considerable difference in construction. Some motors have automatic rewind starters of different construction, while others are equipped with electric starters.

Outboard-motor power heads differ in drive methods; some are equipped with direct drive while others have gear-shift drives. Other points of differences are the fuel supply methods. Some motors have gravity feed, with the fuel tank mounted above the motor; others are equipped with separate remotely-located tanks.

Numerous other power-head differences apply. but since these are not relevant to the disassembly and subsequent repairs and service on the average motor. they will be omitted in the present discussion. In this connection. it should be clearly noted that the following information concerns itself primarily with normal service practice on the average outboard motor. and while certain service pointers may differ due to different construction. a proper fundamental knowledge is all that is required to repair any motor.

A complete servicing job of the motor or any of its components involves the disassembly. parts inspection. and repair or replacement of any parts that may be worn or damaged. When servicing motors. keep small parts in separate containers. such as paper cups. so that they may not become lost or mixed up with other parts. Another method to simplify reassembly and wiring installation is to lay out the various screws and clamps in the order of their proper location.

## DISASSEMBLY OF POWER HEAD

Disassembly. repair. replacement. and reassembly of a power head is primarily a matter of observation of the construction of any given motor. This is in order to establish a schedule or order of disassembly.

Overhauling a power head or any of its components involves a complete tear-down, parts inspection. and repair or replacement of any parts that are worn or damaged. In order to overhaul a power head. remove all other assemblies. such as motor cowling. carburetor. fuel lines, magneto, flywheel, and the entire lower unit.

To separate the power head from the lower unit, simply remove the bolts that secure one to the other. The foregoing procedure will greatly assist in the dismantling process since it is much easier to work on a stripped-down power head than would be the case with the accessories in place.

The general arrangement of parts in typical power heads are shown in Figs. 32 to 40, with the method of disassembly principally as follows:

1. Start disassembly of the power head by removing all brackets and cover plates installed on the cylinder block. This will

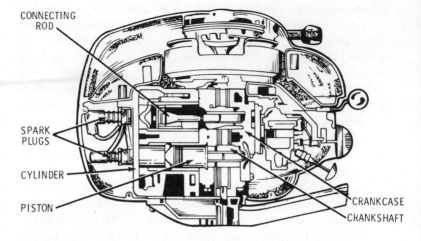

**Fig. 32. Typical power head with a one-piece barrel crankcase and a nonremovable cylinder head.**

include the bypass and exhaust covers. Also remove and discard the gaskets. Never use old gaskets except in extreme emergencies.

2. Remove flywheel.

The next step in the disassembly will depend on the construction of the cylinder and crankcase. There are two principal types of crankcases used. One is known as the split-type which opens vertically, the other is known as the integral-type, and is fitted with cap pieces at top and bottom of the crankcase or, in some instances, a cap piece at only one end of the crankcase so that the crankshaft may be withdrawn from the crankcase. If the crankcase is the split type, proceed as follows:

3. Remove the crankcase screws and separate the crankcase. This also removes the cylinder assembly from the crankshaft with piston and connecting-rod assembly remaining on the crankshaft.

If the crankcase is of the *integral type*, proceed as follows:

4. Remove the cylinder screws and separate the cylinders from the crankcase, leaving the piston and connecting-rod assemblies attached to the crankshaft in the crankcase.

5. In detaching the piston and connecting-rod assemblies from the crankshaft, first scratch a key marking on the inner surface of the piston skirt so that each piston at reassembly will be matched up in the proper cylinder. Connecting rods and caps should be similarly marked or indexed to ascertain their original position in the assembly. This is important since the rod and cap are machined as a matched assembly and will fit properly only when matched as in the original assembly. Use a small file to mark or index the rod and cap.

6. Connecting rods are easier to disconnect if the top, or number one piston, is removed first. On one-piece (integral) crankcases, turn crankshaft until the connecting rod is as far out as it will go, then remove the screws.

7. With the alternate-firing twin- or four-cylinder vertical in-line outboards, it is generally found most convenient to remove the pistons and rods from the top downward.

8. Be careful not to score the cylinder while removing the rings. Pry the ends loose enough to grip them with a pair of long-nosed pliers, then break them away from the piston. Do not attempt to save the rings. Install a complete set of new rings on every power-head service job.

9. When removing wrist pins, observe pin bosses inside of piston and note a small rise embossed on one wrist pin support, or if there is no rise, a prick-punch mark is commonly imbedded in one boss. Some pistons are designed with a slip-fit on one side of the wrist-pin boss and a press fit at the other. This is done to offset distortion of the piston as it expands on reaching normal running temperature. If this is the case, then when driving out the wrist pin, be certain to drive the pin from the side opposite from that marked in order to guard against distortion or damage during the wrist-pin removal operation.

10. To remove the crankshaft on integral-type one-piece crankcases, remove screws that hold the removable bearing assembly in place, and remove it from the crankshaft. On

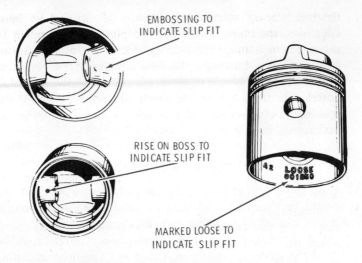

EMBOSSING TO
INDICATE SLIP FIT

RISE ON BOSS TO
INDICATE SLIP FIT

MARKED LOOSE TO
INDICATE SLIP FIT

Fig. 33. Illustrating various wrist-pin installations.

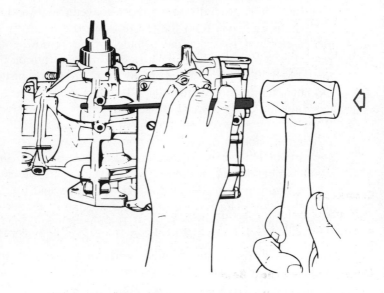

Fig. 34. Removing a center-bearing dowel pin.

some motor types, the lower bearing is removable, and the crankcase studs also attach the bearing assembly. To remove the ball-bearing assembly, tap gently all around its inner edge from the inside with a flat-end punch. Care should be taken not to damage the bearing shield. On motors having cast-in bronze bushings, the bearing cannot be removed. The bearing seal should be replaced. On some motors, hollow dowel pins threaded on the inside are used to secure the bearings. In assemblies of this sort, a special bearing pin puller must be used.

## INSPECTION AND REPAIRS

After the power head has been completely disassembled, all parts should be thoroughly cleaned by immersion in a tank of cleaning solution or by washing with a petroleum solvent.

Inspect all functional parts to determine which parts are to be repaired or replaced to restore the motor to its normal operating condition. Inspect and check the following:

1. Crankcase.
2. Crankshaft for alignment.
3. Crankshaft throws for alignment.
4. Connecting rods for alignment.
5. Wrist pin and crank-pin fits.
6. Ball and needle bearings.
7. Pistons for scoring, cracks, carbon, etc.
8. Piston rings.
9. Cylinders and cylinder block.
10. Reed valves and settings.

### Crankcase

If after careful inspection the crankcase is found to be cracked, it should be replaced. Damaged or broken studs should be replaced. Inspect water passages for obstructions.

### Crankcase Journal Bearings

The journal bearings seldom require replacing. These are cast integrally with the crankcase or with the bearing assemblies. When replacement becomes necessary, replace the entire crankcase or bearing assembly.

## Main Bearings

Needle bearings should always be replaced at servicing and when rust conditions are present. Caged needle bearings should be replaced if they have become wet and rusty. Ball bearings and roller bearings should be cleaned and dried before checking. Do not attempt to check ball or roller bearings by spinning, since a bearing which might otherwise be cleaned and restored to a serviceable condition will very likely be damaged by such practice. Bearings having rusted balls, rollers, or raceways should be discarded. Moderate discoloration of balls and ball tracks will, however, not affect their future use.

*Important:* Always press cartridge type needle bearings into position wtih the "lettered" side up, as opposite side has a greater radius for better installation. Check bearings after installation to see that they are free and not frozen or stuck because of improper installation or tight fit. Inspect roller bearings in particular and check that they are not worn. It is recommended, when repairing motors, that bearings be replaced, as they are relatively inexpensive.

## Pistons

Check ring grooves in piston for carbon accumulation, excessive wear, or damage to ring seats. Carbon deposits on pistons and in ring grooves should be carefully removed. Scratches or other damage to the ring seats results in lack of compression and power.

When cylinders are properly machined and there is proper clearance and lubrication, there is no reason for excessive wear. When

**Fig. 35. Checking piston for roundness with a micrometer.**

any one of the foregoing requirements are not obtained, abnormal wear will result. Normal wear, however, is a result of high speed and temperature, accompanied by the necessary tightness of operation.

If pistons have been scored or metal has been damaged, they must be replaced. Check piston pin bosses for cracks. Replace if cracked or if piston pins are loose. Inspect piston ring grooves for wear, burn, and distortion. It is recommended that new piston rings be installed unless old ones prove to be absolutely free from cracks, burn, carbon, or other abnormal wear. Rings are inexpensive and replacement will insure good repair and future operations. Pins, located in ring grooves, prevent rings from rotating.

NOTE: Before replacing piston rings, clean out the grooves thoroughly, using the recessed end of a broken ring. Also clean any carbon and varnish deposits from the top sides of all pistons with a soft wire brush or carbon remover solution. When wire brushing the top of a piston, do not burr or round the machined edges.

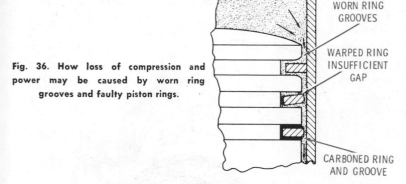

WORN RING GROOVES

WARPED RING INSUFFICIENT GAP

Fig. 36. How loss of compression and power may be caused by worn ring grooves and faulty piston rings.

CARBONED RING AND GROOVE

Gum, varnish, and softer carbon deposits can be removed by soaking in a carbon removal solution *(Gunk), Bendix* parts cleaner, or others. Piston skirt can be polished with crocus cloth to remove burrs. Piston pins are not sold separately because of slight variation in sizes and correct fit into pistons. Check the pin and pin boss, especially if engine has been submerged. If the pin is bent, it elongates the piston pin boss when removed. A new pin would, thus, fit loosely.

POWER HEAD CONSTRUCTION AND SERVICE

If piston-ring grooves are in suitable condition for further service, and the piston otherwise serviceable, check the piston fit in the cylinder. Make certain that the cylinders are round, the same diameter top and bottom, and at right angles to (square with) the base.

The skirt of the piston should be fitted to the cylinder with a clearance of .002 in. in pistons having a diameter of two inches or less, and in pistons having a diameter in excess of two inches the clearance should be .003 in. Failure to provide proper clearance may cause either scored cylinders or freezing, which seizure might pull off the head of a piston or cause the breakage or distortion of other parts, such as pins, connecting rods, etc.

Particular care must be used to give the rings sufficient end and side clearance, since failure to do this might also cause freezing. In reaming the pin holes, the better method is to clamp the reamer and turn the piston around the reamer. If the piston is clamped, it may be distorted, causing the pin holes to be out of alignment when the pressure is released. Furthermore, if a piston is put in a vise, it is apt to be cracked or forced out of round. It is best to buy fitted assemblies.

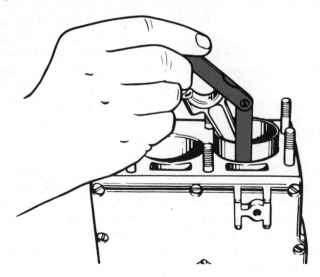

Fig. 37. Checking piston clearance in cylinder block.

In the installation of a piston, never use force on any part of it or in any way. Should it be necessary to place pistons in a lathe or grinder, it is difficult to obtain the greatest accuracy with any device that exerts either inside expansion or outside pressure.

While bell centers or chucks may be used, for best results a universal grinding and turning arbor, or any similar device that will positively maintain uniform roundness while the pressure of tool or grinding wheel is being applied, should be used. This permits an experienced workman to remove accurately even as little as a thousandth of an inch of material from the outer surface.

When reassembling the engine, cleanliness is of the utmost importance. Dirt and chips must be eliminated or all the care used in fitting the various parts may have been useless. Just before installing, dip the piston in oil and be sure that the entire engine is properly lubricated.

## Piston Ring Selection

The piston rings, as previously noted, serve to provide a seal between the piston and cylinder in order to permit the gases to be compressed in the cylinder.

In ring installation, the selection of the proper type piston rings is of great importance in obtaining a satisfactory job. When installing new rings, therefore, only rings of the correct dimensions and clearance as recommended by the manufacturer should be installed.

Rings should be replaced if the face of the ring is glass smooth, has a highly polished appearance, or if the edge of the ring is rounded off. The edges of the ring should be square with the face, not too smooth, and rather dull in appearance if serviceable; if not, install new rings.

## Fitting Piston Rings

When installing new piston rings, first check the ring in the cylinder bore for proper clearance. Square up the ring by pushing it into the cylinder bore with the bottom of the piston. Then check the gap with a feeler gauge. Check each ring in its respective groove for evidence of tightness or binding by rolling the ring around in the piston-ring groove. The ring should roll freely in its groove. When checked with the thickness gauge, the new piston should

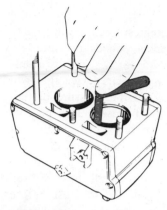

Fig. 38. Checking piston-ring gap in cylinder wall.

have from .0005 to .001 in. clearance between the ring and the side of the groove.

In all cases it is advisable to install the top ring with slightly more clearance than the other rings. Thus, on small gas engines of the type used in outboard application, a minimum clearance of .001 in. is recommended for all rings except the top, and for the top ring a clearance of .002 in. is consistent with good practice.

In outboard-motor applications, the piston-ring end clearance should be at least .003 in. per inch of cylinder diameter. The manufacturer's instruction and recommendations, however, should be strictly adhered to when installing new piston rings.

**Oversize Piston and Piston Rings**

The major purpose for oversize pistons and rings is for salvaging scored cylinder blocks. If the score is over .0075 in. deep, it cannot be effectively rebored for future use.

**Connecting Rods**

The piston, piston rings, and connecting-rod assembly must be properly matched. Engine knocks due to a loose or malfunctioning connecting rod will cause damage to the engine if not corrected.

Check the connecting-rod, wrist-pin, and crank-pin fits. Note the general condition of the wrist-pin and connecting-rod bearings, and if badly scored and worn, they should be replaced. Check the bearing surfaces for rust. Clean the rust off the surface with a fine

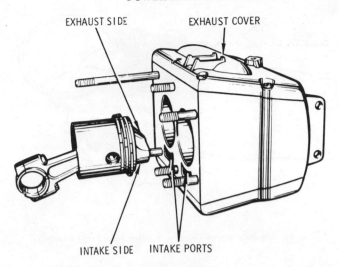

**Fig. 39. Connecting-rod and piston assembly showing correct piston position in the cylinder.**

emery cloth. Rust may leave only stain marks on the surface, but these may be easily removed. To check for excessive looseness of the connecting rod on the crank pin, first check the freeness between the rod and pin by exerting an up and down motion on the rod at right angles to the crank pin.

This check should indicate normal clearance. If excessive clearance or wear is evident, it will be found possible to rock the rod from side to side. Check the wrist-pin fit in the same manner.

### Piston and Connecting Rod

When checking the piston and rod assembly, check for squareness first by installing the assembly on the fixture as shown in Fig. 33. Make certain that the connecting rod is made secure on the protruding pin which simulates the crank pin on the crankshaft. Carefully adjust the position of the piston as it comes to rest against the aligning face of the fixture simulating the walls of the cylinder.

To check for a bend in the rod, adjust the piston to fit against the aligning face with care. Do not use force since it is possible to spring the rod, thus obtaining an erroneous result. If the piston and rod assembly is square (straight connecting rod and straight

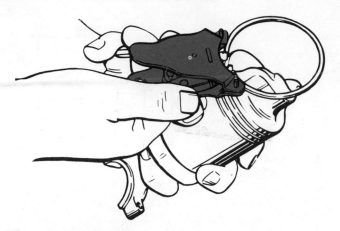

Fig. 40. Installing piston rings on a piston with a ring expander.

piston) the skirt of the piston will be found to rest flatly against the aligning fixture face. When this condition exists, no light will be visible between the skirt of the piston and fixture, except at the ring land area, since these areas are slightly smaller in diameter than the skirt.

To determine if a twist in the connecting rod exist, adjust the assembly on the fixture in an upright position. Then, without disturbing the position of the connecting rod, rock the piston to the right or left, and at the same time observe the possibility of light streaks developing between the piston skirt and aligning surface.

## POWER HEAD REASSEMBLY

Reassembling the power head is essentially the reverse of disassembly. When reassembling the engine, always use new gaskets throughout. Before reassembling the engine, all worn parts should be put into serviceable condition or new parts should be substituted. Make sure that all parts involved in the assembly are clean. Always install new crankshaft oil seals.

### Pistons, Piston Rings, and Connecting Rods

Using a piston-ring expander, assemble the piston rings on the piston in the same order that they were removed. The beveled edge

98

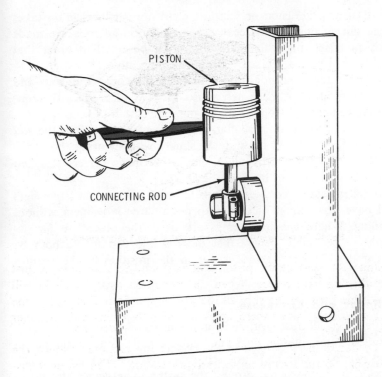

Fig. 41. Checking connecting rod and piston alignment.

of the piston ring should be assembled toward the top of the piston. The ring gaps should be staggered to retard compression loss as much as possible. The ring grooves in many pistons are pinned to secure the position of the ring in the ring groove. This is done to prevent the ends of the ring catching on the edges of the ports in the cylinders.

Lubricate the pistons and cylinder bores and, using a piston-ring compressor, assembly the pistons in the cylinders in the proper position, as previously marked. To prevent the pistons from being installed backwards, note the shape of the piston tops—the small grooved side of the piston is the intake side—the wider, tapered side is the exhaust side.

To install the connecting rod and piston assembly, coat all bearing surfaces, piston-ring grooves, and cylinder walls with oil to guard against abrasion or scuttling until normal lubrication takes place during operation. Because some connecting rods are made with an offset, particular care should be observed in order that the rod and piston intake is assembled correctly.

Remove the connecting-rod caps from the connecting rods and note the position of the match marks for reference. Place the connecting rod carefully on the crank pin, and install the cap with the match mark to match a similar marking on the rod. Bolt the rod and cap together and draw down snugly without using too much force. Connecting-rod openings should be of the correct size and clean, in order not to bind on the shaft.

If roller-bearing connecting rods are used, the correct size rollers will have just enough clearance to permit free movement without binding. Where needle bearings are used, the procedure for assembly is the same, except that the rod and cap should both be smeared with heavy grease to retain the position of the needles during installation.

## Cylinder and Crankcase

Clean out all dust, grit, and foreign matter from the parts to be installed. Lubricate the rings and cylinder walls. Line up the piston rings so that their ends are separated by the lock-pin in each groove or are staggered around the piston. The ring ends should not be on the bypass-port side of the cylinder.

Install the cylinder with a new gasket, if gaskets are used. Tighten the cylinder hold-down nuts securely. In those motors that have removable cylinder heads, install the cylinder head, using a new gasket.

On split-type crankcases, install the upper, center, and lower crankshaft bearings. Install the thrust bearing. Replace all seals and oil rings with new parts. Then install the crankshaft and make sure that the bearings are located on the dowel pins in the crankcase, and that the thrust bearing is in position.

The final assembly includes the installation of the carburetor, flywheel, magneto, fuel pump, starter, spark plugs, etc. Because of the various sizes and types of motors, it will not be possible to supply information as to the procedure to be used when installing the foregoing to the power head.

## Carburetor

If the carburetor has excessive deposits of gum and varnish, it may clog the fuel passages and affect operation. To clean, remove the float, float-valve seat assembly, high- and low-speed needles, and the packing glands. Immerse the carburetor body in a commercial solvent to remove all dirt, grit, and foreign matter.

After careful inspection of all parts, replace or readjust as required. After reassembly of the carburetor, install on the motor crankcase, using a new gasket. If a reed or leaf-type valve is used between the carburetor and crankcase, make sure that the reeds face toward the crankcase side of the engine. Install new gaskets on both sides of the valve assembly.

## Flywheel

Check the crankshaft and flywheel tapers for traces of oil prior to the flywheel installation. This assembly must be perfectly dry. Swab the tapered surfaces with solvent and blow dry with an air stream. Inspect both tapers for burrs or nicks.

Crankshaft key should be assembled to crankshaft with outer edge vertical. Magnetos of the flywheel-mounted type are automatically timed when installed at the factory, thus no further timing will be necessary.

Assembly of the power head is now complete except for the starter, intake manifold, fuel pump, thermostat, motor covers, manual starter linkages, etc. These items can be assembled in the order of disassembly.

Catching a hefty stringer of fish often depends on finding just the right spot. This young angler relies on his fishing outboard to help him where they're bitin'. The engine is a two-cylinder with 10.9 cubic inch displacement. This one can be had in either electrical or manual start.

Courtesy Mercury Marine, Div. of Brunswick Corp.

# Chapter 5

# Lower Unit Construction and Service

The lower unit of an outboard motor contains the stern bracket, drive shaft, casing, and necessary shafting and gearing required to

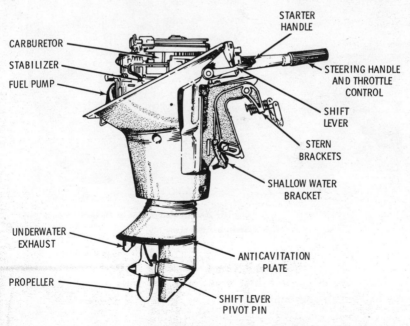

CARBURETOR

STABILIZER

FUEL PUMP

STARTER HANDLE

STEERING HANDLE AND THROTTLE CONTROL

SHIFT LEVER

STERN BRACKETS

SHALLOW WATER BRACKET

UNDERWATER EXHAUST

ANTICAVITATION PLATE

PROPELLER

SHIFT LEVER PIVOT PIN

Courtesy Johnson Motors, Div. of Outboard Marine Corp.

**Fig. 1. Lower unit showing location of components.**

deliver power generated by the power head to the propeller. The lower unit also contains the water pump and associated piping for water circulation through the cooling system. These features are shown in Fig. 1.

The outboard motor is secured to the boat transom by a stern bracket, Fig. 2, which normally is provided with an adjustment mechanism permitting the motor assembly to tilt slightly in case of underwater obstructions striking the projecting motor leg.

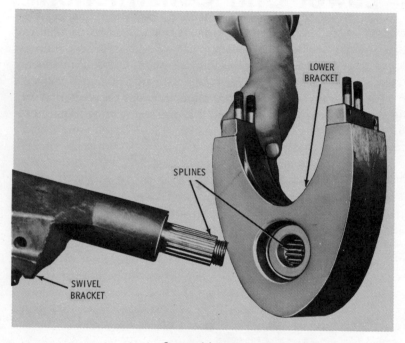

Courtesy Johnson Motors, Div. of Outboard Marine Corp.

**Fig. 2. Stern bracket assembly.**

## GEAR SHIFTS

There are in general three types of lower units, termed according to their operational features:

1. Nonreversible.
2. Full-reversible.

3. Forward-neutral-reverse gear shift.
4. Automatic transmission.

The *nonreversible type* of lower unit provides only a limited arc in pivoting the motor in the pivot bearing and stern bracket, and cannot be used in reverse.

The *full-reversible type* can be pivoted a full turn of 360 degrees. This permits operation in reverse by pivoting the engine through an arc of 180 degrees.

The *forward-neutral-reverse gear-shift type* provides a flexible method of speed control, which functions in a manner similar to that used in certain automotive applications. In order to obtain a forward, neutral, or reverse speed, three gears, a sliding member, and a shifting mechanism are required. The bevel pinion is splined to the drive shaft and rotates constantly when the motor is in operation. The beveled gears, one forward and one aft, floats on the propeller shaft in a manner similar to that of the pinion, and rotates with the motor, one in one direction and one in the other.

In operation, the sliding member is keyed or splined to the propeller shaft and remains stationary, as does the propeller shaft and propeller during (neutral) operation. When forward or reverse operation is desired, the dogs of the sliding member engages like dogs on either gear, depending on which gear is engaged. See Fig. 3.

An *automatic transmission* system employed on outboard motors provides forward, neutral, or reverse speed by merely twisting the steering handle in the desired direction. This fully automatic transmission permits one hand control of steering, speed, and forward-neutral-reverse shifting. Essentially, the transmission consists of a forward and reverse spring, a neutral clutch spring, and an input drum-and-gear assembly that provides for reverse speed. In operation, when the shift-control handle is set in neutral, a reverse pawl moves into contact with the upper end of the neutral clutch spring. This action causes the spring to uncoil and releases its grip on the upper drive shaft, permitting it to revolve freely, disconnecting it from the lower gear transmission.

With the shift-control handle in a forward-speed position, the movable neutral pawl parts with the neutral clutch spring. This, in turn, releases the clutch spring and permits it to recoil, gripping both

105

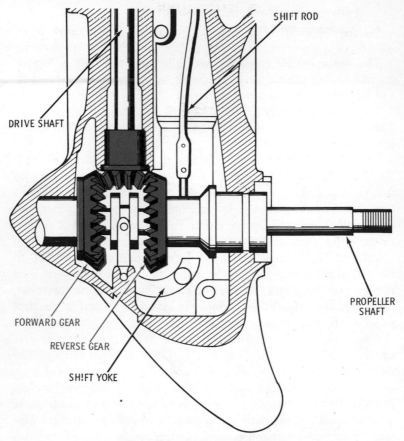

**Fig. 3. Typical reversible gear unit.**

the drive shaft and the hub within the drum-and-gear assembly. With the drive shaft and gear transmission operating as a unit, forward speed will be obtained.

When the shift control is moved into a reverse position, the reverse pawl moves into position against the end of the forward and reverse spring, which, in turn, causes the spring to uncoil and prevents the spring and trunion case from turning. The connection between the drive shaft, input drum, and drum gear are now being completed in such a way as to cause the lower drive shaft to operate in a reverse direction.

## DRIVE-SHAFT HOUSING

The drive-shaft housing may be of tubular construction or of cast aluminum, and provided with flanges at each end for mounting to the engine crankcase and upper part of the gear case. See Fig. 4.

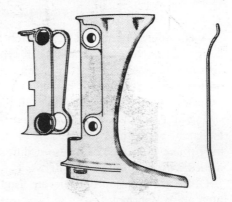

Fig. 4. Drive-shaft housing and water tubing used to conduct water to and from the engine for cooling purposes.

In the case of tubular construction, some form of clamping arrangement is usually provided for attaching the casing to the gear case.

## WATER TUBING

These are contained in the drive shaft housing, and may be plain tubing or cast-in channels. The function of the water tubing is to conduct the water to and from the engine jackets for cooling purposes.

## GEAR CASES

The upper and lower gear-case units are attached and properly sealed to one another to prevent water from entering. The lower gear case is a one-piece unit and contains the bearings, gears, and shafting employed to transmit the power from the engine to the propeller.

The gear case also contains the water-pump impeller and pump housing. The water-pump impeller may be keyed to the drive shaft, or may be located directly behind the propeller and driven by the

107

propeller shaft. The lower gear-case unit is provided with greas seals on both the drive and propeller shaft to retain lubrication an to prevent water from entering.

## PROPELLERS

A considerable amount of research has been made on propelle design to enable water crafts of all types to perform with the bes possible efficiency. Thus, extended tests are constantly made by propeller manufacturers and others in order to supply the prope propeller for the particular boat and engine. For best results, the size and type of boat, motor, and propeller must be properly matched. Sometimes the type of boat, load, and other conditions may make it necessary to use a different propeller than that fur nished with the motor.

Outboard motor propellers are usually cast of bronze or alumi num alloy, and may be of the two- or three-bladed type. The number of blades on a propeller, however, is no indication of efficiency.

### Propeller Size

The size of the propeller is given in two dimensions, namely diameter and pitch. These dimensions are usually stamped on the propeller hub and denoted by figures such as 10 ×12, meaning that the propeller has a diameter of ten inches and a pitch of twelve inches. The two-blade propeller diameter is the distance from the extreme tip of one blade to the tip of the other. In a three-blade propeller the diameter is equal to the diameter of a circle scribed by its revolving blades.

There are only two dimensions of a propeller which concern the owner of an outboard motor boat. Propeller pitch is the theoretical distance a propeller advances through the water in one revolution with no slip. The percentage of slip varies considerably, depending on the boat and load characteristics. Propeller diameter is the propeller-blade distance from the tip of one blade to the tip of an opposite blade. This is shown in Fig. 5.

An example of propeller slippage will be obtained if we assume that a 10 × 12 propeller, instead of advancing 12 inches per revolution through the water, actually advances only a distance of

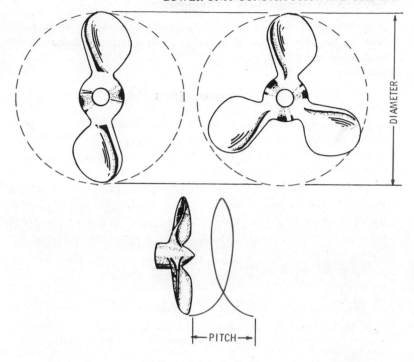

**Fig. 5. Illustrating a typical two- and three-bladed propeller showing the diameter and pitch, respectively.**

eight inches per revolution because of encountered resistance. The percentage of slip in the foregoing example will be 4/12 or 33 1/3 percent, approximately. The percentage loss from slippage depends on several factors, such as type and shape of hull, propeller size, motor rpm, water currents, etc., and may vary from 30 to 60 percent on the average outboard unit.

### Efficiency

Propeller efficiency depends to a great extent on the shape and weight of the hull. Racing hulls are built to offer the least possible resistance to forward motion with a resulting high propeller efficiency. Heavier square-stern types offer a high forward resistance with accompanying low propeller efficiency. Keel interference, angle, and propeller thrust with reference to the line of forward

109

motion, depth of propeller operation, marine growth, and boat loading are other factors which affect propeller efficiency.

## Cavitation

Cavitation is a condition where the propeller is forced to operate in turbulent or greatly disturbed water and has a detrimental effect on propeller efficiency. In most instances, cavitation is brought about by the propeller operating too close to the water surface because of the stern being too high or when turning sharply at high speed.

## Propeller Shear Pin

Shear pins are simple devices to protect the motor and accessories from damage due to underwater obstructions. Under normal operation the shear pin, being inserted in a hole through the shaft to prevent the propeller from slipping, turns with the propeller and shaft.

When, due to conditions beyond the control of the operator, the propeller strikes a foreign object, the shear pin (being purposely made of soft metal) shears off, permitting the propeller shaft to turn while the propeller remains free.

This method of protecting the motor and other parts from damage is usually found in older motor types. Late designs normally incorpoate additional protection in the form of clutches or shock absorbers for motor and propeller protection. One such arrangement consists of a slip clutch having a cone and cone-shaped housing. The cone is attached to the propeller shaft by means of a key or pin. Contact by the propeller with an underwater obstruction causes the cone and propeller to slip, preventing damage to the propeller, gears, or shaft. Other outboard motors provide a neutral slip clutch and shock absorber incorporated in the drive shaft to lessen the possibility of propeller or motor damage when contacting underwater objects.

Late developments in the shock-absorber method has been to simplify construction by inserting a rubber cushion between the propeller and the propeller shaft. This propeller cushion is attached to the propeller shaft by means of a shear pin. When the propeller strikes an obstruction, the rubber cushion (shown in Fig. 6) twists

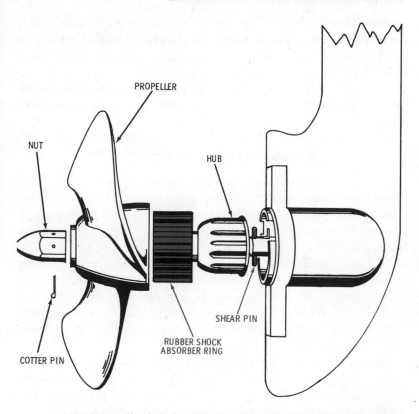

Fig. 6. Propeller-shaft shear pin with rubber shock-absorber ring.

sufficiently to prevent the pin from shearing. When the obstruction has passed, the cushion will twist the propeller back into its normal position.

In this assembly, the drive is through the propeller shaft to the propeller hub. The propeller is driven by the drive pin through the serrated rubber insert which comes to rest in a like serrated section in the propeller. When striking a submerged object, the rubber insert gives or slips in the propeller to absorb the shock which might other wise shear the drive pin. On release of the propeller, the rubber insert resumes its normal position to continue driving the propeller, having engaged slots or serrations in the propeller and on the hub provided for this purpose.

111

## Propeller Clutch

A typical form of propeller shock absorber consists of a pair of sleeves, one of which is keyed to the upper and one to the lower drive shaft. The shock absorbing spring is located within the sleeves, and connects the shafts in such a manner that, when subjected to sudden stress, the spring will coil slightly within the assembly to permit slippage.

## LOWER UNIT SERVICING

The function of the lower unit is to furnish rotative power to the propeller by means of the motor drive shaft and accompanying gear mechanism. The propeller, sometimes called screw or blade, is the unit responsible for transforming the rotary energy of the motor into forward motion of the boat.

Because the design of the lower units vary considerably, caution should be exercised in the disassembly and removal in order not to cause damage to parts during the process. On some outboard motors, the lower-unit housing is a one-piece casting, while in others, two or three castings are bolted together to form the complete housing.

It should also be noted that, while some outboard motors have the cooling water pump located between the lower gear-case housing and the exhaust housing, on other motors the water pump is located in the lower gear case directly ahead of the propeller.

Depending on construction, the lower unit may have one or two drive shafts. Those equipped with a spring-type neutral clutch may have the clutch located on the drive shaft or within the lower gear case on the propeller shaft. Also, some motors may have a direct drive to the propeller while others are equipped with a gearshift mechanism to provide a choice of forward, neutral, or reverse speed. These are only some of the construction differences of the lower units, and it follows from the foregoing that while the operational function of each unit is similar, no procedural information can be put down with respect to lower-unit disassembly.

In this connection it should be noted that, because of the various difficulties which may be encountered in the disassembly and subsequent repairs of the lower unit, any attempt at servicing should not be made unless the owner is satisfied with his ability to cope with the unit in question and also with the knowledge that spare parts are easily available.

## DISASSEMBLY OF LOWER UNIT

The general arrangement of parts in typical lower units are shown in Figs. 7 to 12, with the method of disassembly principally as follows:

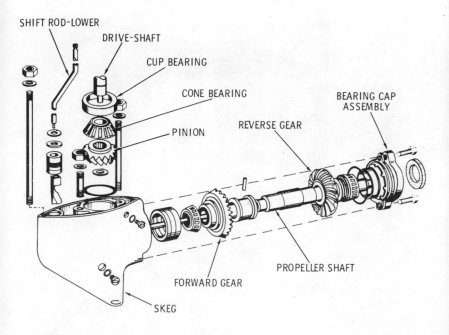

SHIFT ROD-LOWER
DRIVE-SHAFT
CUP BEARING
CONE BEARING
BEARING CAP ASSEMBLY
PINION
REVERSE GEAR
FORWARD GEAR
PROPELLER SHAFT
SKEG

Fig. 7. Parts assembly and lower gear housing of a typical outboard motor.

1. Before disassembly, drain all oil or grease from the gear housing. Clamp the gear housing in a vise in an upright position, gripping the lower skeg in the vise. The use of wooden blocks formed to fit the skeg is advisable in order not to damage the skeg with the vise jaws. Copper jaws may also be used to hold the skegs to avoid markings.

113

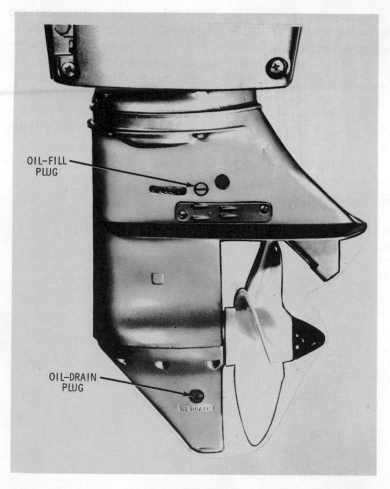

OIL–FILL
PLUG

OIL–DRAIN
PLUG

Fig. 8. Gear lubrication oil-filler and drain-plug location in lower-unit
gear case.

2. Remove the propeller, the water pump, impeller housing,
   and impeller. Remove the impeller pin and the impeller-
   housing plate.
3. Turn the gear housing upside down and hold it in position
   by clamping the drive shaft in a vise with copper jaws.

4. Remove the lower gear case (where used), disconnect and lift up the shift rod just far enough to permit the removal of the propeller shaft, gears, and roller bearings (all in one complete unit) from the gear case. Removal of the complete unit will make all parts accessible for further disassembly.

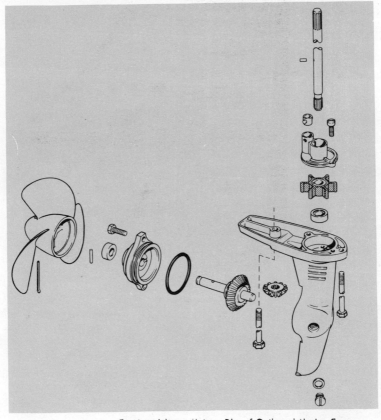

Courtesy Johnson Motors, Div. of Outboard Marine Corp.

**Fig. 9. Exploded view of a typical direct-drive lower unit illustrating arrangement of parts.**

5. Remove all gears, bearings, and seals from the propeller shaft. Remove the gear case from the drive shaft which is still clamped in the vise. Remove the drive shaft from the vise.

6. Remove the pinion gear and roller-bearing assembly. Then remove the pinion roller-bearing cup (where used).

7. To remove the impeller housing from the upper pump housing, gently grasp one of the webs in the housing with a pair of pliers and insert a screwdriver between the impeller housing and the pump housing.

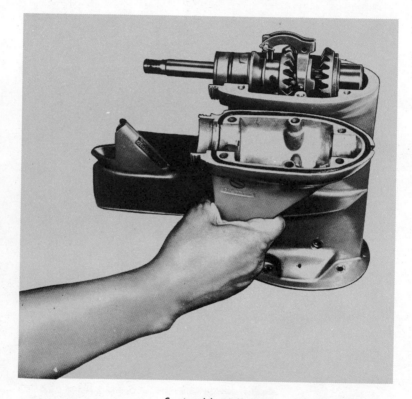

Courtesy Johnson Motors, Div. of Outboard Marine Corp.

**Fig. 10. Cutaway view of the propeller and gear assembly in a full gearshift unit.**

8. Carefully and evenly pull on the pliers and pry with the screwdriver. Exercise the utmost caution during this operation.

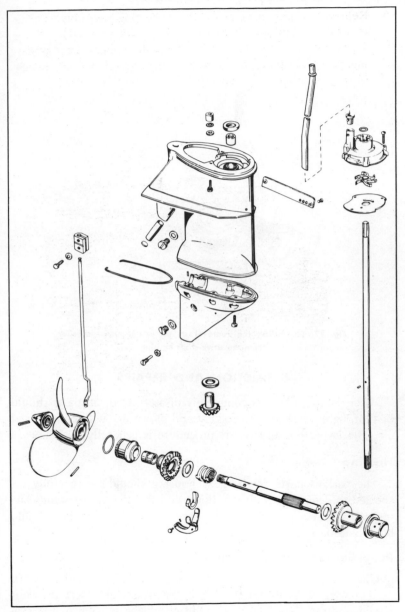

**Fig. 11. Propeller-shaft assembly showing arrangement of gears.**

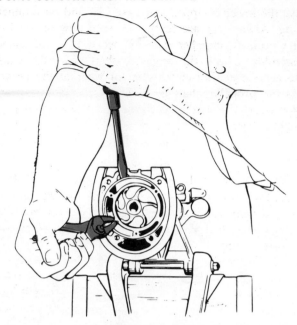

Fig. 12. Illustrating the removal of the water-pump impeller from the drive-shaft housing.

## INSPECTION AND REPAIRS

After the lower unit is completely disassembled, all parts should be thoroughly washed with solvent and blown dry with compressed air. The inspection and repair procedure is generally as follows:

### Housing

The various parts of the gear housing should be carefully inspected to determine their condition and the amount of wear. The inspection will reveal which parts are serviceable and which should be replaced.

### Propeller and Drive Shafts

Check the drive shaft, propeller shaft, and shift-rod seals; if worn or damaged, replace. To check the shift-rod seal, insert the shift rod in position in the gear case and check the tension of the seal on the rod.

118

Remove the lower-to-upper gear-case seal and oil-retainer housing oil ring. Always replace such seals with new ones when reassembling. Check the impeller vanes for wear. If worn, replace with a new assembly. Check the propeller shaft gears for wear. Also check the gears and shift-clutch dog for wear at the point where it engages the propeller-shaft gear. Check the reverse-gear thrust washer for wear. Check the gear-case retainer ring to be sure it has the right tension.

## Bearings

Check the bearings in the gear housing and drive-shaft housing for wear. If the bearings or bushings are of the replaceable type, they can be driven out and preparations made for installation of new bearings and final line reaming; otherwise, if cast-in, new castings will be required.

Check the needle-type roller bearings and replace if worn, pitted, or otherwise damaged. Check the tapered roller bearings and replace bearings and outer race if the rollers or race are pitted and show signs of wear. Be sure that the bearings revolve freely; otherwise they should be replaced.

Installation of new bearings or bushings must be performed with a great deal of care, paying particular attention to alignment to prevent the possibility of cocking, which not only ruins the bearings but, in many instances, the gear case as well.

Note carefully the existence of holes which might have been drilled in the bearing walls for lubrication purposes, and like holes in the bearing walls. These should be in alignment after the bearing has been driven home.

## Gears

When reassembling the gear case, check the drive gears; if worn, or have damaged teeth, replace. Check for free movement of the entire assembly. Bending or excessive drag is the result of insufficient bearing clearance, misalignment of bearings, or improperly meshing gears. Never attempt to mesh an old worn gear with a new gear, but always replace both gears when such conditions occur.

To adjust the gear mesh, lightly tap the end of the propeller shaft with a rawhide mallet to drive the assembly back. Check for a feel of mesh and turn the propeller shaft to make sure no binding occurs at any point.

## Water Pump

Inspect and replace all pump parts that show excessive wear. Replace grease seals and damaged intake screens. When installing the water by-pass plate, make sure that it is installed in the correct position; that is, with the water inlet holes in the plate opposite the water discharge in the housing toward the front of the motor.

## Propeller

Damage common to propellers are bent blades and worn or cracked hubs. When replacing a damaged propeller, it is important that the new propeller be of identical size and characteristics. Slightly bent propeller blades may be straightened to their original shape by the use of a suitable form on which the blades are hammered to shape with a wooden mallet.

## Shear Pin

A broken shear pin normally will result in a sudden racing of the motor and loss of forward motion of the boat. The function of the shear pin is to permit the propeller to be disconnected from the rotating shaft whenever the propeller strikes a foreign object, thus protecting the propeller, motor, and other parts of the mechanism from damage.

It is important that the motor be shut off at the first sign of shear-pin failure. To replace a shear pin, remove the propeller cotter pin and nut, and insert a new pin of identical characteristics. It is normally established practice to be equipped with several spare pins to be used when needed.

## REASSEMBLING LOWER UNIT

Reassembling the lower unit consists essentially of a reversal of the disassembly procedure. One of the most important points to keep in mind is to make sure that the new oil seals and gaskets be put in their respective locations without tearing or rolling.

Many gear cases use seals on the propeller and drive shafts to assist in retaining gear lubricants; otherwise, where not provided, lubricant is actually retained only by the "fit" of the propeller and drive shafts in their respective bearings. In the case of a sealed gear case, it is possible to use a lighter lubricant for better circulation.

The seals (where used) should be installed with care to guard against possible injury to the sealing surfaces which may render them unfit for sealing purposes. Where it is necessary to install the seal over threads, carefully screw the seal over the threaded end of the propeller shaft.

After reassembling the water pump and gear case, make sure of free movement of the entire assembly. Slide the drive shaft into the housing, making sure that the deflector pin is properly inserted in the pump-body groove. Be careful that the drive-gear key is inserted in the proper position.

Reassemble the gear case with utmost care, with the necessary new parts, and using new gaskets coated with a thin layer of non-drying *Permatex* cement. Check for free movement of the entire assembly, since binding or excessive drag is the result of incorrect assembly, insufficient bearing clearance, bearing misalignment, improperly meshed gears, etc.

To adjust the gear mesh, lightly tap the end of the propeller shaft with a rawhide mallet to drive the assembly back, or, if necessary, add shims to secure the correct mesh. When reassembly has been completed, fill the gear housing with the proper grade of lubricant and recheck to see that the shafts are free and that there is no excessive binding. There will, however, be a slight binding if new seals have been used because they should fit snugly on the shafts to prevent any leakage of lubricant.

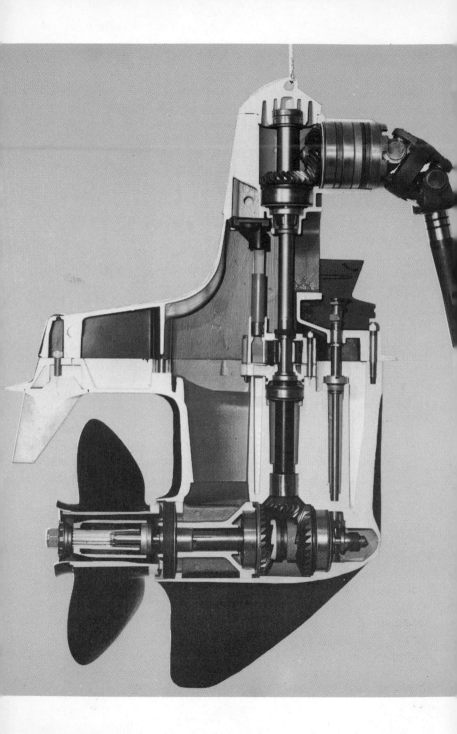

**Chapter 6**

# Cooling Systems

Outboard motors have something in common with other types of internal combustion engines; they must be equipped with some form of cooling system because of the great amount of heat generated by combustion of the fuel. There is no dependable method of measuring the temperature in the combustion chamber during the burning of the fuel, but it is estimated to be about 3,000 degrees F for low-compression engines of the type employed in outboard boating.

Accordingly, it must be evident that the intense heat generated within the gas-engine cylinder would very quickly overheat the metal within the cylinder to such an extent that it would become red hot, resulting in burned and warped valves, seized pistons, overheated bearings, and a breakdown of lubrication.

To avoid these conditions, means must be provided to carry off some of the heat; that is, enough of it to prevent the temperature of the metal of the cylinder rising above a predetermined point and low enough to permit satisfactory lubrication and operation. The excess heat must be carried off by some form of cooling system.

It should be clearly understood, however, that although heat is necessary to cause expansion of the charge which acts on the piston head to produce power, a large part of it goes to waste through the exhaust port and through the cooling system. Thus, for example, it is estimated that only about one-third of the heat energy contained in the fuel is actually converted into useful power, one-third is dissipated through the exhaust, and the remaining one-third is absorbed in the cooling system. Fig. 1 illustrates the temperature difference.

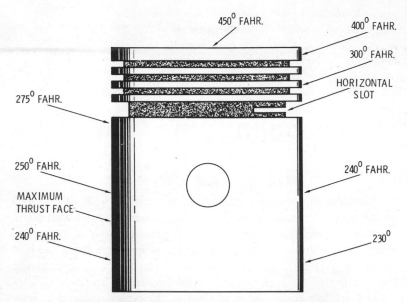

Fig. 1. Working temperatures of different parts of a piston.

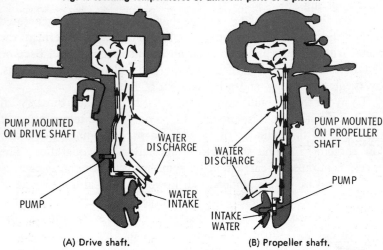

Fig. 2. Water flow diagram for a pump mounted on the drive shaft and on the propeller shaft.

There are two methods of cooling outboard motors; by *water cooling* or by *air cooling*. Water cooling is commonly used and generally employs a pump and associated piping to convey the cooling medium through the cylinder jackets. The water pump may be located either in the lower gear housing directly ahead of the propeller, or in the drive-shaft housing above the drive gears. Two various designs are shown in Fig. 2.

Air-cooled engines usually employ blades incorporated in the flywheel which act to fan or circulate air over the fins cast integrally with the cylinders. Outboard motors using air cooling are available only in the smaller horsepower ranges.

## WATER COOLING SYSTEM

Pumps used to circulate the water through the outboard motor cooling system may be either of the *rotor* or *centrifugal type*. A typical arrangement using a two-stage centrifugal pump is shown in Fig. 3. Here, the water-motivating element consists of two impellers fastened to the motor drive shaft and separated by a stationary deflector. Water enters the pump through slots in the gear housing and is pumped upward through the water tube to jackets around the cylinder. After circulating through the water jackets, the water is discharged through a special water-return tube.

In a typical rotor-pump arrangement (Fig. 4), the rotor (impeller) consists of flexible rubber blades rotating in an aluminum housing into which are cast ports for water discharge. As noted in the illustration, the drive shaft does not center in the impeller or pump housing, but is offset to one side. This causes the impeller blade to flex or bend as they rotate in the housing, curving more while traveling through the area of the narrow side. On the opposite wider side, little curvature occurs.

At a high operating speed, water resistance within the impeller housing is sufficient to prevent the impeller blade from flexing out to maintain contact with the impeller housing; hence, at high speed, simple impeller action results. At a low operating speed, resistance within the impeller housing diminishes and permits the impeller blades to resume normal operation, resulting in a displacement pump action.

125

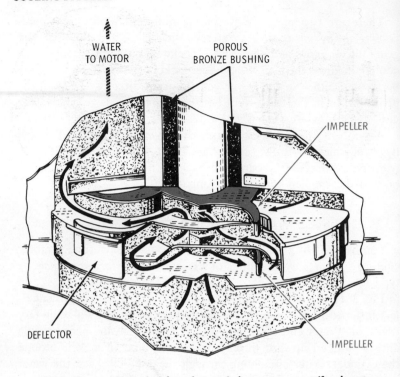

WATER
TO MOTOR

POROUS
BRONZE BUSHING

IMPELLER

DEFLECTOR

IMPELLER

**Fig. 3. Construction principles of a typical two-stage centrifugal water pump assembly.**

The foregoing design permits the pump to operate on a practically constant volume basis to provide an uninterrupted flow of water when operating the motor at slow and intermediate speeds.

## THERMOSTATIC CONTROLS

A thermostatically-controlled cooling system (when used) provides for a temperature-controlled motor regardless of water temperature or operational speeds. The heart of the control system is a thermostat assembly working in conjunction with a pressure-control valve (Fig. 5).

When starting a cold motor, the thermostat is closed and the pressure-control valve by-passes the water back to the water pump as soon as sufficient pressure is built up by the pump to overcome

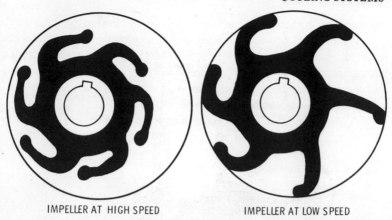

IMPELLER AT HIGH SPEED          IMPELLER AT LOW SPEED

**Fig. 4. A water-pump impeller made of synthetic rubber acts as a water circulator at high speed and as a displacement pump at low speed.**

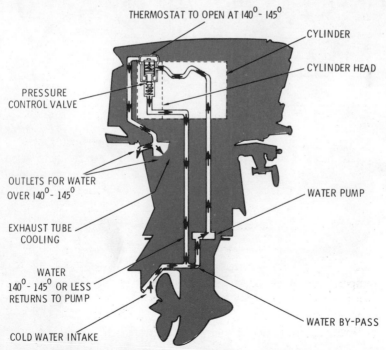

THERMOSTAT TO OPEN AT $140^0$ - $145^0$

CYLINDER

CYLINDER HEAD

PRESSURE
CONTROL VALVE

OUTLETS FOR WATER
OVER $140^0$ - $145^0$

WATER PUMP

EXHAUST TUBE
COOLING

WATER
$140^0$ - $145^0$ OR LESS
RETURNS TO PUMP

WATER BY-PASS

COLD WATER INTAKE

**Fig. 5. Flow diagram showing a thermostatically-controlled cooling system.**

127

the pressure-control valve setting. This recirculation process continues until the proper cylinder-jacket operating temperature is reached, usually a very brief period. When the heated water reaches a temperature of 140 to 145 degrees F, the thermostat valve opens and part of the heated water is discharged to the atmosphere, which in turn also reduces the water pressure.

The *Johnson* 55-HP outboard motor features a *wet-sleeve* exhaust system consisting of an inner and an outer housing with a

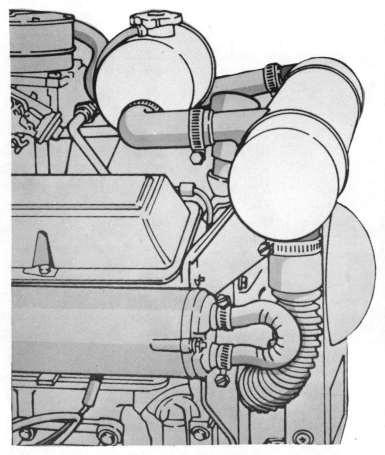

**Fig. 6. A fresh water cooling kit.**

water chamber in between. The water discharged from the engine cooling system fills the space between the exhaust housings and maintains a specified level when the engine is running.

The water drains out when the engine is stopped and tilted above the water line. This chamber of water serves as an effective silencer, quiets the exhaust relief, and cools the outer housing and lower rubber mounts. Exhaust gases are discharged underwater through the propeller hub for efficient silencing and performance. Water inlets in the trim tab scoops up water and directs it back into the exhaust chamber to cool the exhaust gases through the propeller.

A cooling kit shown in Fig. 6 uses fresh water to prevent engine corrosion from salt water. The kit consists of a heat exchanger, tanks and hoses and with the addition of antifreeze makes winter boating possible.

The V-6, 200 HP, and its *baby brother*, the 175 show off their ability to power any size boat. Both have the same 149.4 cubic inch, 90-degree V-block powerhead.
Courtesy Johnson Motors, Div. of Outboard Marine Corp.

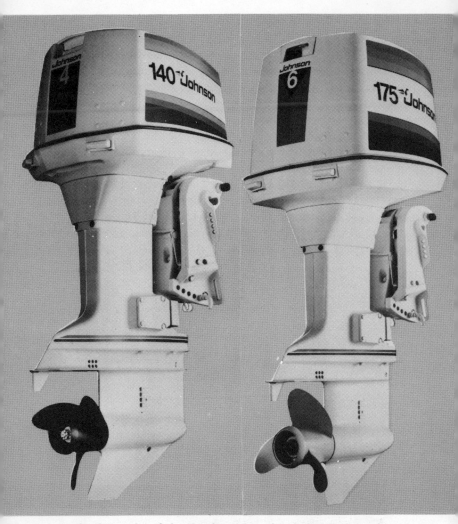

A couple of examples of the "big boys" in outboard motors. Designed to power the larger boats available to fishermen and pleasure craft owners.

Courtesy Johnson Motors, Div. of Outboard Marine Corp.

# Chapter 7

# Carburetors and Fuel Systems

The basic function of a carburetor is to vaporize the fuel and mix it with air in the proper proportions to insure efficient combustion in the cylinder. The basic fundamentals of carburetion are shown in Fig. 1.

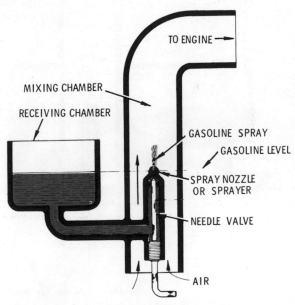

Fig. 1. Elementary carburetor principles.

Carburetion of the fuel is very important. The engine will not deliver top power and efficiency unless the correct amount of a properly combustible mixture reaches the cylinder on each intake stroke. The richest mixture that will burn is about eight parts of air to one part of fuel. The leanest mixture is about twenty-five parts of air to one part of fuel. The ideal mixture is about *fifteen parts of air to one part of fuel.*

If too much air is present for the amount of fuel metered, the mixture is said to be *lean.* A lean mixture will result in poor ignition, hard starting, and poor idling; in fact, if the mixture is too lean, the engine may not start at all, but if it does start, it will not run at high speed.

If, on the other hand, too much fuel is present for the amount of air, the mixture is said to be too *rich.* When this condition exists, incomplete carburetion will result, and excessive carbon deposits will form on pistons, rings, cylinder ports, and exhaust ports. Also, when the mixture is too rich, the engine will have a tendency to *flood* and be difficult to start.

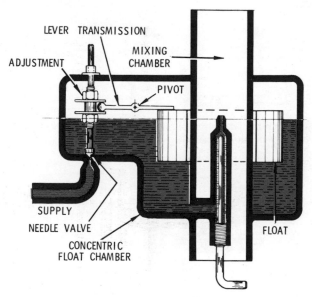

Fig. 2. **Elementary carburetor principles showing fuel-level control by mechanical leverage.**

The first requirement of a carburetor is to have some device to automatically maintain a supply of gasoline in the receiving chamber at very near the same level as the top of the spray nozzle. In most carburetors, fuel-level control is maintained by means of a buoyant element, such as a cork or thin-walled metal float. The float is connected to operate the fuel-inlet valve, usually by means of levers as illustrated in Fig. 2. These are arranged in such a manner that, as fuel enters the float chamber through the inlet valve, the float rises, and in so doing, closes the valve, thus shutting off the supply when fuel reaches the desired level.

The force necessary to bring the fuel mixture from the carburetor into the engine cylinder is due to pressure of the atmosphere, some of which has been removed by the receeding piston, making available a fractional part of the atmospheric pressure as a motive force.

## CARBURETOR FUNDAMENTALS

The carburetor assembly measures the flow of a combustible mixture which, as it passes into the crankcase and cylinders, is

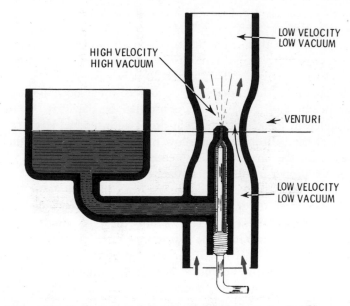

**Fig. 3. Elementary carburetor illustrating venturi principles.**

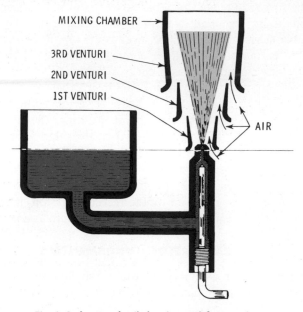

MIXING CHAMBER

3RD VENTURI

2ND VENTURI

1ST VENTURI

AIR

**Fig. 4. Carburetor detail showing a triple venturi.**

controlled by either a check valve, rotary valve, or leaf (reed) valve, depending on the type of carburetion used. The proportion of fuel to air is controlled by needle valves.

In operation, fuel enters the carburetor-float bowl through the inlet needle and seat which is controlled by the float. As fuel is consumed by the engine, the float drops with the fuel level, causing the inlet needle to open and allow more fuel to enter. As the fuel level rises, the float also rises, causing the inlet needle to close when the proper level has been reached.

The amount of fuel which passes from the float bowl through the main nozzle to the *venturi* is regulated or controlled by the fixed high-speed jet which screws into the body casting. As the air enters the carburetor, the restrictions of the venturi causes the air to speed up as it passes over the top end of the main nozzle, reducing the pressure at this point to below atmospheric. See Fig. 3. The difference in atmospheric pressure acting on the fuel in the float bowl causes it to flow upward through the main nozzle. As the throttle is opened, additional air enters the venturi, causing a greater pressure difference and greater fuel flow as required by the engine.

By locating the spray nozzle at the part of the smallest cross-section, as noted, the conditions are favorable for securing better fuel economy as a result of *high* air velocities under *low* pressure. Thus, the greater the pressure drop at the nozzle, accompanied by a proportional increase in the air velocity, the more complete will be the fuel vaporization. The *venturi* principle has been extended to the use of two or more *venturi* tubes arranged in series, as shown in Fig. 4. This is called triple *venturi*.

The idle system of the carburetor is separate from the high-speed system. In the idle system, air enters the idle passage through a small hole located on the right side of the top casting directly behind the idle-adjustment needle. The flow of air is determined by the size of the hole. The air which is allowed to enter the carburetor through the hole, passes over the idle tube, Fig. 5, and picks up fuel from the float bowl. The fuel-air mixture which is available at

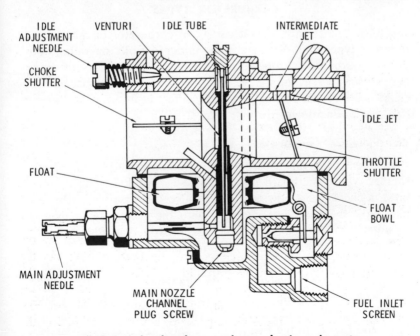

Fig. 5. Typical outboard-motor carburetor showing major parts.

this point is metered through the idle-adjustment needle and passes into the venturi of the carburetor through the idle jet. Additional air passes into the engine and mixes with the fuel entering through the idle jet and through small holes drilled in the throttle shutter. When the engine is running at idle speed, the throttle shutter is completely closed, and all fuel mixture is delivered to the engine through the idle jet.

The intermediate jet located just ahead of the idle passages in the venturi is designed to deliver an additional supply of fuel to the engine at speeds just above idling. Also, by locating the intermediate jet slightly ahead of the throttle shutter (when in he normally-closed position), the shutter when cracked will expose the intermediate jet to the air stream, resulting in additional fuel being passed into the engine cylinders. This increased amount of fuel is necessary to sustain the engine at a higher rate of speed.

## CARBURETOR TYPES

Although there are a great variety of carburetor designs to suit different types and size of engines under various operating conditions, outboard motors normally employ carburetors of either the check-valve or automotive type. Although the number and arrangements of component parts may differ, both types operate on the same basic principle.

### Check-Valve Carburetor

In the check-valve carburetor commonly employed on the smaller type of outboard motors, there is, in addition to the float bowl, a check-valve bowl and check valve. This type of carburetor may have the body cast integrally with the crankcase or may be mounted on the engine separately, as illustrated in Fig. 6.

The float and inlet needle valve regulates the amount of fuel in the bowl. When the engine is running the compression stroke of the piston creates a vacuum in the crankcase and upper part of the check bowl. Normal atmospheric pressure through the carburetor intake opens the check valve, drawing air from the check-valve bowl and fuel from the fuel jet in the valve seat. The fuel-air mixture passes into the crankcase.

136

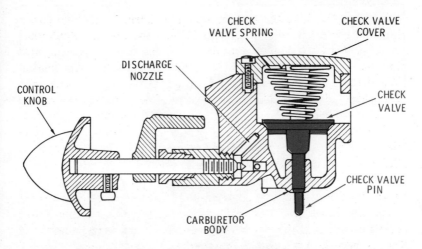

**Fig. 6. Diagrammatic view of a check-valve type carburetor.**

On the firing stroke of the piston, pressure in the crankcase closes the check valve and drives the fuel-air mixture from the crankcase into the cylinder head. On the return stroke of the piston, the fuel-air charge is compressed and exploded. The complete cycle is repeated each revolution of the crankshaft. Running-speed mixtures are controlled by an adjustable tapered needle valve. Priming the check-valve carburetor is done by manually pushing down the float to open the float valve and at the same time opening the check valve. This provides for an extra-rich mixture for quick starting.

## Automotive-Type Carburetors

Automotive type carburetors are used primarily on the larger outboard motors, and differ from the check-valve type mainly in that the fuel admission valve is closed mechanically instead of by spring and pressure action.

The high-speed jet knob is located in the carburetor. The slow-speed jets located in the upper part of the carburetor throat supply fuel when the throttle valve is closed. The proper mixture for slow speed is controlled by the slow-speed adjusting knob near the top of the carburetor.

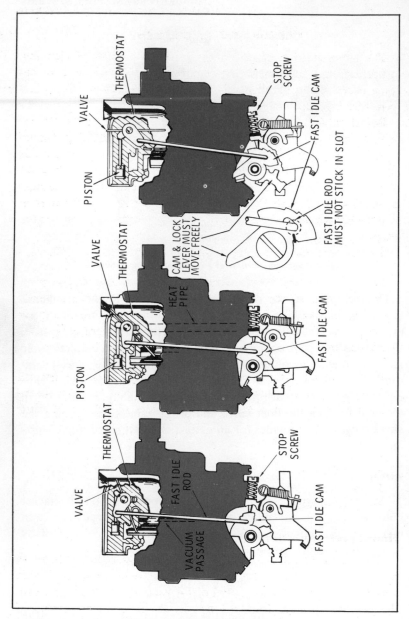

**Fig. 7. Automatic choke operation.**

## CARBURETOR ADJUSTMENT

The major portion of carburetor servicing consists of cleaning, inspection, and adjustment. After considerable usage, it may become necessary to overhaul the carburetor and renew worn parts to restore it to its original operating efficiency.

Before adjusting a carburetor, the ignition system should receive attention. There should be a good spark and the plugs should have the correct gap. The appearance of spark plugs is a good guide in making carburetor adjustments. For precision, install a new set of plugs of the correct heat range and see that the ignition system is functioning properly. Start the engine and run until the normal running temperature is reached. Shut off the engine and remove the plugs.

To test for proper carburetor adjustment, proceed as follows:

Draw a clean white cloth across the electrode end of the plug. A black mark on the cloth indicates a mixture too rich. If barely perceptible, with only a faint gray cloudiness, the mixture is too lean. Correct adjustment is indicated by a distinct gray mark on the cloth.

In the absence of carburetor analyzer equipment, the general procedure to follow is as outlined, varying with the type of carburetor. There are four adjustments on the typical air-valve carburetor as follows:

1. Float-feed valve.
2. Gasoline valve.
3. Air-valve spring.
4. Throttle idling.

### Float-Level Adjustment

The adjustment should be such that the liquid level will be as near the top of the nozzle as possible without overflowing. This reduces to a minimum the initial or lift vacuum necessary to cause the gasoline to issue from the nozzle. If the gasoline persists in overflowing while adjusting, a leaky-float valve is indicated. Regrind or replace.

### Gasoline-Valve Adjustment

Run the engine at an average or normal speed, and with a retarded spark if the spark is manually controlled. Reduce the gasoline supply until the mixture becomes so weak that there is popping in the carburetor, and then note the position of the valve.

Next, increase the mixture until it becomes so rich that the engine begins to choke. Set the adjustment of the gasoline valve halfway between the two points, which will be the approximate setting. Vary the adjustment slightly for a rich or a lean mixture until the speed picks up to maximum and the engine runs smoothly. That will be the correct seting.

### Air-Valve Adjustment

Vary the opening of the air valve by moving the spindle. If the engine speeds up with the additional air, loosen the spring adjustment. If it slows down, the mixture was correct or a little too lean, according to the degree to which the speed is affected.

The spring should be adjusted until the engine speeds up to maximum. The spring has considerable influence on the operation of the carburetor and good adjustment cannot be obtained without the proper spring. Check the adjustment by letting the engine idle and then suddenly open the throttle. If the adjustment is correct, the engine should accelerate quickly and smoothly. If it backfires when the throttle is suddenly opened, the adjustment is faulty.

### Throttle Idling

First, set the throttle-lever adjusting screw at an engine speed corresponding to low idle. Then set the adjustment screw so that the engine fires evenly, without stalling.

## SERVICING THE CARBURETOR

When overhauling a carburetor, several things must be done to assure a good job.

1. The carburetor must be disassembled.
2. The various jet plugs removed.

3. Clean all parts carefully in a recommended solvent, then inspect for damage or wear.
4. Use air pressure only to clear the various orifices and channels.
5. Replace questionable parts with new ones.
6. Use new gaskets at reassembly.

When checking parts removed from the carburetor, it is at times rather difficult to be sure they are satisfactory for further service. It is therefore recommended that *new* parts be used.

## Cleaning Carburetor Parts

The recommended solvent for gum deposits is denatured alcohol, which is easily obtainable. However, there are other commercial solvents which may be used with satisfactory results.

A soft brush should be used to remove gum and carbon deposits while the parts are soaking in the solvent. After cleaning, the parts should be rinsed in clean solvent and then all passages thoroughly blown out with compressed air.

*Note:* Never clean jets with a wire or other mechanical means because the orifices may become enlarged, making the mixture too rich for proper performance.

*Caution:* If the commercial solvent or cleaner recommends the use of water as a rinse, it should be hot. After rinsing, all traces of water must be blown from the passages with air pressure. It is further advisable to rinse the parts in clean kerosene or gasoline to be certain no trace of moisture remains.

## Inspection and Reassembly

*1. Check the throttle shaft for excessive wear in the throttle body.*

If wear is extreme, it is recommended that the throttle-body assembly be replaced rather than installing a new throttle shaft in the old body. During manufacture, the location of the idle-transfer port and spark-advance control ports of the valve is carefully established for one particular assembly. If a new shaft or valve should be installed in an old worn throttle body, it would be very unlikely that the original relationship of these parts to the valve would be obtained. Changing the port relationship would adversely affect normal operation.

*2. Inspect the throttle lever for looseness on the throttle shaft.*
If the lever is loose, it will be impossible to secure proper idle-speed adjustment. Silver-solder or braze the joint to correct this condition, or use a new throttle-body assembly.

*3. Install the idle-mixture needle valve and spring in the body.*
The tapered portion must be straight and smooth. If the tapered portion is grooved or ridged, a new idle needle valve should be used to insure having correct idle-mixture control. In making the idle adjustment, do not use a screwdriver. Make the adjustment with the fingers. Turn the idle-mixture needle valve against its seat, then back off one full turn for the approximate setting.

## CARBURETION

This process may be defined as *the mixing of gasoline in the form of a mist or spray with air in the proper proportions to form the fuel charge for a gas engine.* The character of the fuel charge delivered by a carburetor depends on numerous conditions.

Carburetion is affected by:

1. *Fuel pump*—Controlling the pressure of the fuel fed to the carburetor.
2. *Air cleaner*—If not clean throughout, it will restrict the volume of air taken in by the carburetor.
3. *The carburetor*—Including float-level control, many variations of jets, venturi air valves, throttle valves, choking devices, etc.
4. *The hot spot*—Any device for heating the gas after it leaves the carburetor.
5. *Choke*—The choke affects the volume of air taken in by the carburetor.
6. *Thermostats*—Thermostats controlling choke valve, air valve, or other parts of the carburetion system affect the mixture of air and fuel.

7. *Intake manifold*—Air leaks in the manifold or gaskets change carburetion.

8. *Muffler*—If the muffler or exhaust pipe is restricted, a portion of the burned gases will remain in the cylinder and only a partial charge of fresh gas will be drawn in.

9. *Super charger*—Changes in carburetion due to the use of a supercharger must be taken into consideration when tests are made.

## SERVICE DIAGNOSIS

*Symptom and Possible Cause*          *Possible Remedy*

**Poor Performance—
Mixture Too Lean**

(a) Damaged, worn, incorrect type, or incorrect size of main metering jet.

(a) Disassemble carburetor, then replace main metering jet if in questionable condition.

(b) Damaged tip or bad top shoulder seat of main discharge jet.

(b) Disassemble carburetor, clean and inspect main discharge jet, and replace if necessary.

(c) Vacuum piston worn or stuck.

(c) Disassemble carburetor, and free up stuck piston. If piston is badly worn, replace air-horn assembly.

(d) Corroded or bad seating power jet.

(d) Disassemble carburetor. Clean power jet and channels. If close inspection reveals a faulty seating jet, replacement is recommended.

(e) Incorrect fuel level.

(e) Check fuel level in carburetor. Adjust vertical lip of float to obtain correct level of ⅝ inch from top of fuel to top edge of fuel chamber.

*Symptom and Possible Cause*    *Possible Remedy*

(f) Automatic choke not operating properly.

(f) Check adjustment and operation of automatic choke. If necessary, replace choke to correct this condition.

(g) Worn or corroded needle valve and seat.

(g) Clean and inspect needle valve and seat. If found to be in questionable condition, replace assembly and then check fuel-pump pressure. Pressure should be from 3½ to 5½ pounds.

**Poor Idling**

(a) Carbonized idle tube or poor seating shoulder.

(a) Disassemble carburetor, then clean idle tube and check seating shoulder. Replace idle tube if in a questionable condition.

(b) Idle-air bleed carbonized or of incorrect size.

(b) Disassemble carburetor, then use compressed air to clear idle-air bleed after soaking it in a suitable solvent.

(c) Idle-discharge holes plugged or gummed.

(c) Disassemble carburetor, use compressed air to clear idle-discharge holes after soaking main and throttle bodies in a suitable solvent.

(d) Throttle body carbonized or worn throttle shaft.

(d) Disassemble carburetor, check throttle-valve shaft for wear. If excessive wear is apparent, replace throttle-body assembly with a new unit.

*Symptom and Possible Cause*     *Possible Remedy*

(e) Damaged or w o r n idle needle.

(e) Tighten main body to throttle-body screws securely to prevent air leaks and cracked housings.

(f) Incorrect fuel level.

(f) Check the fuel level in carburetor. Adjust vertical lip of float lever to obtain correct level of $\frac{5}{8}$ inch from top of fuel to top edge of fuel chamber.

(g) Loose main body to throttle-body screws.

(g) Tighten main body to throttle-body screws securely to prevent air leaks and cracked housings.

## Poor Acceleration

(a) Corroded or bad seat on accelerator pump by-pass jet.

(a) Disassemble carburetor. Clean and inspect accelerator pump by-pass jet. Replace by-pass jet if in questionable condition.

(b) Accelerator - pump piston (or plunger) leather too hard, worn, or loose on stem.

(b) Disassemble carburetor. Replace accelerator - pump assembly if leather is hard, cracked, or worn. Test follow-up spring for compression.

(c) Faulty accelerator - pump discharge.

(c) Disassemble carburetor. Use compressed air to clean the discharge nozzle and channels after soaking main body in a suitable solvent. Check the pump capacity.

145

| *Symptom and Possible Cause* | *Possible Remedy* |
|---|---|
| (d) Accelerator-pump inlet check valve faulty. | (d) Disassemble carburetor. Check accelerator-pump inlet check valve for poor seat or release. If necessary, replace faulty part with a new unit. |
| (e) Incorrect fuel level. | (e) Check fuel level in carburetor. Adjust vertical lip of float lever to obtain correct level of $\frac{5}{8}$ inch from top of fuel to top edge of fuel chamber. |
| (f) Worn or corroded needle valve and seat. | (f) Clean and inspect needle valve and seat. If found to be in questionable condition, replace assembly and then check fuel-pump pressure. Pressure should be from $3\frac{1}{2}$ to $5\frac{1}{2}$ pounds. |
| (g) Worn accelerator pump and throttle linkage. | (g) Disassemble carburetor. Replace worn accelerator pump and throttle linkage, then check for correct position. |
| (h) Automatic choke not operating properly. | (h) Check adjustment and operation of automatic choke. If necessary, replace choke to correct this condition. |

**Carburetor Floods or Leaks**

| | |
|---|---|
| (a) Cracked body. | (a) Disassemble carburetor. Replace cracked body, being sure main to throttle-body screws are tight. |

| *Symptom and Possible Cause* | *Possible Remedy* |
|---|---|
| (b) Defective body gaskets. | (b) Disassemble carburetor. Replace defective gaskets, then check for leaks. Be sure the screws are tightened securely. |
| (c) High float level. | (c) Check fuel level in carburetor. Adjust vertical lip of float lever to obtain correct level of ⅝ inch from top of fuel to top edge of fuel chamber. |
| (d) Worn needle valve and seat. | (d) Clean and inspect needle valve and seat. If found to be in questionable condition, replace complete assembly and then check fuel-pump pressure. Pressure should be from 3½ to 5½ pounds. |
| (e) Excessive fuel-pump pressure. | (e) Test fuel-pump pressure. If pressure is in excess of 5½ pounds, replace fuel pump. |

## Poor Performance— Mixture too Rich

| | |
|---|---|
| (a) Restricted air cleaner. | (a) Remove and clean air cleaner. |
| (b) Excess of oil in air cleaner. | (b) Remove and clean air cleaner. Refill oil chamber to required level mark or one pint of SAE 50 engine oil. |
| (c) Leaking float. | (c) Disassemble carburetor. Replace leaking float with a new unit. Check float level, then if necessary, |

147

*Symptom and Possible Cause*      *Possible Remedy*

bend the vertical lip of float lever to obtain a ⅝ inch reading from top of fuel to top of fuel chamber.

(d)  High float level.

(d)  Adjust vertical lip of float as described in (c) above to secure correct float level.

(e)  Excessive fuel-pump pressure.

(e)  Check fuel-pump pressure. Pressure should be from 3½ to 5½ pounds. If pressure is in excess of 5½ pounds, replace fuel-pump assembly.

(f)  Worn main-metering jet.

(f)  Disassemble carburetor. Replace worn metering jet with a new one of the correct size and type.

## AUTOMATIC CHOKE OPERATION

The automatic choke is an integral part of some outboard motor carburetors and is similar to that used on late model cars. See Fig. 7. It automatically regulates the choke valve opening to compensate for temperature variations of the motor. It functions generally as follows:

1.  With the engine cold and not running, the bimetal spring in the choke body and thermostat holds the choke valve closed.
2.  As soon as the engine starts, a vacuum is drawn into the carburetor manifold. The manifold is connected by a hose to a diaphragm and plunger in the choke body and thermostat.
3.  Higher air pressure on one side of the diaphragm and plunger forces the plunger down. This in turn permits a deflector plate (mounted on the same shaft as the bimetal spring) to

turn, and in so doing will open the choke valve enough to keep the engine running until it warms up.

4. Hot air from the exhaust manifold is directed to the bimetal spring so that the spring loses its tension as the engine warms up. This permits the choke to open gradually, and after it reaches full-open position it is held open by the action of the intake manifold on the piston.

5. When the motor is shut off, it will cool down, causing the bimetal spring to contract and coil up in the opposite direction, thus gradually closing the carburetor choke valve.

## FUEL SYSTEMS

The fuel system is an important part of the motor because it feeds the fuel mixture from the tank and into the carburetor. In the carburetor, the fuel is mixed with air and injected into the cylinders where it is ignited to provide power for the propeller.

The transfer of fuel from the tank to the carburetor is normally performed by one of three methods:

1. Gravity.
2. Pressure.
3. Vacuum.

In the gravity-feed type of fuel system, the tank is normally an integral part of the power head, whereas in the pressure and vacuum type, the fuel tank is portable and may be placed in any convenient location.

### Gravity Feed

In cases where the fuel tank is located above the motor (Fig. 8), the fuel is delivered to the carburetor by gravity. This fuel-supply method is used to a considerable extent on the smaller motors where the fuel tank can be mounted on top of the motor. In gravity-feed fuel systems all that is necessary is to provide a fuel line between the tank and the carburetor.

A fuel strainer is usually located in the fuel outlet part of the tank, with a shut-off valve either at the fuel-outlet connection or, in some cases, at the carburetor.

149

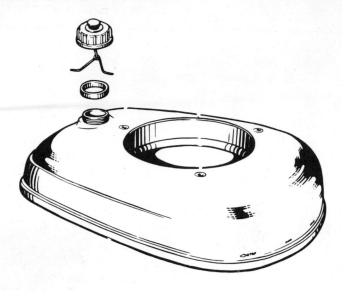

Fig. 8. A typical gasoline tank using gravity feed.

## Pressure Feed

In a pressure-feed fuel system such as shown in Fig. 9, a special air-pressure tube connects the fuel tank with a pressurized check valve attached to the motor crankcase, which is in addition to the conventional liquid-fuel tube connecting the fuel tank with the carburetor.

In operation, pressure is built up in the crankcase when the piston is on its downward stroke. This pressure is transferred to the fuel tank by way of the engine check valve and air-pressure tube. During low-pressure periods of the cycle, the spring forces the valve to its seat, thus preventing loss of air pressure in the tank. During normal motor operation the valve opens and closes in the manner described to provide fuel to the carburetor. In a fuel system of this kind an air-tight filler cap is used, the fuel tank being air-tight with the filler cap in position.

To prevent sludge and foreign matter from entering the carburetor, a fuel filter is usually attached to the fuel line between the tank and carburetor. To insure fuel in the carburetor for starting the engine, the fuel tank is provided with a diaphragm-type *priming*

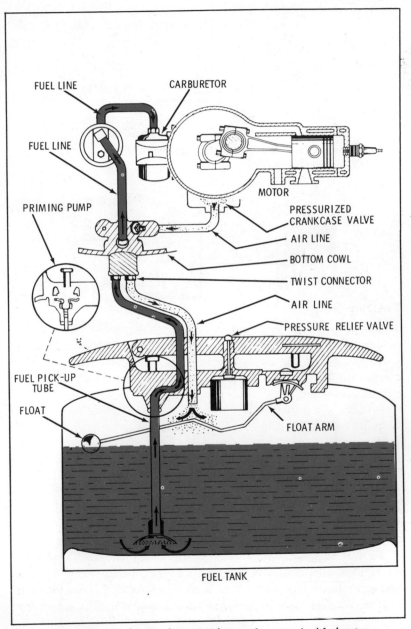

FUEL LINE

CARBURETOR

FUEL LINE

PRIMING PUMP

MOTOR

PRESSURIZED
CRANKCASE VALVE

AIR LINE

BOTTOM COWL

TWIST CONNECTOR

AIR LINE

PRESSURE RELIEF VALVE

FUEL PICK-UP
TUBE

FLOAT

FLOAT ARM

FUEL TANK

**Fig. 9. Diagram showing the essential parts of a pressurized fuel system.**

*pump.* This pumping action is necessary only when the pressure has been released from the tank for refilling, or as a result of standing idle for a period of time.

## Vacuum Feed

In this type of fuel system a special vacuum pump attached to and connected with the engine crankcase provides the necessary pumping action. The pump is operated by crankcase pressure. After priming the fuel system to deliver fuel to the carburetor, the motor is started and the fuel pump continues the flow of fuel from the tank to the carburetor.

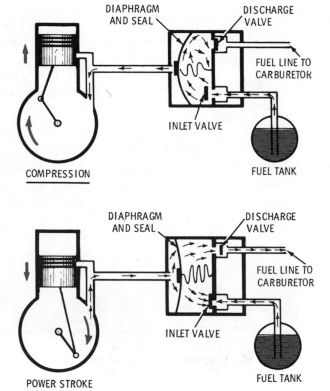

Fig. 10. Operation of a fuel pump used in a vacuum-type fuel system.

In operation, the alternate conditions of vacuum and pressure created by the piston movement in the cylinder are illustrated in Fig. 10. This action is transferred to the pump by the pressure line. The diaphragm in the pump, due to its up-and-down movement, is drawing fuel into the pump and then pumping it into the carburetor, or in the case of a two-stage pump, into the next stage and then into the carburetor. Because the fuel pump is on the motor, and pumps fuel from the tank to the carburetor following the initial priming and starting of the motor, only one flexible fuel line is necessary between the tank and the motor.

Fuel tanks employed in vacuum-tube systems are of the non-pressurized variety, and must be properly vented in order to function properly. To start the engine, most fuel systems of this type provide a separate primer pump consisting of a section of flexible hose and a primer bulb, the latter being a part of the fuel line connecting the fuel tank with the carburetor. Priming is done by squeezing the primer bulb several times or until pressure required to squeeze the bulb increases. This action fills the fuel line and carburetor to permit starting the engine.

## ENGINE VALVES

The fuel-air mixture of the carburetor is controlled by the use of *leaf or rotary valves* located between the carburetor and crankcase, the arrangement of the valves being such that they *open* to

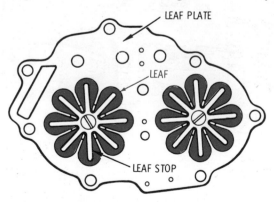

**Fig. 11. Typical leaf-type carburetor valves.**

permit the fuel charge to *enter* the crankcase on the upstroke of the piston, and *close* to *seal* the crankcase and prevent leakage of the fuel charge on the down-stroke of the engine.

## Leaf Valves

Leaf-type valves (Fig. 11) consist of thin metal plates which bear against a leaf plate. As noted in the illustration, the leaf plate has openings which admit the fuel mixture into the crankcase by lifting the leaf from the leaf plate. Thus, injection of the fuel mixture into the motor cylinders is synchronized with the piston movements.

The leaf tension is usually pre-established at the factory with gauges. The degree of leaf opening depends on the crankcase pressure which, in turn, varies with the speed at which the motor is operating. Such action results in a more efficient performance throughout the entire speed range of the motor.

## Reed Valves

A simplified version of the leaf valve, sometimes termed a *reed* valve, is shown in Fig. 12. Basically, the operation and maintenance of this valve is the same as that for the leaf valve.

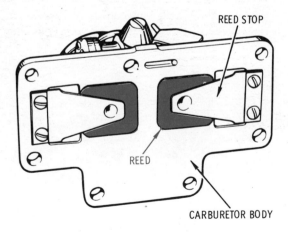

Fig. 12. Typical reed valves employed on two-cycle outboard motors.

## Rotary Valves

These are built into the engine crankshaft and normally consist of passages drilled into the center main-bearing journal. Rotary valves are generally used with automotive-type carburetors.

In operation, the fuel-air mixture charge is drawn into the crankcase on the compression stroke of the piston. As the piston starts down on the firing stroke, a rotary valve, formed by the center bearing and crankshaft, opens to allow the fuel-air charge to be by-passed to the cylinder head where it is compressed and exploded in the following stroke. The rotary valves open and close as the crankshaft revolves to draw the fuel-air charge from the carburetor to the crankcase, and then to force it into the cylinder.

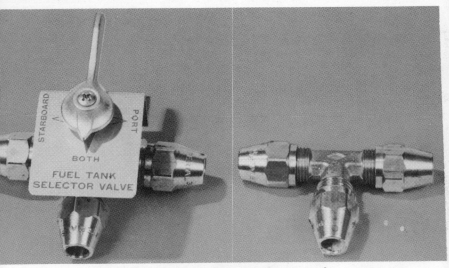

**Tee adapter for fueling two engines from one tank.**

Courtesy OMC.

155

**Single fuel line hookup.**
Courtesy OMC.

**Four-way valve adapter kit making available up to 18 gallons of fuel.**
Courtesy OMC.

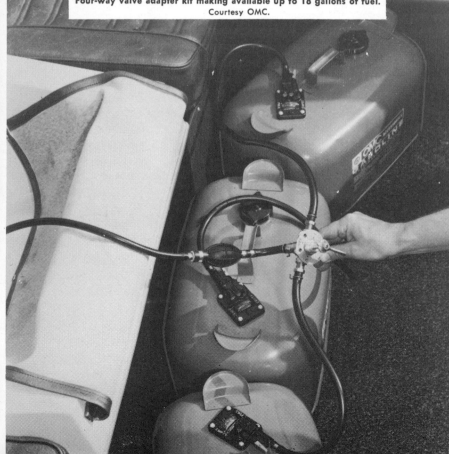

# Chapter 8

# Fuel and Oil Mixtures

A universal all-purpose lubricant to accommodate every conceivable application requirement would certainly have tremendous military and industrial advantages. Yet, lubrication engineers continue to develop ever-wider varieties of special lubricants for special applications.

The familiar words, *good and proper*, are particularly appropriate when applied to lubricants, because *good* ingredients of *proper* chemical composition are necessary to achieve satisfactory performance, reliability, and service life of the equipment in which they are used.

For example, in an automobile such as you drive, the engine alone requires three different kinds of oil, depending on subzero-, cold-, or hot-weather driving conditions; of course multi-viscosity oils combine characteristics to produce an all-weather oil. In the transmission, at least two different kinds of oil are used, depending on whether it is a conventional shift or an automatic transmission. In the rear axle, at least two different types of lubricant are used, depending on whether it is a conventional or a "limited-slip" differential. Isn't it reasonable that the high-precision outboard engine, yielding more horsepower per pound than any standard-production internal combustion engine and admired by the rest of the engine industry as a marvel of compactness and durability, should require a special lubricant?

Quality is only one factor determining the suitability of a lubricating oil for any particular engine. An oil rated as *excellent* for automobile engines would most likely be rated as *unacceptable* for outboard-motor use. One reason is that automobile engine oil contains a dilution inhibitor which resists mixing of the oil with gasoline and with combustion products which are formed in the combustion chamber and escape past the piston rings into the crankcase. This same dilution inhibitor makes the oil extremely resistant to mixing with gasoline as required for outboard-motor fuel.

Gasoline-oil separation puts a layer of oil at the bottom of the tank, with gasoline at the top and various proportions of gasoline and oil between. Since the fuel pick-up is located at the bottom of the tank, the engine may get a high proportion of oil when the tank is full and almost straight gasoline when the tank is nearly empty.

Therefore, the engine may smoke excessively and foul plugs at first, then overheat and possibly score the pistons because the remaining fuel contains insufficient oil. Another reason why high-quality automobile engine oils are unacceptable for outboard-engine use is that the advent of high-compression, high-output, automobile engines presented new lubrication problems which necessitated the addition of metallic detergents to the oil for the purpose of inhibiting varnish formation and possible piston-ring sticking.

In four-cycle engines, the oil is effectively confined to the crankcase and very little leaks past the piston rings into the combustion chamber. In a two-cycle engine, the oil must be mixed with gasoline. Practically all of these metallic detergents enter the cylinders (above the pistons) and form deposits when they come in contact with the hot surfaces of spark plugs, piston crowns, and combustion chambers. These deposits cause pre-ignition and detonation which results in piston-crown burning, piston scuffing, and cylinder-wall scoring.

Frequently, metallic deposits bridge a spark-plug gap so it can not fire and this, in turn, results in the spark plug fouling. To properly evaluate the suitability of oils for various applications, it is necessary to understand something about the nature of oils. For example, no two wells deliver crude oils of identical chemical composition. Crude oils are a product of nature, and according to geographical location, vary in type such as naphthenic, asphaltic, or paraffinic base.

Even beyond this, there are differences in the composition of crudes from different wells in the same geographic location. Consequently, the processes of refining oils and greases vary between individual refineries.

The oil refineries are doing a tremendous job in the very complex processes of blending, compounding, and refining oils to meet a more-or-less uniform standard. Obviously, a universal lubricant standard is impossible, but the art of compounding special lubricants has been developed to the extent that standards set up for specific applications can be satisfactorily met with oils of different base types. To find that an oil compound for one specific application is also completely satisfactory for another application would be pure coincidence.

**Wrestling with this problem for the past 20 years, the *Mercury Marine Corporation* decided to conduct its own oil-processing, canning, and marketing operations, with standardization accomplished as follows:**

1.  Only one selected brand of paraffinic-base oil is used—a base stock which, over a period of years, has been found to be uniform in chemical analysis.
2.  With this base stock, organic detergents rather than inorganic metallic detergents are blended, along with special chemical ingredients necessary for adequate lubrication of high-output, two-cycle engines.
3.  By marketing one quality-controlled oil on a national basis, more consistent duplication of results can be expected, particularly if the brand and type of gasoline is the same from one mix to another.
4.  To date, an oil manufacturer has seen fit to duplicate the general specification set up for two-cycle engine oil to accomplish the following purposes:

    a.  To mix more readily with gasoline and, more thoroughly mixed, to stay mixed, even when the tank is allowed to stand idle for indefinite periods.
    b.  To achieve superior lubricating qualities.
    c.  To incorporate good anti-sticking qualities which keep the piston rings working freely in their grooves.
    d.  To minimize carbon deposits and port clogging.

  e.  To inhibit varnish formation.
  f.  To give results with white marine gasoline and, in emergencies, with good-quality regular gasolines of low lead content.

Remember that many oils carrying a single brand name and sold for example in Florida, do not contain the same ingredients when sold under the same brand name in another part of the country. In some cases, the same brand name may be applied to oils processed from crude oil produced in Texas, California, Pennsylvania, Oklahoma, Saudi Arabia, or other widely-separated areas.

Oil companies save on freight costs by distributing oils from their fields nearest each market area. *Mercury* has gone to great expense to determine the type of oil best able to meet the lubrication requirements of two-cycle engines and to pinpoint the geographical source of the exact type of crude oil required to meet its specifications. Most all two-cycle engine oil comes from a sharply-defined geographical area and this is one reason why its costs are more than ordinary automobile oils.

## GASOLINE

In its original form, petroleum is a liquid bituminous substance composed essentially of carbon and hydrogen. After petroleum is pumped from the oil wells, it is the task of the refinery to extract from it the clean liquid known as gasoline.

Petroleum contains many impurities which must be removed during the refining process before gasoline suitable for use in engines is produced. In the gasoline making process, petroleum is first placed in a closed vessel and heated. During the heating process, the most volatile and lighter parts evaporate first, after which the resulting vapor is passed through a condenser where it is cooled and condensed. It is in this manner that gasoline is obtained as the first distillation product. As the temperature to which petroleum is subjected is increased, the heavier fractions, such as kerosene, gas, and oil are passed off in the same manner.

## Combustion of Gasoline

Gasoline burns either by combustion or detonation. By definition, combustion is a more or less rapid chemical union of carbon with oxygen, whose combination is sufficiently energetic to evolve heat and light. In gas engines, combustion is the steady progressive burning of the charge at a uniform rate.

Detonation is very rapid oxidation; that is, an explosion which causes a very sudden rise in pressure. In gas-engine operation, this occurs after the flame has traveled part way across the combustion chamber. This results in loss of power and over-heating because the rise in pressure is almost instantaneous, and the resulting energy cannot be transmitted to the piston as efficiently as when the pressure rise is more gradual. When detonation takes place, it provides a hammer-like blow against the piston head, and the engine is said to knock.

Detonation may harm an engine in several ways. In extreme cases, pistons have been shattered, and rings and cylinders damaged. Other effects of detonation may be over-heating, broken spark plugs, over-loaded bearings, high fuel consumption, loss of power, and frequent need for overhaul.

## Octane Rating

In the development of antiknock fuels by improved refining processes, it becomes necessary to establish some standards of rating, resulting in the octane method. In this method, two hydrocarbons—octane and heptane—are used.

The ability of a fuel to resist detonation is measured by its octane rating. The tendency of a fuel to detonate, however, varies in different engines and in the same engine under different operating conditions. The octane rating of a gasoline is not important when used in an outboard motor. Ethyl or other top-price gasolines usually contain more tetra-ethyl lead than regular gasoline, which may tend to form more deposits on the spark plugs.

In general, there is no advantage in using the ethyl or premium gasoline in an outboard engine. Marine white gasoline, which may be difficult to obtain in certain locations, will probably give very satisfactory service and may be tried if excessive spark-plug fouling has been experienced. Switching to a different brand of regular gasoline, or even trying several brands may eventually provide a satisfactory result. *CAUTION: Never use gasoline dopes such as advertised oil additives, top cylinder lubes, etc., since they are all harmful in the operation of outboard motors.*

It is the practice of gasoline manufacturers to vary the volatility of gasoline with the season. Thus, gasoline furnished during the spring and fall will usually be more volatile than those furnished during the hot summer months. Similarly, gasoline furnished during the cold winter months will be even more volatile than those obtained during the spring and fall. From the foregoing, it follows that difficulties experienced in starting and idling a motor in very cold weather may be due to the use of gasoline purchased during the previous summer.

It is for this reason that fresh fuel is preferred for best service, and the practice of leaving the gasoline in the outboard motor tank for a long period of time may lead to starting and idling difficulties.

## Fuel Mixing

For normal operation, the oil and gasoline should be mixed in the proportions recommended by the engine manufacturer. These proportions may vary a great deal, depending on the size (horsepower rating) and other factors. Two-cycle outboard motors operate on a mixture of oil and gasoline. The oil mixed with the gasoline lubricates the internal parts of the power head while the gasoline is the fuel necessary for combustion.

Using the correct gas and oil is of the utmost importance for top performance and trouble-free operation. Because the oil and gasoline are mixed together, it is self-evident that the oil used must be of a quality that will lubricate and at the same time be combustible so that harmful deposits will not form. The oil must, in addition, be readily mixable with gasoline and remain mixed during extended storage.

## LUBRICATION CHART

Oil companies are usually very helpful in providing information about suitable gasoline together with the quantity of oil required per gallon of gasoline.

The following lubrication chart is by courtesy of *Texaco, Inc.,* and shows the proper amount of gasoline-to-oil for most outboard motors. The *ounces of oil per gallon of gasoline* shown are for engines which are already broken in. A mixture using 50 percent more oil is recommended during the break-in period of new engines.

In making these recommendations, *Texaco* lubricating engineers enjoyed the full cooperation of the marine engine and gear manufacturers. The products listed are for normal operating temperatures. It should be remembered that SAE numbers are viscosity limits only. For cold-weather operation, the next lower viscosity grade should be used. In cases of very high temperatures and loads, it may be necessary to use the next higher viscosity grade.

Recommendations are also based on the assumption that engine speeds and loads are normal, and that engines are in good mechanical condition. Mechanical faults, such as worn pistons and loose bearings cannot be corrected with oil, although frequently the use of a heavier grade will offer temporary relief.

## GASOLINE-TO-OIL MIXTURE CHART

| NAME AND MODEL | Product | Ounces of Oil Per Gallon of Gasoline | Pints Per 6 Gallon Tank |
|---|---|---|---|
| AMERICAN MARC (Diesel) | Havoline SAE 30 | (Do not mix oil & fuel) | (Do not mix oil & fuel) |
| BRITISH SEAGULL (All Models) | OB-30 | 12 | 4½ |
| BUCCANEER (See Gale) | | | |
| CHRYSLER | | | |
| 3.5 hp | OB-30 | 8 | 3 |
| 4.4-105 hp | OB-30 | 2½ | 1 |
| CLINTON (All Models) | OB-30 | 4 | 1½ |
| CROFTON (All Models) | Havoline SAE 30 | (Do not mix oil & gasoline) | (Do not mix oil & gasoline) |
| ELGIN (See Sears-Roebuck) | | | |
| ESKA (See Tecumseh) | | | |
| EVINRUDE | | | |
| Fleetwin: 4434, 4443, 4447, 7512, 7574, 7516, 7518, 7520, 7522, 7524 | OB-30 | 8 | 3 |
| Lightfour: 4315, 4318, 4322, 4325, 4383, 4386, 4389, 4393 | OB-30 | 12 | 4½ |
| Speedifour: 7031 | OB-30 | 12 | 4½ |
| Speeditwin: 6039 | OB-30 | 12 | 4½ |
| All other models prior to 1964 | OB-30 | 5½ | 2 |
| All Models 1964-1969 | OB-30 | 2½ | 1 |
| FAGEOL (Crofton) (All Models) | | | |
| Separately Lubricated | Havoline SAE 30 | (Do not mix oil & gasoline) | (Do not mix oil & gasoline) |

## GASOLINE-TO-OIL MIXTURE CHART (Cont'd.)

| NAME AND MODEL | Product | Ounces of Oil Per Gallon of Gasoline | Pints Per 6 Gallon Tank |
|---|---|---|---|
| **FIRESTONE** | | | |
| 2 hp through 8 hp ................................ | OB-30 | 8 | 3 |
| 12 hp through 40 hp .............................. | OB-30 | 5½ | 2 |
| **FISHER PIERCE** (Bearcat) ..................... | Havoline SAE 30 | (Do not mix oil & gasoline) | (Do not mix oil & gasoline) |
| **GALE** | | | |
| All Models (prior to 1961) ................. | OB-30 | 8 | 3 |
| All Models (1961-1963) ..................... | OB-30 | 5½ | 2 |
| Except 3 HP ................................ | OB-30 | 8 | 3 |
| **HOMELITE** (All models) | | | |
| Separately Lubricated ..................... | Havoline SAE 30 | (Do not mix oil & gasoline) | (Do not mix oil & gasoline) |
| **JOHNSON** | | | |
| All Models (Prior to 1964) ................ | OB-30 | 5½ | 2 |
| 1964-1969 (All Models) ..................... | OB-30 | 2½ | 1 |
| **McCULLOCH** | | | |
| 1950 through 1962—3.5 hp | | | |
| 1950 through 1959—6 and 7.5 hp | | | |
| All 1949 and earlier Scott-Atwater Models | OB-30 | 6½ | 2½ |
| All other models from 1950 to the present, | | | |
| incl. 3.5 hp (from 1963 to 1965) ......... | OB-30 | 2½ | 1 |
| **MERCURY**** | OB-30 | 5½ | |
| **MONTGOMERY WARD**—Sea King | | | 2 |
| All models (1956-1963) ..................... | OB-30 | 8 | 3 |
| 1964-1969 3½ hp | OB-30 | 8 | 3 |
| 1964-1966 6 and 9 hp ...................... | OB-30 | 8 | 3 |
| 1967-1969 6 and 9.2 hp .................... | OB-30 | 5½ | 2 |
| 1964-1969 20 thru 80 hp ................... | OB-30 | 2½ | 1 |
| **NEPTUNE** (All Models)..................... | OB-30 | 8 | 3 |
| **SEA KING**—See Montgomery Ward | | | |
| **SEARS ROEBUCK** | | | |
| Sears (All models) ........................ | OB-30 | 2½ | 1 |
| Elgin—1959-62, 3.5 through 7.5 hp ......... | OB-30 | 8 | 3 |
| All other models .......................... | OB-30 | 5½ | 2 |
| **TECUMSEH** ................................ | OB-30 | 8 | 3 |
| **WEST BEND** | | | |
| 1956 through 1965— | | | |
| 2 through 9 hp ............................ | OB-30 | 8 | 3 |
| 1956 through 1960—12 hp ................... | OB-30 | 8 | 3 |
| 1961 through 1963—12 hp ................... | OB-30 | 5½ | 2 |
| 1956 through 1964—10 and 16 | | | |
| through 80 hp ............................ | OB-30 | 5½ | 2 |
| 1965—20 through 80 hp ..................... | OB-30 | 2½ | 1 |
| **WESTERN AUTO** (See Wizard) | | | |
| **WIZARD** | | | |
| 1959 (All Models) ......................... | OB-30 | 8 | 3 |
| 1960 through 1962 (All Models | | | |
| except 3.6 hp) ........................... | OB-30 | 5½ | 2 |
| 1960 through 1962—3.6 hp .................. | OB-30 | 8 | 3 |
| 1963-1964 (All Models) .................... | OB-30 | 5½ | 2 |
| 1965—3.5, 6, and 9 hp ..................... | OB-30 | 8 | 3 |
| 1965—20 hp ................................ | OB-30 | 2½ | 1 |
| 1966-1967-1968-1969 3.5 hp ................ | OB-30 | 8 | 3 |
| 1966-1967-1968-1969 6.0, 9.2 and 20 hp ... | OB-30 | 5½ | 1 |
| **Mercury—During warranty period follow manufacturer's recommendation. | | | |

## Outboard Fuel Mix Guide

Many outboarding trips, particularly with small engines, require less than a full tank of fuel. This chart shows the approximate quantity of BIA certified oil which should be mixed with various smaller quantities of fuel for outboards that operate on a "50-to-1" ratio. Use an accurate measuring cup.

| Gasoline | Oil |
|---|---|
| 1 quart | $\frac{1}{24}$ pt. ( .7 oz.) |
| $\frac{1}{2}$ gallon | $\frac{1}{12}$ pt. (1.3 oz.) |
| 1 gallon | $\frac{1}{6}$ pt. |
| 2 gallons | $\frac{1}{3}$ pt. |
| 3 gallons | $\frac{1}{2}$ pt. |
| 4 gallons | $\frac{2}{3}$ pt. |
| 5 gallons | $\frac{5}{6}$ pt. |
| 6 gallons | 1 pt. |

Keep in mind that all of *Johnson's* late model engines use a 50-to-1 fuel mix. This is true of all of *Chrysler's* engines with the exception of the 3.6 horsepower which uses 25 to 1. *Mercury* engines vary and therefore should be checked before mixing the fuel. For instance the *Mercury Competition* outboards vary. The Twister II uses a 18:1 ratio as does the 650X. The *Mercury 25SS* uses a 25:1 mixture. It is always best to check out the specifications before mixing fuel.

*Outboard Motor Gears*—Use Outboard Gear Oil EP 90 for clutch and shift models when an SAE 90EP oil is specified by the manufacturer. Special products are supplied by outboard manufacturers for electric-shift models. Outboard Gear Grease is recommended when a grease-type product is required. When an SAE 30 or 40 oil is recommended, use Outboard Motor Oil or Havoline of the prescribed viscosity.

## LOWER-UNIT LUBRICATION

The lower unit of an outboard motor requires grease or oil in the gear case. It is important that the motor manufacturer's recommendation with respect to lower-unit lubricants be followed in each

## STERN AND OUTBOARD DRIVES

| NAME AND MODEL | Lubricant Recommended (Normal Operation) |
|---|---|
| **BRENNAN** | |
| Upper case (spiral bevels) ........................................................ | Gear Lube EP 90 |
| Lower case (straight bevels) ..................................................... | Outboard Gear Grease |
| **CHRYSLER**—Drive 90 ................................................................ | Gear Lube HD 90 |
| Volvo 250 ................................................................................... | Havoline Motor Oil 10W-30 |
| **EATON** | |
| Powernaut ................................................................................ | Gear Lube HD 90 |
| Interceptor Mod. 200 up to Ser. 219752 .............................. | Gear Oil 3450 |
| Interceptor Mod. 200 after Ser. 219752 ............................... | 10W-30 (Havoline) |
| **HARNISCHFEGER** (Napco) | |
| Power Hawk ............................................................................. | Outboard Gear Oil EP 90 |
| **HOLMAN AND MOODY** ............................................................ | Havoline 10W-30 |
| **HYDRO DRIVE** ......................................................................... | Texamatic Fluid |
| **MERCURY** | |
| Mercruiser ............................................................................... | Outboard Gear Oil EP 90 |
| **MUNCIE** (MGW-Flexidrive) ...................................................... | Gear Lube HD 90 |
| **OSCO** (see Muncie) | |
| **PERKINS** ................................................................................... | Gear Oil 3450 |
| **RANGER** .................................................................................... | Universal Gear Lube EP 90 |
| **SHARK-O-MATIC** (Montgomery Ward & Chrysler) .................. | Outboard Gear Oil EP 90 |
| **UNIVERSAL**—Sabre V-6 and Super V-6............................... | Gear Lube HD 90 |
| **VOLVO AQUAMATIC** | |
| 80, 100, 110 and 120 up to Serial No. 219751 ................... | Outboard Gear Oil EP 90 |
| Model 200 from Serial No. 219751 ....................................... | Havoline Motor Oil 10W-30 |
| Model 250 from Serial No. 219751 ....................................... | Havoline Motor Oil 10W-30 |

individual case, since motors and operating conditions vary greatly.

Outboard lower units normally contain several screw-plug type openings. On the nongear-shift engine, filling is usually accomplished through the lower of the two openings after both the lower and upper screw plugs have been removed.

The gear housing is serviced by removing the air-vent screw and lubricant-filler plug. Insert the gear-lubricant tube into the filler-plug hole and inject lubricant until an excess starts to flow out of the air-vent screw hole, indicating that the housing is filled. Make sure that the plug gaskets are properly located when replacing plugs, so that water will not leak past the threads and into the gear housing. When a complete change of lubricant is required, place the motor in a vertical position and remove the oil drain plug and gasket on the bottom of the gear case. Permit the oil to drain out completely before refilling.

# Chapter 9

# Troubleshooting

The *outboard motor,* like other types of internal combustion engines, must perform the work of drawing in and compressing its charge before energy is developed in its cylinder, and some special device is required to start it. To start an outboard motor, therefore, requires the use of power from an external source. For most motors it is necessary to disengage the propeller during the starting period.

Small outboard two-cycle engines are usually started by a cord, by turning the flywheel, or by a special hand gear. The latter must have a ratchet or clutch which will release or throw it out of gear as soon as power is developed. The electrical or self-starting system is usually employed on larger engines and is similar to that used in automobiles. This starting system usually consists of a small electric motor which is mechanically connected to the engine shaft through a set of gears, and electrically connected to a storage battery which furnishes the current required for starting.

The battery is kept charged by an electric generator which is driven by means of a set of pulleys from the engine. The generator also assists the battery in supplying the current requirements for ignition and lights during normal operating conditions. The battery should be kept charged at all times. The state of charge should be checked by making specific-gravity readings with a battery hydrometer. It is suggested that specific-gravity readings and checking for replacement of water be made every two weeks. If the battery has been standing for 30 days, it should be recharged before being placed into service to assure reliable starting. Charge the battery up to the specific gravity recommended by the battery manufacturer.

Proper water level should be maintained at all times. Never add acid except when acid has been lost by spilling.

Fuel and ignition systems are the most common causes of motor troubles. When a motor fails to start, the trouble in a majority of cases is to be found in the ignition system, such as magneto or spark-plug failure, a run-down battery, an open electrical circuit, but only rarely in the fuel or cooling system. The proper performance of all outboard motors, whether two- or four-cycle, depends on a supply of correct fuel mixture, good compression, and an adequate spark to ignite the mixture at the proper time.

Troubles and remedies in two-cycle outboard motors are similar to those of the four-cycle automotive type, the difference being mainly due to the method of getting the fuel and air mixture into the combustion chamber. In two-cycle motors, the fuel mixture passes through the crankcase and enters the combustion chamber through ports uncovered by the piston. It should be clearly understood that the "Remedies" section of this chapter explains *what to do*—not *how to do*. To give service technique here would be a useless repetition of instructions given in other sections of this book.

## SERVICE DIAGNOSIS & MOTOR NOISE

| *Symptom & Possible Cause* | *Possible Remedy* |
|---|---|
| **Motor Will Not Start** | |
| (a) Empty fuel tank. | (a) Fill tank with a fresh clean mixture of oil and gasoline. |
| (b) Weak battery. | (b) Recharge and test battery as outlined in other parts of this book. If necessary, replace battery with a new one. |
| (c) Dirty or corroded distributor contact points. | (c) Clean and inspect contact points; if badly burned or pitted, replace points and condenser. Adjust gap to manufacturer's specifications. |

| *Symptom and Possible Cause* | *Possible Remedy* |
|---|---|
| (d) Defective coil. | (d) Replace weak coil with a new one. Then check conditions of contact points and replace if necessary. See (c) above. |
| (e) Broken or loose ignition wires. | (e) Replace broken ignition wires and those with cracked insulation. Tighten all connections at distributor. Be sure the spark-plug wires are secure in distributor cap. |
| (f) Fouled spark plugs. | (f) Clean and tighten spark plugs. Adjust gaps to manufacturer's specifications. |
| (g) Improper spark-plug gap. | (g) See (f) above. |
| (h) Improper spark timing. | (h) Check ignition timing. Replace parts as necessary to correct this condition. |
| (i) Dirt or water in fuel line or carburetor. | (i) Disconnect lines and clean with compressed air. Remove and clean carburetor. Drain and refill fuel tank with fresh gasoline-oil mixture. |
| (j) Carburetor flooded. | (j) Check carburetor float level and needle-seat assembly. Check float for leaks and replace parts as necessary to correct this condition. |
| (k) Fuel level in carburetor bowl not correct. | (k) Check fuel level and compare with that given by the carburetor manufacturer. |
| (l) Defective starting motor. | (l) Repair or replace defective starting motor. |

| *Symptom and Possible Cause* | *Possible Remedy* |
|---|---|
| (m) Open ignition - switch circuit. | (m) Turn on ignition switch; if ammeter shows a slight discharge, it indicates that current is flowing. A glance at the fuel gauge (if used) will indicate whether or not there is fuel in the tank. If no indication is shown when turning the ignition switch, the circuit is faulty and should be repaired. |

## Motor Stalls

| | |
|---|---|
| (a) Idling speed too low. | (a) Reset throttle adjustment until engine idles at its normal idling speed. |
| (b) Incorrect fuel mixture. | (b) Check to see that oil and gasoline are mixed in the correct proportions. |
| (c) Dirt or water in fuel line or carburetor. | (c) Disconnect lines and clear with compressed air. |
| (d) Incorrect carburetor fuel level. | (d) Carburetor fuel level should be as per manufacturer's specifications. |
| (e) Improper choke adjustment. | (e) Readjust choke. |
| (f) Carburetor icing (cold weather). | (f) Open throttle as motor starts to stall. Keep motor at fast idle until conditions clear. |
| (g) Weak battery. | (g) Recharge and test battery. If necessary, replace battery with a new one of the same type and capacity. |

170

| *Symptom and Possible Cause* | *Possible Remedy* |
|---|---|
| (h) **Spark** plugs dirty or gaps incorrectly set. | (h) Clean and tighten spark plugs. Adjust spark-plug g a p s to manufacturer's specifications. |
| (i) Defective magneto coil or condenser. | (i) Check magneto coils on the stator plate. Before checking, however, the stator must either be removed from the engine or the poles of the magnetic rotor must be in a neutral position away from the stator field, or the magnetic influence will result in an incorrect conclusion. |
| (j) Magneto breaker points dirty or incorrectly set. | (j) Clean and adjust breaker points and set gap or gaps according to manufacturer's specifications. Replace condenser if necessary. |
| (k) Leaks in ignition wiring. | (k) Replace broken ignition wires and those with cracked insulation. Tighten all connections at coil, breaker, and i g n i t i o n switch. Check spark-plug wires for proper terminal contacts. |
| (l) Motor overheating. | (l) Refer to Chapter COOLING SYSTEM for various causes of engine overheating. |

(a) Incorrect carburetor mixture setting.

(a) Check carburetor mixture setting. If carburetor mixture setting is too rich, motor will run rough or sluggish. If the mixture is too lean, motor will spit or backfire and slow down or stop.

(b) Leaks in ignition wiring.

(b) Wipe spark-plug wires clean and inspect for broken or worn insulation or broken wires, especially under clamps. Be sure wires are tight at the magneto end and on the spark plugs.

(c) Moisture on ignition wires, cap, or plug.

(c) Dry the wet ignition system with compressed air or a clean dry cloth. Remove individual spark-plug wires from cap; dry cavity and wire ends thoroughly. Inspect inside of cap and remove all traces of moisture and dirt.

(d) Weak battery.

(d) Recharge and test battery. If necessary, replace battery with new one of the same type and capacity.

(e) Low grade of fuel.

(e) Use only fuel mixtures of a type approved by the motor manufacturer.

(f) Incorrect breaker-point gap.

(f) Check breaker-point gap and readjust if necessary. Inspect the points carefully,

*Symptom and Possible Cause*          *Possible Remedy*

and if they are burned or dirty it will be necessary to clean or replace.

(g)  Defective distributor rotor.     (g)  Check distributor-cam play. Replace parts as required to correct this condition. Replace worn distributor shaft.

## Motor Misfires While Idling

(a)  Incorrect spark-plug gap.        (a)  Clean and tighten spark plugs. Adjust gaps to manufacturer's specifications.

(b)  Defective or loose spark plug.   (b)  See (a) above.

(c)  Spark plugs of incorrect heat range.  (c)  Exchange spark plugs for size and gap range as recommended by engine manufacturer.

(d)  Sticking breaker arm.            (d)  Remove, clean, and inspect for damage. Replace with new one if necessary.

(e)  Incorrect breaker-point gap.     (e)  Adjust gap to manufacturer's specifications.

(f)  Breaker points not synchronized. (f)  If magneto has been removed from engine, it must be accurately retimed to engine upon reassembly. Proper timing of magneto to the engine produces an ignition spark in each cylinder at the exact instant that the fuel mixture should be ignited for best engine performance. This dis-

*Symptom and Possible Cause*         *Possible Remedy*

tance, which is accurately determined by the engine designers, is usually designated as a given number of degrees of angular travel of crankshaft before piston reaches its uppermost position in the cylinder.

(g) Loose wires in primary circuit.

(g) Check for worn or damaged wiring between battery, ammeter, ignition switch, and coil. Check for loose terminal connections. Replace wiring if necessary.

(h) Corroded or pitted breaker points.

(h) To adjust the breaker-point gap, loosen the screw on the stationary bracket, and move either one way or the other after checking with feeler gauge for proper gap setting.

(i) Cracked distributor cap.

(i) Cracked distributor caps are dangerous because of leakage or high-voltage flashover. If the leakage is heavy, or if more than one path occurs, it is recommended that the part be discarded.

(j) Leaking or broken high-tension wires.

(j) Dry off wet ignition system with compressed air or a clean dry cloth. Remove the individual spark-plug wires from cap; dry cavity and wire ends thoroughly.

*Symptom and Possible Cause*  *Possible Remedy*

Inspect inside of cap and remove all traces of moisture and dirt.

(k)  Weak magnet.

(k)  Check magneto with magnetic analyzer and, if necessary, re-magnetize.

(l)  Worn distributor or magneto-shaft bushings.

(l)  Check distributor-shaft play. Replace worn distribtor cam shaft. Make adjustments or replace parts as conditions require.

(m) Defective coil or condenser.

(m) Replace defective coil or condenser with new ones, then check the condition of contact points and replace if necessary. Adjust gap to manufacturer's specifications.

(n)  Defective ignition switch.

(n)  Replace defective ignition switch.

(o)  Spark timing out of adjustment.

(o)  See (f) above.

(p)  Dirt or water in fuel.

(p)  Refill tank with the proper mixture of fresh gasoline and oil.

(q)  Reed valve open or broken.

(q)  Check and replace reeds as required.

## Motor Misfires at High Speed

(a)  Distributor points dirty or incorrectly spaced.

(a)  Clean and adjust contact points; if badly burned or pitted, replace points and condenser. Adjust point gap to manufacturer's specifications.

175

| *Symptom and Possible Cause* | *Possible Remedy* |
|---|---|
| (b) Coil or condenser defective. | (b) Replace defective coil or condenser with new ones, then check conditions of contact points and replace if necessary. Adjust gap to manufacturer's specifications. |
| (c) Incorrect ignition timing. | (c) Check and reset ignition timing. Replace parts as necessary to correct this condition. |
| (d) Spark plugs dirty, damp, or gap set too wide. | (d) Clean and tighten spark plugs. Adjust gap according to manufacturer's specifications. |
| (e) Wrong spark plugs. | (e) Check manufacturers's recommendation. The plug which is installed originally in the motor, for standard or normal use, is the one that will give best service under operating conditions. |
| (f) Dirty carburetor. | (f) Remove, clean, and recondition carburetor. Replace parts as necessary. |
| (g) Lean carburetor adjustment. | (g) Reset idle-adjustment screw as per manufacturer's recommendations for correct idle mixture. |

## Motor Backfires

| | |
|---|---|
| (a) Cracked spark-plug porcelain. | (a) Replace cracked spark plug with one of identical size and gapping. |
| (b) Carbon path in distributor cap. | (b) Remove carbon and clean distributor parts. |

| *Symptom and Possible Cause* | *Possible Remedy* |
|---|---|
| (c) Crossed spark-plug wires. | (c) Reverse wire connection at spark plugs only. |
| (d) Improper timing. | (d) Check and reset ignition timing. |
| (e) Poor quality fuel. | (e) Clean fuel tank and refill with an approved oil and gasoline mixture. |
| (f) Improper ignition timing. | (f) Check and reset ignition timing. Replace parts as necessary to correct this condition. |
| (g) Engine pre-ignition. | (g) See (f) above. |
| (h) Improperly seated or broken reed valves. | (h) Check reeds thoroughly and replace as required. A reed must seat tightly against the reed plate along the entire reed length and should completely cover holes in the reed plate. |

**Piston Ring Noise**

| | |
|---|---|
| (a) Broken ring. | (a) Replace broken ring as required. Check to determine causes of breakage and correct as necessary. |
| (b) Top ring striking cylinder ridge. | (b) Remove ridge at top of cylinder as required, using suitable ridge reamer. Check rings and piston for possible damage and replace parts necessary. |
| (c) Broken ring lands. | (c) Replace piston if needed. Check for ridge at top of cylinder wall and remove, using suitable ridge reamer. |

| Symptom and Possible Cause | Possible Remedy |
|---|---|
| | Check rings and piston for possible damage and replace parts as necessary. |

## Piston Noise

| | |
|---|---|
| (a) Piston-pin fit too tight. | (a) Refit piston as required. Fit pins at normal room temperature, thumb-press fit. |
| (b) Excessive piston-to-bore clearance. | (b) Replace piston as required. Check cylinder walls for excessive wear and, if necessary, recondition cylinder walls and install new pistons and rings. |
| (c) Carbon accumulation in head. | (c) Remove cylinder head and clean carbon from chamber, pistons, and valves. Drain and refill tank with a recommended grade of oil and gasoline. |
| (d) Collapsed piston skirt. | (d) Replace pistons as required. Check cylinder walls for possible scoring. Recondition as necessary to correct. |
| (e) Insufficient clearance at top ring land. | (e) Check piston clearance. If necessary refit pistons to correct this condition. |
| (f) Broken piston, skirt, or ring land. | (f) Replace pistons as required. Check cylinder walls for possible scoring or damage. Recondition walls if necessary and install new pistons. |

| *Symptom and Possible Cause* | *Possible Remedy* |
|---|---|
| **Reed Valve Failures** | |
| (a) Incorrect reed-valve setting. | (a) Inspect reeds and replace any that are cracked, broken, or warped. The reeds should seat lightly against the reed plate around the entire perimeter of each lobe and should completely cover the holes in the reed plate. |
| (b) Broken or weak reed valve. | (b) Inspect and replace as required. If reed breakage occurs, the broken portion of the reed will usually be found in the crankcase or in the transfer port passages. If the piece is small enough, it will generally pass through the combustion chamber and be discharged with the exhaust. |
| (c) Improper valve opening. | (c) Check reed valves for possible damage. Check reed opening with that listed by the manufacturer. Check reed-stop adjustment by measuring distance from the reed plate to the lower side of the reed stop. Correct or replace as necessary. |
| (d) Corrosion of reed valve. | (d) Remove corrosion from reed valve, reinstall, and adjust. Replace reeds if necessary. |

179

*Symptom and Possible Cause*

*Possible Remedy*

(e)  Poor valve seat.

(e)  Remove deposits on valve seat. Replace valve reeds as required.

## Connecting Rod Noise

(a)  Misaligned rods.

(a)  Check rods for alignment. If necessary, straighten rod or install a new one to correct this condition. Check bearing and journal for excessive wear. Replace parts as required.

(b)  Excessive bearing clearance.

(b)  Replace worn bearings as required. Fit connecting-rod bearings to the desired clearance.

(c)  Eccentric or out-of-round crank-pin journal.

(c)  Replace and regrind shaft as necessary. Replace with new undersize bearings after grinding operation is completed.

## Main Bearing Noise

(a)  Loose flywheel.

(a)  Tighten flywheel to a torque of 55 to 60 foot-pounds, then check engine for noise.

(b)  Excessive bearing clearance.

(b)  Replace worn bearings as required. Fit main bearings to the desired clearance.

(c)  Eccentric or out-of-round journals.

(c)  Replace crankshaft or regrind journals as necessary. Replace with new undersize bearings when grinding operation is completed.

180

| *Symptom and Possible Cause* | *Possible Remedy* |
|---|---|
| (d) Bent or twisted crankshaft. | (d) Replace or straighten crankshaft as necessary, then check condition of bearings; replace as required. |

## Broken Piston Rings

| | |
|---|---|
| (a) Wrong type or size. | (a) Replace rings as required after checking cylinder walls for possible scoring or grooving. When replacing rings. use only those that are factory engineered and inspected and the correct type and size for the engine being worked on. |
| (b) Undersize pistons. | (b) Fit new pistons and rings. Check cylinder walls for possible scoring or grooving. Recondition walls as required. |
| (c) Ring stroking top ridge. | (c) Replace rings as required after checking cylinder walls for possible scoring or grooving. Remove ridge and recondition walls, if necessary. |
| (d) Worn ring grooves. | (d) Fit new pistons and rings after checking cylinder walls for possible scoring or grooving. Recondition cylinder walls as required. |
| (e) Broken ring lands. | (e) Fit new pistons and rings, checking cylinder walls for possible scoring or groov- |

| *Symptom and Possible Cause* | *Possible Remedy* |
|---|---|
| | ing. Recondition cylinder walls if necessary. |
| (f) Insufficient gap clearance. | (f) Replace rings as required. Check walls for damage and recondition if necessary. Correct ring gap should be .007 to .015 inch. |
| (g) Excessive side clearance in groove. | (g) Replace broken rings as required. Inspect cylinder walls for damage, and recondition if necessary. |

## Broken Pistons

| | |
|---|---|
| (a) Undersize pistons. | (a) Recondition cylinder walls if necessary; then check walls with a micrometer and fit new pistons and rings. |
| (b) Eccentric or tapered cylinder. | (b) Recondition cylinder walls and fit new pistons and rings. |
| (c) Misaligned or tapered cylinders. | (c) Recondition cylinder walls if necessary. Then fit new pistons and rings. Realign connecting rods. |
| (d) Engine overheating. | (d) Recondition cylinder walls if necessary; then fit new pistons and rings. Refer to Chapter on COOLING SYSTEMS for possible causes and remedies of engine overheating. |

# Chapter 10

# Electrical Systems

A knowledge of electricity and magnetism is of great importance to owners of outboard motor boats and servicemen because it enables them to grasp more clearly the operating principles of the various units comprising the electric starting, lighting, and ignition systems associated with outboard motors.

## ELECTROMAGNETISM

Electricity and magnetism have a close relationship with each other. Every time an electric current flows, it sets up a magnetic field. Also, every time a magnetic field is increased, decreased, or changed in direction, an electric voltage is set up in any nearby conductor. Thus, if electricity flows through a wire coil around an iron core, it will make an electromagnet out of the iron core. If the direction of magnetism passing through the iron core is reversed, a voltage will be generated in the winding of a coil of wire around this core.

Such an electromagnet is a magnet only when current flows through its coil. When the current is interrupted, the iron core returns almost to its natural state. This loss of magnetism is, however, not absolutely complete since a very small amount called *residual magnetism* remains for a longer or shorter period of time.

Certain substances, particularly special alloy steel, retain a substantial part of their magnetism after the magnetic field used to magnetize them has been removed, and are therefore called *permanent magnets*. Other substances, like soft iron, remain magnets only when they are in the field of another permanent magnet and become demagnetized after removal. Such magnets are called *temporary magnets*.

A magneto, such as used in the ignition system of some outboard motors, is simply a specialized form of electric generator which uses the magnetic principles in order to generate electricity. Permanent magnets are used to produce the magnetic field.

## MAGNETO ESSENTIALS

In order to produce a working magneto, it is necessary to have an armature plate which is attached to a soft-iron laminated core and pole-shoe assembly, a coil with a primary and secondary winding, a condenser, and breaker points.

The magneto coil, as normally used, consists of two windings termed the *primary* and *secondary*. The primary is made up of about 175 turns of heavy wire. One end of the primary is connected to the frame of the magneto as ground, and the other is connected to the live insulated breaker point. The secondary usually has about 10,000 turns of very fine wire wound on outside of the primary. The inside end of the secondary is grounded along with the primary ground. The outer end is connected to the spark-plug wire.

The condenser is a storage reservoir for electricity and acts to prevent arcing of the breaker contacts. It consists essentially of two strips of foil with paper insulation between them, and wound together so that one of the strips of foil can be grounded and the other strip connected to the live breaker point. At the instant of breaker-point opening, the insulating paper between the two strips of foil acts as a storage reservoir for electricity during an extremely small fraction of a second before the arc across the breaker points are extinguished.

## GLOSSARY OF COMMON ELECTRICAL TERMS

An *insulator* is a substance which offers tremendous resistance to the passage of an electric current.

Two kinds of wire *conductors* are copper wire (low resistance) and resistance wire (high resistance).

*Volts, amperes,* and *ohms* are three units that form the basis of Ohm's law.

A *volt* is the unit of electric pressure called electromotive force. It is that electric pressure which produces a current of one ampere against a resistance of one ohm.

An *ampere* is the unit of electric current. It is that current produced by a pressure of one volt against a resistance of one ohm. (It is that quantity of electricity that will deposit .005084 grain of copper per second.)

A *coulomb* is the quantity of electricity delivered by a current of one ampere maintained for one second of time. Hence, one ampere is a rate of current flow equal to one coulomb per second of electricity when the current is turned on. See Fig. 1.

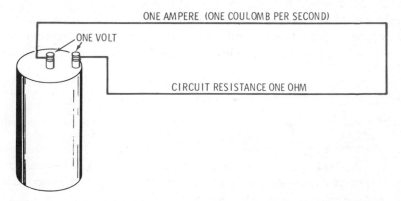

**Fig. 1. A simple circuit showing the relation between volts, amperes, coulombs, and ohms.**

An *ohm* is the resistance offered to an unvarying current by a column of mercury at 32 degrees F., 14.4521 grams in mass of a constant cross-sectional area of one square millimeter and 100.3 centimeters long.

*Ohm's law* gives the relations between volts, amperes, and ohms. It is usually stated as: The amount of current in amperes is equal to the pressure in volts divided by the resistance in ohms; that is:

$$I = \frac{E}{R}$$

$$R = \frac{E}{I}$$

$$E = I \times R$$

where:
I equals current in amperes,
R equals resistance,
E equals voltage.

*Direct current* is electron flow in only one direction.

*Alternating current* is electron flow first in one direction and then in a reverse direction.

*Primary current* comes directly from the source.
*Secondary current* occurs when the voltage and amperage of a primary current have been changed by an induction coil.

*Low-voltage* current is called low-tension; *high-voltage* current is called high-tension current.

An *insulated circuit* is one in which the wires are covered with insulating material to prevent leakage.

A *short circuit* is one in which the current leaks and returns to the source without doing its work. Electric current always takes the path of least resistance.

*Magnetism* is the property that some bodies have to attract iron and steel, and those bodies having this property are called magnets. Magnets have two opposite kinds of magnetism or magnetic poles. One of these poles tends to move toward the north pole and the other toward the south. They are accordingly called the north and south poles. See Fig. 2.

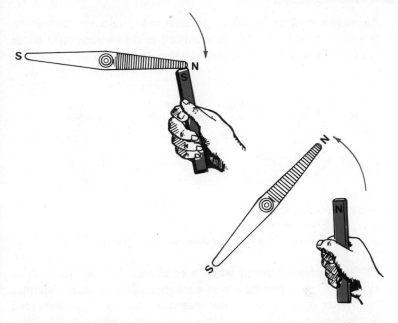

**Fig. 2. Effect of unlike and like poles. Unlike poles attract each other, like poles repel each other.**

The two laws relating to magnetic *poles* are: (1) Unlike poles attract each other; and (2) like poles repel each other.

A *permanent magnet* is a magnet made of hard steel which holds its magnetism almost indefinitely.

An *electromagnet* is a magnet made up of an iron core around which is wound a number of turns of insulated wire. When an electric current flows through the winding, the core becomes magnetized and strong magnetic poles are produced.

A *solenoid* is a spiral conductor of numerous turns with or without an iron core which forms a magnet when current passes through the coil. (The core greatly increases the magnetic strength of the solenoid.)

A *magnetic field* is the region surrounding a magnet in which magnetic force acts.

*Electromagnetic induction* is the tendency of electric currents to flow in a conductor when it is moved in a magnetic field so as to cut lines of magnetic force. See Fig. 3.

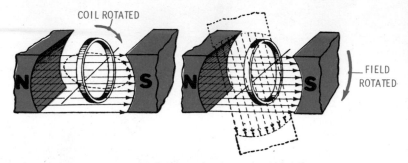

**Fig. 3. Example of electromagnetic induction.**

*Cut lines of force* occur when a conductor forming part of an electric circuit is moved across a magnetic field in such a manner as to alter the position of the magnetic lines of force embraced by the circuit. (The current thus produced is called the *induced current,* and that part of the wire moved in the magnetic field is the *inductor.*)

A *cell* is a device for producing electricity through the action of two dissimilar metal plates placed in an exciting fluid called the electrolyte. (The two dissimilar plates are called the elements.)

A *battery* consists of two or more cells joined together so as to form a single unit.

The difference between *primary cells* and *secondary cells* is that cells are said to be primary when they produce a current of themselves; secondary is when they must first be charged from an external source, storing up a current supply which is afterward yielded in the reverse direction to that of the charging current. (Accordingly, an assembly of secondary cells joined together is known as a storage battery.)

*Cell circuits* are three methods of connecting cells: In series, in parallel, and in series-parallel, as shown in Fig. 4.

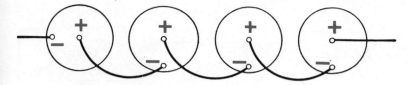

(A) Series.

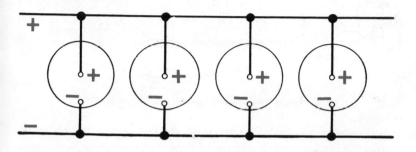

(B) Parallel.

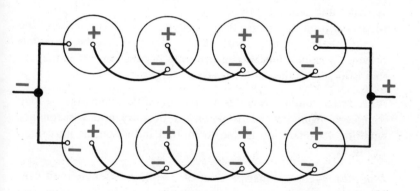

(C) Series-parallel.

**Fig. 4. Battery connections.**

A *primary inductor coil* is a type of coil that consists of a long iron core around which is wound a considerable length of low-resistance insulated copper wire. Its operation is due to self-induction. See Fig. 5.

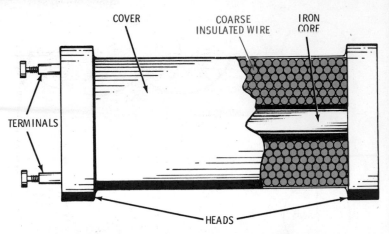

COVER    COARSE    IRON
INSULATED WIRE    CORE

TERMINALS

HEADS

**Fig. 5. Primary induction coil used for low-tension ignition.**

*Self-induction* is the property of an electric current which tends to resist any change in its rate of flow. Self-induction is brought into action by the making and breaking of the circuit connected to the source. The primary induction coil is used in low-tension or make-and-break ignition.

In an ignition hook-up, the spark occurs at the instant the circuit breaks, not at the instant of making. When the current is flowing, it cannot be stopped instantly because of self-induction; that is, it acts as though it possesses weight.

A *secondary induction* coil is a type of coil that consists of a long iron core around which is wound a primary and a secondary winding. Its operation is due to mutual induction, as illustrated in Fig. 6.

*Mutual induction* is that product of a voltage in one circuit provided by a changing current in a neighboring circuit, even though no apparent connection exists between the two circuits. The circuit to which the current is applied is called the *primary circuit* and the circuit in which a current is induced is called the *secondary circuit*. In an actual coil, the primary and secondary circuits are made up of heavy and fine insulated wire, respectively. The property of a secondary coil that makes it of great value

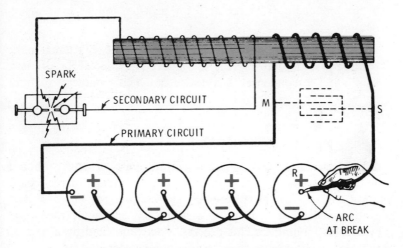

Fig. 6. Production of spark with a secondary coil.

for most purposes is its *mutual induction* by which the voltage of the induced current may be increased or diminished to any extent, depending on the relation between the number of turns in the primary and secondary winding.

The approximate ratio of the voltage of an induced current is to the voltage of the primary current as the number of turns of the secondary winding is to the number of turns of the primary winding. This makes it possible to obtain the very high voltage

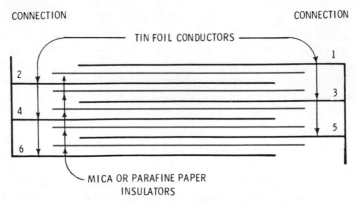

Fig. 7. Construction of a typical condenser.

of the induced current required for high-tension or jump-spark ignition.

A *condenser* is necessary in the secondary coil of a jump-spark ignition system to absorb the self-induced current of the primary winding. The condenser is a device designed to absorb or hold an electric charge. See Fig. 7.

## IGNITION SYSTEMS

The electrical system is an important part of any outboard motor, because it provides instant starting by means of fuel-spark ignition. As the fuel mixture enters the combustion chamber and is compressed by the piston, it is necessary that some means be provided for igniting it. This process is accomplished by a part of the electrical system known as the *ignition system*.

There are two types of ignition systems used on outboard motors:

1. Magneto ignition.
2. Battery ignition.

In the *magneto ignition* system, magnetism is used to generate the voltage required to cause the spark to ignite the fuel mixture. The *battery ignition* system differs from the *magneto ignition* system, mainly because the chemical reaction within the battery provides the necessary voltage for the fuel-ignition spark.

From the foregoing, it is apparent that magneto ignition requires no assistance from an outside source of electricity, such as a dry cell or storage battery, to produce the necessary spark action. The electrical energy is generated by the rotation of the flywheel on the magneto and is imparted to the spark plugs to cause combustion in the cylinder for continuous motor operation.

### Magneto Fundamentals

In order to fully comprehend what makes the spark in a magneto ignition system, it is necessary to know not only what causes magnetism, but also the interaction, or relationship, between magnetism and electricity. See Fig. 8.

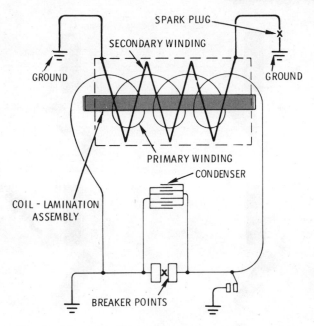

**Fig. 8. Schematic diagram showing a typical magneto-ignition circuit.**

Magnetism and electricity have a close relationship with each other. Any time electricity flows through a wire, it sets up a magnetic field around that wire. If this magnetic field is disturbed by an increase or decrease in its strength, or if its direction is changed, an electric voltage is created in any nearby conductor. Thus, if electricity is made to flow through a coil around an iron core, it will make an electromagnet out of the iron core. Also, if the direction of magnetism passing through an iron core is reversed, a voltage will be generated in the windings of a coil of wire around this core.

In this connection, it should be noted that when a piece of iron or any of its alloys is charged with electricity in order to form a permanent magnet, certain changes take place within the metal that cause the magnet to have two distinct ends which are called *poles*. These poles are called the *south* and the *north* poles of the magnet, as shown in Fig. 9.

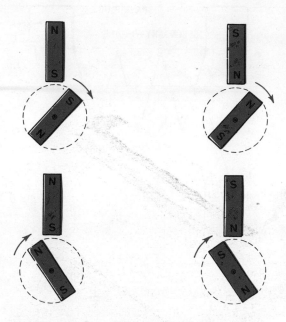

Fig. 9. Showing how like poles of permanent magnets
tend to repel one another while unlike poles tend to
attract one another.

The direction of the lines of force in the magnetic field is from the north pole to the south pole. Like magnetic poles, such as two south or two north poles, repel one another, whereas magnets having opposite poles (a south and a north) attract one another when brought into close proximity.

## Condensers

A condenser, as used in ignition circuits, acts as a storage reservoir for electricity. It consists essentially of two strips of foil with paper insulation between them and wound together so that one of the strips of foil can be grounded and the other strip of foil connected to the live breaker point. At the instant of breaker-point opening, the insulating paper between the two strips of foil acts as a storage reservoir for electricity during an extremely small fraction of a second before the arc across the breaker points is ex-

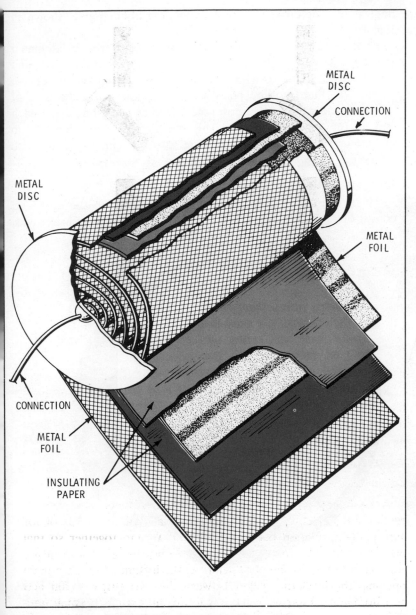

METAL
DISC

CONNECTION

METAL
DISC

METAL
FOIL

CONNECTION

METAL
FOIL

INSULATING
PAPER

Fig. 10. Details of a typical ignition condenser.

tinguished. The construction of an ignition condenser is shown in Fig. 10.

As the magnetic field will readily pass through iron, a laminated iron core is used to provide a controlled pathway to support and direct the magnetic field. The magnets are placed on the engine flywheel so that opposite poles will always line up at the ends of the core, and so that the north pole will alternately line up at each end as the flywheel rotates. This causes the magnetic field to change direction as each succeeding set of magnets line up with the core.

## Ignition Coils

The windings of the ignition coil are wound on the core and consist of a primary winding having a number of turns of heavy wire

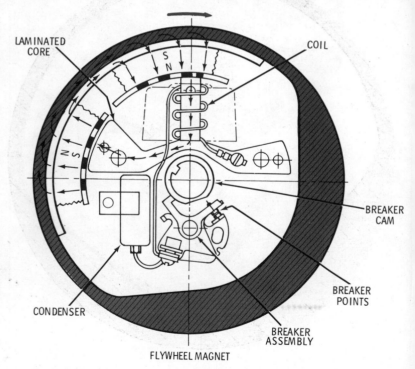

Fig. 11. Illustrating the component parts and direction of magnetic lines in a typical ignition magneto.

and a secondary winding having a greater number of turns of finer wire. The primary is grounded at cne end, and is attached to the breaker points and to the condenser at the other. The secondary is also grounded at one end, and is attached directly to the spark plug at the other.

When the magnets are lined up with the core, the direction of the magnetic lines of force through the core is from the north pole to the south pole, as noted in Fig. 11. As the flywheel continues to rotate, the strength of the magnetic field will drop slightly

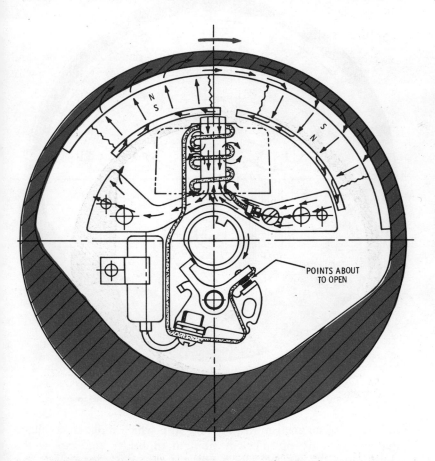

POINTS ABOUT
TO OPEN

Fig. 12. Diagram showing an ignition magneto with points about to open.

which, in turn, creates a primary voltage. When the next set of magnets line up with the core, the voltage in the primary sets up its own magnetic field which resists the change in direction of the magnetic field through the core. See Fig. 12.

The points will then open, as noted in Fig. 13, and the current will cease to flow through the primary winding. This, in turn, results

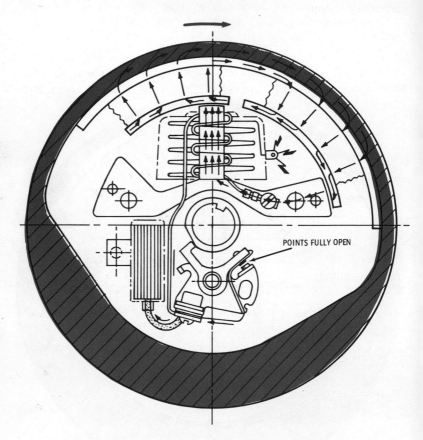

POINTS FULLY OPEN

Fig. 13. Diagram showing an ignition magneto with points open.

in a surge of magnetism through the core which induces a voltage in the secondary of sufficient strength to bridge the gap at the spark plug.

At the same instant the breaker points open, the condenser acts as a reservoir for the surge of current in the primary which would otherwise tend to arc across the breaker points. Once the points are opened, the current in the condenser will be discharged back through the primary, which further contributes to the change in the magnetic field in the coil and core, and to the voltage of the secondary output.

## MAGNETO TYPES

There are two general types of outboard-motor magnetos—the flywheel type in which the magnet is contained in the flywheel, and

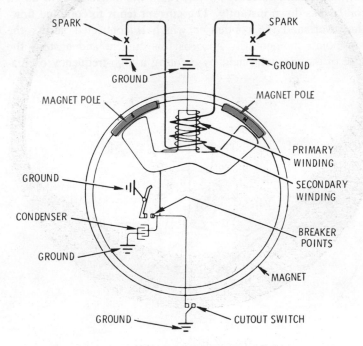

Fig. 14. Diagram showing the circuit arrangement in a typical fly-wheel magneto.

the rotor type with the magnet contained in the rotor. The flywheel and rotor types are shown in Figs. 14 and 15.

## Flywheel-Type Magnetos

With reference to Fig. 16 (showing a flywheel-type magneto) it will be noted that the magneto consists essentially of an armature base, often called the stator plate, with the coils, condenser and breaker-point assembly mounted on the base. A permanent magnet mounted inside the flywheel completes the assembly.

In operation, as the permanent magnet poles pass over the pole shoes of the coil laminations, a magnetic field causes a current to flow through the primary winding of the coil. This current is normally grounded through the closed breaker points. When the breaker points open (actuated by a cam on the crankshaft), the flow of the primary current is broken and the magnetic field about the coil breaks down instantly. The current tends to continue flowing, however, and the condenser which is connected across the breaker points momentarily absorbs this current and hastens the collapse of the magnetic field by creating a high-frequency oscilla-

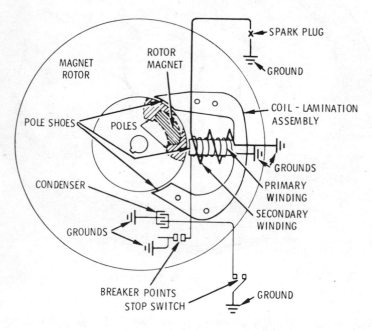

Fig. 15. Schematic circuit arrangement in a typical rotor magneto.

tion in the current. The condenser also reduces pitting of the breaker points by absorbing any sparking across them.

In the secondary winding of the coil, this collapsing magnetic field induces a very high voltage which is carried by the high-tension spark-plug wire to the spark plug, where it jumps the plug gap and ignites the fuel charge in the cylinder. This cycle is repeated for each revolution of the crankshaft in a two-cycle engine and every other revolution in a four-cycle engine. The speed at

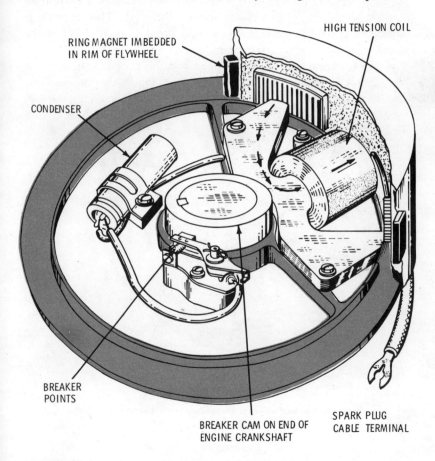

**Fig. 16. Flywheel magneto with permanent rotating magnet embedded in rim of engine flywheel.**

which the ignition process takes place can be calculated from the fact that, with an engine running at 3600 rpm, the entire cycle is repeated sixty times a second.

In this connection it should be noted that one complete coil, condenser, and breaker-point circuit is required for each engine cylinder. Thus, for a two-cylinder, alternate-firing engine, it is necessary to have two sets of contact points, two ignition coils, and two condensers, as shown in Fig. 17. For a four-cylinder out-

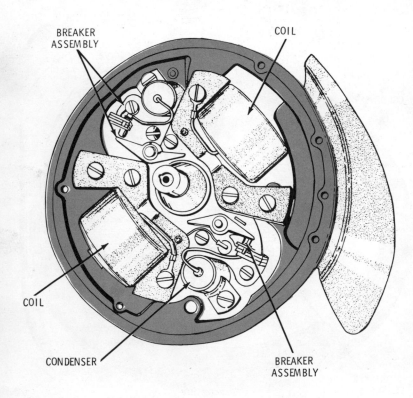

Fig. 17. Typical flywheel magneto for twin-cylinder alternate-firing motor.

board motor, the magneto has two sets of contact points, and two ignition coils with two spark plug leads from each coil. A separate condenser is used with each coil.

## Rotor-Type Magnetos

Certain smaller size outboard motors employ a coil, lamination assembly, and rotor magnet arrangement, as shown in Fig. 15, to produce the magnetic field. The rotor has an integral permanent magnet and pole pieces. Rotation of the permanent magnet through the field of the primary windings produces the primary current.

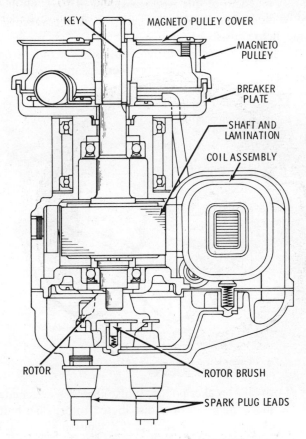

Fig. 18. Cutaway view of a typical belt-driven type aircraft magneto.

The rotary magneto differs from the flywheel type mainly in the method used to produce the magnetic field. As will be noted from the illustrations, the circuit arrangements are similar with respect to the armature plate, ignition coil, and breaker points.

## Aircraft-Type Magnetos

Some engine manufacturers have replaced the conventional fly-wheel-type magnetos with a self-contained engine-driven aircraft magneto. A magneto of this type, as shown in Figs. 18 and 19, is attached to the power head and is belt driven at crankshaft speed.

The magneto consists of a four-pole field (an aluminum housing having two alnico magnets), an ignition coil of standard design, a rotor shaft, and a lamination and breaker assembly which includes

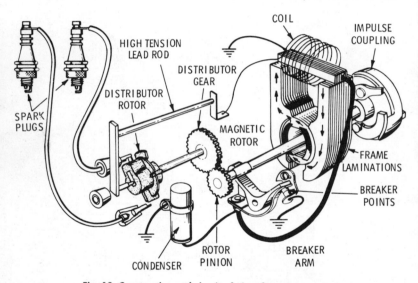

Fig. 19. Construction and circuit of aircraft-type magneto.

two sets of primary breaker points. It also includes a secondary distributor assembly made up of a distributor rotor, distributor cap, and four spark-plug leads. Basically, this ignition system functions in the same manner as that of the previously described flywheel- and rotor-type magnetos.

As noted in Fig. 19, the distributor rotor which controls the proper ignition timing is fastened to the distributor gear. It is driven by a smaller gear (rotor pinion) located on the drive shaft of the

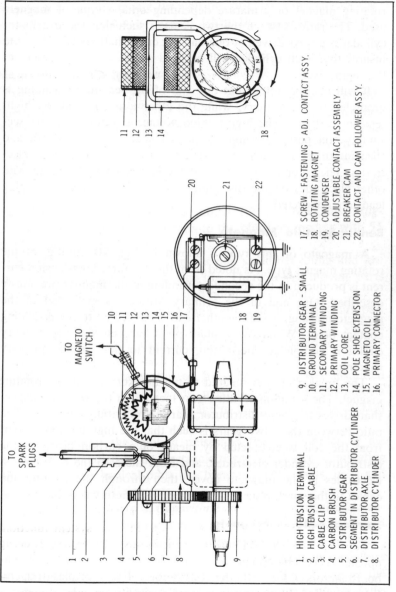

17. SCREW - FASTENING - ADJ. CONTACT ASSY.
18. ROTATING MAGNET
19. CONDENSER
20. ADJUSTABLE CONTACT ASSEMBLY
21. BREAKER CAM
22. CONTACT AND CAM FOLLOWER ASSY.

9. DISTRIBUTOR GEAR - SMALL
10. GROUND TERMINAL
11. SECONDARY WINDING
12. PRIMARY WINDING
13. COIL CORE
14. POLE SHOE EXTENSION
15. MAGNETO COIL
16. PRIMARY CONNECTOR

1. HIGH TENSION TERMINAL
2. HIGH TENSION CABLE
3. CABLE CLIP
4. CARBON BRUSH
5. DISTRIBUTOR GEAR
6. SEGMENT IN DISTRIBUTOR CYLINDER
7. DISTRIBUTOR AXLE
8. DISTRIBUTOR CYLINDER

TO MAGNETO SWITCH

TO SPARK PLUGS

Fig. 20. Schematic diagram showing the *Bendix-Scintilla* type of ignition magneto.

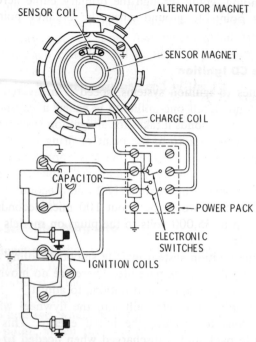

SENSOR COIL

ALTERNATOR MAGNET

SENSOR MAGNET

CHARGE COIL

CAPACITOR

POWER PACK

ELECTRONIC SWITCHES

IGNITION COILS

Fig. 21. Ignition system which is independent—requires no battery to operate.

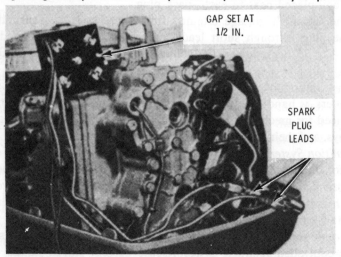

GAP SET AT 1/2 IN.

SPARK PLUG LEADS

Fig. 22. A spark checker may be used to check ignition output.

pacitor to the ignition coil. The system is independent and requires no battery to operate.

This ignition system is extremely durable in normal use but can be easily damaged by improper operating, testing and servicing procedures. The following precautions should be observed:

1. Make certain that all wiring connections are clean and tight.
2. Make certain that wires do not bind moving parts or touch metal edges where they may chafe through insulation.
3. Do not open or close any electrical circuits while the engine is running.
4. Do not use an electric tachometer other than those recommended by the manufacturer.
5. Do not hold spark plug wires while checking for spark.

### Troubleshooting

Use only approved methods to prevent damage to components. Before inspecting ignition system, make sure that trouble is not coming from contaminated fuel or improper carburetor adjustment.

### Checking for Spark

Disconnect spark plug leads at spark plugs and connect them to a needle point spark checker in Fig. 22 . Spark checker gap should be set at ½-inch. Crank engine with ignition switch "ON" and observe spark checker. A strong, steady spark firing one gap and then the other indicates system functioning correctly.

Weak, inconsistent spark or spark from only one coil; suspect, sensor coil or ignition coil. Weak, inconsistent spark from both coils; suspect charge coils. No spark at all; suspect ignition switch, wiring from ignition switch or power pack.

### Wiring

Engine missing, surging and failure to start or run can be caused by loose or corroded electrical connections. Check all terminals and plug-in connectors for tight clean contact. Also check all wiring for short to ground.

### Sensor Coil

The sensor coil may be checked with an ohmmeter. Disconnect black/white lead wire from #6 terminals on power pack assembly (Fig. 23) and tage them to avoid confusion. Meter should indicate 10 to 20 ohms resistance between sensor coil leads. Use ohmmeter to inspect sensor for short to ground. Sensor coil is not available separately, timer base (3) with sensor coil is renewed as an assembly.

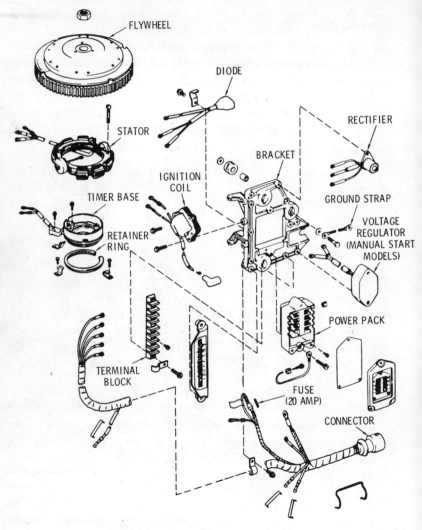

FLYWHEEL

DIODE

RECTIFIER

STATOR

BRACKET

IGNITION COIL

GROUND STRAP

TIMER BASE

VOLTAGE REGULATOR (MANUAL START MODELS)

RETAINER RING

POWER PACK

TERMINAL BLOCK

FUSE (20 AMP)

CONNECTOR

**Fig. 23. Component parts of an ignition system.**

## Charge Coils

To inspect charge coils, disconnect light brown lead wire from #1 terminal on power pack. Resistance to ground through brown wire should be 800 to 950 ohms. Charge coils are renewed as an assembly with stator (2) after removal of the flywheel.

## Ignition Coils

Ignition coils may be checked with a standard ignition coil test equipment available from several sources. Operating instructions and coil test specifications are included with the testers.

Suppliers of test equipment are:

> Graham Testers, Inc.
> 4220 Central Avenue, NE
> Minneapolis, Minnesota 55421
> Merc-O-Tronic Instruments Corp.
> 215 Branch Street
> Alton, Michigan 48003

## Shift Diode

In the 1971 and 1972 models failure of the shift diode may cause the lower unit to shift into forward gear immediately after ignition switch is turned "OFF."

Shift diode may be inspected with an ohmmeter or a continuity light with no more than a 12-volt power source. Disconnect the diode leads at terminal block (12). Connect tester leads to purple/green wire and to yellow wire from diode. Reverse connection. Tester reading with a good shift diode will indicate indefinite resistance with one connection and no resistance in other direction. Repeat this test with purple/green wire and yellow/gray wire. Again, diode should show no resistance in one direction and infinite resistance in other direction.

## Stator and Timer Base Assembly

Stator (2) and timer base (3) of Fig. 23 may be serviced after removal of the flywheel. Stator assembly is secured to the power head by four screws. The timer base may be removed after the stator by removing the four screws and clips along the outside edge.

When reassembling the unit, make certain that wiring does not restrict free movement of the timer base. Inspect taper on the crankshaft and the taper in the flywheel. Install the flywheel key with flat of key parallel to the center line of the crankshaft *not* surface of taper. Torque the flywheel nut to 100-105 ft. lbs.

## Timing

Connect a power timing light to #1 (top) cylinder. Ignition should be fully advanced (19°-20° BTDC) at a minimum of 3500 rpm with the motor in gear. See Fig. 24. Should adjustment be necessary, stop the engine and turn spark advance stop screw, Fig. 25. One full clockwise turn of the screw will retard the ignition approximately one degree.

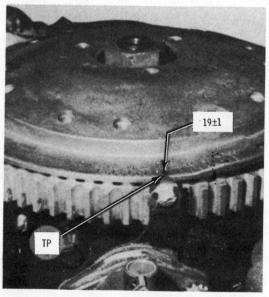

Fig. 24.. Full ignition advance (18°-20°) should occur at a minimum of 3500 RPM.

## BATTERY IGNITION

The storage battery, because of its ability to supply auxiliary power, has replaced the conventional magneto as a source of

**Fig. 25. Maximum spark advance is adjusted by turning stop screw.**

ignition in many instances. This is particularly evident on larger outboard installations due to the need for additional electrical energy, such as for lighting, radio, and other power-consuming accessories.

Battery ignition systems may be divided into two groups or types, depending on the starting method:

1. Manual starting.
2. Automatic starting.

Manual-starting engines require cranking, as by pull-rope, in the same manner as the conventional magneto-equipped engines, but with the battery furnishing the ignition spark. Automatic starting, or *electric starting*, as it is usually termed, provides an electric starting motor which engages a ring gear on the flywheel and turns it over until the engine fires. Ignition systems of this type are similar to that employed on automobiles.

## Ignition Circuits

With reference to Fig. 26, a typical battery ignition circuit consists essentially of a storage battery, an ignition coil with an iron core, primary and secondary windings, a distributor containing contact points, a cam to open the points at the correct intervals, a condenser, a rotor, and a distributor cap.

Electrically, the ignition system is composed of two circuits, termed the *primary* and *secondary*. The primary is the low-voltage and the secondary the high-voltage circuit. The component parts of the primary circuit are the battery, the ammeter, the ignition switch, the primary winding of the ignition coil, and the cam and breaker points.

The secondary or high-voltage circuit is composed of the *secondary winding* of the *ignition coil*, the *distributor,* the *spark-plug* leads, and the *spark plugs.* The breaker points are activated by a

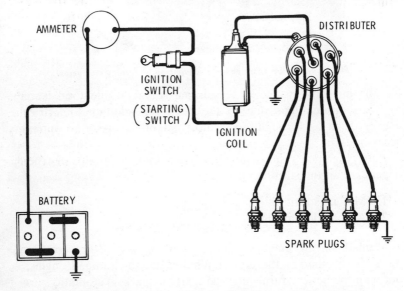

AMMETER

IGNITION
SWITCH

(STARTING)
SWITCH

IGNITION
COIL

DISTRIBUTER

BATTERY

SPARK PLUGS

**Fig. 26. Wiring diagram of a typical six-cylinder battery ignition circuit.**

cam on the crankshaft or distributor shaft. As the shaft rotates, the breaker points will open and close in relation to the position of the piston in the cylinder. Thus, when the piston reaches the top of the compression stroke, the cam will cause the breaker points to open.

When the points are closed, current will flow from the ballast, through the primary windings of the ignition coil, through the points, to ground, and back to the battery. As the current passes through the primary, a magnetic field is formed around the primary and secondary windings. When the piston reaches the top of its stroke, the breaker points open, and current ceases to flow through the primary. This causes the magnetic field to collapse, cutting across the turns of wire in the secondary. The collapse of the magnetic field induces a high voltage in the secondary windings that is strong enough to jump the gap at the spark-plug electrodes.

The condenser prevents the current from arcing across the points as they are opened. As the points open, the current will flow into the condenser momentarily and will then discharge back through the magnetic field. The cam is located on the distributor shaft, and is driven indirectly by the engine crankshaft. The distributor usually runs at one-half the engine speed. Thus, one complete revolution of the engine crankshaft is equal to half a revolution of the distributor shaft. The cam will ordinarily have as many lobes as there are cylinders in the engine.

Within the time necessary for one revolution of the cam, the primary circuit has been interrupted once for each cylinder. Thus, the cam and breaker points located in the distributor are in reality a timing device, and it is in this manner that the distributor, to the extent that it is a rotary switch in the secondary circuit, must make contact with a spark plug each time a high-voltage surge is developed in the secondary.

## ELECTRIC STARTING SYSTEMS

The electric starting system employed on outboard motors consists of a starting motor, starter and choke solenoid, starter and choke switches, mercury or limit switch, storage battery, and the necessary interconnecting cables and wires. Fig. 27 illustrates the wiring diagram of a typical electric starting system.

In operation, when the ignition key (starter switch) is turned to the START position, current will flow from the battery to the ignition switch, and to both the ignition and solenoid terminals. From the solenoid terminal, current will flow through a throttle and a mercury switch on the shifting mechanism which is placed in the circuit as a safety measure. Both of these switches must be closed in order for the starter motor to operate. They are adjusted so that they will close only when the shift is in neutral and the throttle retarded to the START position.

From the limit switches, current will then flow through a coil in the starter solenoid to ground, and back to the battery. The current passing through the coil causes the coil to act as a magnet to close the gap between two terminals on the solenoid. Attached to these two terminals are the cables from the positive terminal on

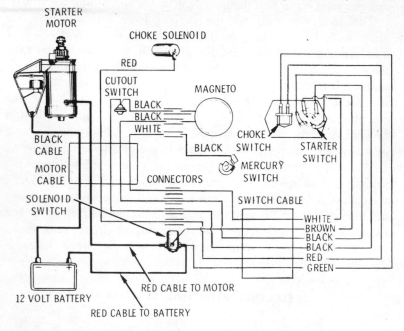

**Fig. 27. Wiring diagram of a typical electric-starting system.**

the battery and the cable that leads to the starter motor. As soon as these two terminals are bridged, current will flow to activate the starter motor, which will crank the engine.

When the engine has started and the ignition key snaps back to the ON position, current will no longer flow through the solenoid coil, and the circuit between the battery and the starter motor will be opened.

## Starter Solenoids

The starter solenoid contains windings which cause a plunger to rise when the starter switch is pushed. The movement of the solenoid plunger causes a circuit to be completed between the battery and the motor terminal, energizing the starter motor. When the starter switch is released, the solenoid plunger is de-energized, causing it to move back to its original position, thus opening the circuit between the battery and the starter motor, which becomes de-energized.

## Mercury Switches

The mercury switch is a safety device which is operated by the throttle, and opens the starting motor switch circuit to prevent accidental engagement of the starter motor when the throttle lever is set beyond the half-throttle position.

## Ignition Cut-On Switch

Outboard motors of larger horsepower are usually equipped with an automatic vacuum cut-out that prevents a motor from increasing in speed to a point that could be harmful to the motor itself. Thus, when the motor is idling, the gear shift is in neutral, the switch will prevent an excessively high-motor speed by cutting out the ignition to one of the spark plugs.

## Starting Motors

All outboard-engine starting motors consist of a supporting frame, the field assembly, armature, and cranking system or drive. Although starting motors resemble generators, they are different in construction and operation. Many general parts, like field coils, armature, and brushes are common to both, but the design of these parts are different. Also, in a generator, mechanical energy is converted into electrical energy, whereas in a motor, electrical energy is converted into mechanical energy.

The starting motor is a low-voltage, series-wound, direct-current motor that converts electrical energy from the battery into mechanical energy for cranking the engine when the circuit between the battery and the motor is closed.

The means for coupling the motor to the engine when starting is known as the *cranking system*. The cranking system is generally composed of the following units:

1. Battery and battery cables.

2. Cranking motor, including the drive assembly which engages the flywheel gear during cranking operation.

3. Cranking motor solenoid switch mounted on the cranking motor for shifting the drive assembly and closing the motor circuit.

In operation, the drive-assembly pinion is moved into engagement with the flywheel ring gear by action of the solenoid on the shift lever, which engages the shift collar of the drive assembly by pushing on the clutch spring. This serves as a cushion in case the pinion and gear teeth butt instead of meshing. The helical splines assist in obtaining proper pinion engagement.

The drive pinion is pulled out of engagement after the engine

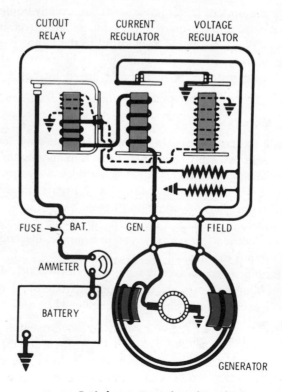

Fig. 28. Typical generator and regulator circuit.

starts by action of the shift-lever return spring. The shift lever is connected to the solenoid-switch plunger by a link and adjusting screws.

## Automotive Electric System

An automotive type generating system employed on outboard motors contains in addition to conventional electric units, a two-brush generator and a regulator. The function of the regulator (Fig. 28) is to control the generator output in accordance with the demands of the electrical system. The generator is commonly mounted on a bracket on the side of the engine and driven by a belt from the engine flywheel.

The function of the generator is to keep the battery in a charged condition, thus eliminating the necessity of removing the battery for charging at frequent intervals. The generator regulator contains a *cutout relay, current regulator,* and *voltage regulator,* which is usually mounted in one complete unit and enclosed by a sheet-metal cover.

Most generators of this type are shunt-wound, with the regulator connected as illustrated. A typical generator consists essentially of an armature revolving within a magnetic field, a commutator, spring-loaded brushes, shaft, and bearings, all mounted within a sturdy frame.

## Essential Controls

In any electric system such as that shown in Fig. 28, where there is a generator and battery, two control elements are necessary for the proper working of the system. They are:

1. Means for preventing current reversal when the generator is charging the battery.
2. Means for limiting the generator voltage.

The generator cutout relay acts as an automatic switch to connect the generator to the battery when the generator voltage exceeds that of the battery. When the battery voltage exceeds that of the generator, the cutout-relay contacts open to prevent the battery from discharging through the generator.

The voltage and current portion of the regulator controls the amount of current the generator produces, allowing the generator to produce a high current when the battery is in a discharged condition. When the battery is charged, and the electrical accessories are disconnected, the regulator reduces the current produced to the amount needed to meet the operating requirements of the system.

## Magneto-Alternator

This type of electrical system consists principally of a low-voltage magneto and alternating-current generator unit combined with the engine flywheel. The magneto-alternator starting system differs from the automotive ignition arrangement mainly in that the current obtained from the generator is of the alternating type whose frequency is directly proportional to the speed of the rotor shaft, the number of poles for the alternator being given.

The alternating current produced by the generator is converted into direct current for battery charging by means of a rectifier connected as indicated. In certain systems of this type, the output is controlled in accordance with the battery, and engine and external load demand, by an automotive-type three-unit regulator, such as shown in Fig. 28, which incorporates both current and voltage control.

In operation, the alternating current generated in the stator windings passes to the rectifier. This, in turn, converts the alternating current into direct current. The negative side of the rectifier circuit is grounded, with the positive passing to the ignition switch and to the negative battery terminal. The starter circuit consists of a cranking motor and starter-engagement mechanism. A starter solenoid prevents the full starting current from passing through the ignition switch. As the ignition key is turned on, a circuit is completed through the generator field winding located in the engine flywheel. As the flywheel is rotated, an intense magnetic field is developed in the poles of the field-winding and passes through the laminated iron in the stator. This causes alternating current to be generated in the stator coils, and it flows through the three leads to the rectifier where it is converted into direct current and delivered to the system.

## STORAGE BATTERIES

The storage battery is an electrochemical device for converting chemical energy into electrical energy. The amount of electrical power in a storage battery is determined in part by the amount of chemical substance in the battery. When these substances have been used up, they are restored to their original chemical condition by passing an electric current through the battery.

In an outboard motor, the storage battery (when used) supplies the electric current which operates the starting motor and other accessories until the generator becomes activated. In a generating system using voltage and current regulators, the battery controls the voltage of the electrical system. The storage battery is usually considered the central unit of the electrical system because the various circuits or paths which carry electricity to the various operating units begins and terminates there. Thus, in tracing circuits and in hunting trouble, the battery is the reference point from which other observations and tests are conducted.

### Storage-Battery Construction

Storage batteries employed in outboard-motor installations equipped with automotive-type starting are normally of the 6-volt, 100-ampere, or 12-volt, 50-ampere rating. A storage battery of this type consists of three or more cells, depending on the voltage desired. Thus, a battery with three cells of two volts each, connected in series, is known as a 6-volt battery, and one of six cells connected in series is known as a 12-volt battery.

Each cell of the battery consists of a hard-rubber compartment into which are placed two kinds of lead plates, known as *negative* and *positive*. These plates are insulated from each other by suitable separators and are submerged in a solution of sulfuric acid and water. Fig. 29 illustrates the parts of a storage battery. After the plates have been formed, they are connected into *positive* and *negative* groups. The negative group of plates has one more plate than the positive group to provide a negative plate on both sides of all positive plates.

The assembly of a positive and negative group, together with the separators, is called an *element*. Because storage battery plates

221

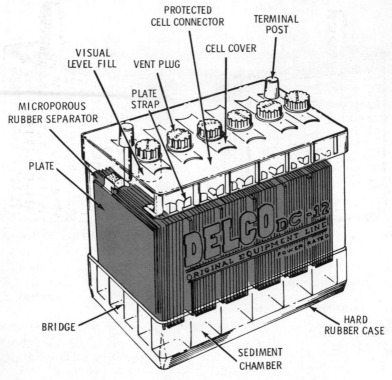

**Fig. 29. Construction details of a typical lead-acid storage battery.**

are more or less of standard size, the number of plates in an element is roughly a measure of battery capacity. The distance between the plates of an assembly element is approximately one-eighth of an inch. To prevent the plates from touching one another and causing a short circuit, sheets of insulating material, usually wood, porous rubber, or spun glass, are inserted between the plates. These separators are thin and porous so that the electrolyte will easily pass between the plates.

With the elements in place, the covers are pressed on and the compartments are sealed. The cells are then connected together by short heavy bars of lead, called top connectors, as shown in Fig. 30. A top connector is fused or "burned" to the positive post of one element and the negative post of the element in the adjoining

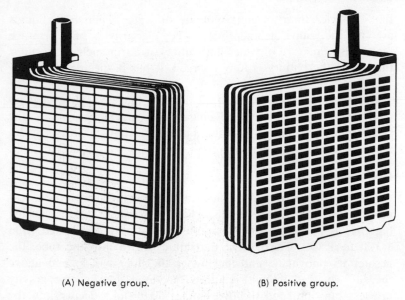

(A) Negative group.       (B) Positive group.

**Fig. 30. Negative and positive groups of storage-battery plates and separators.**

cell. When all top connectors are in place, there will be one un-connected positive and negative post at each end of the assembly. These are known as the *terminal posts*. It is to these terminal posts that the cables of the electric circuit are attached.

## Electrolyte

When the assembly is completed, the electrolyte is poured into the cells to cover the plates and insulation. The electrolyte is prepared by mixing chemically-pure sulfuric acid and pure water. In a fully-charged battery, the proportions are approximately five parts of water to two parts of sulfuric acid. After the plates have soaked in this solution for a short period of time, the battery is connected to a suitable source of electric current and charged.

## Specific Gravity

*Specific gravity* is the weight of a substance compared to the weight of the same volume of chemically-pure water at a temperature of 4° C. The specific gravity of sulfuric acid is 1.835

223

times heavier than an equal volume of water when both liquids are at the same temperature. The electrolyte of a storage battery is a mixture of water and sulfuric acid in such proportions that when the battery is fully charged, it has a specific gravity of 1.280.

Because the amount of sulfuric acid in the electrolyte changes with the amount of electrical charge, the specific gravity of the electrolyte also changes with the amount of charge. This provides a convenient way of measuring the degree of charge in a battery.

## Hydrometers

The specific gravity of an electrolyte can conveniently be measured by a hydrometer syringe. The hydrometer used for testing batteries is provided with a specific-gravity scale graduated from 1.100 to 1.300. The heavier the liquid drawn into the tube, the greater its buoyancy, and the higher the float will extend above the surface of the liquid. Liquids having a low specific gravity are less buoyant, and the hydrometer float sinks deeper into the liquid.

A fully-charged battery has a specific-gravity reading of 1.280 to 1.300, while the specific gravity of a discharged battery may be as low as 1.150. A specific-gravity reading of 1.200 and 1.215 indicates that the battery is more than half discharged. For convenience, the reading is spoken of as being 1150, 1200, 1280, etc., instead of 1.150, 1.200, 1.280, etc., which is the true specific gravity. After measurement, the electrolyte is returned to the cell by compressing the bulb, after which the reading of the next cell can be taken.

## Temperature Corrections

In this connection it should be noted that the specific-gravity reading of a battery varies with the temperature of the electrolyte. Hydrometers are generally calibrated so as to give accurate readings at 80° F for the electrolyte. This refers to the temperature of the liquid itself and not the temperature of the surrounding atmosphere.

Correction can be made for temperature by adding .004 (usually referred to as 4 "points of gravity") to the hydrometer reading for every 10° F that the electrolyte is above 80° F, or subtracting .004 for every 10° F that the electrolyte is below 80° F. If the electrolyte temperature is not too far from the 80° F standard, or if only an approximate idea of the specific-gravity reading is required, it will not be necessary to make the temperature correction. There are hydrometers available which have built-in thermometer and temperature-scale correction which simplifies the operation of obtaining a true specific-gravity reading.

## Chemical Action

When a cell is fully charged, the active material of the negative plates consists of spongy lead ($P_b$) and the active material on the positive plates is lead peroxide ($P_bO_2$). The specific gravity of the electrolyte (sulfuric acid, $H_2SO_4$ and water $H_2O$) is then at its maximum and the cell is capable of delivering electricity when connected to a circuit.

## Discharge

As the cell is delivering current, that is, discharging, the chemical action that takes place changes both the lead ($P_b$) of the negative plate and the lead peroxide ($P_bO_2$) of the positive plate to lead sulphate ($P_bSO_4$) and the sulfuric acid ($H_2SO_4$) to water ($H_2O$).

The decomposition of the sulfuric acid and the formation of water dilutes the remaining acid, thus lowering the specific gravity of the electrolyte. As the discharge progresses, the negative and positive plates finally contain considerable lead sulfate. The discharge should always be stopped before the plates have become entirely changed to lead sulphate.

## Charge

To charge the cell, an external source of direct current must be connected to the battery terminals. The chemical reaction is then reversed and the lead sulfate on the positive plates is converted back into lead peroxide ($P_bO_2$), while the lead sulfate on the negative plates is changed back to sponge lead ($P_b$). The $SO_4$ from the plates combines with hydrogen to form sulfuric acid ($H_2SO_4$), and the electrolyte gradually becomes stronger until no

225

more sulfate remains on the plates. The electrolyte will then be of the same specific gravity as before the discharge.

## Battery Charging Methods

A storage battery can be charged with direct current only. If only alternating current is available, a motor-generator or a rectifier must be used to convert it into direct current.

When connecting the battery terminals to the charging equipment, the positive wire of the charging circuit must always be connected to the positive terminal of the battery, and the negative wire to the negative terminal. The electrolyte in each cell should be brought to the proper level by addition of pure water before the battery is connected for charging.

If several batteries are to be charged at the same time, and are to be connected in series, the positive terminal of one battery should be connected to the negative terminal of the next battery. The positive terminal of the end battery of the series is then connected to the positive terminal of the charging source, and the negative terminal of the series of batteries is connected to the negative terminal of the charging source.

There are two methods of charging batteries, namely the constant-current and the constant-potential. The constant-current method is used extensively, particularly where the condition of the battery is not fully known. There are no exact values as to the charging rate, but a safe rate would be equal to one half of the number of plates in the cell. Thus, for example, the charging current of a 13-plate cell would be 6.5 amperes, and for a 17-plate cell, 8.5 amperes approximately. Also, where several batteries are connected in series for charging, the charging current is determined by the size of the smallest battery in the circuit.

The temperature of the battery should be watched carefully during all stages of the charging process. It should be checked frequently with a thermometer, and if it rises above 110° F, either the current should be shut off until the battery is cool or the charging rate reduced. Proper ventilation should be provided when charging batteries.

As a battery approaches a charged condition, gas bubbles commence to appear at the surface of the electrolyte. This is known as gassing. All cells should gas freely when the battery is fully charged. If a cell does not gas, either the cell is not charged or else there is some internal trouble. Excessive charging will damage the battery, particularly the positive plates. Depending on the charging rate, most batteries can be charged in 12 to 16 hours, although batteries with sulphated plates may require a charging period of up to 24 hours.

Constant-potential charging, as the name implies, maintains the same voltage throughout the charging period, and as a result, the current is automatically reduced as the battery approaches full charge. When properly done, this method has been found generally satisfactory for recharging batteries which are in good working condition, and it has the advantage of completing the charging process in a minimum of time. A badly sulfated battery may not, however, come up to charge when this charging method is being used.

## Battery Ratings

All batteries are given a normal capacity rating according to the number of ampere-hours obtained from the battery under certain working conditions. The 20-hour rating has been accepted as standard by the *American Society of Automotive Engineers* for automotive batteries. To measure the capacity, a battery is discharged continuously at a specific rate until the voltage drops too low for efficient use. Thus, for example, a battery that will deliver 6 amperes for 20 hours is said to have a capacity of 120 ampere-hours.

This measurement is of particular interest because it indicates what may be expected of a battery in the way of satisfactory performance. The capacity of a battery depends on the amount of active material that can react with the electrolyte. Obviously, this depends on the thickness and design of the plates, hence the number of plates is not always an accurate index of the capacity.

Also, one of the characteristics of a storage battery is that its total ampere-hour capacity is dependent on the rate of discharge. The lower the rate of discharge, the greater the ampere-hour capacity will be; whereas, the higher the discharge rate, the lower will be the capacity. Thus, a battery having a 120-ampere-hour

227

capacity at a 6-ampere discharge rate will ordinarily have a capacity of over 120 ampere-hours at a lower discharge rate.

## THUNDERBOLT IGNITION SYSTEM

The *Thunderbolt* ignition, invented by *Mercury* engineers and manufactured by *Mercury*, features a specially designed rotating metal disc to take the place of the switching action of conventional breaker points. See Figs. 31 and 32. There are no breaker points to wear out.

With no breaker points, the need for periodic checks and adjustments to plugs and points is eliminated, since the breaker system needs no timing correction with use. Once correctly set, the timing never needs resetting, since there is no breaker cam or cam follower to wear, no points to pit, erode, or need re-gapping.

Courtesy Mercury Marine, Div. of Brunswick Corp.

Fig. 31. New distributor design using no points for *Mercury Thunderbolt* 4-cylinder ignition system.

An integral part of the new *Thunderbolt* ignition system is *Mercury's* new *Polar-Gap* spark plug. This is a very "cold" spark plug. Operating temperature of the electrodes and ceramic insulator is 800 to 1000° F cooler than conventional spark plugs. This means that the *Polar-Gap* plug does not glow red hot in the combustion chamber as do conventional plugs. Consequently, deposits from the use of leaded fuels do not reach pre-ignition temperature levels. The center electrode receives the high voltage from the coil.

A ceramic insulator forms the gap, and large masses of metal form an outer ring, which is the other electrode. The spark travels from the center electrode to the outer electrode, making it a 360-degree electrode gap. This reduces the rate of electrode erosion, partially accounting for the greatly increased life of the spark plug.

*Thunderbolt* ignition and *Polar-Cap* plugs go together. It takes the *Mercury* ignition to fire these plugs. The *Thunderbolt* ignition gives them a super spark and vastly improves the idle. This ignition

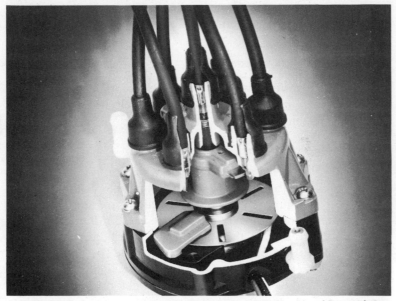

Courtesy Mercury Marine, Div. of Brunswick Corp.
**Fig. 32.** New breakerless distributor ignition system used in Mercury 6-cylinder outboard motors.

system maintains an even output under all conditions of boat speed, load, and battery charge. It cannot be burned out by an overcharged battery. In tests, this ignition operated equally well in ranges from 1 rpm to over 10,000 rpm, and in temperatures from minus 100° to plus 300° F.

*Thunderbolt* ignition is a complete fully-integrated system that makes use of space-age technology and solid-state components capable of producing spark-voltage far surpassing any conventional system, and in mere millionths of a second—so quickly that practically no energy is lost through current leakage caused by spark-plug deposits. Thus, it can fire plugs that are "fouled" by conventional standards.

## ELECTRICAL SYSTEM SERVICE

The main function of the electrical system is to provide spark-plug ignition after the fuel has entered the combustion chamber and has been compressed by the piston. There are two types of ignition systems used on outboard motors, namely:

1. Magneto ignition.
2. Battery ignition system.

The manual-starting types of outboard motors are usually provided with magneto ignition, whereas the electric-starting types have battery ignition.

### Magneto Ignition

Normally, magnetos are not difficult to service, nor are magneto troubles difficult to diagnose. When a magneto ignition system does not operate properly, a visual inspection will, in a great many instances, reveal the source of trouble. See Fig. 33. Particular attention should be given to the spark plugs, distributor, cables, etc., since trouble of this sort may easily be remedied.

First, check other engine components to be sure they are functioning properly, and try to isolate the trouble by the process of elimination. For example, the carburetor, the suction reed valves, the shaft seal, or a plugged gas-tank vent may actually be the prime reason for poor performance.

With the magneto mounted on the engine, the first step is to check whether the magneto is producing a spark. In this test, the spark-plug leads should be detached and the terminal supported one eighth of an inch from the metal of the engine block while cranking the engine slowly. Remove the spark plug so the engine will crank easily. If a spark appears, the winding of the magneto and breaker may be regarded as being in good condition.

If no spark is produced, inspect the breaker contacts for condition and spacing. Check the magneto switch and primary circuit

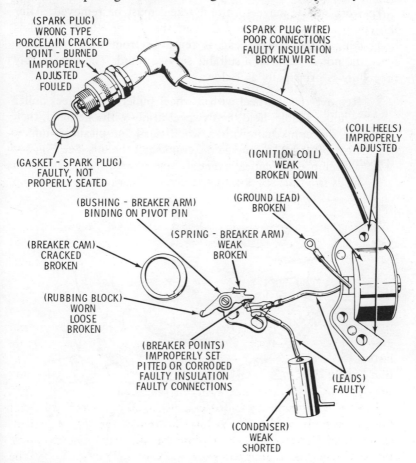

Fig. 33. Typical magneto ignition trouble spots.

231

for high resistance or damaged insulation. When spare parts are available, the coil or condenser may be checked by the comparison method, provided the parts can be readily removed. Install parts which are known to be in good condition in place of the parts suspected to be defective. If no improvement is found by the check as outlined, and no spark is produced, the magneto must be removed from the engine for shop service.

## Magneto Servicing

To work on the magneto, the flywheel must be removed. After the cowl, or cover, is removed from the motor, the flywheel is accessible. If the power head is removed from the lower unit, place the power head on a suitable service stand. The disassembly procedure is principally as follows:

1. Remove the flywheel with a wheel puller. If a wheel puller is not available, hold the flywheel firmly with one hand, then tap the crankshaft with a wood, lead, or plastic hammer. Be careful not to damage the crankshaft threads. See Fig. 34.
2. To remove the entire magneto, first remove the high-tension leads from the spark-plug terminals. Then remove the clamp

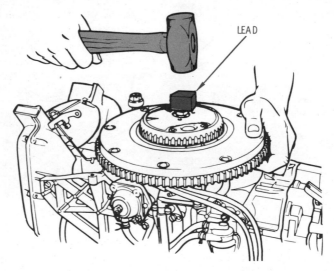

Fig. 34. Removing flywheel without a flywheel puller.

screws which hold the high-tension leads to the cylinder block. Loosen the screws below the magneto stator plate in order to lift off the magneto.

3. Observe the condition and action of the breaker assembly. Fig. 3. The rocker or shuttle may be sticking or worn, points may be pitted, worn, burnt, improperly set, or cocked. Replace as necessary.

4. Check the point setting with a feeler gauge. The correct point setting is usually .020 inch, but may vary on different engines. The setting is usually stamped on the stator plate, or breaker box, or may be found in the engine service bulletin.

5. If replacement points are not available, they can be stoned, using care to keep the surfaces flat and parallel. They should be removed separately and rubbed against the stone. Do not use a file as this may contaminate the points with iron particles. After setting the breaker points, recheck the magneto at cranking speed. This check may eliminate the necessity for removing the coil and condenser and is the most effective method of determining if the magnet is operating satisfactorily.

6. If the coil and condenser are functioning normally, and if the points are in good condition, then check the wiring system carefully. Look for grounds caused by broken insulation, or broken or cracked insulation washers. Do not overlook the possibilities of broken wires under the insulation, loose connections, or open circuits because of corroded connections. Check every wire on the armature plate if necessary, and resolder with firm clean connections.

## Replacement of Coil

To replace the coil on the core, press the coil by hand as far as possible. Do not bend the magneto core, which, being laminated, is quite easily distorted. The core must be supported under its center leg while the new coil is pressed on. Be sure the coil is "bottomed" before bending the tab. When putting a new coil in place on the stator plate, be careful to see that the primary leads are in the proper position.

Align the core with the bosses on the stator plate carefully, or the flywheel magnets will strike and cause damage to the flywheel or magneto assembly. Check the ground connection to be sure it is making good contact both under the screw and at the crimped end of the terminal. Check for good contact at the live terminal ends.

## Magneto Testing

A convenient method of testing a magneto under operating conditions consists in removing the entire unit from the engine and operating it at various speeds on a suitable test stand. The following procedures are for the more common types of magnetos for industrial engines:

1. Clamp the magneto on the test-stand table, fastening it securely so that it cannot slip when driven by the test-stand motor.
2. Connect the magneto to a test-stand motor and run it at approximately 1000 rpm. Check for arcing at the breaker contacts which indicates that the primary circuit is in good condition. Check the condenser capacity if the breaker arcing is bright and spitting. If no secondary spark is produced, remove the distributor block and note whether sparks jump the safety gap when the magneto is run at operating speed. If the spark jumps the gap when the distributor block is off, and does not jump when the block is on, renew the distributor block.
3. If the magneto is still inoperative after the previous tests, check the coil using a suitable test instrument.

## Coil Testing

Fundamentally, the coil tester provides a source of primary current intercepted by a built-in breaker to induce high-voltage current in the secondary winding of the coil to be tested. Primary current is controlled manually by a rheostat in the test unit, giving a definite amperage for each coil unit.

When testing any coil mounted on the armature plate, disconnect the condenser and separate the breaker points by a strip of paper. One primary lead from the test unit is connected to the armature plate, with the other connected to the breaker bracket. This completes the primary circuit for testing purposes.

If the coil is in good condition and suitable for use, the induced high-voltage current to the spark plugs should be of sufficient strength to consistently spark across the gap on the test unit, with the primary current adjusted to the amperage specified for the particular coil.

An irregular, seemingly weak or hesitating spark across the gap indicates a weak coil or a damp and partially broken down secondary. Under no condition should an attempt be made to improve this spark by increasing the primary current. The coil is inoperative if it cannot be made to spark properly on the specified amperage. A completely dead coil is indicated by no visible spark.

## Battery Ignition

The battery ignition system differs from the magneto ignition system because a battery provides the electricity necessary to produce the ignition spark. Because of additional service provided in electric-starting systems, with accompanying higher cost of equipment, it is normally used only in medium and large outboard-motor installations. In this connection it should be noted that a complete electric-starting system is similar to that used in automotive service. See Figs. 35 and 36.

The battery ignition system consists of the battery, ignition coil, distributor, condenser, ignition switch, spark plugs, and the necessary low- and high-tension wiring. In the foregoing, the battery is merely a source of energy to be used until the engine fires and the generator takes over. The function of the ignition coil is to transform the camparatively low voltage obtained from the battery to a voltage of sufficient strength to jump the spark-plug gap. The ignition distributor opens and closes the primary ignition circuit, and distributes the high-tension charge to the spark plugs.

*Adjusting Distributor Breaker Contacts*—The breaker contacts not only serve to open the primary circuit and cause a high-voltage spark, but they regulate the length of time that the current flows in the coil. This has a direct effect on the value of the spark at the spark plugs, and with the higher speeds and compression pressures of modern engines, this affects the power and speed.

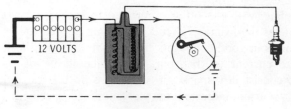

(A) Magnetic field build-up in ignition coil.

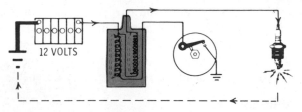

(B) Magnetic field collapses and spark is produced at spark plug.

**Fig. 35. Diagram of a typical battery ignition system.**

The manufacturer's specifications should always be followed when adjusting the breaker contacts to insure that the proper amount of separation is provided. If the contact points are set too close, they will tend to burn and pit rapidly, while points with too much separation will cause ignition failure at high speed.

After considerable use, contact points may not appear smooth and bright, but this is not necessarily an indication that they are not functioning properly and giving good ignition. They should not be disturbed as long as proper operation is obtained. Should the points become pitted or burned in operation, rub lightly with a dry oilstone. Points can also be dressed with a clean ignition file without removing them from the distributor.

*Oxidized Contact Points*—This condition may be caused by high resistance or loose connections in the condenser circuit, oil or foreign materials on the contact surfaces, or most commonly, high voltages. Check for these conditions where burned contacts are experienced.

*Contact-Point Pressure*—This pressure should be within the limits given. Weak tension will cause point chatter and ignition miss at

236

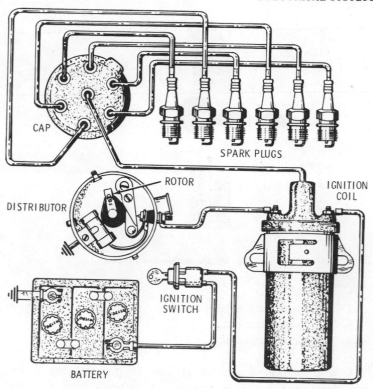

**Fig. 36. Battery ignition circuit for 6-cylinder engine.**

high speed, while excessive tension will cause undue wear of the contact points, cam, and rubbing block. Most data tables specify breaker-arm spring tension at 17 to 20 ozs.

*Dwell*—The contact points in a modern distributor must be adjusted under actual running conditions with a dwell-angle meter. By definition, the dwell angle is: *The angle of cam rotation through which the distributor points remain closed.* The points must remain closed long enough to insure saturation and build-up of the ignition coil. Eccentricity and bearing wear will cause variation of dwell angle. See Fig. 37.

*Condenser*—There are four factors which affect condenser performance, and each must be considered in making condenser tests. They are:

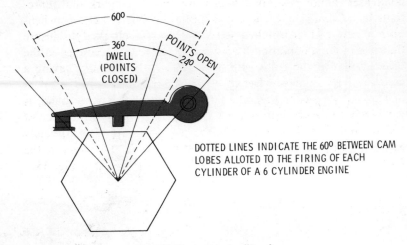

DOTTED LINES INDICATE THE 60° BETWEEN CAM
LOBES ALLOTED TO THE FIRING OF EACH
CYLINDER OF A 6 CYLINDER ENGINE

Fig. 37. Illustrating dwell angle.

1. Breakdown.
2. Low insulation resistance.
3. High series resistance.
4. Low series resistance.

Low insulation resistance or leakage prevents the condenser
from holding a charge. A condenser with low insulation resistance
is said to be weak. All condensers are subject to leakage, which up
to a certain limit is not objectionable. When it is considered that
the ignition condenser performs its function in approximately
1/12,000 of a second, it can be seen that leakage can be large
without detrimental effects, but must be considered, however, in
making tests.

*Relationship of Coil to Condenser*—The condenser controls the
action or output of the coil. Its purpose is to induce high-voltage
current in the secondary winding of the coil which is essential to
proper ignition. The condenser may, therefore, be considered an
integral part of the coil because without it the coil cannot function.

Obviously, therefore, a condenser with improper capacity, or one
which leaks, is failing to perform its proper function in the operation with the coil, and consequently the coil with an inefficient

238

condenser cannot possibly deliver to the plugs, a spark that represents its maximum efficiency. It is important, therefore, that whenever a new coil is installed the condenser is checked to insure that it is in good condition. As previously noted, the voltage in the primary part of the coil circuit is very low, the primary having a comparatively small number of turns of heavy wire.

The voltage on the secondary coil circuit, on the other hand, is very high, the secondary having a comparatively great number of turns of fine wire. The voltages in the coil sides vary approximately as the turn ratios, being between 10,000 and 25,000 volts in the secondary and usually 6 or 12 volts in the primary. See Fig. 38.

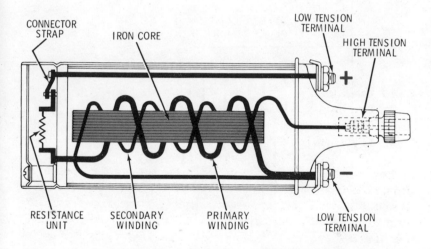

**Fig. 38. Ignition coil details showing windings and terminals.**

## STARTING MOTOR SERVICE AND TESTS

An electric-starting system consists of the *battery, starting switch,* and *starting motor.* The battery supplies the energy, the switch completes the circuit allowing this energy to flow to the starting motor, and the starting motor engages the ring gear on the flywheel and turns it over until the engine fires. Because of its action in cranking the engine, the starting motor is commonly called the cranking motor.

The starting-motor assembly consists of the motor, drive assembly, shift lever, and solenoid switch. When the solenoid is energized, the starter armature spins, feeding the pinion on the threaded sleeve until it meshes with the flywheel gear. See Fig. 39.

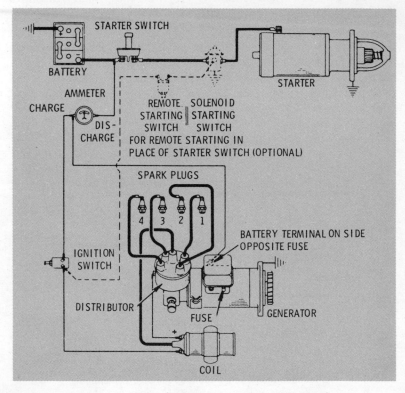

Fig. 39. Wiring diagram of a typical electric-starting system.

When the cranking motor is not operating, the pinion is in a disengaged position. As soon as the cranking-motor switch is closed, the armature begins to operate, picking up speed rapidly. The pinion, however, does not pick up speed instantly and, as a result, the screw shaft turns with the pinion. This forces the pinion to move laterally toward the end of the shaft and into mesh with the flywheel ring gear. As the pinion moves into mesh with the ring, it reaches the pinion stop. Since it can travel no further, it is

240.

forced to rotate with the armature. thus turning the flywheel and cranking the engine.

The shock of engagement of the pinion and flywheel ring gear is absorbed by the drive spring. After the engine starts, the flywheel ring gear turns the starter pinion faster than the armature. At a predetermined speed, the gear is released and forced back along the sleeve threads to its normal position.

*Starting Motor Troubles*—In many respects, a starting motor is similar to a generator, and the inspection for location of troubles is similar for both. Starting motor action is indicative, to some extent, of the starting motor condition. A starting motor that responds readily and cranks the engine at normal speed when the control circuit is closed is usually in good condition.

If the motor does not develop rated torque and cranks the engine slowly (or not at all), check the battery, battery terminals and connections, the ground cable, and battery-to-cranking motor cable. Corroded, frayed, or broken cables should be replaced and loose or dirty connections corrected. The starting solenoid should be checked for burned contacts and the contacts replaced if necessary.

If there are burned bars on the commutator, it may indicate open-circuited armature coils which prevent proper cranking. Inspect the soldered connections at the commutator riser bars, resolder these connections, and turn down the commutator as necessary. An open armature will show excessive arcing on the no-load test at the commutator bar which is open.

Tight or dirty bearings will reduce armature speed or prevent the armature from turning. A worn bearing, bent shaft, or loose pole shoe will allow the armature to drag, causing slow speed or failure of the armature to rotate. Check for these conditions.

If the brushes, bearings, commutator, battery, and external circuit appear in good condition, and the cranking motor still does not operate correctly, remove the cranking motor and submit it to the no-load and torque test.

*Interpretation of No-Load and Torque Test Results*—The following indications apply:

1. Rated torque, current draw, and no-load speed indicates a normal condition of the cranking motor.

2. Low free speed and a high current draw with a low developed torque may result from:
   a. Tight, dirty, or worn bearings, bent armature shaft, or loose field-pole screws which allow the armature to drag.
   b. Shorted armature. Check armature further on growler.
   c. A grounded armature or field. Check by raising the grounded brushes and insulating them from the commutator with cardboard, then check with a test lamp between the insulated terminal and the frame. If the test lamp lights, raise the other brushes from the commutator and check the fields and commutator separately to determine whether it is the fields or armature that is grounded.

3. Failure to operate with high current draw indicates:
   a. A direct ground in the switch, terminal, or fields.
   b. Frozen shaft bearings which prevent the armature from turning.

4. Failure to operate with no current draw indicates:
   a. An open field circuit. Inspect the internal connections and trace the circuit with a test lamp.
   b. Open armature coils. Inspect the commutator for badly burned bars. Running at free speed, an open armature will show excessive arcing at the commutator bar which is open.
   c. Broken or weakened brush springs, worn brushes, high mica on the commutator, or other causes which would prevent good contact between the brushes and commutator. Any of these conditions will cause burned commutator bars.

5. Low no-load speed, with low torque and low current draw indicates:
   a. An open field winding. Raise and insulate the ungrounded brushes from the commutator and check the fields with a test lamp.
   b. High internal resistance due to poor connections, defective leads, dirty commutator, and causes listed under 4c.

6. High free speed with low developed torque and high current draw indicates shorted fields. There is no easy way to detect shorted fields, since the field resistance is already low. If

shorted fields are suspected, replace the fields and check for improvement in performance.

*Field Coil Test for Continuous Circuit*—Place the test prod leads on the field coil leads. If the test lamp lights, the field coils are all right. If the test lamp does not light, there is an open circuit in one or both of the field coils.

*Field-Coil Test for Ground*—Place one test prod lead to the frame and the other to the field-coil lead. If the test lamp does not light, the field coils are in good condition. If the test lamp lights, one or both of the field coils are grounded.

*Individual Field-Coil Test for Ground*—Break the soldered connection between the two field coils and test each one separately, replacing the field coil found to be grounded.

*Field-Coil Leads Inspection*—Inspect the field-coil leads where they are soldered at the starting-switch terminal to be sure that they are tight.

*Armature Test for Ground*—Place one test-prod on the armature and the other on the commutator. If the test lamp lights, the armature is grounded and should be replaced. If the test lamp does not light, the armature is in good condition.

*Armature Test for Short Circuit*—Place the armature on the growler, and with a saw-blade over the armature core, rotate the armature and test. If the saw-blade does not vibrate, the armature is in good condition. If the saw-blade vibrates, the armature is short-circuited and should be replaced.

*Commutator*—Inspect the commutator for roughness. If it is rough, turn it down on a lathe until it is thoroughly cleaned, then sand off with 00 sandpaper.

*Insulated Brush-Holder Test for Ground*—Place one test-prod lead to the cover and the other on the brush holder. If the test lamp lights, the brush holder is grounded and should be replaced. If the test lamp does not light, the brush holder is in good condition.

*Brushes*—Check condition of the brushes, and if they are pitted or worn, they should be replaced. Check the tension of the brush-holder springs; they should have enough tension to hold the brushes snugly against the commutator.

*Brush Ground Leads*—Disconnect the brush ground leads from the end frame and clean all terminals and replace. Check the insulation of the brush to field-coil leads. The insulation should not be broken.

*Drive-Housing Bushing*—Check the condition of the drive-housing bushing. The armature shaft should fit snugly in this bushing, if it is worn it should be replaced.

To facilitate the service diagnosis, the following basic trouble pointers together with their possible causes and remedies are given:

## STARTER MOTOR TROUBLES

*Symptom and Possible Cause*          *Possible Remedy*

### Starter Fails to Operate

(a) Corrosion at battery posts.

(a) Remove battery cables and clean terminals and clamps. Check clamps for corrosion and replace if necessary.

(b) Loose battery cables.

(b) Clean battery posts and cable clamps. Tighten securely for good contact.

(c) Dead battery cell.

(c) Replace defective battery with a new one. Check voltage regulator and generator output.

(d) Defective starter or solenoid switch.

(d) Replace starter and ignition switch and check starting-motor solenoid for operation. Replace if necessary.

(e) Defective starter.

(e) Remove and test starting motor. Replace parts as required or the complete unit.

(f) Weak battery.

(f) Test specific gravity of battery and check for dead cell.

| *Symptom and Possible Cause* | *Possible Remedy* |
|---|---|

## Starter Fails and Lights Dim

| | |
|---|---|
| (a) Weak battery. | (a) Test specific gravity of battery and check for dead cell. |
| (b) Loose connections. | (b) Tighten loose connections as required, being sure to check terminals for corrosion. |
| (c) Dead battery cell. | (c) Replace defective battery with a new one. Check voltage regulator and generator output, which may have contributed to the battery failure. |
| (d) Battery terminals corroded. | (d) Remove battery cables and clean terminals and clamps. Check clamps for corrosion and replace if necessary. |
| (e) Internal ground winding. | (e) Remove starting motor and test. |

## Starter Turns But Does Not Engage

| | |
|---|---|
| (a) Broken drive spring. | (a) Remove starting motor and install new drive spring. Check screw shaft for excessive wear or burring; replace if necessary. |
| (b) Broken teeth on flywheel ring gear. | (b) Replace flywheel ring gear; be sure and check the teeth on mating pinion for wear and replace if necessary. |
| (c) Grease or dirt on screw shaft. | (c) Remove starting motor and clean screw shaft in clean kerosene. |

## GENERATOR SERVICING

The generator is a machine used to convert mechanical energy into electrical energy. The function of the generator is to restore to the battery the current used in cranking the engine and, in addition, to supply current for lights, ignition, radio, horn, etc., up to the limit of the generator's capacity. Basically, direct-current-type generators used on outboard motors are similar in construction to that of cranking motors previously noted. The generator may be connected directly or by a belt and pulley to the crankshaft.

To control the amount of electricity produced by the generator, a regulator is used. The regulator contains three electrical devices whose purposes are as follows:

1. To automatically connect the generator to the battery when the generator is operating fast enough to charge the battery, and to disconnect the generator from the battery when the generator slows or stops, thus preventing discharge of the battery through the generator.
2. To limit the maximum current output of the generator to a safe value.
3. To limit the voltage output of the generator to a value that will be safe for the battery, radio, and other accessories.

As a general rule, the generator should be inspected and tested at frequent intervals to determine its condition. High-speed operation, excessive dust and dirt, high temperature, and operation of generator at or near full output over an extended period of time are all factors which increase bearing, commutator, and brush wear.

When a generator fails to operate properly, and it has definitely been determined that the trouble is in the generator and not in some other part of the circuit, the generator should be removed from the engine and taken to a suitable test-stand for examination.

### Inspection

The following inspection will disclose whether the generator is in proper condition for service or if it should be removed for repairs. Proceed as follows:

1. Using a good light and a mirror, inspect the commutator through the openings in the commutator end frame. Low or irregular output may result if the commutator is coated with grease or dirt, is rough, out of round, or has high mica between the bars. If the commutator bars are burned, an open circuit is indicated.

2. Inspect the commutator end of the generator for throw solder, indicating the generator has been overheated due to excessive output. Excessive output usually results when the generator field is grounded either internally or at the regulator. If this is indicated, disconnect the FIELD terminal of the generator or regulator and run the engine at medium speed. If the generator output drops off, the regulator is at fault, but if the output remains high, the generator field is grounded internally. If the field is found to be grounded, the regulator usually will be damaged.

3. Check the condition of the brushes; make sure that they are not binding in the holders and that they are resting on the commutator with sufficient tension to give good, firm contact. Brush leads and screws must be tight. If the brushes are worn down to one half their original length compared with new brushes, the generator must be removed for installation of new brushes.

4. If the commutator or brushes are in bad condition, other than being dirty, the generator should be removed for repairs. If these parts are only dirty, however, they may be cleaned without removal of the generator.

5. Check the belt for condition and proper tension; make sure that all generator mounting bracket and brace bolts are tight. A loose belt will permit belt slippage, resulting in rapid belt wear and low or erratic generator output. An excessively tight belt will cause rapid belt wear and rapid wear of the generator and bearings. If the belt requires adjustment, first loosen the belt so that the generator pulley is free, then check the pulley for tightness and check the generator bearings for freeness of rotation and excessive sideplay. Rough or excessively worn bearings should be replaced.

6. Inspect and manually check all wiring connections at the generator, regulator, charge indicator, junction block, and battery to make certain that all connections are clean and tight.

## GENERATOR REGULATOR SERVICE

Generators being attached and driven by the engine run at variable speed, with a resulting variable output in the absence of an output control. Accordingly, regulators are necessary to keep the current and voltage within proper limits, as well as to prevent reversal of current. See Fig. 40.

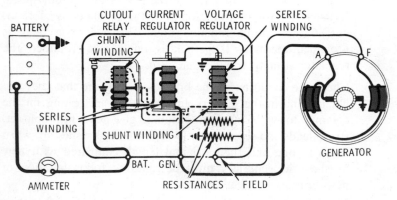

Fig. 40. Wiring diagram of a typical voltage regulator.

Before testing and adjusting the generator regulator, it is advisable to first test the generator output and the charging circuit wiring. If the generator output or charging-circuit voltage drops are not within normal limits, repairs should be made before testing the regulator.

The following is the general procedure when making tests and adjustments of the *cutout relay, voltage regulator,* and *current regulator* in the order named:

### Cutout Relay

*Air Gap*—Disconnect regulator. Measure the air gap between the armature and the center of the winding core with the contact points held closed. Bend the spring hanger until both sets of points meet at the same time. If the air gap does not agree with specifications, adjust by loosening the two adjusting screws. Raise or lower the armature as required.

*Point Opening*—Measure the point opening. If it does not agree with specifications, bend the upper armature stop until it does.

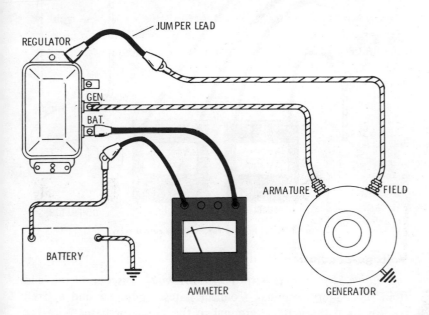

Fig. 41. **Meter hookup for checking generator output.**

*Closing-Voltage Check*—Connect the regulator to the proper generator and battery. Connect a voltmeter between the regulator GENERATOR terminal and the regulator base. Connect an ammeter between the battery and the regulator BATTERY terminal. Slowly increase the generator speed until the points close. If the closing voltage is not according to specifications, bend the spring-post until it is. Decrease the generator speed and note the reverse current necessary to open the points. If not according to specifications, adjust by changing the air gap. Increasing the air gap lowers the reverse current setting. See Fig. 42 for the proper meter connections.

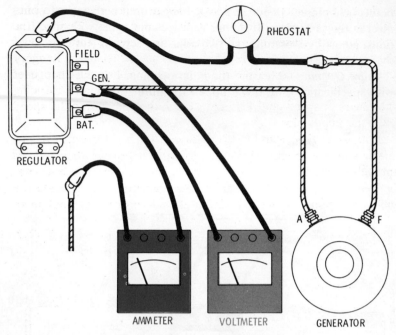

RHEOSTAT

FIELD

GEN.

BAT.

REGULATOR

A F

AMMETER    VOLTMETER    GENERATOR

Fig. 42. Meter hookup for checking cutout relay.

## Voltage-Regulation Relay

*Voltage Setting, Fixed-Resistance Method*—Disconnect the lead from the battery terminal. Connect a test voltmeter and a fixed resistor from the battery terminal to the regulator base. With the regulator at operating temperature, run the generator at charging speed and note the voltage setting. If the setting does not agree with specifications, adjust by bending down one spring hanger until it does. Bending the hanger down increases the setting, bending the hanger up lowers the setting. Confine the adjustment to one spring unless the regulator is badly out of adjustment.

For complete adjustment, remove the second spring. Connect a voltmeter from the GENERATOR terminal to the regulator base. Open the voltage-regulator points by hand, and increase the generator speed until the voltmeter reads approximately one-half the specified operating voltage (open circuit). This establishes the approximate generator speed at which the adjustment should be made. Let the points close and adjust the first spring hanger to one-half the total voltage setting. Install the second spring. Connect the voltmeter and resistance as illustrated. Complete the adjustment of the second spring hanger (without changing the first spring hanger) until the correct voltage setting is obtained. After each change of setting, check the adjustment by replacing the cover and reducing the generator speed until the points open, then increasing the speed until the points close.

*Voltage Setting, Variable-Resistance Method*—Connect an ammeter and a ¼-ohm variable resistor between the battery and the BATTERY terminal, as illustrated in Fig. 43. Connect a voltmeter between the BATTERY terminal and the regulator base. Operate the generator at medium speed. If less than 8 amperes are obtained,

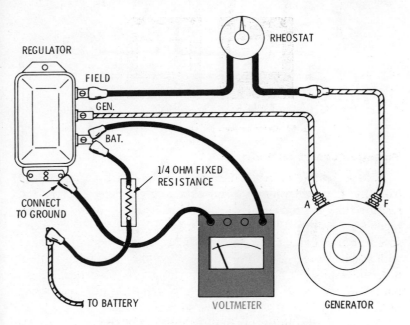

**Fig. 43. Meter hookup for checking voltage relay.**

turn on all lights and accessories to permit a higher output. Cycle the generator and note the setting. Adjust as in the fixed-resistance method.

251

*Air Gap*—Disconnect the regulator. Open the points by hand and release the armature slowly until the points just touch, then measure the air gap. If not according to specifications, adjust by loosening the two mounting screws and raise or lower the contact brackets as required. See Fig. 43 for proper meter connections.

## Current-Regulation Relay

*Current Setting*—Connect the regulator to the generator and battery. Remove the regulator cover and connect a jumper across the voltage-regulator points. Connect an ammeter as indicated. With the regulator at operating temperature, turn on all lights and acces-

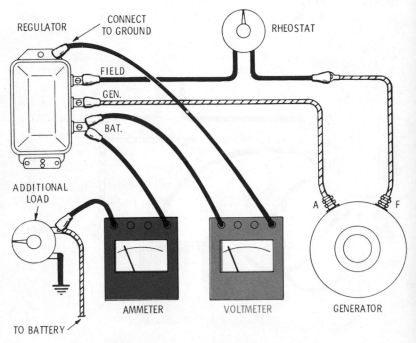

Fig. 44. Meter hookup for checking current relay.

sories. Run the generator at medium speed and note the current setting. If not according to specifications, adjust by bending the spring hanger of one spring until it is adjusted properly. Bending the spring hanger up decreases the current setting. Bending the hanger down increases the current setting. Confine the adjustment to one spring unless the regulator is completely out of adjustment.

For complete adjustment, remove one spring and adjust the remaining spring hanger to one-half the specified setting. Reinstall the first spring and adjust its spring hanger to the full current setting.

*Air Gap*—Disconnect the regulator and open the points by hand. Release the armature slowly until the points just touch, then measure the air gap. If not according to specifications, adjust by loosening the two contact mounting screws and raise or lower the contact bracket as required. See Fig. 44 for the proper meter connections.

## ALTERNATORS

Alternating-current generators (usually called *alternators*) used on some outboard motors are usually connected in "Y" or delta and consist of a rotating field which is part of the flywheel, and a stationary armature containing the power-generating windings. The field excitation current is carried to the field through a brush assembly mounted on the breaker plate and a brass slip-ring mounted to the underface of the flywheel.

The three-phase alternating current produced by the generator is converted into (pulsating) direct current by means of a full-wave, three-phase, bridge rectifier. The generator output is controlled in accordance with the battery, engine, and external load demand by an automotive-type, three-unit regulator which incorporates both the current and voltage control and is similar to the previously described regulators used with direct-current generators.

## BATTERY MAINTENANCE

For trouble-free operation, the battery must be properly maintained. Most present-day outboard-motor electrical systems require a 12-volt battery. New storage batteries which are not fully charged initially will not supply the required energy to the starting motor. This condition usually results in insufficient motor speed for engine starting. Charge the battery to the specific-gravity level recommended by the manufacturer. An overnight trickle charge of three to four amperes maximum will usually fully restore a battery.

Lead-acid batteries have an inherent self-discharge characteristic which necessitates recharging every 30 to 45 days when not in use. Failure to do so will result in plate sulfation which will permanently damage the battery. New dry-charge outboard-motor batteries should not be filled with electrolyte until ready for service. After the battery has been filled, the correct specific-gravity reading should be obtained after about 15 minutes. If not, the battery must be brought up to full charge before being put into service.

When adding distilled water to the battery, be extremely careful not to fill to more than about three-sixteenth of an inch above the perforated baffles appearing inside the battery. Battery solution or

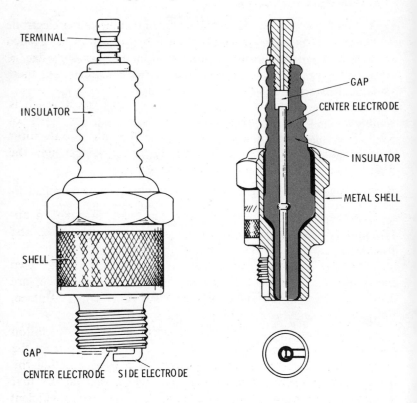

**Fig. 45. Construction of a typical spark plug.**

electrolyte expands from heat caused by charging. Overfilling, therefore, will result in overflow.

## SPARK PLUGS

Spark plugs are a small but very important part of the outboard motor. Without proper spark-plug operation, satisfactory engine performance cannot be obtained. Outboard motors are equipped with spark plugs of special electrode design, and differ from the automotive type in that the side electrode is considerably shorter, extending only about half-way across the center electrode.

### Spark-Plug Construction

With reference to Fig. 45, it will be noted that the center electrode is insulated from the spark-plug shell by means of a molded insulator. The side electrode projects from the bottom edge of the spark-plug shell and is positioned in such a manner that there is a gap between it and the center electrode.

This gap is known as the spark-plug gap, the size of which is determined by the manufacturer to suit the various types of engines. It follows that the plug recommended by the manufacturer for a certain type of motor is generally one that will give the best service under normal operating conditions.

### Perma-Gap Spark Plugs

Thunderbolt CD ignition is a necessary factor in enabling application of surface-gap spark plug design. *Mercury* uses the *Perma-Gap* spark plug across the line.

Essentially, spark plug construction is misleadingly simple. Two metal parts, a threaded base and a slender center electrode, are separated and protected by a porcelain insulator. When in place, the plug is sealed to the cylinder head by a metal gasket.

The plug serves as a conductor of electricity from the ignition lead up to its tip. Then the current flashes across the gap from the center electrode to the ground electrode, the base, creating the ignition spark. There are many external and internal factors that can hamper or prevent this directional flow and retard efficient spark formation. Attention to critical areas by electrical engineers

Fig. 46. This type of spark plug offers a path for the arc all around the center electrode.

produced a plug design that has reduced or completely done away with the old bugaboos such as tip fouling, too hot or too cold temperature range, preignition, periodic cleaning and regapping. For modern outboard engines, the former side-electrode replacement plug has joined the propeller shear pin as a museum piece.

256

Evolution has produced the optimum spark plug insofar as *Mercury* is concerned. They are convinced the *Perma-Gap* is the one plug for all of their engines. Fig. 46.

The ground electrode of a surface-gap design is an adaptation of the idea that in numbers there is security. The spark can leap the radial gap in any direction since the electrode surrounds the firing tip full circle. Side electrode plugs have a limited area in which to receive the jumping spark and if the gap is fouled or the electrode is bent, the spark will be weak or fail.

Spark plug fouling is virtually impossible. Self cleaning characteristic results in dependable ignition at all engine speeds. Electrode cleaning and regapping is eliminated. No heat range problems—a cooler running engine is a longer-running engine. Only two plug styles are required for a full range of engines. Longlife plugs eliminate need for periodic inspection or replacement. Plugs last longer.

## Spark-Plug Classification

Spark plugs are classified into various types in accordance with the temperature at which they are designed to operate:

1. Hot plugs.
2. Cold plugs.

The hot plug illustrated in Fig. 47A has a long core section exposed to the flame within the cylinder and is designed to operate on motors where the operating temperature and speeds are low. The cold plug (Fig. 47B) is designed to operate under extreme high temperatures, having a short cross-section exposed to the flame within the cylinder, and is for use where the operating temperature and speeds are high.

Because of the various operating conditions, spark plugs are made in a number of heat ranges. This will enable plugs to maintain the proper temperature for the type of service to which the motor is subjected. There are no sharp lines of distinction between the "hot" and "cold" spark plugs, and each group has several classifications with relation to the temperature at which they are designed to operate.

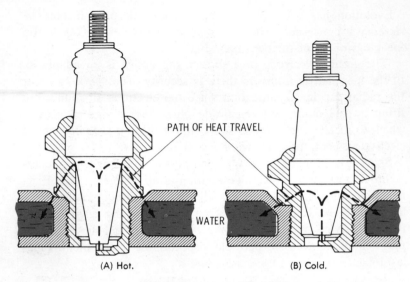

(A) Hot.                                    (B) Cold.

**Fig. 47. Heat range of spark plugs.**

The use of a *cold* plug in a *low-speed* engine will result in consistent fouling, while the use of a *hot* plug in a *high-speed* engine will result in pre-ignition, causing the engine to "ping" or to "surge." In extreme cases the plug may be hot enough to result in complete motor stoppage or burning of the piston head.

The appearance of spark plugs removed from the cylinder block will indicate whether it is *too hot* or *too cold* for the motor. If the plug is operating at its most efficient temperature, the porcelain part which projects inside the cylinder will be dark brown, chestnut, or coffee-colored. If the porcelain is chalky white, or has flaky blisters, the plug is *too hot*.

The reason for the use of different type plugs is because of the conditions under which the plugs must operate. The end of the plug is subjected to intense heat from the explosions of the fuel mixture, and this heat is dissipated by conducting along the porcelain end of the plug, and then to the cylinder jacket. If the porcelain part of the plug is comparatively long, the heat cannot be dissipated rapidly, and the plug will run hot. If the plug is short, the heat can pass through it more quickly, and the plug will run cold. See Fig. 48.

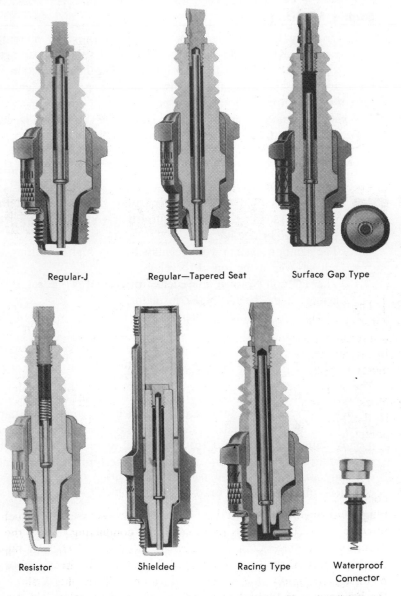

Regular-J          Regular—Tapered Seat          Surface Gap Type

Resistor          Shielded          Racing Type          Waterproof Connector

Courtsey Champion Spark Plugs

**Fig. 48. Internal view of various type plugs.**

### Engine Misfiring

To properly fire the charge, a combustible mixture must be present in the cylinder. In addition, a spark of sufficient strength must be supplied to ignite the fuel mixture. The main function of the spark plug, therefore, is to transmit the energy of the ignition system in the form of an adequate spark.

When a normal fuel charge fails to ignite, the spark plug is said to be "misfiring." Causes for misfiring are usually as follows:

1. The plug gap may be so small that there is a burnable mixture between the electrodes.
2. On the other hand, the plug gap may be so wide that the ignition system is unable to furnish a voltage of sufficient strength to bridge it.
3. The ignition system voltage may be too high, resulting in a flash-over at the top of the plug.
4. The ignition voltage may leak to ground as a result of a mechanical break in the insulator.
5. Because of conducting deposits on the firing surface of the insulator, the ignition voltage may leak to ground. In this case, energy is drained away and the ignition system cannot build up sufficient voltage to bridge the gap.

Most misfiring results from shorting due to deposits on the insulator nose surface. When these are removed by cleaning, the spark plugs firing ability is usually restored. This type of short-circuiting usually causes considerable trouble, since it can occur without being noticed. Only a slow decrease in performance and fuel economy will result by the occasional misfiring of one or more cylinders due to burned or dirty spark plugs.

### Spark-Plug Inspection

Ignition troubles usually result from a variety of causes and may only seldom be traced to faulty spark plugs. Instead, they are usually due to poor plug installation, unsuitable heat range selection, or poor engine maintenance.

A close inspection will usually reveal good installation practice, the methods being to check each plug and its gasket as they are removed from the engine. A gasket which is compressed to about three quarters of its original thickness, with smooth parallel surfaces, indicates that the plug was properly installed and tightened.

## Spark-Plug Analysis

*Normal*—Correct heat range turns insulator to light tan or gray in color. Few deposits are present. Electrodes are not burned.
 Change plugs at regular intervals, using type of recommended plug for heat range.

*Wet Fouling*—Damp or wet, black carbon coating over entire firing end, forming sludge in severe cases.
 Wrong spark-plug heat range (too cold).
 Prolonged trolling operation.
 Low-speed carburetor adjustment too rich.
 Improper ratio of fuel mix.
 Induction manifold bleed-off return passage obstructed.
 Worn or defective breaker points resulting in lack of voltage.

*Overheating*—Electrodes badly eroded. Premature gap wear. Insulator has gray or white "blistered" appearance.
 Incorrect spark-plug heat range (too hot).
 Carburetion too lean (hi-speed adjustment).
 Ignition timing overadvanced.
 "Sticky" piston rings.
 Prop not suited to boat load of motor (lugging motor).
 Worn or defective water pump.
 Restricted water intake.
 Scale, salt, or mud in water jackets causing restriction in cooling system.

*Aluminum "Throw-Off"*—Metallic "gob" of gray pot metal adhering to electrodes and plug bore. Very rare.
 Caused by pre-ignition source within cylinder melting aluminum alloy off piston. Do not install new plugs until source of pre-ignition is determined and piston examined.

*Core-Bridging*—Electrodes not badly burned. Bottom of side electrode usually coated with ashlike deposits. Insulator nose "peppered" with tiny beads or small chunks fused to firing end. Sometimes have the appearance of glasslike bubbles.

*Gap Bridging*—Spark gap shorted out by combustion particles wedged or fused between electrodes.

Both "core bridging" deposits and "gap bridging" are caused by excessive combustion-chamber deposits striking and adhering to the spark-plug's firing end. They originate from the piston, shedding excessive deposits from its crown. These deposits are caused by one of a combination of the following:

Excessive carbon in cylinder.
Use of nonrecommended oils.
Immediate high-speed operation after prolonged and excessive trolling.
Improper ratio of fuel mix.

*NOTE*: Most outboard manufacturers market a combustion chamber "purging" solvent which can be run in the engine to clean out troublesome deposits. In extreme cases, cylinders and pistons may have to be cleaned manually, as new plugs may give only temporary relief.

### Spark-Plug Types

Although the spark plugs are normally gapped at the factory, it is a good practice to check for proper setting. Resetting may become necessary after continued use. To ascertain the proper spark-plug gap, check the gap with the proper size of feeler gauge. The gauge should slide snugly between the two points. If an adjustment is required, bend the side electrode until the proper gap is obtained.

Table 1 provided by the *Champion Spark Plug Company* lists the spark-plug types and gap openings for plugs used in most outboard motors of recent manufacture.

**Table 1.    Type of Champion Spark Plug and Gap
for Various Outboard Motors**

| MODEL | Spark Plug | Plug Gap |
|---|---|---|
| **AERO MARINE** | | |
| 1971-73 AM9000 (9 h.p.) ......................................................CJ-8 | | .025 |
| 1971-73 Jet Pak ...........................................................................J-13Y | | .035 |

| MODEL | Spark Plug | Gap Plug |
|---|---|---|
| 1970-73 AM4000 (4 h.p.) | J-14Y | .035 |
| 1970-73 AM7500M, AM7500E (7.5 h.p.) | CJ-8 | .035 |
| 1970-72 AM5000M, AM5000E (5 h.p.) | H-10J | .035 |
| **AIRBOY** | | |
| 20, 40, 90 (B&S) | J-8J | .030 |
| 90 (OMC) | F-14Y | .030 |
| 50 | J-6J | .030 |
| 120 | H-8J | .030 |
| **ALDENS** | | |
| 1970-71 5, 7 h.p. | J-13Y | .035 |
| 1968-69 5, 7 h.p. except Model 1186 | J-8J | .035 |
| 1969 Model 1186 - 7 h.p. | J-13Y | .035 |
| 1961-67 All 3, 5, 7 h.p. models | J-8J | .030 |
| **ALSPORT** | | |
| 14mm Heads | L-3G | .020 |
| 18mm Heads | K-8G | .020 |
| **ANZANI (British)** | | |
| Minor, Pilot | L-10 | .020 |
| Super-Single | D-16J | .020 |
| **APACHE** | | |
| J-5 | TJ-8J | .030 |
| J-9 | J-12J | .030 |
| **ARCHIMEDES-PENTA** | | |
| 1975 450 | UL-17V | ...... |
| Thru 1974 450 | L-78 | .020 |
| 600, 700, 970 | UL-17V | ...... |
| 90, 120, 140, 250 | L-88A | .020 |
| U22, 80 | L-85 | .020 |
| **ARCHIMEDES-PENTA—Continued** | | |
| 35, 39, 40, 50, 50a | L-81 | .020 |
| 360, 550X | L-78 | .020 |
| 252 | UL-82Y | .020 |
| **ARROW** | | |
| 4, 5.5, 7.5 h.p. | J-13Y | .030 |
| **BOATIMPELLER** | | |
| 18mm Heads | D-9 | .020 |

| MODEL | Spark Plug | Plug Gap |
|---|---|---|
| **BRITISH SEAGULL** | | |
| 1966-73 Silver Century | D-16 | .020 |
| 1966-73 Silver Century Plus | D-16 | .020 |
| 1956-73 Forty Plus | D-16 | .020 |
| 1955-73 Forty Minus, Forty Featherweight | D-16 | .020 |
| 1957-70 Century Plus | D-16 | .020 |
| 1956-70 Century | D-16 | .020 |
| **BROOKLURE** | | |
| 14mm Heads | J-6J | .030 |
| **CARNITI** | | |
| 90 h.p. | L-78 | .025 |
| **CHAMPION** | | |
| A, 1B, 1J, 1K, 1L, B1F, D1C, D1D, D1E, D1F | D-16 | .025 |
| R1C, S1C, S1D, S1E, S1F, 2B, 2G, 2H, 2J | D-16 | .025 |
| 2K, 2M, 2N, 2I-HD, 2MM, D2C, D2D, D2F | D-16 | .025 |
| M2G, S2C, S2D, S2F, D3D, 4L, 4L-HD | D-16 | .025 |
| 1H, D1G, M1G, S1G, 3G, 3H, D4G, M4G, S4G | H-10J | .025 |
| 3M-GS, 3MM-GS, 3NS, 4M-GS, 4MM-GS, 4N-D | J-7J | .030 |
| 6M-D, 6M-GS, 6M-HD, 6MM-GS, 6M-SGS, 4N-D | J-8J | .030 |
| 4KS, 4LS, 4LS-1X Normal | D-6 | .030 |
| 4KS, 4LS, 4LS-1X, 6N-HR Racing | K-60R | .020 |
| 4M-HR, 4MM-HR, 6M-HR, 6MM-HR | J-62R | .020 |
| **CHIEF** | | |
| 1974   K-500, K-700, K-750 | J-13Y | .030 |
| J-5 | TJ-8J | .030 |
| J-9 | J-12J | .030 |
| J-200, J-300, J-350, J-400, J-500, J-700 | CJ-8 | .030 |
| K-150, K-200, K-300, K-400, K-990 | CJ-8 | .030 |
| Thru 1973: K-500, K-700, K-750 | CJ-8 | .030 |
| **CHRIS-CRAFT** | | |
| Challenger, Commander | J-8J | .028 |
| **CHRYSLER** | | |
| **Models with Magnapower Ignition:** | | |
| 1975   60, 105, 120, 135 h.p. | UL-18V | ...... |
| 1974-75 75, 90 h.p. | L-20V | ...... |
| 1972-75 150 h.p. | L-20V | ...... |
| 1971-75 45 h.p. | UL-18V | ...... |
| 1969-75 55 h.p. | UL-18V | ...... |

| MODEL | Spark Plug | Gap Plug |
|---|---|---|
| 1974    60 h.p. w/Mag. II | UL-18V | ...... |
| 1974    60 h.p. w/Mag. I | L-20V | ...... |
| 1974    135 h.p. | L-20V | ...... |
| 1970-74 120 h.p. | L-20V | ...... |
| 1968-74 105 h.p. | L-20V | ...... |
| 1972-73 130 h.p. | L-20V | ...... |
| 1969-73 70, 85 h.p. | L-20V | ...... |
| 1970-71 135 h.p. | L-20V | ...... |
| 1968    75 h.p. | L-20V | ...... |

**Models with Standard Ignition:**

| MODEL | Spark Plug | Gap Plug |
|---|---|---|
| 1974-75 5 h.p. | L-10 | .030 |
| 1974-75 10, 15 h.p. | L-4J | .030 |
| 1973-75 25, 30 h.p. | L-4J | .030 |
| 1971-75 6, 8 h.p. | L-4J | .030 |
| 1970-75 3.6 h.p. | H-8J | .030 |
| 1968-75 20, 35, 45 h.p. | L-4J | .030 |
| 1967-75 55 h.p. | L-4J | .030 |
| 1971-73 12.9 h.p. | L-4J | .030 |
| 1968-73 9.9 h.p. | L-4J | .030 |
| 1969-70 5, 7 h.p. | L-4J | .030 |
| 1966-69 3.5 h.p. | H-8J | .030 |
| 1968    4.4, 6.6 h.p. | L-4J | .030 |
| 1966-67 9.2, 20, 35, 45, 75, 105 h.p. | J-4J | .030 |
| 1966-67 6 h.p. | H-10J | .030 |
| 1966    50 h.p. | J-4J | .030 |

**CLINTON**

| MODEL | Spark Plug | Gap Plug |
|---|---|---|
| 1974    K-500, K-700, K-750 | J-13Y | .030 |
| J7, J-8 | H-10J | .030 |
| J-9 | J-12J | .030 |
| J-5 | TJ-8J | .030 |
| AJ-9, BJ-9, J-200, J-300 | CJ-8 | .030 |
| J-350, J-400, J-500, J-700 | CJ-8 | .030 |
| K-150, K-200, K-300, K-400, K-990 | CJ-8 | .030 |
| Thru 1973: K-500, K-700, K-750 | CJ-8 | .030 |
| W-100, W-140, W-250 | L-81 | .025 |

**COMMODORE**

| MODEL | Spark Plug | Gap Plug |
|---|---|---|
| 2 h.p. | H-10J | .030 |
| 7.5, 10 h.p. | H-8J | .030 |
| 18, 40 h.p. | J-4J | .030 |

| MODEL | Spark Plug | Gap Plug |
|---|---|---|
| **CORSAIR** | | |
| 3.6, 4, 5, 7.5 h.p. | H-10J | .035 |
| 1953-56 10 h.p. | H-10J | .035 |
| 1950-52 10 h.p. | CJ-8 | .035 |
| 16 h.p. | D-9J | .035 |
| 1956 30 h.p. | J-6J | .030 |
| **ELGIN** | | |
| 58201, 58202 (2 h.p.) 58401 (2.5 h.p.) | J-12J | .050 |
| 58561, 58562, 58571, 58651 (5 h.p.) | J-12J | .050 |
| 58641, 58642, 58652 (6 h.p.) | J-12J | .050 |
| 58821, 58822, 58823, 58824 (16 h.p.) | J-12J | .050 |
| 58841, 58843, 58844, 58851, (16 h.p.) | J-12J | .050 |
| 5833, 58221, 58231, 58250, 58711 (2 h.p.) | J-11J | .050 |
| 58211, 58501 thru 58551 (7.5 h.p.) | J-11J | **.050** |
| 58601 thru 58621, 58741 (7.5 h.p.) | J-11J | .050 |
| 58701 thru 58731, 58751 (7.5 h.p.) | J-11J | .050 |
| 58761, 58771, 58772, 58781 (7.5 h.p.) | J-11J | .050 |
| 58241, 58321, 58331, 59241 (2 h.p.) | H-10J | .030 |
| 6002, 6003, (3.5 h.p.), 6001 (5.5 h.p.) | H-10J | .030 |
| 58563, 59501, 59521, 59541 (55 h.p.) | H-10J | .030 |
| 6006 (6 h.p.), 6009, 6010 (7.5 h.p.) | H-10J | .030 |
| 6005, 6068 (6 h.p.) | H-10J | .035 |
| 6008, 6060, 6061 (7.5 h.p.) | H-10J | .035 |
| 58341, 58741, 59791, 59701, 59721 (7.5 h.p.) | H-8J | .030 |
| 59011 (8 h.p.), 59891 (10 h.p.) | H-8J | .030 |
| 58801, 58891, 58902, 58912 (12 h.p.) | H-8J | .030 |
| 58941, 58951, 58961, 58971, 59561 (12 h.p.) | H-8J | .030 |
| 58991, 59881 (12 h.p.) | H-8J | .030 |
| 59601, 59861, 59871 (25 h.p.) | H-8J | .030 |
| 59421, 59431, 59621 (30 h.p.) | H-8J | .030 |
| 59631, 59801, 59811 (30 h.p.) | H-8J | .030 |
| 59402, 59403, 59412, 59413 (35 h.p.) | H-8J | .030 |
| 59441, 59451, 59831 (35 h.p.) | H-8J | .030 |
| 59821, 59901, 59911 (35 h.p.) | H-8J | .030 |
| 6012 (12 h.p.) | J-6J | .035 |
| 6013, 6014, 6015, 6069 (14 h.p.) | J-6J | .035 |
| 6025, 6028, 6032 (25 h.p.) | J-6J | .035 |
| 6033, 6035 (27.7 h.p.) | J-6J | .035 |
| 6034, 6036, 6037, 6038 (28 h.p.) | J-6J | .035 |
| 6040, 6043-6047 (40 h.p.) | J-6J | .035 |
| 6060 thru 6063 (60 h.p.) | J-6J | .035 |

| MODEL | Spark Plug | Plug Gap |
|---|---|---|
| 59661, 59671 (18 h.p.) | J-4J | .030 |
| 6070 (28 h.p.) | J-4J | .030 |
| 594001, 594011, 59421 (40 h.p.) | J-4J | .030 |
| 594031, 59461, 59471 (40 h.p.) | J-4J | .030 |
| 6052, 6053 (43.7 h.p.) | J-4J | .035 |
| 6072, 6073 (75.2 h.p.) | J-4J | .035 |
| 6054, 6055, 6056, 6057 (45 h.p.) | J-4J | .035 |
| 6074, 6075, 6076, 6077 (75 h.p.) | J-4J | .035 |
| 60900 (2 h.p.), 6092 (3.5 h.p.) | TJ-8J* | .030 |
| *Engines without special connector | CJ-8 | .030 |
| 6091 (3.5 h.p.), 6066, 6067 (9 h.p.) | CJ-8 | .030 |
| 6062, 6063 (45 hp.), 6064, 6065 (75 h.p.) | UJ-17V | ...... |

## ELTO

| MODEL | Spark Plug | Plug Gap |
|---|---|---|
| Fisherman, Lightwin, Imperial | K-15J | .025 |
| Service "A", Super "A", Foldlight (2.75 h.p.) | K-15J | .025 |
| Fleetwin (8.5 h.p.) | K-15J | .025 |
| Senior Speedster (13.7 h.p.) | K-15J | .025 |
| Single, Super Single (2.2 h.p.) | K-15J | .025 |
| Big Quad, Speeditwin, Super "C" | D-9J | .025 |
| Senior Quad, Junior Quad | D-9J | .025 |
| Handifour, Lightfour, Imperial | D-9J | .025 |
| Special Speedster (9 h.p.) | UD-16/D-16 | .025 |
| Speedster (1949)(12 h. p.) Sportster (5 h.p.) | J-6J | .025 |

## ESKA

| | MODEL | Spark Plug | Plug Gap |
|---|---|---|---|
| 1975 | 1973 (3 h.p.), 1974 (4.5 h.p.) | J-13Y | .035 |
| 1975 | 1975 (5.5 h.p.), 1976 (7.5 h.p.) | J-13Y | .035 |
| 1975 | 1974 (7.5 h.p.), 1978 (9.9 h.p.) | J-13Y | .035 |
| 1975 | 1979 (15 h.p.) | J-13Y | .035 |
| 1969-74 | All except 1703, 1703A, 1705 | J-13Y | .035 |
| 1969-74 | All except 1713, 1713A, 1715 | J-13Y | .035 |
| 1969 | 1703, 1703A, 1705, 1713, 1713A, 1715 | J-8J | .035 |
| 1961-68 | All except 1123, 1126, 1146, 1157 | J-8J | .030 |
| 1961-68 | All except 1159, 1167, 1168, 1170 | J-8J | .030 |
| 1967 | 1167, 1168, 1170 | TJ-6J | .030 |
| 1966 | 1157, 1159 | TJ-6J | .030 |
| 1965 | 1146 | TJ-6J | .030 |
| 1962 | 1123, 1126 | TJ-8J | .030 |

## EVINRUDE

| | MODEL | Spark Plug | Plug Gap |
|---|---|---|---|
| 1975 | Evinrude 135 (135 h.p.) | UL-77V* | ...... |
| 1975 | Evinrude 115 (115 h.p.) | L-77J4† | .040 |
| 1975 | Evinrude 85 (85 h.p.) | L-77J4† | .040 |

ELECTRICAL SYSTEMS

| MODEL | Spark Plug | Plug Gap |
|---|---|---|
| 1975 Hustler (75 h.p.) | L-77J4† | .040 |
| 1975 Evinrude 70 (70 h.p.) | L-77J4† | .040 |
| 1975 Sizzler (50 h.p.) | L-77J4† | .040 |
| 1975 Evinrude 50 (50 h.p.) | L-777J4† | .030 |
| 1975 Evinrude 40 (40 h.p.) | L-4J | .030 |
| 1975 Evinrude 25 (25 h.p.) | J-4J | .030 |
| 1975 Evinrude 15 (15 h.p.) | L-7J | .030 |
| 1975 Evinrude 9.9 (9.9 h.p.) | L-7J | .030 |
| 1975 Evinrude 6 (6 h.p.) | J-6J | .030 |
| 1975 Evinrude 4 (4 h.p.) | J-6J | .030 |
| 1975 Evinrude 2 (2 h.p.) | J-6J | .030 |
| 1974-75 Silver Starflite (135 h.p.) | UL-77V* | ...... |
| 1974-75 Strangler (135 h.p.) | UL-77V* | ...... |
| 1974 Triumph, Hustler (70 h.p.) | UL-77V* | ...... |
| 1974 Sizzler (50 h.p.) | UL-77V* | ...... |
| 1974 Norseman (40 h.p.) | UL-4J | .030 |
| 1974 Fastwin (15 h.p.) | UL-4J | .030 |
| 1974 Sportwin (9.9 h.p.) | UL-4J | .030 |
| 1973-74 Starflite (85-115 h.p.) | UL-77V* | ...... |
| 1973-74 Starflite S (135 h.p.) | UL-77V* | ...... |
| 1973-74 Sportster (25 h.p.) | UJ-4J | .030 |
| 1971-74 Lark (50 h.p.) | UL-77V* | ...... |
| 1964-74 Yachtwin (3.4-4 h.p.) | J-6J | .030 |
| 1956-74 Fisherman (5.5-6 h.p.) | J-6J | .030 |
| 1956-74 Mate (1.5-2 h.p.) | J-6J | .030 |
| 1952-74 Lightwin (3-5.2 h.p.) | J-6J | .030 |
| 1973 Fastwin (18 h.p.) | UJ-4J | .030 |
| 1972-73 Triumph (65 h.p.) | UL-77V* | ...... |
| 1972-73 Norseman (40 h.p.) | J-4J | .030 |
| 1956-73 Sportwin (9.5-10 h.p.) | J-4J | .030 |
| 1969-72 Sportster (25 h.p.) | J-4J | .030 |
| 1969-72 Starflite (85 h.p.) | L-76V | ...... |
| 1967-72 Starflite (100-125 h.p.) | L76-V | ...... |
| 1950-72 Fastwin (14-18 h.p.) | J-4J | .030 |
| 1971 Surf-Six-O (55-60 h.p.) | L-76V | ...... |
| 1968-71 Triumph | L-76V | ...... |
| 1965-71 Ski-Twin (33-40 h.p.) | J-4J | .030 |
| 1958-70 Ducktwin (3 h.p.) | J-6J | .030 |
| 1956-70 Lark (30-40 h.p.) | J-4J | .030 |
| 1951-70 Bigtwin (25-40 h.p.) | J-4J | .030 |
| 1968 Speedifour (85 h.p.) | L-76V | ...... |
| 1968 Sportfour (65 h.p.) | L-76V | ...... |

| MODEL | Spark Plug | Plug Gap |
|---|---|---|
| 1967-68 Starflite (80-85 h.p.) | J-4J | .030 |
| 1967-68 X-115 (115 h.p.) | L-76V | ...... |
| 1965-68 Angler (5 h.p.) | J-6J | .030 |
| 1964-67 Sportfour (60 h.p.) | J-4J | .030 |
| 1963-67 Speedifour (14mm Hds.) (75-80 h.p.) | J-4J | .030 |
| 1958-66 Starflite (50-100 h.p.) | J-4J | .030 |
| 1962-64 Speeditwin (28 h.p.) | J-4J | .030 |
| 1958-59 Four-Fifty (50 h.p.) | J-4J | .030 |
| 1950-58 Fleetwin (7.5 h.p.) | J-6J | .030 |
| 1953-54 Super Fastwin (5.2 h.p.) | J-6J | .030 |
| 1948-51 Sportwin (3.3 h.p.) | J-6J | .030 |
| 1939-50 Speedifour (18mm Hds.) | D-9J | .030 |
| 1945-49 Zephyr (5.4 h.p.) | J-6J | .030 |
| 1942-49 Light Four (9.7 h.p.) | D-9J | .030 |
| 1946-47 Ranger (1.1 h.p.) | H-10J | .030 |
| 1966-70 Aquanaut Diving Unit (2 h.p.) | CJ-14 | .030 |

*For fouling use L-2G or L-77J4 (.040" gap)
†For sustained full throttle use, install UL-77V

## FAGEOL

| 44 | J-6J/J-6 | .025 |
|---|---|---|

## FEDERAL

| 1971-72 3.5, 5, 7 h.p. | J-13Y | .035 |
|---|---|---|

## FIRESTONE

| 1966 Featherweight 5 | J-12J | .030 |
|---|---|---|
| 1960-62 2 h.p. | H-10J | .030 |
| 1960-62 7.5, 8, 12, 25, 30 h.p. | H-8J | .030 |
| 1956 30 h.p. | J-6J | .035 |
| 1953-56 10 h.p. | H-10J | .035 |
| 1950-52 10 h.p. | CJ-8 | .035 |
| 3.6, 4, 5, 7.5 h.p. | H-10J | .035 |
| 16 h.p. | D-9J | .035 |
| 40 h.p. | J-4J | .030 |

## FISHER-PIERCE

| Bearcat 55 | J-6 | .025 |
|---|---|---|
| Bearcat 85 | N-4 | .025 |

## FOREMOST

| 3.5 h.p. | H-8J | .030 |
|---|---|---|
| 6 h.p. | H-10J | .030 |
| 9.2 h.p. | J-4J | .030 |

| MODEL | Spark Plug | Plug Gap |
|---|---|---|
| **GALE** | | |
| Buccaneer 3, 5, 5.5, 12, 15, 25 h.p. | J-6J/J-4J | .030 |
| Buccaneer 35, 40, 60 h.p. | J-4J | .030 |
| Sovereign 35, 40, 60 h.p. | J-4J | .030 |
| **GAMBLES** | | |
| 1970    3.5, 5, 7 h.p. | J-13Y | .035 |
| 1969    3.5, 5 h.p. | J-8J | .035 |
| 1969    7 h.p. | J-13Y | .035 |
| **GOLDEN JET** | | |
| (SEE ESKA) | | |
| **GRANTS (Seacruiser)** | | |
| 1971-74 3.5, 5, 7, 7.5, 9.9, 14, 15 h.p. | J-13Y | .035 |
| **HIAWATHA** | | |
| 1958-62 12, 25 h.p. | J-6J | .035 |
| 1958-62 38, 40, 60 h.p. | J-4J | .035 |
| 1956-62 3, 3.6, 5, 7.5 h.p. | H-10J | .035 |
| 1956-60 16 h.p. | D-9J | .035 |
| 1957    35 h.p. | J-6J | .030 |
| 1956    30 h.p. | J-6J | .030 |
| **HOMELITE** | | |
| (SEE FISHER-PIERCE) | | |
| **HONDA** | | |
| 75 Twin, 45 Twin | P-8Y | .025 |
| **JOHNSON** | | |
| **Models with Magflash CD Ignition:** | | |
| 1975    50ES, 50ESL, 70ES, 70ESL | L-77J4† | .040 |
| 1975    75ESR, 75ESLR, 85ESL, 115ESL, 115ETL | L-77J4† | .040 |
| 1975    135ESL, 135ETL | UL-77V* | ...... |
| 1974    135ETL, 115ETL, 70ES, 70ESL, 70ESLR | UL-77V* | ...... |
| 1973-74 85ESL, 135ESL, 115ESL | UL-77V* | ...... |
| 1971-74 50ES, 50ESL | UL-77V* | ...... |
| 1973    65ESLR | UL-77V* | ...... |
| 1972-73 50R, 50RL, 65ES | UL-77V* | ...... |
| 1971-72 100ESL, 125ESL | L-76V* | ...... |
| 1969-72 85ESL | L-76V* | ...... |
| 1970-71 60ES, 60ESL | L-76V | ...... |
| 1969-70 115ESL | L-76V | ...... |
| 1969    55ES, 55ESL | L-76V | ...... |
| 1968    TR10S | L-76V | ...... |

| MODEL | Spark Plug | Plug Gap |
|-------|-----------|----------|
| 1968    GT | L-76V | ...... |
| 1967-68 V4TL | L-76V | ...... |
| 1964-68 VX, VXH | L-76V | ...... |

*For fouling use L-2G or L-77J4 (.040" gap)

†For sustained full throttle use, install UL-77V

**Models with Standard Ignition:**

| MODEL | Spark Plug | Plug Gap |
|-------|-----------|----------|
| 1975    40E, 40EL, 40R, 40RL | L-4J | .030 |
| 1975    25E, 25EL, 25R, 25RL | J-4J | .030 |
| 1975    15E, 15EL, 15R, 15RL | L-7J | .030 |
| 1975    10E, 10EL, 10R, 10RL | L-7J | .030 |
| 1971-75 2R, 6RL | J-6J | .030 |
| 1969-75 4R, 4W, 6R | J-6J | .030 |
| 1974    40R, 40RL, 40E, 40EL | UL-4J | .030 |
| 1974    9R, 9RL, 9E, 9EL | UL-4J | .030 |
| 1974    15R, 15RL, 15E, 15EL | UL-4J | .030 |
| 1973-74 25E, 25EL, 25R, 25RL | UJ-4J | .030 |
| 1973    20R, 20RL | UJ-4J | .030 |
| 1971-73 9RL, 40EL, 40RL | J-4J | .030 |
| 1969-73 9R, 40R, 40E | J-4J | .030 |
| 1972    25E, 25EL | J-4J | .030 |
| 1971-72 20RL, 25RL | J-4J | .030 |
| 1969-72 20R, 25R | J-4J | .030 |

**JOHNSON— (Models with Standard Ignition)—Continued**

| MODEL | Spark Plug | Plug Gap |
|-------|-----------|----------|
| 1969-70 1R | J-6J | .030 |
| 1969-70 33R, 33E, 40ES | J-4J | .030 |
| 1968    SC | J-6J | .030 |
| 1967-68 JHF, JWF | J-6J | .030 |
| 1965-68 LD | J-6J | .030 |
| 1965-68 RXE | J-4J | .030 |
| 1964-68 MQ | J-4J | .030 |
| 1962-68 RX | J-4J | .030 |
| 1958-68 V4, V4A, V4M, V4S, VX, VXH | J-4J | .030 |
| 1956-68 FD, FDE | J-4J | .030 |
| 1954-68 CD, JH | J-6J | .030 |
| 1952-68 JW | J-6J | .030 |
| 1951-68 RD, RDE, RDS, RJE, RK | J-4J | .030 |
| 1952-66 TN, AD, QD, V4H, V4ML | J-4J | .030 |
| Air Buoy Diving Unit | CJ-14 | .025 |

**K-MART**

| MODEL | Spark Plug | Plug Gap |
|-------|-----------|----------|
| 1971    5, 7 h.p. | J-13Y | .035 |
| 1970    3.5, 5, 7 h.p. | J-13Y | .035 |

| MODEL | Spark Plug | Plug Gap |
|---|---|---|
| **K & P** | | |
| (SEE MINI MOTOR) | | |
| **KONIG** | | |
| Racing | L-57R | .016 |
| 500cc 75 h.p. model | L-54R | .016 |
| **MAJESTIC** | | |
| 1MB, 2MB, 4MB, 1MBB | UD-16/D-16 | .030 |
| M2L, M2LL, M2N, M4LGS | UD-16/D-16 | .030 |
| M3LGS, M3LLGS, M3NGS, M4LLGS, M4NGS | J-7J | .030 |
| M6LLGS, M6NGS | J-8J | .030 |
| **MARINER** | | |
| (SEE CHAMPION) | | |
| **MARTIN** | | |
| 20 (2.3 h.p.), 100 (10 h.p.) | J-6J | .035 |
| 40, 45 (4.5 h.p.), 75 (7.5 h.p.) | J-8J | .035 |
| 60, 66 (7.2 h.p.) | J-8J | .035 |
| 60 Hi-Speed (7.5 h.p.) Gasoline | J-6J | .035 |
| 60 Hi-Speed (7.5 h.p.) Alcohol Mixture | J-57R | .020 |
| 200 Silver Streak (17 h.p.) | J-62R | .023 |
| **McCULLOCH** | | |
| 1964-69 3.5, 7.5 h.p. | H-10J | .035 |
| 1964-69 4 h.p. w/long shaft | H-10J | .035 |
| 4 h.p. | J-14Y | .035 |
| 9 h.p. | CJ-8 | .035 |
| 9.5 h.p. | J-7J | .035 |
| 14 h.p. | J-4J | .035 |
| 28, 45 h.p. Manual Start | J-4J | .035 |
| 45 h.p. Electric Start | UJ-17V | ...... |
| 590/630 | J-4J | .035 |
| 75 h.p. | UJ-17V | ...... |
| **MERCURY** | | |
| **Merc Series with Thunderbolt Ignition:** | | |
| 1975    650XS (65 h.p.) | L-76V | ...... |
| 1975    45 (4.5 h.p.) | L-78V | ...... |
| 1975    75 (7.5 h.p.), 110 (9.8 h.p.) | L-78V | ...... |
| 1972-75 402 (40 h.p.) | L-76V | ...... |
| 1970-75 200 (20 h.p.) | L-78V | ...... |
| 1970-75 500 (50 h.p.), 650 (65 h.p.) | L-76V | ...... |
| 1970-75 850 (85 h.p.), 1150 (115 h.p.) | L-76V | ...... |

| MODEL | Spark Plug | Plug Gap |
|---|---|---|
| 1970-75 1500 (150 h.p.) | L-76V | ...... |
| 1974    75 (7.5 h.p.), 110 (9.8 h.p.) | L-76V | ...... |
| 1970-74 40 (4 h.p.) | L-78V | ...... |
| 1970-73 75 (6-7.5 h.p.), 110 (9.8 h.p.) | L-78V | ...... |
| 1970-73 800 (80 h.p.), 400* (40 h.p.) | L-76V | ...... |
| 1970-73 1350 (135 h.p.), 1400 (140 h.p.) | L-76V | ...... |

*1970-71 Merc 400 only requiring
conventional type plug use L-77J (gap .030")

**1966-69 Merc Series with Thunderbolt Ignition:**

| | | |
|---|---|---|
| 500SS (50 h.p.), 650SS (65 h.p.) | L-76V | ...... |
| 800 (80 h.p.) | L-76V | ...... |
| 950, 950SS (95 h.p.) | L-76V | ...... |
| 1000PP, 1000SS (100 h.p.) | L-76V | ...... |
| 1100, 1100SS (110 h.p.) | L-76V | ...... |
| 1250BP, 1250SS (125 h.p.) | L-76V | ...... |

**1967-69 Merc Series with Standard Ignition:**

| | | |
|---|---|---|
| 39 (3.9 h.p.), 40 (4 h.p.) | L-9J | .030 |
| 60 (6 h.p.) 75 (7.5 h.p.) | L-7J | .030 |
| 110 (10 h.p.) 200 (20 h.p.) | L-4J | .030 |
| 500M, 500S (50 h.p.), 650S (65 h.p.) | L-4J | .030 |
| 950 (95 h.p.), 1100 (110 h.p.) | L-4J | .030 |

**Merc Series w/Std. Ignition 1960-1966:**

| | | |
|---|---|---|
| 39 (3.9 h.p.) | J-8J | .025 |
| 60 (6 h.p.), 100, 110 (10 h.p.) | J-7J | .025 |
| 150 (15 h.p.) | J-7J | .025 |
| 350 (35-40 h.p.) (Thru 1965) | J-6J | .025 |
| 350 (35-40 h.p.) (1966) | J-4J | .025 |
| 200 (20-22 h.p.), 350 (25 h.p.) | J-6J | .025 |
| 300 (35 h.p.), 400 (40-45 h.p.) | J-6J | .025 |
| 500 (50 h.p.), 600 (60 h.p.), 700 (70 h.p.) | J-6J | .025 |
| 650, 650S (65 h.p.), 850 (85 h.p.) | J-4J | .025 |
| 900 (90 h.p.), 1000 (100 h.p.) | J-4J | .025 |
| 800E (80 h.p.) Ser. No. 1403610 and under | J-2J | .025 |
| 800EL (80 h.p.) Ser. No. 1405606 and under | J-2J | .025 |
| 800E (80 h.p.) Ser. No. 143611 and above | J-4J | .025 |
| 800 EL (80 h.p.) Ser. No. 1405607 and above | J-4J | .025 |

**Mark Series thru 1959:**

| | | |
|---|---|---|
| 20H (16 h.p.), 55H (40 h.p.) | J-62R/J-57R | .025 |
| 5 (5 h.p.) 6 (6 h.p.) 7 (7.5 h.p.) | J-7J | .025 |
| 10, 15 (10 h.p.) 15A (15 h.p.) | J-7J | .025 |

| MODEL | Spark Plug | Plug Gap |
|---|---|---|
| 20 (16 h.p.) 25 (25 h.p.) 28 (22 h.p.) | J-6J | .025 |
| 58 (45 h.p.) 30, 30H (31 h.p.) | J-6J | .025 |
| 35A (35 h.p.) 50, 50H, 55 (40 h.p.) | J-6J | .025 |
| 75 (60 h.p.) 78 (70 h.p.) | J-6J | .025 |
| **MID-JET** | | |
| M-2, M-3 | J-4J | 030 |
| M-4 | L-4J | .030 |
| **MINI MOTOR (K & P)** | | |
| 1973   Aqua Bug II | DJ-6J | .025 |
| 1972-73 Aqua Bug | CJ-8 | .030 |
| 1969-73 Mini Motor | CJ-14 | .030 |
| **MONO** | | |
| M-50 | J-6J | .030 |
| M-75 | J-10Y | .030 |
| M-5A, M-6A | J-8J | .030 |
| **MOTO ATTREZZI** | | |
| Mac 10 (Wankel) | L-86 | .025 |
| **MUNCIE** | | |
| 11B1, 15B1, (1.5 h.p.) | J-11J | .025 |
| 11B4, 11B6, 11B10, 15B4, 17B1 | J-6J | .025 |
| 11B2, 15B2 (2 h.p.) 11B16 (16 h.p.) | K-15J | .025 |
| A1, A1A, AA1A, WC-1, 500 (1.7 h.p.) | J-8J | .015 |
| **NEPTUNE** | | |
| OB1, 2, 2C, 3, 4, 31, 32, 51, 63 | UD-16/D-16 | .025 |
| OB15, 16, 17 (16 h.p.) | K-57R | .015 |
| OB11, 12, 34, 64, 65, 102, 112, 238, 239 | K-15J | .025 |
| 438, 439, 638, 639, 1016, 1638, 1639 | K-15J | .025 |
| 10A16, 11A16, 11A2, 16A39 | K-15J | .025 |
| 101, 189, 139, 1A39, 10A1 | J-8J | .025 |
| 111, 11A1, 15A1 | J-11J | .025 |
| 104, 106, 113, 114, 116, 539, 938, 939 | J-6J | .025 |
| 1010, 1110, 4A39, 5A39, 9A39, 10A4, 10A6 | J-6J | .025 |
| 11A3, 11AA3, 11AA10, 10A10, 11A6, 11AA6 | J-6J | .025 |
| 15A3, 15AA3, 15A6, 15AA6, 15A9, 15AA9 | J-6J | .025 |
| 17A1, 17A2, 17A3, A1, AA1, AA1A | J-6J | .025 |
| A2, AA2, AA4, AA6, AA10 | J-6J | .025 |
| **OLIVER** | | |
| Challenger: J, J-2 (5.5 h.p.) | J-8J | .030 |
| Challenger: J-3, J-4, J-5, J-6 (6 h.p.) | J-8J | .030 |
| Commander: K, K-2 (15 h.p.) | H-8J | .030 |

| MODEL | Spark Plug | Plug Gap |
|---|---|---|
| Commander: K-3, K-4, K-5, K-6 (16 h.p.) | H-8J | .030 |
| B, B-2, B-3 (35 h.p.) | D-9J | .030 |
| **OTASCO** | | |
| 1970-74 5, 7, 7.5, 9.9, 15 h.p. | J-13Y | .035 |
| 1969 7 h.p. | J-13Y | .035 |
| 1969 3.5, 5 h.p. | J-8J | .035 |
| 1968 5, 7 h.p. | J-8J | .035 |
| **OTTERBINE** | | |
| Jet Drive (2 h.p.) (B&S Eng.) | CJ-8 | .025 |
| **OUTBOARD JET** | | |
| J55, J55B (5.5 h.p.) | J-6J | .030 |
| **PEERLESS** | | |
| J-5 | TJ-8J | .030 |
| J-9 | J-12J | .030 |
| **PENTA** | | |
| (SEE ARCHIMEDES-PENTA) | | |
| **PERKINS** | | |
| 1962-65 4.5, 6.5 h.p. | J-8J | .028 |
| 1962-65 18 h.p. | H-8J | .028 |
| 1962-65 30, 40 h.p. | L-86 | .035 |
| 1961 35 h.p. (14mm Heads) | L-86 | .035 |
| 1959-61 6 h.p. | J-8J | .028 |
| 1959-61 16 h.p. | H-8J | .028 |
| 1959-61 40 h.p. | L-86 | .035 |
| 1959-60 35 h.p. (18mm Heads) | D-9J | .035 |
| **RILEY** | | |
| 75 h.p., Four Cycle, 5 Cylinder Radial | J-6 | .025 |
| **SCOTT (McCulloch)** | | |
| 1962-63 Flying Scott (75 h.p.) | UJ-17V | ...... |
| 1962-63 Royal Scott (Electric) (45 h.p.) | UJ-17V | ...... |
| 1962-63 Royal Scott (Manual) (45 h.p.) | J-4J | .035 |
| 1962-63 Sports Scott (28 h.p.) | J-6J | .035 |
| 1962-63 Fleet Scott, Power Scott (14 h.p.) | J-6J | .035 |
| 1962-63 Fishing Scott (7.5 h.p.) | H-10J | .035 |
| 1961-62 Scotty (3.5 h.p.) | H-10J | .035 |
| 1961 75.2 h.p. Custom | UJ-17V | ...... |
| 1961 43.7, 75.2 h.p. | J-4J | .035 |
| 1961 27.7, 14.1 h.p. | J-6J | .035 |
| 1961 7.6 h.p. | H-10J | .035 |
| 1959-60 12, 25, 40, 60 h.p. | J-6J | .035 |

275

| MODEL | Spark Plug | Plug Gap |
|---|---|---|
| 1959-60 3.6, 6, 7.5, 10 h.p. | H-10J | .035 |
| **SCOTT-ATWATER** | | |
| 1958    22-25, 40, 60 h.p. | J-6J | .035 |
| 1953-58 10 h.p. | H-10J | .035 |
| 1956    33 h.p. | J-6J | .030 |
| 1955    30 h.p. | J-6J | .030 |
| 1950-52 10 h.p. | CJ-8 | .035 |
| All 3.6, 4, 5, 7.5 h.p. | H-10J | .035 |
| All 16 h.p. | D-9J | .035 |
| **SEA-BEE (Goodyear)** | | |
| 1960    All models | J-6J/J-4J | .030 |
| 1946-59 All models | J-7J | .030 |
| **SEACO** | | |
| 1973-74 4.5, 7.5, 9.9, 15 h.p. | J-13Y | .035 |
| **SEA-DOO** | | |
| Jet-Powered Aqua Scooter w/Rotax Engine | K-9 | .025 |
| **SEAGULL** | | |
| (SEE BRITISH SEAGULL) | | |
| **SEA-KING (Montgomery Ward)** | | |
| 1975    35, 55 h.p. | L-4J | .030 |
| 1974-75 10, 15, 25 h.p. | L-4J | .030 |
| 1972-75 6 h.p. | L-4J | .030 |
| 1968-74 9.6, 20, 35, 55 h.p. | L-4J | .030 |
| 1967-71 6 h.p. | H-10J | .030 |
| 1964-70 3.5, 5.8 h.p. | H-8J | .030 |
| 1969    5 h.p. | J-8J | .035 |
| 1969    7 h.p. | J-13Y | .035 |
| 1966-69 9.2 h.p. | J-4J | .030 |
| 1964-67 20-80 h.p. | J-4J | .030 |
| 1964-65 9 h.p. | H-8J | .030 |
| All 1.5-25 h.p. models | J-6J/J-4J | .030 |
| All 35-60 h.p. models | J-4J | .030 |
| **SEARS** | | |
| 2.0 h.p. 58241, 58250 | J-11J | .030 |
| 3.0 h.p. 58540, 58541, 58543, 58544 | J-13Y | .035 |
| 3.5 h.p. 6091 to 1965 | TJ-8J | .030 |
| 3.5 h.p. 6091 from 1966 | CJ-8 | .030 |
| 3.5 h.p. 6094, 59501, 59900 | CJ-8 | .030 |

| MODEL | Spark Plug | Plug Gap |
|---|---|---|
| 3.5 h.p. 60020, 60030, 6003 | H-10J | .030 |
| 3.5 h.p. 59860, 59861, 58510, 58511 | J-8J | .035 |
| 3.5 h.p. 58560, 58542, 58550, 59862 | J-13Y | .035 |
| 3.6 h.p. 58512, 58513 | J-8J | .035 |
| 3.6 h.p. 58514 | J-13Y | .035 |
| 3.6 h.p. 6001, 60000 | H-10J | .030 |
| 4.0 h.p. 58580 | J-13Y | .035 |
| 4.5 h.p. 59460, 59461, 59462, 59463, 59564 | J-13Y | .035 |
| 4.8 h.p. 58970, 58971 | J-13Y | .035 |
| 5.0 h.p. 58520, 58521, 58610, 58620 | J-13Y | .030 |
| 5.0 h.p. 58962, 58990, 58991, 58992, 59310 | J-13Y | .035 |
| 5.0 h.p. 59311, 59673, 59680 | J-13Y | .035 |
| 5.0 h.p. 59670, 59671, 59672 | J-8J | .035 |
| 5.0 h.p. 59520, 58960, 58961 | J-8J | .035 |
| 5.5 h.p. 59430, 59431, 59432, 59433 | J-13Y | .035 |
| 6.0 h.p. 6004, 6005, 60060 | H-10J | .030 |
| 7.0 h.p. 58830, 58531, 58532 | J-13Y | .035 |
| 7.0 h.p. 58870, 59440, 59480 | J-13Y | .030 |
| 7.0 h.p. 58530 | J-13Y | .035 |
| 7.5 h.p. 6008, 6010, 6012 | H-10J | .030 |
| 7.5 h.p. 60070, 60090, 60100 | H-10J | .030 |
| 7.5 h.p. 58820, 58880, 59450 | J-13Y | .035 |
| 7.5 h.p. 58821, 58881, 58890, 58882 | J-13Y | .035 |
| 7.5 h.p. 58850, 59491 | J-13Y | .035 |
| 9.9 h.p. 58710, 58711 | J-13Y | .035 |
| 10.5 h.p. 58720, 58721 | J-13Y | .035 |
| 12.0 h.p. 5927 | H-8J | .030 |
| 14.0 h.p. 6015 | J-6J | .030 |
| 14.1 h.p. 6013, 60140, 60150 | J-6J | .030 |
| 15.0 h.p. 58760, 58761 | J-13Y | .035 |
| 27.7 h.p. 6033, 6035 | J-6J | .030 |
| 28.0 h.p. 60370, 60380 | J-4J | .030 |
| 28.0 h.p. 6037, 6038, 60340, 60360 | J-6J | .030 |
| 35.0 h.p. 5941 | J-4J | .030 |
| 43.7 h.p. 6044, 6045, 6050, 6051 | J-6J | .030 |
| 45.0 h.p. 6056, 6057, 6058 | J-4J | .030 |
| 45.0 h.p. 60540, 60550 | J-4J | .030 |
| 75.0 h.p. 6078, 60740, 60750 | J-4J | .030 |
| 75.2 h.p. 6070, 6071 | J-6J | .030 |
| 75.2 h.p. 6076, 6077 | J-4J | .030 |
| **SPRITE** | | |
| J-5 | TJ-8J | .030 |

277

| MODEL | Spark Plug | Plug Gap |
|---|---|---|
| **SUZUKI** | | |
| DT300 (16 h.p.) | L-81 | .020 |
| D100, DT100 | L-86 | .025 |
| **TAS** | | |
| T0B-12 | CJ-8 | .025 |
| **TERRY TROLLER** | | |
| T4T | J-8J | .025 |
| T5T | H-10 | .025 |
| **TOMOS** | | |
| 4, 5 (5 h.p.) | L-85 | .025 |
| **TRITON** | | |
| 4, 5.5, 7.5 h.p. | J-13Y | .030 |
| **VIKING** | | |
| 1968-71 9.6, 20, 35, 55 h.p. | L-4J | .030 |
| 1965-71 3.5, 15 h.p. | H-8J | .030 |
| 1965-71 6 h.p. | H-10J | .030 |
| 1966-70 9.2 h.p. | J-4J | .030 |
| Thru 1967 20, 35, 50 h.p. | J-4J | .030 |
| Thru 1965 All models except 9 h.p. | J-8J | .025 |
| 1965 9 h.p. | H-8J | .030 |
| **VOLVO-PENTA** | | |
| Aquamatic BB70 - Low Speed | J-6/J-6J | .028 |
| Aquamatic BB70 - Sustained High Speed | J-4J | .028 |
| Aquamatic 100 | L-5 | .028 |
| **VOYAGER** | | |
| 1VA, 2VA, 1VB, V2L, V4GS, V2LL, 2N | UD-16/D-16 | .030 |
| V3LGS, V3NGS, V4NGS, V3LLGS, V4LLGS | J-7J | .030 |
| V6LLGS, V6NGS | J-8J | .030 |
| **WARDS** | | |
| (See "Sea-King") | | |
| **WEST BEND** | | |
| 1964-65 35, 50 h.p. | J-4J | .030 |
| 1963-65 6 h.p. | H-10J | .030 |
| 1962-65 3.5, 9, 10 h.p. | H-8J | .030 |
| 1961-65 20, 45, 80 h.p. | J-4J | .030 |
| 1958-63 12 h.p. | H-8J | .030 |
| 1956-63 7.5, 25, 30 h.p. | H-8J | .030 |
| 1961-62 40 h.p. | J-4J | .030 |

| MODEL | Spark Plug | Plug Gap |
|-------|-----------|----------|
| 1960-62 18 h.p. | J-4J | .030 |
| 1961 6 h.p. | H-8J | .030 |
| 1959-61 2 h.p. | H-10J | .030 |
| 1958-60 8, 16, 35, 40 h.p. | H-8J | .030 |
| 1957-59 6 h.p. | H-10J | .030 |
| 1956-58 2 h.p. | J-11J | .050 |
| 1957 8 h.p. | H-8J | .035 |
| 1956-57 12 h.p. | H-8J | .025 |
| 1956 5.5 h.p. | H-10J | .035 |
| 1955 5 h.p. | J-12J | .050 |
| 1955 7.5 h.p. | J-11J | .050 |

**WESTERN AUTO**
(SEE WIZARD)

**WHITE AUTO STORES (Seahawk)**

| | | |
|-------|-----------|----------|
| 1972-74 5, 7, 7.5, 9.9, 15 h.p. | J-13Y | .035 |

**WIZARD**

| | | |
|-------|-----------|----------|
| 1970-74 3.5, 5, 7, 7.5, 9.9 h.p. | J-13Y | .035 |
| 1968-71 20 h.p. | L-4J | .030 |
| 1966-71 9.2 h.p. | J-4J | .030 |
| 1965-69 3.5 h.p. | H-8J | .030 |
| 1965-71 6 h.p. | H-10J | .030 |
| 1969 7 h.p. | J-13Y | .035 |
| 1969 5 h.p. | J-8J | .035 |
| 1965-67 20 h.p. | J-4J | .030 |
| 1965 9 h.p. | H-8J | .030 |
| 1959-64 3.5, 6, 7.5, 10 h.p. | H-10J | .035 |
| 1959-64 12, 14, 25 | J-6J | .035 |
| 1959-64 40, 60 h.p. | J-4J | .035 |
| WD3, WD3S, (3.2 h.p.), WF4, WG4 (6 h.p.) | J-8J | .025 |
| WF7, WG7, WH7, WG7A, WJ7 (10 h.p.) | J-8J | .025 |
| WD4, WD4S (6 h.p.), WH6, WH6-1 (5 h.p.) | J-7J | .025 |
| WK7, WM7, WM7A (10 h.p.) | J-7J | .025 |
| WN7, WN7A (12 h.p.), WH6A (5 h.p.) | J-6J | .025 |
| WA25, WA25E (25 h.p.) | J-6J | .025 |
| OC575, OC585 (5.5 h.p.) | J-8J | .030 |
| OC1575, OC1585 (15 h.p.) | H-8J | .030 |
| OC 3585 (35 h.p.) | D-9J | 0.30 |

**YAMAHA**

| | | |
|-------|-----------|----------|
| Model P-95 | L-81 | .025 |
| All other models | L-86 | .025 |

279

| MODEL | Spark Plug | Plug Gap |
|-------|-----------|----------|
| **ZUNDAPP** | | |
| 5 h.p. .................................................................................................. | L-85 | .025 |

Table 2 provided by the *Champion Spark Plug Company* lists the spark-plug types and gap openings for plugs used in most inboard motors of recent manufacture.

### Table 2. Type of Champion Spark Plug and Gap for Various Inboard Motors

| MODEL | Spark Plug | Plug Gap |
|-------|-----------|----------|
| **AEROJET** | | |
| All Models .......................................................... | J-6/UJ-6 | .025 |
| **AERO MARINE** | | |
| 1971-On 265, 320 Series ................................ | RBL-8 | .032 |
| 1970-71 375 Series ........................................ | RBL-8 | .032 |
| 1969-70 265 Series ........................................ | J-6/RJ-6 | .032 |
| 1966-70 320, 350, 375 Series ...................... | N-6/RN-6 | .032 |
| 427 Jet, 454 Series ........................................ | RBL-8 | .032 |
| 455 Series ...................................................... | J-6/RJ-6 | .032 |
| 304, 360 Jet .................................................. | N-9Y | .032 |
| 482 Series ...................................................... | RN-9Y | .032 |
| **AMECO** | | |
| 302, 351W Ford Engines .............................. | F-10 | .030 |
| **AMERICAN CHALLENGER** | | |
| Eagle 400, 600, 800 .................................... | BL-13Y | .020 |
| **BARR (Conversions)** | | |
| **BUICK ENGINES:** | | |
| 1971-74 455 cu.in. ........................................ | RBL-12 | .035 |
| 1970 455 cu. in ............................................ | RBL-8 | .030 |
| 1967-69 400, 430 cu.in. ................................ | RBL-8 | .030 |
| **CHEVROLET ENGINES:** | | |
| **6-Cyl. Engines:** | | |
| 1970-74 250 cu.in. ........................................ | RBL-12 | .035 |
| 1970-74 292 cu. in ........................................ | RBL-8 | .035 |

| MODEL | Spark Plug | Gap Plug |
|---|---|---|
| 1970    230 cu.in. | RBL-8 | .035 |
| 1963-69 292 cu.in. | RN-6 | .035 |
| 1962-69 194, 230, 250 cu.in. | RN-12Y | .035 |
| **V-8 Engines:** | | |
| 1971-74 350, 400 cu.in. | RBL-8 | .035 |
| 1971-73 307 cu.in. | RBL-12 | .035 |
| 1971-72 427 cu.in. | BL-7Y | .035 |
| 1970    400 cu.in. | RJ-12Y | .035 |
| 1970    350 cu.in. (4-bbl.) | RJ-10Y | .035 |
| 1967-70 350 cu.in. (2-bbl.) | RJ-12Y | .030 |
| 1968-70 307 cu.in. | RJ-12Y | .035 |
| 1967-69 302 cu.in. | RJ-10Y | .035 |
| 1961-69 327 cu.in. | RJ-6 | .035 |
| 1955-67 283 cu.in. | RJ-12Y | .035 |
| **CHRYSLER ENGINES:** | | |
| 1972-74 440 cu.in. | J-11Y | .035 |
| 1968-71 383 cu.in. (4-bbl.) | J-11Y | .035 |
| 1966-71 440 cu.in. (350 h.p.) | J-13Y | .035 |
| 1966-71 440 cu.in. (375 h.p.) | J-11Y | .035 |
| 1960-71 383 cu.in. (2-bbl.) | J-14Y | .035 |
| 1966-67 383 cu.in. Hi-Perf. | J-11Y | .035 |
| 1963-65 413 cu.in. | J-14Y | .035 |
| 1963-65 413 cu.in. Hi-Perf. | J-11Y | .035 |
| 1963-64 413 cu. in. (Two 4-bbl.) | RJ-11Y | .035 |
| **OLDSMOBILE ENGINES:** | | |
| 1972-74 455 cu.in. Hi.-Perf. | RJ-12Y | .040 |
| 1971-74 350 cu.in. | RJ-12Y | .040 |
| 1972-74 455 cu.in. (4-bbl.) | RJ-18Y | .040 |
| 1971    455 cu.in. (4-bbl.) | RJ-12Y | .040 |
| 1971    455 cu.in. (2-bbl.) | RJ-18Y | .040 |
| 1970    455 cu.in. (4-bbl.) | RJ-12Y | .030 |
| 1968-70 350 cu.in. (4-bbl.) | RJ-10Y | .030 |
| 1968-70 350, 455 cu.in. (2-bbl.) | RJ-12Y | .030 |
| **PONTIAC ENGINES:** | | |
| 1972-74 400, 455 cu.in. | RBL-12 | .040 |
| 1971    455 cu.in. (2-bbl.) | RJ-18Y | .035 |
| 1970-71 455 cu. in. (4 bbl.) | RJ-12Y | .035 |
| 1967-71 400 cu.in. | RJ-12Y | .035 |
| 1967-69 428 cu.in. | RJ-10Y | .035 |
| 1960-67 389 cu.in. | RJ-12Y | .035 |
| 1963-66 421 cu.in. | RJ-10Y | .035 |

ELECTRICAL SYSTEMS

| MODEL | Spark Plug | Plug Gap |
|---|---|---|
| **B & W** | | |
| LH4, LH6, LH Deluxe, 45 | W-14 | .025 |
| LH Super, LH Super Special | J-6/UJ-6 | .025 |
| LH Master, LH Dual Ignition | J-6/UJ-6 | .025 |
| Standard Models | W-18 | .025 |
| Mystic, Engineer Models | W-14 | .025 |
| B&W Series: 30, 35, 60, 105 | J-6J | .025 |
| B&W Series: 135, 155, 165 | J-6J | .025 |
| **BRENNAN** | | |
| 100, 125, with 7/8" Heads | W-14 | .025 |
| 100, 125 with 18mm Heads | UD-16/D-16 | .025 |
| CE, B70, E4, EE4, M4, N4 | UD-16/D-16 | .025 |
| 90, 150, 175, B100 | UD-16/D-16 | .025 |
| NEO, 60, 70, 75, 100R | W-14 | .025 |
| Light Six, Fisherman | W-14 | .025 |
| Kid | J-8/J-8J | .025 |
| Imp | H-10/H-10J | .025 |
| Imp II, Junior, Frontenac | J-7/J-7J | .025 |
| Gold Cup, Master 6, E-4 | J-7/J-7J | .025 |
| **BUCHANAN (Canada)** | | |
| 1955-66 Junior 4A, 4B (14mm Heads) | J-8J | .028 |
| 1955-63 Rocket K, Meteor KL | J-8J | .028 |
| 1950-55 Comet | J-6 | .025 |
| 1937-55 Meteor | J-8 | .025 |
| 1932-55 Junior Four (18mm Heads) | D-16 | .025 |
| 1936-41 Rocket | J-8 | .025 |
| Comet M, Comet ML, Sabre MCL, Jupiter | J-8J | .028 |
| Model 110 | N-6 | .035 |
| Models 185, 283, 327 | UJ-6 | .028 |
| Models 430, 431 | F-9Y | .035 |
| **BUEHLER** | | |
| Jetstream using Chrysler 273, 428 cu.in. | RN-6 | .035 |
| Jetstream using Chrysler 318 cu.in. | XJ-10Y | .035 |
| **CASTOLDI** | | |
| 1974 2261E | N-8 | .035 |
| 1974 2264E | N-9Y | .035 |
| 1974 1966cc. (113 h.p.) | RF-9Y | .035 |
| 1974 2614E | RN-9Y | .025 |

282

| MODEL | Spark Plug | Plug Gap |
|---|---|---|
| **CHEVROLET** | | |
| **MOR MARINE CONVERSIONS:** | | |
| **6-Cylinder Engines** | | |
| 1970-74 250 cu. in. | RBL-12 | .035 |
| 1970-74 252 cu.in. | RBL-8 | .035 |
| 1970 230 cu. in. | RBL-8 | .030 |
| 1963-69 292 cu.in. | RN-6 | .035 |
| 1962-69 194, 230, 250 cu.in. | RN-12Y | .035 |
| **V-8 Engines** | | |
| 1971-74 350, 400 cu.in. | RBL-8 | .035 |
| 1971-73 307 cu.in. | RBL-12 | .035 |
| 1971-72 427 cu.in. | BL-7Y | .035 |
| 1970 400 cu.in. | RJ-12Y | .035 |
| 1970 350 cu.in. (4-bbl.) | RJ-10Y | .035 |
| 1967-70 350 cu.in. (2-bbl.) | RJ-12Y | .030 |
| 1968-70 307 cu.in. | RJ-12Y | .035 |
| 1967-69 302 cu.in. | RJ-10Y | .035 |
| 1961-69 327 cu.in. | RJ-6 | .035 |
| 1955-67 283 cu.in. | RJ-12Y | .035 |
| **CHRIS-CRAFT** | | |
| A, B, BA, C, H, K, KB w/Regular Hds. | UJ-6/J-8J | .028 |
| A, B, BA, C, H, K, KB w/Alum. Hds. | H-10/H-10J | .028 |
| KBL, KC, KFL, KL, KLC w/Regular Hds. | UJ-6/J-8J | .028 |
| KBL, KC, KFL, KL, KLC w/Alum. Hds. | H-10/H-10J | .028 |
| LC, LD, M, MB, MBL w/Regular Hds. | UJ-6/J-8J | .028 |
| LC, LD, M, MB, MBL w/Alum. Hds. | H-10/H-10J | .028 |
| MC, MCL, ML, W, WB w/Regular Hds. | UJ-6/J-8J | .028 |
| MC, MCL, ML, W, WB w/Alum. Hds. | H-10/H-10J | .028 |
| 181 thru Ser. No. 603191, 153 | RN-5 | .035 |
| 181 from Ser. No. 603192 | RBL-9Y | .035 |
| 225 Series | J-10Y | .035 |
| 283, 302, 307, 327 Series w/gasket Hds. | UJ-6 | .025 |
| 307, 350, 454 Series w/Tapered seats | RBL-9Y | .035 |
| 350 Hi-Perf. | RBL-8 | .035 |
| 427, 431 Series | F-10Y | .030 |
| 430 Series | F-9Y | .030 |
| **CHRYSLER** | | |
| **4-Cylinder Engines:** | | |
| M91D, M91F | N-9Y | .035 |
| M122A | L-5 | .035 |

| MODEL | Spark Plug | Plug Gap |
|---|---|---|
| **CHRYSLER—Continued** | | |
| **6-Cylinder Engines:** | | |
| 1975 M225B | RBL-9Y | .035 |
| Thru 1974 M225B | RN-6 | .035 |
| M46-3, M46S-3, M46-4 | RJ-7 | .035 |
| M47-3, M47S-3, M47-4 | RJ-7 | .035 |
| M265, M265A | RJ-7 | .035 |
| M170 | RN-6 | .035 |
| M225A, M225GD, MH225D | RN-6 | .035 |
| M183B | L-5 | .035 |
| **V-8 Engines:** | | |
| M44, M44-3 | RJ-7 | .035 |
| M45, M45S, M45-3, M45S-3, M45SP-3 | RN-6 | .035 |
| M81, M413E | RN-6 | .035 |
| M273A, M273B | RN-9Y | .035 |
| LM318B, LM318BT, LM318D | RN-9Y | .035 |
| LM340B, LM340BV, LM340BT, LM360BT | RN-9Y | .035 |
| M80, M318A, M318B, M318C, M318GD | XJ-10Y | .035 |
| M383B, M400B | XJ-10Y | .035 |
| M413B, M413D | XJ-10Y | .035 |
| M426B, M426D | XJ-10Y | .035 |
| M440B, M440BV, M440D, M440S, M440SV | XJ-10Y | .035 |
| **CHRYSLER VOLVO** | | |
| 110, 115, 120, 130, 165, 170 | L-5 | .028 |
| **CLIMAX** | | |
| 98 cu.in. | RN-9Y | .030 |
| 302, 351 cu.in. | F-10 | .030 |
| 460 cu.in. | RF-11Y | .030 |
| **CROFTON** | | |
| 1959-On 53 V-drive, 53 V.I.P. | J-6J | .025 |
| **CRUSADER** | | |
| 1974-75 307 cu.in. | RBL-8 | .035 |
| 1974-75 454 cu.in. | RBL-8 | .035 |
| 1971-75 292, 350 cu.in. | RBL-8 | .035 |
| 1971-73 307 cu.in. | RBL-12 | .035 |
| 1971-72 427 cu.in. | BL-7Y | .035 |
| Mark: 140, 170, 200, 225 | UJ-6 | .025 |
| Models: 170J, 185, 200J, 210, 230, 230J | UJ-6 | .025 |
| Mark: 275, 300, 325 | J-4J | .032 |

| MODEL | Spark Plug | Plug Gap |
|-------|------------|----------|
| **CRUSADER—Continued** | | |
| Mark 240 Model 280 | N-6 | .032 |
| CS 100, 150, 165, 280 | N-6 | .032 |
| CS 180, 220, 250 CM Cadillac | UJ-6 | .032 |
| CS 320 | N-5 | .032 |
| **DAYTONA** | | |
| Models 100, 150 | N-6 | .035 |
| Models 200, 300 | UJ-6 | .035 |
| Models 400, 400 Turbo | N-4 | .035 |
| Models 427, 427 Turbo (Heavy Service) | N-3 | .035 |
| Models 427, 427 Turbo (Light Service) | N-4 | .035 |
| **DEARBORN** | | |
| (SEE INTERCEPTOR) | | |
| **DETLOFF** | | |
| Model M | RJ-10Y | .035 |
| **EATON** | | |
| (SEE INTERCEPTOR) | | |
| **ECON-O-POWER** | | |
| (SEE LEHMAN) | | |
| **EMPEROR** | | |
| 4-15, 4-25, 4-55, 4-70 | J-8/UJ-8 | .025 |
| 6-70, 6-90, 6-95, 6-145 | J-8/UJ-8 | .025 |
| 4-40, 4-50, 4-60, 6-125 | W-14 | .025 |
| V-8: 215, 235, 280, 300, 315, 345 cu.in. | J-10Y | .035 |
| Buick 300 & V-6 | UJ-6 | .035 |
| Chevrolet 283, 327, 409 cu.in. | UJ-6 | .035 |
| Chrysler 6-cyl., 170 cu.in. | N-14Y | .035 |
| Ford Engines (18mm) | F-9Y | .035 |
| Jeep Engines | J-8/UJ-8 | .030 |
| **ESCORT** | | |
| (SEE FORD MARINE ENGINES) | | |
| **EVINRUDE** | | |
| DU Series | J-4J | .030 |
| CU, SU Series | N-6 | .035 |
| HU Series | J-10Y | .035 |
| KU Series | J-6 | .035 |
| NU Series | N-9Y | .025 |
| TU-14, TU-15, TU-16 | J-10Y | .035 |
| TU-17 and up | J-6 | .035 |

285

| MODEL | Spark Plug | Plug Gap |
|-------|-----------|----------|
| **FLAGSHIP** | | |
| 1971-72  292  cu.in. | RBL-11Y | .035 |
| 1971-72  307, 350 cu.in. | RBL-9Y | .035 |
| 1971-72  427, 454 cu.in. | RBL-7Y | .035 |
| 66, 96 | J-11/J-11J | .030 |
| 136 | J-11/J-11J | .035 |
| 85, 90, 100, 118 | UJ-6/J-6 | .030 |
| 145, 150, 185, 190, 220, 225 | UJ-6/J-6 | .035 |
| 240, 250, 283, 310, 327, 350M | UJ-6/J-6 | .035 |
| Model 300 (427 cu.in.) | N-4 | .035 |
| Model 155 (292 cu.in.) | N-6 | .035 |
| **FORD** | | |
| 1975      302, 351W, 460 cu.in. | RBL-11Y | .035 |
| 1975      534 cu.in. | RF-10 | .030 |
| Thru 1974 302, 351W, 427, 534 cu. in. | RF-10 | .030 |
| 460, 429 cu. in. | RBL-13Y | .035 |
| **GOFF** | | |
| 1973      GMP  455 | RJ-18Y | .040 |
| 1969-73 GMP  225 | J-12Y | .035 |
| 1971-72 GMP  455 | RJ-12Y | .040 |
| 1961-70 GMP  455 | RJ-10Y | .030 |
| **GRAYMARINE** | | |
| **Lugger Series** | | |
| Four 69, Seascout 91, Seascout 45 | J-11J | .035 |
| Four 22, 52, 112 | UD-16/D-16 | .025 |
| Four 40, 75, 80, 85TD, 140, 162 | D-14 | .025 |
| Six 51, 121, 186, 226, 330 | D-16 | .025 |
| Six 91, 244 | D-14 | .025 |
| Six 71, 77 | D-9/D-9J | .025 |
| **Express Series** | | |
| Four 140, 162 | D-9/D-9J | .025 |
| Four 52, 112 | D-14 | .025 |
| Six 121, 186; Super 117, Super 427 | D-9/D-9J | .025 |
| Six 71, 77, 80, 111, 427 | D-14 | .025 |
| Six 91, 224 | D-6 | .025 |
| Sea Scout 91 | J-11J | .035 |
| **Phantom Series** | | |
| Four 45 | J-7/J-7J | .025 |
| Four 62 | D-9/D-9J | .025 |

| MODEL | Spark Plug | Plug Gap |
|-------|------------|----------|
| **GRAYMARINE (Phantom Series)—Continued** | | |
| Four 75, 85, 86, 162 | D-14 | .025 |
| Six 88, 90, 103, 104, 112, 125 | D-9/D-9J | .025 |
| Six 115, 135, 200 | D-6 | .025 |
| Six 70, 80, 100, 109, 109TD 110, 116, 118 | D-14 | .025 |
| Six 120, 122, 135, 136, 150, 165, 175 | D-14 | .025 |
| Six 185, 205, 620, 750 | D-14 | .025 |
| **Fireball Series** | | |
| Four 50 | J-8/J-8J | .025 |
| Four 90 | D-14 | .025 |
| Six 140, 160 | D-10 | .020 |
| Six 116, 150, Super 330 | D-9J | .020 |
| Six 116, 150 for hi-speed use | K-60R | .020 |
| V-8 Models C, CF, CH, 135, 138, 138A | UJ-6 | .025 |
| V-8 Models 170, 175, 178, 178B, 188 | UJ-6 | .025 |
| V-8 Models 195, 215, 220, 225, 238 | UJ-6 | .025 |
| V-8 Models 260, 280, 310, 427 | UJ-6 | .025 |
| V-8 Models 304, 360 | N-12Y | .025 |
| Misc. & Racing: FB-244MS | XMJ-14 | .025 |
| Misc. & Racing: FB-455 | J-12Y | .030 |
| Racing 91 | J-2J/J-57R | .020 |
| Racing 225, 244 | K-54R | .020 |
| Misc: Six 136, 160 | L-85/L-12Y | .025 |
| Six 232, Stern Drive & Reverse gear | N-9Y | .025 |
| Rolls Royce engine | N-5 | .025 |
| **HALL SCOTT** | | |
| All models | D-16 | .020 |
| **HAMILTON TURBO-PAC** | | |
| (SEE FORD MARINE ENGINES) | | |
| **HARBOR MASTER** | | |
| (SEE MURRAY & TREGURTHA) | | |
| **INTERCEPTOR** | | |
| V-4 104, V-6 122 | UL-82Y | .030 |
| 144, 170 Side draft carb. Normal operation | F-11Y | .030 |
| 144, 170 Side draft carb. Cont. hi-speed | F-9Y | .030 |
| 170 Down Draft carb. | F-10 | .030 |
| 200, 256, 272, 289, 292, 312, 352 | F-10 | .030 |
| 221, 427 (330 h.p.) | F-82 | .030 |
| 260 | F-83Y | .030 |
| 390, 302 | F-9Y | .030 |

| MODEL | Spark Plug | Plug Gap |
|---|---|---|
| **INTERCEPTOR—Continued** | | |
| 427 (300 h.p.) Normal Operation | F-10 | .030 |
| 427 (300 h.p.) Cont. hi-speed | F-82 | .030 |
| 427 (400 h.p.) Normal Operation | F-9Y | .030 |
| 427 (400 h.p.) Cont. hi-speed | F-82 | .030 |
| **INTERNATIONAL** | | |
| (SEE PALMER-GREENWICH) | | |
| **JOHNSON** | | |
| DU Series | J-4J | .030 |
| CU, SU Series | N-6 | .035 |
| HU Series | J-10Y | .035 |
| KU Series | UJ-6 | .035 |
| NU Series | N-9Y | .025 |
| TU: -14, -15, -16 | J-10Y | .035 |
| TU: -17 & up | J-6 | .035 |
| **KERMATH** | | |
| Sea Pup, Sea Twin | J-11 | .025 |
| **KING** | | |
| 1973    454 cu.in., 450 h.p. | RBL-8 | .035 |
| 1972-73 455 cu.in., 410 h.p. | RJ-10Y | .035 |
| 1972-73 455 cu.in., 325 h.p. | RJ-12Y | .040 |
| 1971-73 455 cu.in., 270 h.p. | RJ-18Y | .040 |
| 1971-73 350 cu.in., 240 h.p. | RJ-12Y | .040 |
| **KOHLER** | | |
| Model L-160 | J-8/UJ-8 | .025 |
| **LATHROP** | | |
| (SEE B&W) | | |
| **LEHMAN ECON-O-POWER** | | |
| **FORD ENGINE CONVERSIONS:** | | |
| **6-Cylinder Engines** | | |
| 1972-73 155 (Capri) | RN-9Y | .035 |
| 1960-73 300, 250, 240, 200 cu.in. | RF-12 | .035 |
| 1960-73 170 | RF-12 | .035 |
| **V-8 Engines** | | |
| 1970-73 460, 429, 351 CID, 14mm | RBL-13Y | .035 |
| 1968-73 460, 429, 351, 302 CID, 18mm | RF-12 | .035 |
| 1969-71 302 CID, 14mm | RBL-7Y | .035 |

| MODEL | Spark Plug | Plug Gap |
|---|---|---|
| **LEHMAN ECON-O-POWER (Ford Engine Conversions)—Continued** | | |
| 1963-68 289, 260 CID | RF-12 | .035 |
| 1958-68 428, 427, 410, 390 CID | RF-12 | .035 |
| 1956-62 312 292 CID | 870 | .035 |
| 1954 256 CID | H-10 | .035 |
| **CHEVROLET ENGINE CONVERSIONS** | | |
| 1971-73 400 CID | RBL-8 | .035 |
| 1971-73 350, 307 CID | RBL-12 | .035 |
| 1957-70 400, 350, 327, 307, 283 CID | RJ-6 | .035 |
| **MARINE DRIVES SYSTEMS (MDS)** | | |
| Stern Drive Models 85, 110 | UL-82Y | .025 |
| **MERCRUISER** | | |
| **Stern Drive Engines:** | | |
| 60 | L-85 | .025 |
| 80 | N-9Y | .025 |
| 90 | RN-9Y | .032 |
| 110, 140-6, 150, 160, 200 | RN-6 | .035 |
| 120 thru Ser. No. 3825578 | RN-6 | .035 |
| 120 from Ser. No. 3825579 on | RBL-8 | .035 |
| 140-4 thru Ser. No. 3826282 | RN-6 | .035 |
| 140-4 from Ser. No. 3826283 on | RBL-8 | .035 |
| 165 thru Ser. No. 2771483 | RN-6 | .035 |
| 165 from Ser. No. 2771484 on | RBL-8 | .035 |
| 215, 255, 888 | F-10 | .030 |
| 190 | RJ-6 | .035 |
| 225 thru Ser. No. 3385720 | RJ-6 | .035 |
| 255 from Ser. No. 3385721 on | F-10 | .030 |
| 250 | J-19V | ...... |
| 250 Shielded | RMJ-3 | .035 |
| 255 thru Ser. No. 4175499 | F-10 | .030 |
| 255 from Ser. No. 4175500 on | RBL-11Y | .035 |
| 270 thru Ser. No. 2959703 | J-19V | ...... |
| 270 thru Ser. No. 2959703 Shielded | RMJ-3 | .035 |
| 270 from Ser. No. 3077736 on | RBL-8 | .035 |
| 280 (Jet), 400 (Jet) | RBL-8 | .035 |
| 310 | N-3 | .035 |
| 325 thru Ser. No. 2761141 | N-19V | ...... |
| 325 from Ser. No. 3043030 on | BL-3 | .035 |
| 475, Typhoon KT, Tempest | BL-21V | ...... |

| MODEL | Spark Plug | Plug Gap |
|---|---|---|
| **MERCRUISER—Continued** | | |
| **Inboard Engines:** | | |
| 30, 55 | L-85 | .025 |
| 215, 255 | F-10 | .030 |
| 255 thru Ser. No. 3415950 | J-19V | ...... |
| 225 from Ser. No. 3415950 Shielded | RMJ-3 | .035 |
| 225 from Ser. No. 3515951 on | F-10 | .030 |
| 250 | J-19V | ...... |
| 255 thru Ser. No. 4178299 | F-10 | .030 |
| 255 from Ser. No. 4178300 on | RBL-11Y | .035 |
| 270 thru Ser. No. 2904164 | J-19V | ...... |
| 270 thru Ser. No. 2904164 Shielded | RMJ-3 | .035 |
| 270 Ser. Nos. 3077336 to 3077495 | RBL-8 | .035 |
| 270 Ser. Nos. 3077496 to 3077735 | J-19V | ...... |
| 270 Ser. Nos. 3077496 to 3077735 Shielded | RMJ-3 | .035 |
| 270 from Ser. No. 3077736 on | RBL-8 | .035 |
| 325 thru Ser. No. 2762441 | J-19V | ...... |
| 325 from Ser. No. 3042731 on | BL-3 | .035 |
| 350 | BL-3 | .035 |
| 475 | BL-21V | ...... |
| **MILLER** | | |
| (SEE BARR CONVERSIONS) | | |
| **MURRAY & TREGURTHA** | | |
| 04H | J-6/J-6J | .025 |
| 041 | J-8/J-8J | .030 |
| 02, OB ⅞" Heads | W-14 | .025 |
| 02, OB 18mm Heads | D-14 | .025 |
| Other ⅞" Heads | W-18 | .025 |
| **NORDBERG** | | |
| (SEE UNIVERSAL) | | |
| **NORSEMAN** | | |
| (SEE UNIVERSAL) | | |
| **ONAN** | | |
| MCCK, MKH, MAJ | H-8/H-8J | .025 |
| MUK, MGO | J-8/UJ-8 | .025 |
| MTK | K-15J/D-14 | .025 |
| MPG | J-6/UJ-6 | .025 |
| MJB | H-8 | .025 |
| MJB Shielded models | XEH-8 | .025 |

| MODEL | Spark Plug | Plug Gap |
|---|---|---|
| **O.M.C.** | | |
| 1974      All models: Tapered seat, 18mm Hds. | RF-10 | .030 |
| 1973-74 All models: Tapered seat, 14mm Hds. | RBL-8 | .035 |
| 1973-74 All models: ¾" Reach Hds. | N-6 | .035 |
| Model 480 | J-4J | .030 |
| DU Series | J-4J | .030 |
| CU, GU, LU, SU, VU Series | N-6 | .035 |
| HU Series | J-10Y | .035 |
| KU Series | UJ-6 | .035 |
| NU Series | N-9Y | .025 |
| TU-14, -15, -16 | J-10Y | .035 |
| TU-17 & up | J-6 | .035 |
| TU-20D | RBL-8 | .035 |
| XU-20S | J-6 | .035 |
| XU-20C | RBL-8 | .035 |
| JU, WU, XU, TUFR, TUFM, TUFP | RBL-8 | .035 |
| **Inboards** | | |
| TT, TJ, AJ | J-6 | .035 |
| AT Series, ⅜" Reach Heads | J-6 | .035 |
| AT Series, ½" Tapered Seat Heads | RBL-8 | .035 |
| **OWENS** | | |
| (SEE FLAGSHIP) | | |
| **PALMER-GREENWICH** | | |
| M-60, P-60 | D-15Y | .030 |
| PA 190, PA220, PA225 | RF-10 | .032 |
| PA350 | RBL-13Y | .032 |
| M304, M345, MKIV-115, MKVI-150, Normal Serv. | UJ-6 | .030 |
| M304, M345, MKIV-115, MKVI-150, Light Serv. | UJ-8 | .030 |
| MKVIII: 200, 225, 275, 300 Normal Serv. | UJ-6 | .030 |
| MKVIII: 200, 225, 275, 300 Light Serv. | UJ-8 | .030 |
| M196, M265, M392, M549, M345B, M392B | UJ-6 | .030 |
| PW27, 18mm Heads | D-21 | .030 |
| PW27, 14mm Heads | J-10Y | .030 |
| Y304, Y345, Y392 | UJ-6 | .030 |
| PB-V-215 (V-8) | L-85 | .035 |
| P302, P351 | F-9Y | .030 |
| MKVID-110, MD188, MD301, MD301SM (Diesel) | AG-40 | ...... |
| **REVLEY** | | |
| Models R225, R300, R401 | J-10Y | .035 |

| MODEL | Spark Plug | Plug Gap |
|---|---|---|
| **ROLLS-ROYCE** | | |
| LM-841 | N-8 | .035 |
| **SEAMASTER** | | |
| 300, 534 | F-10 | .030 |
| 534 Turbo | F-57R | .035 |
| **STAR MARINE** | | |
| (SEE EMPEROR) | | |
| **TURBO-MARINE** | | |
| 1973   Ford 302 cu.in V-8 Escort | RF-10 | .028 |
| 1973   Ford 104 cu.in 4-cyl. | RN-9Y | .025 |
| 1971-73 Kohler K-399-2 | K-8 | .020 |
| **UNIVERSAL** | | |
| All 18mm Heads except BR Racer | UD-16 | .025 |
| BR Racer | D-9/D-9J | .025 |
| Atomic Four, Master Six (After Aug. '59) | J-8 | .035 |
| UJ, UJ-4, HF, HFR, HFVD | J-8 | .035 |
| OK, OKR, OKH, OKHR, OKVD, OKHVD | J-8 | .035 |
| OL, OLH, OLR, OLHR, OLVD, OLHVD | J-8 | .035 |
| Explorer Six | J-8 | .035 |
| Z, ZH, ZHR, ZR, ZVD, ZHVD | J-6 | .035 |
| ZS, ZSH, ZSR, ZSHR, ZSVD, ZSHVD | J-6 | .035 |
| Super Six, Commodore, Super Six Stevedore | J-6 | .035 |
| Z Super Six Express | J-6 | .035 |
| EV, EV15, EV20, EV25, EV30 | H-10/H-10J | .035 |
| NKEV 277 h.p. Big King | F-9Y | .035 |
| LEV, LEVH 188 h.p. Little King | UJ-6 | .028 |
| Strato-King | UJ-6 | .028 |
| Knight, Tarpon, Marlin | J-7/J-7J | .030 |
| Bullett, Arrow, Bluefin | J-7/J-7J | .030 |
| Colt | J-8J | .028 |
| Z-Drive, Elf | J-8 | .032 |
| Super Sabre | J-12Y | .035 |
| Sabre 140 h.p., 198 cu.in. | J-10Y | .035 |
| Super Sabre 155 h.p., 225 cu.in. | J-10Y | .035 |
| **VOLVO-PENTA** | | |
| C5, C10, C23 | D-16/UD-16 | .025 |
| AQ80, AQ180, BB25, BB70, MB36A, MB36B | J-6/UJ-6 | .025 |
| AQ90, B18A, B18C, BB30B, BB100, BB100A | L-85 | .025 |
| AQ105A, AQ110, AQ115A, AQ120, AQ130A | L-81Y | .025 |

| MODEL | Spark Plug | Plug Gap |
|---|---|---|
| **VOLVO-PENTA—Continued** | | |
| AQ130B, AQ130C, AQ165A, AQ170A, AQ170B | L-81Y | .025 |
| BB115A, BB165A, BB170A, BB170B | L-81Y | .025 |
| MB10A | L-92Y | .025 |
| AQ95, AQ95A, AQ100, MB20A | L-87Y | .025 |
| AQ150, AQ150A, AQ150B | J-10Y | .035 |
| B16A, B16C | J-7 | .025 |
| AQ210A thru Ser. No. 177314 | UJ-6 | .025 |
| AQ210A from Ser. No. 177315 on | RBL-9Y | .025 |
| AQ200A, AQ225A | RBL-9Y | .025 |
| Kerosene Eng.: AQ60F, BB30F, MB18F | L-10 | .035 |
| **WAUKESHA** | | |
| 155 h.p. WRA, WLA, 302/2b | F-10 | .035 |
| 165 h.p.: WRE, WLE | F-10 | .035 |
| 165 h.p.: 302/2a | RF-10 | .035 |
| 185 h.p.: WRB, WLB | F-10 | .035 |
| 185 h.p.: 302/2 | RF-10 | .035 |
| 215 h.p.: WRD, WLC, 302/4 | F-10 | .035 |
| 255 h.p.: WRD, WLD, 351/4 | F-10 | .035 |
| 350 h.p.: WRF, WLF | BL-11Y | .035 |
| 350 h.p.: 460/4 | RBL-11Y | .035 |
| **WEST BEND** | | |
| Shark-O-Matic (Stern drive) | J-4J | .030 |
| **WISCONSIN** | | |
| ABM, AEM, AKM, TFM, VH4M | D-16J | .025 |
| **XTERMINATOR** | | |
| 101, 202, 303, 404 | J-12Y | .025 |

This *Mercury Thruster* electric outboard is designed as a trolling motor for boats powered by higher horsepower marine engines. The electric can also be used to maintain boat position in a desirable fishing spot affected by wind or current. The *Thruster*'s reduction gearing permits optimum motor and propeller speeds to provide higher prop thrust in relationship to battery current drain.

# Chapter 11

# Motor Tune-Up

There are two kinds of tune up applicable to the gas engine; minor and major. A minor tune up applies mainly to the ignition system and a major tune up applies to a complete diagnosis or overall check and servicing.

## MINOR MOTOR TUNE-UP

A minor tune up is intended as a preventive measure for motors which are in fairly normal condition. This tune up should be done rather frequently in order to maintain the standard performance originally built into the motor. If a motor does not perform satisfactorily after a minor tune up, a major tune up, which includes a compression test, may be necessary.

A minor tune up includes tests and servicing of:

1. Battery (when used).
2. Spark plugs.
3. Magneto.
4. Wiring circuits.

### Battery

Inspect the battery cable and ground strap for broken insulation, corroded and broken strands, and loose or corroded terminals. Repair broken or chafed insulation with loom or tape. If the cable strands are broken or loose at the terminals, the cable should be replaced.

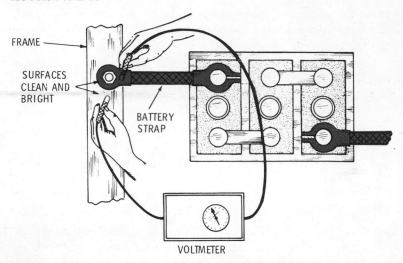

FRAME

SURFACES
CLEAN AND
BRIGHT

BATTERY
STRAP

VOLTMETER

Fig. 1. Testing the efficiency of the battery ground connections.

Clean and tighten all cable connections. Test for a weak battery.
Make a voltage test of the battery cells as shown in Fig. 1, and
add distilled water if needed. Tighten all primary and high-tension
wire connections, particularly at the ignition-starter switch, ammeter, and voltmeter.

*Battery Cable Test*—Connect the positive test lead of a voltmeter to the positive battery post, and the negative test lead to the
battery cable terminal on the starter switch. Crank the engine for
15 seconds while observing the voltmeter reading. If the voltmeter
shows more than 0.2-volt drop, recheck for loose and dirty terminals. If the terminals are tight and clean, check the cable and
replace if needed.

The battery ground-cable test is shown in Fig. 1. This test
is made in the same manner as the battery cable test except that
the negative lead of the voltmeter should be connected to the
engine frame, and the positive test lead of the voltmeter connected
to the positive battery post.

## Spark Plugs

Most marinas are equipped with complete testing facilities,
including spark-plug testers. In testing, the pressure applied should

equal the maximum compression pressure as rated by the manufacturer. Before testing, however, the points should be adjusted to the proper gap as specified by the engine manufacturer.

Carefully inspect the insulators and electrodes of all spark plugs. Replace any plug which has a cracked or broken insulator or has loose electrodes. If the insulator is worn away from the center electrode, or if the electrodes are burned or worn so they cannot be adjusted to the proper gap, the plug should be replaced. For further spark-plug information, see Chapter 10.

*Surface-Gap Spark Plugs*—Surface-gap spark plugs are becoming more common as original equipment in outboards. Their unusual design gives them not only exceptional antifouling characteristics, but freedom from overheating and pre-ignition. Surface-gap plugs cannot be used indiscriminately in two-cycle engines, but must be mated by the engine manufacturer to a customized ignition system. Special thermostatic cooling and fuel/oil mixtures are also essential for optimum performance.

Surface-gap plugs incorporating an internal series gap are identified by the prefix letter "U," such as the UJ-17V. Because of the high-voltage requirements of this design, special high-output ignition systems are required. This unique combination of high voltage, series gap, and surface-gap firing provides the "U" type surface-gap plug with unusually great fouling protection.

Since it is impossible to seat the insulator almost flush with the firing end of the plug, the plug runs comparatively cool during high-speed engine operation. Combustion deposits which shed from the piston or chamber do not cling or fuse to the firing end of the plug. Thus, one source of misfire and pre-ignition is eliminated. It is important to note that *Champion's* surface-gap plugs can be used only in the engines which are designed for this innovation. Successful operation of the plugs depends not only on a high-voltage (35,000 volts) ignition, but also on the use of very lean fuel/oil mixtures and thermostatically-controlled head temperatures.

## Magnetos

In most two-cycle engines, the magneto is seldom the cause of trouble. Sometimes, however, magnetism may be lost due to carelessness or abuse, such as dropping the magnet rotor, or else due to storage of the engine for an extended period of time. In such cases, remagnetizing may be necessary.

To remagnetize a magnet rotor proceed as follows:

    a. Remove magnet rotor from magneto.

    b. Determine polarity of both magnet rotor and magnetizer by means of a compass.

    c. Place magnet rotor between jaws on tester as noted in Fig. 2. Note that unlike poles of both the magnet rotor

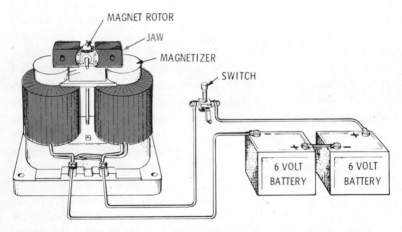

Fig. 2. Typical magnet rotor remagnetizer showing the wiring of the essential components.

    and magnetizer must be placed together; that is, the jaw at the north-pole end of the magnet rotor must rest on top of the south pole of the magnetizer.

    d. With magnetizer properly connected to the switch, allow current from batteries to flow through magnet rotor for about five seconds, then disconnect current for about three seconds. Repeat the foregoing procedure.

After disassembly of the magneto, all metal parts should be thoroughly cleaned in gasoline and dried. All parts should be inspected for damage or wear.

Every roadway leading to boating waters presents an opportunity to enrich one's life, with just a single hitch. If you don't have a trailerable rig, you're left behind.
Courtesy Mercury Marine, Div. of Brunswick Corp.

Mercury also makes a 175 HP outboard, V-6. Here it is powering a larger offshore-type hull-23 footer.
Courtesy Mercury Marine, Div. of Brunswick Corp.

Half of this bass fishing duo has tied into the first catch of the day. For powering this fishing machine, they have a 140 horsepower compact four-cylinder stern drive powerplant with plenty of zip. In this 15.5-foot boat, the 140 HP package gets two anglers to their favorite fishing hole at a top speed of 48 mph.

Courtesy Mercury Marine, Div. of Brunswick Corp.

perceptible voltage drop because of the drain on the battery. Such performance indicates a satisfactory circuit.

## MAJOR MOTOR TUNE-UP

A major tune up comprises an overall check and service as required, in addition to the tests and servicing included in a minor tune up. A major tune up includes such items as:

1. Battery (when used).
2. Cylinder blocks.
3. Reed-valve adjustments.
4. Compression tests.
5. Carburetor adjustment.
6. Ignition system.
7. Cooling system.

### Battery

Clean and tighten the battery connections. Replace any worn or frayed cables. Check all connections leading from the battery to the various instruments and starting devices. Specific-gravity readings of the electrolyte must be taken before adding water, as water will not mix with the electrolyte immediately and a true reading will not be obtained.

If the specific gravity drops below 1.150, check the battery for the cause and then recharge. When specific gravity reaches 1.280, discontinue charging. Add pure distilled water to bring the level of the electrolyte to one-quarter inch above the plates in each cell.

### Cylinder Blocks

Inspect the cylinder block thoroughly for cracks and condition of the cylinder bore. Check all pistons for scoring, cracks, carbon, etc. If any pistons are scored or metal has been damaged, they must be replaced.

Check the piston-pin bosses for cracks and replace if cracked or if piston pins are loose. Inspect the piston ring grooves for wear, burn, or distortion. It is recommended that new piston rings be installed unless old ones prove to be absolutely free from cracks, burn, carbon, or other abnormal wear.

Before replacing the piston rings, however, clean out all grooves thoroughly, using the recessed end of a broken ring. Also, clean any carbon and varnish deposits from the top and sides of the piston with a soft wire brush or with carbon removal solution. When wire brushing the top of the piston, do not burr or round the machine edges.

Gum, varnish, and softer carbon deposits can be removed by soaking in a carbon removal solution. Piston skirts can be polished with crocus cloth to remove burrs. Check the piston pins and pin bosses, especially if the engine has been submerged. If a piston pin is bent, it will elongate the piston-pin base as it is removed. A new pin will therefore fit loosely.

If the cylinder walls are scored, they should be rebored. In this connection it should be noted that, when the depth of the score exceeds .0075 in., it cannot, in most instances, be effectively rebored for future use. If sleeves have been scored, but not out-of-round, or if for some other reason the sleeve is rough, it can be polished with a cylinder hone. Polishing should be done with a finishing hone. Carbon can be removed from the top of the cylinder with a closed cup brush.

## Reed Valves

Check for chipped, bent, or damaged reed valves and replace when necessary. Never bend a reed valve to obtain a setting, as bending will cause leakage. Always check the reed-stop opening dimensions carefully, as larger openings can cause breakage and smaller openings will not allow sufficient fuel to enter at high engine speeds. When reassembling, be sure that all gaskets are in place and bolts are tightened in sequence.

## Compression Tests

Satisfactory engine operation depends on adequate and uniform compression in all cylinders. Loss of compression results in loss of power, and nonuniform compression in cylinders causes unsatisfactory or jerky operation. To obtain the true operating condition of an engine, a compression test is necessary.

Test the compression with a suitable compression gauge. If the compression varies greatly from one cylinder to another, it indicates troubles in pistons, rings, cylinders, etc., and the engine should be disassembled and checked. When making the test, it is essential that the engine be at its operating temperature and the fuel mixture be of the proper grade. To make the compression test, proceed as follows:

1. Remove the spark plug of each cylinder to be tested and, with the engine warmed up to its working temperature, the throttle open and the ignition switch off, apply the compression gauge to the spark-plug hole and crank the engine by hand or with the starter. A check valve in the tester holds the compression in the gauge until released by the operator, permitting an accurate reading to be made.

2. Test each cylinder and record each reading. In this connection it should be noted, however, that a small variation in pressure may always exist, even with engines in perfect operating condition. This variation is principally due to the lack of uniformity in combustion chambers, even in cylinders of exactly the same size. When the difference in pressure exceeds the manufacturer's normal allowance, the cause should be found and remedied.

## Carburetor Adjustment

When adjusting the carburetor, be sure that the engine is at its normal operating temperature. Use either a vacuum gauge or combustion analyzer for accurate adjustment. To insure normal engine performance, the following adjustments should be made or checked:

1. Idle adjustment.
2. High-speed adjustment.
3. Slow-speed adjustment.
4. Float-level adjustment.

*Idle Adjustment*—The fuel mixture is controlled by the idle needle valve which, when turned clockwise, gives a leaner mixture, and when turned counterclockwise, gives a richer mixture.

*High-Speed Adjustment*—After the motor has been properly warmed up, set the throttle to the fast position on all motors, and shift to forward gear. Complete the high-speed adjustment as follows:

1. Slowly turn the high-speed adjustment clockwise until the motor commences to slow down (mixture becoming too lean).

2. Determine the critical lean point as closely as possible, then back the needle out slightly. It is better to set the mixture slightly rich, when in doubt, rather than too lean. An excessive lean mixture will cause overheating and loss of power. Sustained full throttle with this setting may cause motor damage and burned spark plugs.

*Slow-Speed Adjustment*—After the motor has been warmed up and the high-speed adjustment completed, proceed as follows:

1. Place the throttle in the shifting range on slow position and the gear shift (if so equipped) in forward gear. Turn the idle-adjustment screw clockwise until the motor starts to slow down or fires unevenly due to the mixture becoming too rich because of lack of air.

2. Turn the adjustment screw counterclockwise until the motor picks up speed and fires evenly. Do not adjust leaner than necessary to attain a reasonable smooth idling. Again it is preferable to set the mixture a little rich, rather than too lean.

3. For the final adjustment, alternately open and close the throttle a few times as a test. If acceleration hesitance or stalling at idle speed occurs, it will be necessary to repeat the entire adjustment procedure.

*Float-Level Adjustment*—In order to provide the carburetor with a constant controlled supply of fuel, it may be necessary to adjust the float setting. When adjusting the float setting, proceed as follows:

1. Remove the fule bowl and gasket from the carburetor body. Then with the carburetor body held upside down, the float

should be level, or horizontal with the plane of the carburetor body.

2. If resetting is necessary, do not bend the brass float arm by pulling or pressing on the cork float. Instead, bend the brass tabs, holding the cork float, until the required adjustment has been obtained.

3. Assemble the float in the carburetor and recheck the float setting. If an inspection indicates that the fuel level continues to rise beyond the float setting point, remove the inlet needle and seat, and clean the seating surfaces with a soft cloth. Before reassembling, make sure that the hole in the float is centered around the speed nozzle so that there is no restriction to the movement of the float during operation.

*Throttle-Cam Setting*—The throttle-cam setting is important on twin-cylinder engines. On many twin-cylinder outboards, the throttle-cam setting is the most important of all linkage adjustments. A throttle actuator (roller or bar) rides the ramp on the side of the magneto housing to open or close the carburetor butterfly as the magneto housing rotates.

There is a degree-for-degree relationship in the throttle-plate opening and the spark advance—the throttle must not lead or lag the spark. If this "sync" is out of adjustment, hard starting and poor midrange outboard operation will result. Many outboards have a reference mark on the throttle-advance cam. On some, only the center of the link or roller has to be aligned with this mark. Others use "sight" marks on the crankcase housing. Before you take aim, consult the manufacturer's service manual on procedure and adjustment.

Most hard starting can be attributed to worn out or fouled plugs—or to carburetor overchoking. Improper "sync" of the spark advance to the carburetor throttle-plate opening is also high on the list.

Here's another good tip. Disconnect the fuel line when the engine is not in use. Many complaints of hard starting are due to carburetor flooding when the engine is tilted, as in launching or trailering. Fuel tanks exposed to the sun or trailed over rough roads will also develop considerable pressure. In some cases, this pressure will be great enough to over-ride the float needle when the motor is tilted, allowing raw fuel to enter the intake manifold. This, of course, provides far too rich a mixture, and hard starting will result.

## Ignition System

If you want a silken-smooth idle, and more all-around action, then "sync" your points. The ultimate aim in dual breaker points on 2-cylinder outboards is to fire the top plug exactly 180 degrees after the bottom plug. If the breakers open a few degrees too early or too late, the maximum piston "push" is not shared by both cylinders.

Unless both breakers are radically out of adjustment, you'll get near-normal performance. But, for added zip and extra rpm's, perfectly synchronized twin-breaker points will give outboards perfect trolling and hydroplane "feel."

To achieve better point installation on "twins," *Mercury* dealers use a customized protractor scale. *Johnson, Evinrude,* and *Gale,* on the other hand, use special timing indicators that fit over the magneto housing. With a test light or continuity meter across the points, the breakers are adjusted to open exactly 180 degrees apart. V-4 magnetos can be "synced" 90 degrees apart, as each set of breakers fires two plugs. A test light and the pulley cover provide reference marks for an accurate 90-degree lineup with the housing.

*Mercury's* coil-battery 6-cylinder engines divide the ignition task among two coils and two sets of points. Each coil and breaker fires 3 spark plugs. The distributor cam is 3-lobed, with each set of breakers firing 120 degrees apart. The second set, however, fires at 60-degree intervals. (One set fires at 0, 120, and 240 degrees; the other at 60, 180, and 300 degrees.)

*Rough Idle*—Do not dismantle an outboard carburetor or magneto until you've checked some common causes for rough idle.

1. Stale or improperly mixed fuel.
2. Improper carburetor setting.
3. Pinched or kinked fuel lines.
4. Fouled or improperly gapped plugs.
5. Out-of-sync carburetor or magneto.
6. Defective fuel pump.

If you have checked these items and the engine is still sputtering, you might have to probe deeper into the situation.

1. Look for a bent gear or exhaust housing.
2. Check the points and timing.
3. Check the reeds for flat contact with the reed plate.
4. Clean the oil-drain screen in the reed-plate base.
5. Inspect the carburetor needle and float valve.
6. Check for dirt in the coil.

Great fluctuations in rpm at idle are usually attributable to sticking piston rings or scored cylinder walls.

*Centrifugal Advance*—Sticking centrifugal weights due to broken or stretched springs can cause poor acceleration, loss of top speed, and even detonation. Here is one way to spot-check the centrifugal advance. Grip the distributor shaft (or rotor) and twist in the direction of rotation, then release. The shaft (or rotor) should snap back to its original position. If it hangs up, or returns sluggishly or slowly, chances are the distributor weights and springs need overhauling.

## Lubrication

Proper distributor action is greatly dependent on proper lubrication. Top engine performance and economy are "hair-triggered" by centrifugal and vacuum movement. A few drops of oil twice a season on the distributor-shaft wick, or in the oil hole of the breaker plate (if so equipped), and at the side of the distributor will work wonders. Lightly lubricating the cam with an approved material will promote rubbing-block life and preserve the gap settings. Remember, however, over-lubrication, causing oil to be thrown against the points, is sudden death to breakers.

## Primary Leads

A frayed primary wire or broken insulation can cause misfiring—even stop a boat dead in the water. Always check the primary lead from the coil terminal to the breaker contacts for ragged or cracked insulation. Wires inside the distributor are constantly flexing with breaker-point movement. Make certain the breaker-point leads and condenser pigtails are not chafing or interfering with the distributor-plate action. Some breaker plates have a grounding wire to the distributor housing. Be sure it is in good condition.

## Cooling System

The water-pump impeller is keyed to the drive shaft and turns within a cam-shaped cavity in the water-pump body. In case of water-pump failure, it will be necessary to disassemble that part of the lower unit which contains the pump assembly. To disassemble the water pump, proceed as follows:

1. Supporting the gear-housing assembly in a vise, remove the screws which attach the water-pump body to the gear housing, and lift off the pump.
2. Slide the water-pump top plate and impeller up and off of the drive shaft, and remove the water-pump impeller drive key.
3. Lift the water-pump back plate and gasket up and off of the drive shaft.
4. Inspect all of the water-pump parts for water or damage. Look for wear or sand scores on the water-pump impeller, deflector, and housing. Replace any parts that are worn or damaged. Install a new water-pump gasket and the water-pump back plate to the gear housing. Clean out all passages in the pump body, and replace the intake screen when necessary.

# Chapter 12

# Engine Horsepower
# Measurement

By definition, one horsepower is a unit of power numerically equal to a rate of 33,000 foot-pounds of work per minute, or 550 foot-pounds per second. The horsepower of an engine may be expressed in several ways, depending on how it is measured.

According to definitions and the manner in which it is measured, horsepower may be classed as:

1. Brake horsepower.
2. Indicated horsepower.
3. SAE horsepower, etc.

Other types of horsepower used in the various branches of engineering are: *boiler horsepower, hydraulic horsepower, electrical horsepower*, etc. One of the simplest means to determine usable horsepower of a small engine is by means of the Prony-brake method, which consists of the engine flywheel rotating against a braking device.

## PRONY BRAKE

The output of a small and medium size engine is frequently determined by means of a Prony brake. The method of assembling such a device is shown in Fig. 1. It consists essentially of two

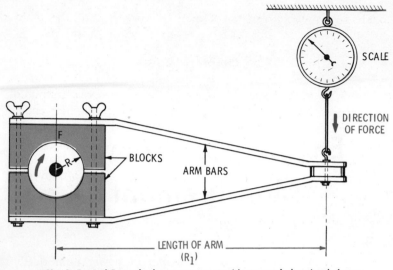

SCALE

DIRECTION OF FORCE

BLOCKS

ARM BARS

LENGTH OF ARM
$(R_1)$

**Fig. 1. Typical Prony-brake arrangement with suspended spring balance.**

blocks of wood shaped to fit around the flywheel of the engine. The pressure of the blocks may be adjusted by means of tightening or loosening the bolts holding the blocks in place. The two bars fastened at the top and bottom of the brake form an arm which is attached to a scale. When the engine turns, the friction between the flywheel and the wooden blocks converts the power supplied by the engine into heat.

The heat generated by the flywheel as it turns under the pressure of the blocks is absorbed by a stream of water applied to the flywheel rim. In developing the expression for the horsepower converted into heat, let $R$ represent the radius of the flywheel in feet, and $F$ the force supplied at the surface of the flywheel. Then, when the flywheel completes one revolution, the force $F$ moves a distance of $2\pi R$ feet, and therefore $F2\pi R$ foot-pounds of work is done.

When the flywheel rotates at $N$ revolutions per minute, $FN2\pi R$ foot-pounds of work is being done. Since one horsepower is developed for every 33,000 foot-pounds of work done per minute, we may write:

$$\text{Horsepower} = \frac{FN2\pi R}{33,000}$$

which, after reduction of terms, may be written:

$$\text{Horsepower} = \frac{FNR}{5255}$$

*Example*—It is desired to measure the horsepower output of a gas engine by means of a Prony brake attached to the engine flywheel. Compute the horsepower output, with the engine running at its rated speed of 750 rpm, a lever length of 36 inches, and a scale deflection of 50 pounds.

*Solution*—The power output may easily be computed by substituting numerical values in our formula for horsepower, or

$$\text{Horsepower} = \frac{FNR}{5255} = \frac{50 \times 750 \times 3}{5255} = 21.4$$

## ROPE BRAKE

For comparatively small engines, various forms of rope brakes are often employed. In such cases, a weight is hung from one end of the rope and a spring-scale fastened to the other, as shown in Fig. 2. In order to compute the horsepower in brake systems of

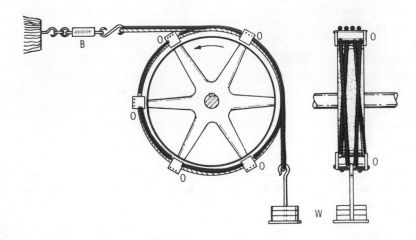

Fig. 2. Side and end view of a typical rope brake.

311

this sort, multiply the difference between the weight $W$ and the weight registered on the spring balance $B$ by the number of revolutions of the flywheel per minute, and by the circumference of a circle passing through the center of gravity of the rope expressed in feet. Finally divide the product by 33,000.

This type of brake is easily constructed of material at hand, and being self-adjusting, needs no accurate fitting. For large powers, the number of ropes may be increased. It is considered a most convenient and reliable brake. In Fig. 2, the spring balance $B$ is shown in a horizontal position. This is not necessary; if convenient, the vertical position may be used. The ropes are held to the pulley or flywheel face by blocks of wood $O$. The weight $W$ may be replaced by a spring balance if desirable. To calculate the brake horsepower, subtract the pull registered by the spring balance $B$ from the weight $W$. The lever arm is the radius of the pulley plus one-half the diameter of the rope. The formula is:

$$BHP = \frac{2\pi RN\,(W-B)}{33,000} = \frac{RN\,(W-B)}{5255}$$

*where*

    $R$ is the radius in feet from the center of the shaft to the center of the rope,

    $N$ is the revolutions per minute,

    $W$ is the weight in pounds,

    $B$ is the spring balance, in pounds.

## TORQUE

The torque of an engine is usually expressed in pound-feet, and is the measurement of the turning effort exerted by the flywheel at a radius of one foot from the center of rotation.

The turning effect produced by an engine does not depend on the magnitude only, but also on the radial distance through which the force acts. If torque is represented by $T$, and is expressed in pound-feet, it may be written:

$$T = FR$$

where

$F$ equals force in pounds.

$R$ equals radial distance in feet through which the force acts.

We also have

$$HP = \frac{FNR}{5255}$$

which, after substitution, may be written as

$$HP = \frac{TN}{5255}$$

From the foregoing it will be noted that, since the horsepower is a product of torque and rotation speed, the horsepower at any given rpm will vary directly with the torque. Thus, for example, if at a constant engine speed the torque is doubled, the horsepower output will also be doubled.

Actually, however, the torque does not remain constant throughout the various speeds of an engine, but after a short rise, begins to fall off. This falling off of torque as the speed increases above a certain point is caused by the inability of the engine to obtain as full a charge of gas as at a lower speed.

## DYNAMOMETER

Another device for measuring the developed horsepower of an engine is commonly known as a dynamometer. This is a very convenient method of power measurement and consists of an electric generator connected to the main shaft of the engine to be tested.

If the efficiency of the generator is known at the particular speed and output at which it is to be operated, a very accurate method of measuring the power of the engine becomes available. Since the amount of electrical power delivered will vary according to the speed at which the armature revolves, and this in turn is dependent on the power of the engine under test, it is evident that the power delivered to the engine can be read directly from the instrument recordings.

For direct-current generators, brake horsepower is equal to the product of amperes multiplied by volts and divided by the product of 746 times the efficiency of the generator. By formula,

$$HP = \frac{Current \times Voltage}{746 \times Efficiency}$$

For dependable test results, the two machines should be of comparative size, and the generator loaded accordingly by suitable power-consuming devices. Another means employed to measure the power of an engine is by means of a so-called hydraulic brake. In this system, the engine shaft delivers power to a paddle wheel revolving in a fluid which is designed to offer enough resistance to absorb all the power furnished by the engine.

## INDICATED HORSEPOWER

This method of measuring engine horsepower is used mainly for experimental and laboratory purposes, and is a measurement of the force delivered by the expanding gas to the piston inside the cylinder.

Briefly, indicated horsepower is based on the pressure exerted on the piston during the power stroke obtained from an indicator diagram, area of the piston head, length of stroke, and the number of power strokes in a given period.

To express the indicated horsepower of an engine the following formula is used:

$$IHP = \frac{PLAN}{33,000} \times K$$

where

$P$ is the mean effective pressure in lbs. per sq. in. acting on the piston (as shown by indicator diagram),

$L$ is the length of stroke in feet,

$A$ is the area of piston in square inches,

$N$ is the number of working strokes per min.,

314

$K$ is the coefficient equal to ½ times the number of cylinders in gas engines, and 2 times the number of revolutions in double-acting steam engines.

## SAE HORSEPOWER

The "SAE" horsepower formula was developed by the *Society of Automotive Engineers,* and is used in certain States to determine the tax for auto license plates. The assumption upon which this formula for brake horsepower is based, is that all gas engines will, or should deliver their rated horsepower at a piston speed of 1000 feet per minute, that the mean effective pressure in such engine cylinders will average 90 lbs. per sq. in., and that the mechanical efficiency will average 75 percent. The formula, as presently employed, is written as follows:

$$BHP = \frac{D^2 N}{2.5}$$

where

$D$ is the cylinder-bore diameter in inches,
$N$ is the number of cylinders.

It should be noted that this formula, while being of value in the early days of the automobile with its inefficient engine, is today very misleading, since modern engines develop about four times the horsepower computed by using this formula. A more suitable method of determining the auto license tax is by weight, as has been adopted by most States, instead of so-called horsepower.

### Efficiency

The term "efficiency," as applied to an engine or any other power-producing machine, is generally meant to be the relationship between the output and input, both measured in the same units. It is commonly written

$$\text{Efficiency} = \frac{\text{Power ouput}}{\text{Power input}}$$

315

Since the power output of any power-producing machine is always smaller than its input, it follows that the quotient in the foregoing equation will always be less than one. Efficiencies of machinery are commonly given as a percentage factor of one, such as 28, 52, 92 percent, etc., and while some power-conversion methods result in comparatively high efficiencies, others, particularly all forms of thermal power-conversion machinery, have a low efficiency.

## Thermal Efficiency

The overall thermal efficiency of a gas engine is the relationship between the fuel input and the power output. This relationship is commonly expressed in "heat units" or "British thermal units" (abbreviated BTU). It has been found experimentally that one BTU equals 778 foot-pounds of work. It is therefore a simple matter to convert the horsepower output of an engine into BTU.

The thermal efficiency of an engine is written as follows:

$$\text{Thermal efficiency} = \frac{\text{output in BTU}}{\text{input in BTU}}$$

*Example*—An engine delivers 50 brake horsepower for a period of one hour, and in that time consumes 30 lbs. (approximately 5 gallons) of gasoline. Assuming that the gasoline has a heat value of 18,500 BTU per pound, calculate the thermal efficiency of the engine.

*Solution*—From the foregoing data, the energy developed by the engine at 50 horsepower for one hour equals 50 horsepower-hours.

BTU per HP hour $= 33,000 \times 60 \div 778 = 2545$

BTU output per hour $= 50 \times 2545 = 127,250$

BTU input per hour $= 30 \times 18,500 = 555,000$

$$\text{Thermal efficiency} = \frac{\text{Power output}}{\text{Power input}} = \frac{127,250}{555,000}$$

$$= 0.23 \text{ or } 23\%$$

## Mechanical Efficiency

The mechanical efficiency of an engine is the ratio of brake horsepower to indicated horsepower. It is written

$$\text{Mechanical Efficiency} = \frac{\text{Brake horsepower}}{\text{Indicated horsepower}}$$

The factor which has the greatest effect on mechanical efficiency is the friction between moving engine parts. Since the friction between the moving parts of an engine remains practically constant throughout its speed range, it follows that the mechanical efficiency will be highest when the engine is running at a speed which develops the maximum horsepower.

## Piston Displacement

Piston displacement generally means the number of cubic inches of cylinder space displaced by the pistons during a single stroke. Since the length of the stroke and the cylinder-bore diameter are both measurable, it is a comparatively simple matter to obtain this piston displacement.

## Volumetric Efficiency

The quantity of charge drawn into the cylinder of an internal-combustion engine is always less than the theoretical quantity of charge which would fill the working volume of the cylinder at atmospheric pressure and temperature. The ratio of the actual to the theoretical quantity is termed volumetric efficiency.

$$\text{Piston displacement} = \frac{\pi D^2}{4} \times L \times N$$

where

$D$ is the cylinder-bore diameter in inches,
$L$ is the length of stroke in inches,
$N$ is the number of cylinders.

*Example*—An eight-cylinder, 250-horsepower automotive engine, according to specifications has a 4.125 × 3.4-inch bore and stroke. What is the piston displacement?

*Solution*—Substituting values in our previously developed formula, we may write

$$\text{Piston displacement} = \frac{3.14(4.125)^2}{4} \times 3.4 \times 8$$

$$= 363.5 \text{ cu. in.}$$

*Example*—A four-cylinder gas engine with a capacity of 104 cubic inches has a stroke length of 3.13 inches. Calculate the cylinder-bore diameter.

*Solution*—Using the previously derived formula

$$\text{Piston displacement} = \frac{\pi D^2}{4} \times L \times N$$

$$104 = \frac{3.14 \times D^2}{4} \times 3.13 \times 4$$

$$D^2 = \frac{104 \times 4}{3.14 \times 3.13 \times 4} = \frac{104}{9.83} = 10.58$$

$$D = \sqrt{10.58} = 3.25 \text{ in.}$$

The foregoing 104-cubic-inch engine accordingly has a 3.25 × 3.13-inch bore and stroke, respectively.

It is usually impractical, however, to employ more than eight cylinders in automotive application because of the greater length of the power plant and the much stronger and heavier crankshaft required. When the number of cylinders are increased above six, the solution for the best arrangement is found in two sets of cylinders inclined at an angle, thus providing an engine of the same length but increased power. This engine is called the V-type. In this type of engine, the angle between the cylinders usually varies from 90° to 45°. The advantages of multiple cylinders are decreased vibration, greater flexibility, overlapping power strokes, lighter reciprocating parts, and higher speeds.

This fiberglass fisherman's boat is powered by an 85 horsepower outboard by *Johnson*. It gets you to your fishing location in a hurry.

Courtesy Johnson Motors, Div. of Outboard Marine Corp.

Boating safety programs sponsored by many boating groups, under Coast Guard and various state agency supervision, make it possible for youngsters to acquire the savvy and knowledge for safe boat operation without supervision.

Courtesy Mercury Marine, Div. of Brunswick Corp.

# Chapter 13

# Boat Trailers

Thanks to the trailer, today's average boat owner is a mobile boatman. No longer tied to one lake or one river, he and his family are limited to waters only by how far they want to drive. It may be a small river just down the road, or the big lake halfway across the continent—but the boat trailer has made the outboarder a sort of nautical gypsy, free to chase his choice of waters across the map.

Trailering a boat is not difficult. Like driving an automobile, there are a few common sense tips that should be followed. First, and most important, according to the *Johnson Motors News Bureau,* make sure the boat and trailer are not too heavy for the tow car. A good rule of thumb to follow is that the loaded trailer should not weigh more than the automobile pulling it.

Next, consider the car itself. Most experts now recommend an automatic transmission as best for pulling a boat trailer because it permits smoother shifting and can handle steep grades easier. For a heavy load being pulled a considerable distance, a heavy-duty cooling system, heavy-duty brakes, and heavy-duty springs would be in order, though not absolutely necessary. The hitch that connects the trailer to the car is also very important, for it must receive and transmit all the stresses of towing.

There are many good, reliable hitches on the market. One that distributes the weight so the tow car's front wheels and the trailer's wheels are sharing the burden is by far the best. The ultimate responsibility for trouble-free trailering must lie with the tow car's driver. Driving with a large boat and trailer hooked on behind is far different than navigating the family car down to the corner grocery, so driving sense can make all the difference between a happy outing and a bad memory.

Give yourself braking room, swing wide on corners to clear curbs, and follow local trailering rules. Practice backing before you head out onto the open road—it's not as difficult as some say, but it *does* take a little practice. Trailing a boat is a simple open-door to boating fun. Just a little common sense and the proper equipment is all it takes.

## BOAT TRAILER DESIGN

Boat trailer design is improved. Trailered boats ride more safely, are more secure, and are easier to handle. Many trailers are tailor-made for a kind of boat. Built-in quality is found in most of today's namebrand trailers. However, they do require care from their owners. Typical boat trailers are shown in Figs. 1 and 2.

## LUBRICATION

After long trips or immersion of the trailer in water, its bearings should be lubricated. This must be done regularly if the trailer is used in salt water.

## TRAILER CHECK

Before starting out on a trip, be sure all bolts are tightened. Check tire pressure—underinflation is worse than overinflation. Check for adequate slack in the safety chain. Inspect the tie-downs to see that they are secure. To prevent damage to the boat, see that the rollers, bolsters, and other areas of contact conform to the shape of your boat's bottom.

## LAUNCHING THE BOAT

When launching the boat, pick a sloping shoreline to ease the operation. Be sure that your car tires are on ground firm enough to provide enough traction to pull out with the weight of the trailered boat.

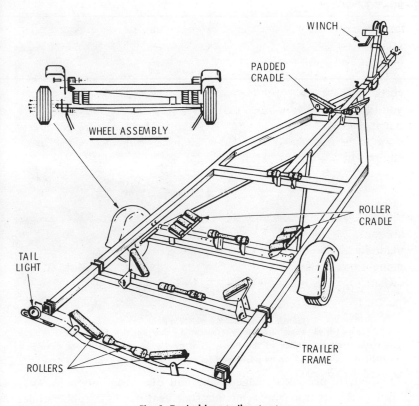

WINCH

PADDED CRADLE

WHEEL ASSEMBLY

ROLLER CRADLE

TAIL LIGHT

TRAILER FRAME

ROLLERS

**Fig. 1. Typical boat-trailer structure.**

## TRAILER SIZE

Trailer manufacturers usually describe their models in terms of load capacity or the maximum weight the trailer will carry. Since the weight of the boat depends on its size, trailer catalogs generally provide, in addition to load capacity, such necessary items as boat length and boat width.

For trouble-free operation, the trailer should be designed to support the hull throughout its length, preferably under the keel. This will prevent the hull from sagging during long periods of storage or when additional weight is placed in the boat during transport. Adjustable, well-padded support blocks or cradles should

323

Fig. 2. Stern drive boats are easily trailerable, due to the compactness of the powerplant and the ability of the Power Trim device on the *MerCruiser* drive unit to be positioned for easy launching.

fit snugly to prevent damage to the hull due to vibration. A well-equipped boat trailer may include such features as a rubber-roller transom support with transom tie-down, electric tail light, completely-equipped boat winch with rope and attachment hooks, automotive-type wheels and brakes, shock absorbers, etc.

## STATIC LOAD CAPACITY

The static load capacity of a trailer is the weight of the boat, motor, and gear that will be included when loading a trailer. Many boat owners will pile luggage and camping equipment into their boat. This must be considered as a part of the static load. When on the road, this equipment should be well distributed and secured to prevent shifting.

It is recommended that the boat, motor, and equipment be weighed to determine the exact weight since there are too many variations of boat models and gear to rely totally on average weights. From the foregoing, it follows that when considering trailer load capacity, the weight of the outboard motor and necessary gear should be added to the weight of the empty boat.

## GROSS WEIGHT

Road and bridge weight limits are always based on gross weight and not on static load capacity. The gross weight is the weight of the boat, motor, gear, and trailer, and is the weight actually supported by the tires.

## WINCH MOUNTING

The trailer winch assembly shall be so mounted that it will be symmetrical with the recommended standards for bow eyes. It is advantageous to be able to lift upward slightly with the winch cable when loading the boat onto the trailer. On the other hand, it is preferred to pull down slightly with the winch cable if the winch is to be used to hold the bow of the boat when trailering.

## WHEELS AND BEARINGS

To facilitate boat-trailer operation, it is necessary that the wheels, bearings, and tires be of standard size, in addition to being equipped with effective water seals to prevent the entrance of water in the wheel bearings. With respect to trailer tire pressure, manufacturer's recommendation should be followed in each instance, because of the relationship between speed, load, tire size, and inflation.

## TIE-DOWNS

Before hitching up the trailer it is necessary that the boat be properly tied down. Trailers should be furnished with appropriate tie-downs capable of holding the boat securely against the rollers or bolsters. If, while trailering, separation occurs between the boat and rollers or bolsters, shock loads will be introduced which may result in damage to both the boat and trailer.

## SERIAL NUMBERS AND LICENSE PLATES

A plate carrying the manufacturer's name and serial number for that particular trailer shall be permanently attached to each trailer, or the serial number shall be permanently stamped on the trailer frame. Boat-trailer manufacturers make available a bracket or location for the mounting of a standard vehicle license plate.

## STATE REQUIREMENTS

Although individual state laws applicable to boat trailers may vary, they all require certain minimum safety measures. Boat-trailer manufacturers usually make brakes and safety chains available to meet individual state requirements. Trailer brakes are of sufficient size only when they adequately control the movement of, and can stop and hold the trailer. They shall be so designed as to be applied by the driver of the towing motor vehicle from the driver's seat, and connected so that in case of accidental break-away of the towed vehicle, the brakes shall be automatically applied.

### Taillight Requirements

Most states require at least one tail lamp on the rear of every trailer. Generally, the statutes do not specify what size the lamp must be, but there are specifications on color (red), range of visibility (most frequently, 500 feet to the rear), and location.

### Stop-Light Requirements

Most states require one red stop lamp on every trailer weighing more than 3000 pounds gross; and one on every trailer 3000 pounds gross or less if so loaded or of such dimensions as to obscure either the stop light on the towing vehicle, or hand signals by the driver of the towing vehicle.

### Directional-Light Requirements

Most states require two red or amber signal lights on the rear of every trailer under one or more of the following conditions:

1. If the trailer is so loaded or constructed as to prevent hand and arm signals by the operator of the towing vehicle, or

mechanical turn signals of the towing vehicle, from being visible both from front and rear.

2. If the distance from the center of the steering wheel of the towing vehicle to the rear limit of the trailer body or load exceeds 14 feet.

3. If the distance from the center of the steering wheel to the left outside limit of the trailer body or load exceeds 24 inches.

## Reflector-Light Requirements

Many states differentiate between trailers having a gross vehicle weight exceeding 3000 pounds and trailers weighing 3000 pounds gross or less as to the number of reflector lights required.

Typically, as many as six reflectors are required on every trailer over 3000 pounds gross, with two on each side, one amber at or near the front and one red at or near the rear, and two on the rear, one on each side. On every trailer of 3000 pounds gross or less, usually two red reflectors, one on each side of the rear, are required. In most states, reflectors are not required to be of any specific size, but they must be of such size and characteristics and so maintained as to meet prescribed visibility requirements. They must be readily visible at night from all distances within 50 to 500 feet from a following vehicle when directly in front of the lawful upper beams of its headlamps.

## HIGHWAY PRECAUTIONS

Before going on the highway, it is recommended that the boat, motor, and accessories, together with the trailer, be carefully inspected. This inspection covers points to be checked when initially matching the boat and trailer, as well as items to cover before each trip.

Assuming the boat owner is about to commence the trailer-boat trip, the following prehighway check should be made:

1. Check to see that the rollers, bolsters, and other contact points are adjusted to the boat contour.

2. Check to see that no part of the boat makes contact with the vehicle when making a turn with the steering wheel turned to its maximum limit.

3. Check for proper slack in the safety chains to permit maximum turns.
4. Make sure that the trailer lights, brakes, and license conform with the legal requirements of the state.
5. Check to see that all parts, nuts, and bolts are tight, and that all moving parts are properly lubricated.
6. All tires should be inflated to the correct pressure, and all tie-downs properly secured.
7. Check to see that the trailer is properly hitched and that the safety chains are secure.
8. Check the motor to see that it is tightly secured on the transom and that the tilt mechanism is in proper position.
9. If baggage or equipment is to be carried in the boat, it must be properly distributed and secured.
10. It is recommended that gas tanks be left empty on long trips and filled upon arrival at the destination. If gas tanks cannot be emptied, keep them tightly closed.

It should be noted that all of the foregoing items should be checked periodically or as often as deemed necessary while on the trip.

## CARTOPPING

The boatman who transports his boat on the top of his car has the advantage of launching wherever his fancy takes him. If the idea of cartopping appeals to you, and you're a new boatman, pick your outfit with care. A 100-lb. boat is about all that one person can handle. But, with help, you should be able to manage a 150-lb. craft. Cartoppers come in flat or round bottoms with a variety of bow shapes. Flat bottoms suit river drafting. For pond and lake fishing, a V-hull of aluminum or fiberglass is a better choice.

Aluminum cartoppers are lighter than fiberglass, require practically no maintenance, and are very popular. Fiberglass boats require far less maintenance than wood. Both aluminum and fiberglass require flotation to assure safety. Wood hulls float without added flotation. They are quiet, but do demand the care and service inherent to wood.

Cartoppers are best powered with outboard motors ranging from 1½ to 10 HP. The little motors are ideal for trolling. Folding motors are handy when cartopping and conserve car-trunk space. When transporting your boat, be sure it is securely fastened fore and aft as well as from side to side. At highway speeds, your car develops a lifting force capable of lifting your cartopper off of the car.

# Chapter 14

# Outboard Boating Fundamentals

There are rules for boat handling that are a must before any attempt is made to operate an outboard-motor boat. A thorough understanding of the boat and its action under different conditions of loading, weather, and currents are basic fundamentals, but this knowledge does not qualify a person as a *safe* boat operator.

The only way to learn about proper boat handling is by actual practice. Theory and reading of literature on the subject go a long way, but will never replace the knowledge obtained in actual practice.

## DIRECTIONAL TERMS

There are a large number of nautical terms which may be useful, particularly when dealing with large vessels such as operate on oceans and on the Great Lakes. On boats operated by outboard motors, however, only a few selected terms will be needed since these will assist in the operational functions of the boat.

With reference to Fig. 1, it should be noted that there are four main terms dealing with the various directions while aboard. These are *bow, stern, port,* and *starboard.* As illustrated, the bow is the forward or front part, while the stern is the aft or rear part of the boat. The port and starboard refer to the sides of the boat, the port side being on the left hand and the starboard side on the right

331

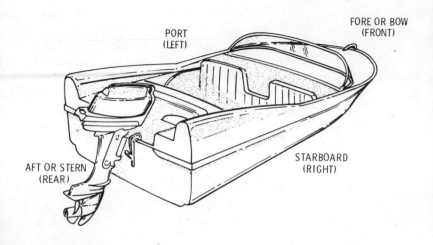

PORT
(LEFT)

FORE OR BOW
(FRONT)

AFT OR STERN
(REAR)

STARBOARD
(RIGHT)

Fig. 1. Directional references or terms commonly used on all types of waterborne crafts.

hand of a person when standing aboard facing the bow or front part of the boat.

Because of the constantly increasing popularity and consequent traffic hazards of boating, certain so-called "rules of the road" are necessary. Traffic rules on the water are somewhat similar to those on land, and it is for the sake of highway safety that a strict set of enforced rules and regulations have been promulgated. Thus, the license to operate a motor vehicle in the United States is obtained only after a person has proved before duly appointed officials the ability to operate the vehicle according to a prescribed set of safety rules.

A similar set of rules and regulations are in effect for the safety and guidance of motor boats operated on navigable waters in the United States. These include Federal Regulations imposed by the Motor Boat Act and its amendments, which set forth the minimum requirements concerning lights, safety equipment, and other regulations for motor vessels under 65 feet in length.

In general, the Federal Motorboat Act states that motor boats (outboards and inboards) operating on navigable waters in or opening into the Great Lakes, an ocean, or gulf, and all navigable waters tributary to such waters upstream to the first lockless dam, are under federal regulation.

In order to make the foregoing regulation enforceable, any motorboat operated on a body of water classed as "navigable" must be registered with the United States Coast Guard and bear its assigned registration number on each side of the bow. All motorboats more than 16 feet in length, or having a motor larger than 10 horsepower, whether inboard or outboard-powered, must comply with this rule.

## BOAT NUMBERING

Under the Federal Boating Act, all motor boats powered by more than 10 horsepower will be required to secure and display a boat number (or secure a new number if already numbered) if operated at any time on navigable waters in the United States. Under provisions of the act, some states have assumed the numbering function from the federal government, and in these states boats will be numbered by state agencies instead of by the United States Coast Guard. These state systems, where in effect, may also include other types of motor boats or small craft.

## POWER-BOAT CLASSIFICATION

The Motor Boat Act divides power boats into four classes, as follows:

Class A:   Boats less than 16 feet in length.
Class 1:   Boats 16 to 26 feet in length.
Class 2:   Boats 26 to 40 feet in length.
Class 3:   Boats 40 to 65 feet in length.

Most pleasure-type motor boats will fall into Class A and 1. All Class 1 boats must be registered with the United States Coast Guard (except those used for racing purposes only) within ten days after purchase.

From the foregoing, it follows that it is not necessary to register an outboard motor boat on federal waterways (sea coasts and tributary waters, the Great Lakes, and rivers or lakes touching more than one state, etc.) unless the boat is more than 16 feet in length, or unless the motor is larger than 10 horsepower. If the boat is more than 16 feet in length, or if the motor is in excess of 10 horsepower, and used on Federal waters, the nearest Coast Guard office should be contacted for information about boat registration. This boat registration is simple, and there is no charge for this service.

The Motor Boat Act prescribes the equipment to be carried by all outboard motor boats when navigating in federal waters. They are as follows:

All motor boats, whether inboards or outboards, must have a life preserver or a buoyant seat cushion for every person aboard. These should carry the Coast Guard's stamp of approval. If the boat has any enclosed spaces, an approved type of fire extinguisher must be provided.

All Class 1 boats must have a whistle, horn, or other mechanical sound-producing device capable of producing a blast of two seconds or more in duration. Lights are required to be displayed on the bow and stern from sunset to sunrise.

The bow light is a combination light that shows green to starboard and red to port. The light must be visible for one mile straight ahead and through an angle of 112.5 degrees on each side. (See Fig. 2.) The stern light must be a white light visible from all directions for a distance of two miles, and mounted in such a way that it is higher than the bow light.

## ADDITIONAL EQUIPMENT

In addition to the running lights required by law, there are a number of other items that should be aboard every boat, regardless of its size and how it is used. Proper planning includes having at least two anchors (one light and one heavy), together with appropriate anchor lines.

Always carry additional rope or line. A spare coil of a couple of hundred feet or so, may become essential, together with a ring lifebuoy in case of emergency. Most outboards, in common with other boat types, have a tendency to leak slightly, and should therefore be provided with an efficient bilge pump or other means for water bailing.

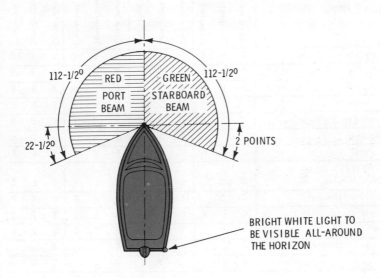

Fig. 2. Light combination required in the bow of a vessel.

To the foregoing should be added a sizeable tool kit, some spare engine parts such as shear pins, spark plugs, etc., extra fuel, and a good portable light. Food and a supply of fresh water are other essential necessities. If, during an extreme emergency, the boat should overturn, remember to stay with it. Don't try to swim to shore; it may be a good deal farther than it looks from the boat. It is important to realize that, even filled with water, the boat will stay afloat (metal boats have air chambers to prevent them from sinking) and provide support until help arrives.

Table 1 sets forth the recommended additional equipment by class of vessel and area of operation, such as open waters, semi-protected waters, and protected waters. Items are shown as "E" essential, or "D" desirable.

## Table 1. Recommended Additional Equipment

| Item | Class A (to 16') | | | CLASS 1 (16' to 26') | | | Class 2 (26' to 40') | | | Class 3 (40' to 65') | | |
|---|---|---|---|---|---|---|---|---|---|---|---|---|
| | Open waters | Semiprotected | Protected | Open waters | Semiprotected | Protected | Open waters | Semiprotected | Protected | Open waters | Semiprotected | Protected |
| Anchor(s) | E | E | E | E | E | E | E | E | E | E | E | E |
| Anchor cable (line, chain, etc.) | E | E | E | E | E | E | E | E | E | E | E | E |
| Bailing device, (pump, etc.) | E | E | E | E | E | E | E | E | E | E | E | E |
| Boat hook | .. | .. | .. | D | D | D | E | E | E | E | E | E |
| Bucket (fire fighting/bailing) | E | E | E | E | E | E | E | E | E | E | E | E |
| Coast pilot | .. | .. | .. | D | D | .. | D | D | .. | D | D | .. |
| Compass | E | E | D | E | E | D | E | E | E | E | E | E |
| Course protractor or parallel rules | D | D | .. | E | E | D | E | E | E | E | E | E |
| Deviation table | D | D | .. | E | E | D | E | E | E | E | E | E |
| Distress signals | E | E | E | E | E | E | E | E | E | E | E | E |
| Dividers | D | D | .. | E | E | D | E | E | E | E | E | E |
| Emergency rations | E | .. | .. | E | .. | .. | E | .. | .. | E | .. | .. |
| Emergency drinking water | E | D | .. | E | D | .. | E | D | .. | E | D | .. |
| Fenders | D | D | D | D | D | D | D | D | D | D | D | D |
| First-aid kit and manual (10- to 20-unit) | E | E | E | E | E | E | E | E | E | E | E | E |
| Flashlight | E | E | E | E | E | E | E | E | E | E | E | E |
| Heaving line | .. | .. | .. | .. | .. | .. | D | D | D | D | D | D |
| Lantern, kerosene | .. | .. | .. | .. | .. | .. | D | D | D | D | D | D |
| Light list | D | D | .. | E | E | D | E | E | E | E | E | E |
| Local chart(s) | E | D | .. | E | E | E | E | E | E | E | E | E |
| Megaphone or loud hailer | .. | .. | .. | .. | .. | .. | D | D | D | D | D | D |
| Mooring lines | E | E | E | E | E | E | E | E | E | E | E | E |
| Motor oil and grease (extra supply) | .. | .. | .. | D | D | D | D | D | D | D | D | D |
| Nails, screws, bolts, etc. | D | D | D | D | D | D | D | D | D | D | D | D |
| Oars, spare | E | E | E | E | E | E | .. | .. | .. | .. | .. | .. |
| Patent log | .. | .. | .. | D | .. | .. | D | .. | .. | D | .. | .. |
| Pelorus | .. | .. | .. | .. | .. | .. | D | D | D | D | D | D |
| Radar, reflector, collapsible | D | D | .. | D | D | .. | D | D | .. | D | D | .. |

## Table 1. Recommended Additional Equipment (Cont'd)

| | Class A (to 16') | | | CLASS 1 (16' to 26') | | | Class 2 (26' to 40') | | | Class 3 (40' to 65') | | |
|---|---|---|---|---|---|---|---|---|---|---|---|---|
| | Open waters | Semiprotected | Protected | Open waters | Semiprotected | Protected | Open waters | Semiprotected | Protected | Open waters | Semiprotected | Protected |
| Radio direction finder | .. | .. | .. | D | .. | .. | D | .. | .. | D | .. | .. |
| Radio, telephone | D | .. | .. | D | D | .. | D | D | .. | D | D | .. |
| Ring buoy(s) (additional) | D | D | D | D | D | D | D | D | D | D | D | D |
| RPM table | .. | .. | .. | D | D | D | D | D | D | D | D | D |
| Sounding device, (lead line, etc.) | D | D | .. | D | D | E | E | E | E | E | E | E |
| Spare batteries | D | D | D | D | D | D | D | D | D | D | D | D |
| Spare parts | E | D | .. | E | E | D | E | E | D | E | E | D |
| Tables, current | .. | .. | .. | .. | .. | .. | .. | D | D | .. | E | E |
| Tables, tide | .. | .. | .. | .. | .. | .. | .. | D | D | .. | E | E |
| Tools | E | D | .. | E | E | D | E | E | D | E | E | D |

### TRAFFIC RULES

To provide safety and to avoid collisions, there are traffic rules afloat as well as on land. The fundamental *rules of the road* which apply to outboard motor boats are the same as for large motor yachts, lake freighters, and ocean-going liners.

In most cases, collisions may be avoided by complying with the rules of the road and traffic regulations, at the same time taking into consideration the effects of existing weather conditions and tides, the maneuverability of the vessel, and the traffic load in the vicinity. The fundamental rules of the road are as follows:

1. *Meeting*—When two boats are approaching each other head-on, or nearly so, it will be the duty of each to steer to starboard (bearing right) so as to pass to the port side of one another, as illustrated in Fig. 3.
2. *Overtaking*—When one boat is overtaking another, the boat being overtaken has the right of way. See Fig. 4.

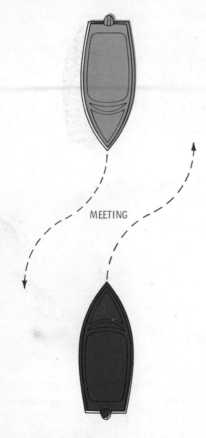

MEETING

Fig. 3. The law requires that it shall be the duty of each to pass on the port side of the other.

3. *Crossing*—When two boats are crossing, and there is risk of collision, the boat which has the other on the port side has the right of way and will hold the same course and speed, as shown in Figs. 5 and 6.

4. *Sailboats* and *rowboats* without motor attachment always have the right of way over all motor boats.

5. *Fishing boats,* whether underway or anchored, have the right of way.

6. Boats coming out of a slip or moving from docks or piers, do not have the right of way until they are entirely clear of the slip or pier.

338

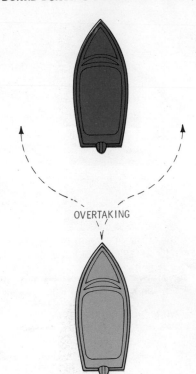

7. Caution should be exercised at all times. Never take chances by relying entirely on the speed and maneuverability of your boat or by guessing the capability of another. In case of accidents or collisions between boats, it is the duty of each to stand by and give every necessary assistance in every possible form, including towing to the nearest port, if required.

## ANCHORING

For the sake of safety, every boat should carry at least two anchors to be used in emergencies. Anchors are designed in such a manner that they, by virtue of their own weight and the pull exerted by the boat, will drive themselves deeper into the bottom

339

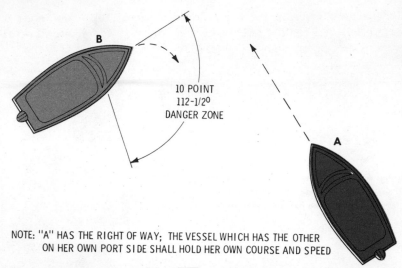

NOTE: "A" HAS THE RIGHT OF WAY; THE VESSEL WHICH HAS THE OTHER
ON HER OWN PORT SIDE SHALL HOLD HER OWN COURSE AND SPEED

Fig. 5. Two boats approaching each other at right angles. In this case, the boat which has the other to her own port side shall hold her course and speed.

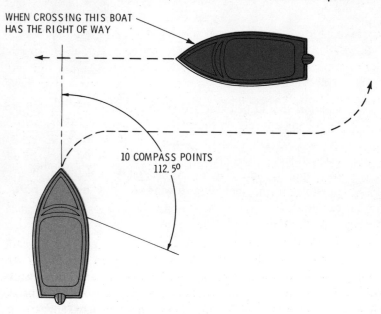

Fig. 6. Another illustration showing the rules of the road.

to increasingly secure the boat. To be efficient, an anchor must grip firmly and swiftly, but yet be capable of quick release. Two various designs are shown in Fig. 7.

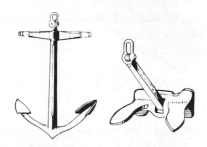

Fig. 7. Two typical boat anchors.

When getting ready to release the anchor, make sure that the water is deep enough to keep the boat afloat regardless of changing tides. On the other hand, too deep an anchoring spot may be dangerous if insufficient line is available. In moderate weather, a safe ratio of length of anchor line to depth of water is about six-to-one. Thus, for example, when anchoring in 8 feet of water, approximately 48 feet of anchor line will be required.

To make sure that the anchor line will be of sufficient length, careful soundings with the lead-line should be taken to ascertain the depth of the water. Other factors to be considered is to have the anchor line attached properly to the boat and anchor, and to see that the line is properly coiled and clear for running before releasing the anchor. Tides, current, and sudden squalls must always be taken into consideration when anchoring the boat. It is good practice to back up the boat slowly when dropping the anchor. This will avoid fouling the line and will properly secure the anchor to the bottom.

## Pulling Up Anchor

To pull up the anchor, start the engine and proceed slowly until the boat is vertically above the anchor, hauling up the line in the process. If the anchor is "stuck" temporarily, secure the shortest possible line to the bow of the boat and proceed slowly ahead. When the anchor becomes loose, stop the boat and bring the anchor aboard.

## DOCKING AND MOORING

By definition, a dock is a slip or waterway extending between two piers or projecting wharves, or cut into the land for the reception of ships. From the foregoing, it follows that a dock differs from a wharf or pier in that it occupies the space between two piers or projecting wharves.

In approaching piers, wharves, or floats, proceed at slow speed, with proper regard for winds, tides, and currents; the speed need only be sufficient for proper control of the boat. Also, remember to protect the hull with fenders before contacting the landing area. With the wind sternwise when approaching the pier, always attempt to bring the bow into the wind or current before coming alongside. Reverse the engine just before the boat is parallel to the pier, keeping in mind that when reversing, the stern tends to swing to port or left.

The mooring, or the process of tying up the boat to the wharf, pier, or float, is a comparatively simple matter provided the proper approach has been made. See Fig. 8. Most landing areas are

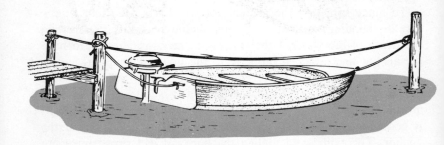

Fig. 8. Typical method of tying up or securing a boat.

provided with rings, cleats, or bollards around which to fasten or take a turn with the line. When making fast to a wharf or pier in tidal waters, provide enough slack in the line to allow for the rise and fall of the tide. This is particularly essential when boating in waters where the difference between high tide and low tide may be several feet during a 24-hour period.

Mooring to floating buoys in protected harbors requires that the buoy be securely anchored to a line or chain to prevent shifting due to winds, waves, or currents. The chain or line should be of sufficient length to keep the wood or metal buoy from being pulled down when the waves are high or when mooring in tidal waters. A double set of buoys is sometimes beneficial, particularly in crowded harbors; that is, the boat is tied up from both bow and stern.

## MOORING KNOTS

Successful boating requires knowledge about tying a few common knots of the type used in scouting work. Depending on the docking facilities available, whether simple cleats, bollards, or rings are used, the ability to quickly and safely secure the boat is essential. The most frequently used knots are the clove-hitch, half-hitch, fisherman's bend, bowline, square knot, cleat-hitch, etc. A few of these knots are shown in Fig. 9.

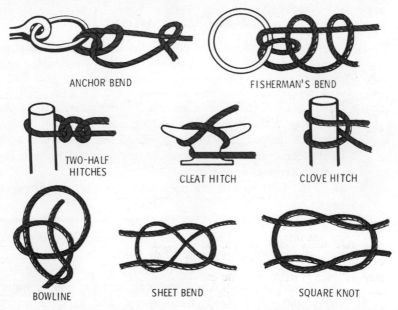

ANCHOR BEND     FISHERMAN'S BEND

TWO-HALF HITCHES    CLEAT HITCH    CLOVE HITCH

BOWLINE    SHEET BEND    SQUARE KNOT

**Fig. 9. Typical mooring knots used in securing a boat to piers.**

In securing the line to a cleat, wrap the line around the cleat and take a half-hitch over one prong. The clove-hitch, one of the easiest knots to make, is somewhat deceptive in that it will work itself loose unless constant strain is provided. A good knot to use in making fast to a bollard, post, or pilings is two half-hitches. Useful knots when fastening lines to an anchor are the fisherman's bend and bowline. The square knot, being the most common, is preferred when tying ropes or lines of equal thickness together.

## BOAT FENDERS

A useful item for small boats is the boat fender. It can be difficult to determine just what type or size to buy, because there are so many sizes, shapes, and materials available. For a small outboard motor boat you might check on the canvas-covered sponge rubber or all-plastic stripping for attaching to the gunwales. You might install a wooden rub rail capped with half-oval aluminum moulding.

## COMMON SENSE AFLOAT

An outboard motor boat, whether for fishing, hunting, camping, or just cruising around, will provide the utmost in relaxation and pleasure if a few common-sense rules are followed:

1.  Load tackle boxes, fuel cans, etc., into the boat from the dock. Keep arms free when climbing into the boat.
2.  Step into the center of the boat. When changing seats, walk in the center-line of the boat. Steady yourself by keeping both hands on the sides of the boat.
3.  Hold the boat against the dock while people are getting in or out.
4.  Be careful not to overload the boat. Boat manufacturers do not intend all the seats to be used at once. Three people is a full load for the average 12 or 14-foot boat.
5.  Be sure there is a life jacket or buoyant cushion for everyone aboard, a pair of oars, and a tin can for bailing water.
6.  Carry extra fuel, food, fresh water, and tools, even on contemplated short trips.

7. Use common sense. A portable radio is useful to obtain weather reports. When a storm is approaching, get ashore without delay. Keep clear of other boats, and be particularly careful around bathing beaches.
8. Check out your fire extinguisher and flashlight or lantern.
9. It is suggested that an extra propeller be carried as a spare.

You must, necessarily, heed a few little inconveniences in order to safely enjoy the waterways. It is advisable, therefore, to check with authorities in regard to local, state, and federal boating regulations and restrictions. Some boating precautions are repeated here for the obvious reason that "the life you save may be mine."

Keeping practicing water safety night and day by observing the following simple rules:

Do not operate boat near swimmers, skin divers, or fishermen.

Keep clear of sailing craft and rowboats, yielding right-of-way.

Always keep to the right; show courtesy at all times.

A boat which is being overtaken has the right-of-way.

Practice boat turns to test for "stern swing" of the boat.

Test for stopping distance at various boat speeds to be prepared for any unusual situation involving braking.

When reversing, stern will dip, so ask passengers to move forward in the boat to guard against swamping. When reversing, motor will not tilt up when striking a submerged object, thus be alert so that the transom will not be damaged.

Back away from the dock slowly in reverse gear.

Approach a dock slowly and, if possible, into the wind, waves,

Fig. 10. Method of tying boat to dock to avoid buffeting.

or current. Avoid buffeting by securing to dock as shown in Fig. 10.

Any flag or light which is all or part red is a warning that bad weather is developing or exists.

When heading into rough water while boat is on plane, decrease speed but maintain plane to prevent water from entering boat. Alter direction of attack on waves until it feels right.

"Danger Zone" is a 112.5-degree arc which is measured from dead ahead to off the starboard or right-hand side. A boat must yield the right-of-way to other craft which approach it within the danger zone shown in Fig. 5.

*Signposts*—Know the channel markers to follow a safe and confident course. See Fig. 11.

BLACK CAN
AND SPAR BUOYS

RED NUN
AND SPAR BUOYS

OBSTRUCTION
MARKER

MID-CHANNEL
BUOY

RED
WHITE
BLACK

Fig. 11. Channel markers are signposts for your protection.

When returning, keep the red buoys on your right; black buoys on your left.

Black-and-white vertically striped buoys indicate middle of channel; always pass close to them, either side.

Black-and-red horizontally striped buoys indicate obstruction; give them a wide berth.

## Respect these flags

*Danger*. The sport divers flag indicates a diver is in the water. You should keep a minimum of 30 yards between your boat and this flag. A life is worth more than a few feet of water.

*Distress*. The distress flag indicates a boat or passenger in serious trouble. When seeing this, you should respond and render any

assistance possible. Remember—it could be your boat displaying this flag. See Fig. 12.

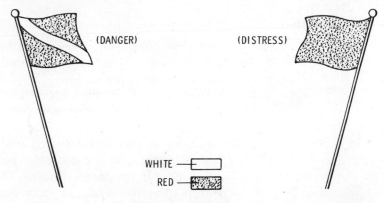

(DANGER)        (DISTRESS)

WHITE ——
RED ——

Fig. 12. Danger and distress flags.

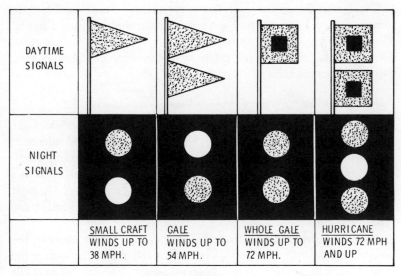

| | | | | |
|---|---|---|---|---|
| DAYTIME SIGNALS | | | | |
| NIGHT SIGNALS | | | | |
| | SMALL CRAFT WINDS UP TO 38 MPH. | GALE WINDS UP TO 54 MPH. | WHOLE GALE WINDS UP TO 72 MPH. | HURRICANE WINDS 72 MPH AND UP |

RED ——
WHITE-
BLACK-

Fig. 13. Weather warning system.

*Weather warning system.* Thoroughly familiarize yourself with weather bureau warning system signals and waterway traffic signs, as shown in Fig. 13.

## Safety Check

Any time is the time to check your present safety equipment for serviceability. Children's life jackets come in different sizes, rated to support youngsters in different weight ranges. Compare your children's weight against figures printed on the jacket labels to make sure the tops haven't exceeded their jacket weight capacities.

See that jacket straps are readjusted to fit comfortably on those rapidly growing wearers. Check the condition of the buckles and see that the straps are securely fastened to the jackets. Buoyant life cushions used by adults need inspection, too. Compare yours with new ones. Are they noticeably flattened? If so, it would be wise to test their buoyancy by actual immersion.

Check two things on your fire extinguisher. Those which have pressure gauges should show pressure within the designated limits. Then study the handle and trigger assembly. If something is bent, jammed, or corroded, or the safety seal is broken, you should have a qualified person set it in order.

## Parking Rules

Absence of "No Parking" signs does not mean that boaters are free to anchor anywhere and everywhere. Good judgment and consideration for others is called for when selecting a parking place. Most boaters know it's against the rules to anchor in channels. It's also unlawful to tie up to government navigation buoys. A boat moored to a buoy can hide it from sight and could send some other boat aground.

On rivers, especially narrow winding ones, boaters observe the common sense rule of always keeping to the right. But when the time comes to anchor, some boaters forget this and drop their hooks just around a sharp bend. Anchor far enough beyond any bend in the river so that boats rounding the bend on the same side of the river can see you in time to turn away or reduce their speed to avoid an accident.

## Children in Boats

Although boating is a true family sport, it is a good idea to insure good times for the younger set. This can be done by keeping their interest peaked. In other words, get them involved. You can assign duties like keeping a supply list, keeping a log book or checking instruments and recording data.

You can make a game of reading buoys, finding landmarks, and taking a bearing. You can ease the tension of long runs by a quick trip ashore for a cookout or a swim from the beach. Keep simple fishing gear aboard for the children's use. Make a game of testing the children on identifying different types of boats. Docking and shoving off are always tests of skill. Assign duties to these operations in keeping with the youngster's capacities. There's nothing dull about boating unless you make it so. Keep the children happy by keeping them constructively busy.

## TYPES OF OUTBOARD BOATS

The outboard motor can be adapted to power almost any floating object that is sufficiently large to accommodate motor and occupants. A large selection of motors will be found among the various boat types suitable for outboard motor service.

Outboard hulls may be classified with respect to materials used in their construction as:

1. Wood.
2. Metal.
3. Plastic.
4. Plywood.
5. Fiberglass.

They may be further classified (Fig. 14) with respect to shapes of hull as:

1. Flat-bottom.
2. Vee-bottom.
3. Round-bottom.

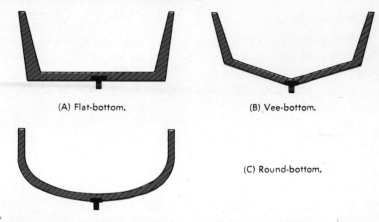

(A) Flat-bottom.

(B) Vee-bottom.

(C) Round-bottom.

**Fig. 14. Types of hulls that are suited for outboard motors.**

In general, outboard hulls may also be classified with respect to type or size as:

1. Rowboats and skiffs.
2. Prams and dinghies.
3. Runabouts.
4. Utilities.
5. Cruisers.

## Rowboats and Skiffs

The familiar flat-bottom rowboat or skiff, although originally powered by a pair of oars, is today often equipped with an outboard motor. The rowboat is the work horse of the small boat fleet, and is easy to build and relatively inexpensive, whether it is constructed of wooden planks and ribs, plywood, or aluminum.

The bottom may be flat, vee, or round, in sizes of up to about 18 feet. Boats of this type are generally suited for small outboard motors of up to about 10 horsepower. The flat-bottom skiff makes a satisfactory utility or fishing craft on small protected lakes and shallow streams.

## Prams and Dinghies

The main characteristic of prams and dinghies is their light-weight and portability. They are approximately 8 to 10 feet in length and weigh from about 50 up to 150 lbs. The difference between a pram and a dinghy is that prams are constructed with snub-nosed bows, while dinghies have round or pointed bows.

Because of their limited size, they usually carry a maximum of two persons, and are suitable for outboard motors of up to 3 horsepower. They are often carried on top of the family car for vacation use, and are also commonly employed as tenders for larger vessels, such as cabin cruisers and sailing yachts. Materials of construction are usually aluminum, fiberglass, and plywood.

## Runabouts

These are light outboard boats commonly used for sports, as for towing water skiers, on day outings, for commuting, etc. The average size is from 12 to about 20 feet. The bottoms are usually of the vee or rounded type and are suitable for motors of from 5 to 50 horsepower, depending on the boat size.

Runabouts are frequently termed the "sport boats" of the water, and are broad of beam to offer stability and to induce planing. When equipped essentially for sports, the boat is normally furnished with a long foredeck, which frequently includes a full or split center deck, and such deluxe appointments as upholstered seats, remote controls, windshields, etc. Construction materials vary and may be plywood, metal, plastic, or fiberglass.

## Utilities

These boats are for general service use, and are normally completely open or with a short forward deck. Their size varies and may be anywhere from about 12 to 18 feet. Utilities are powered with motors from 5 to 50 horsepower, depending on size.

## Cruisers

The outboard cruiser has been growing in popularity, since it provides additional inboard space normally required for the motor compartment. Because of the added weight of cabins and superstructure, the size of the hull for outboard cruisers is usually from 16 to about 22 feet.

The cruiser, although a great deal costlier than conventional boat types, provides most of the amenities of the home, being equipped with all the normal utilities required, including electricity, water, toilets, refrigeration, and sleeping facilities for up to six people.

Hulls are usually framed with oak and may be planked with mahogany or waterproof plywood. Motor horsepower requirements vary with the size of the hull. Smaller cruisers may use only about 25 horsepower, whereas larger types may use twin motors.

## Hull Construction

Construction of the hull largely determines the manner in which the boat moves through or over the water. The various designs are known as displacement, semidisplacement, and planing.

The main difference between the displacement and planing designs that the former is built to run through the water, while the latter is built to run on top of the water. The displacement-type boat usually has a curved keel and narrow stern, and in plowing through the water, floats at rest only after it has displaced an amount of water equivalent in weight to that of the boat, passengers, motor, load, and all equipment. Because of its design features, the speed of the displacement-type boat is limited and it is usually equipped with motors of small to medium size.

Semidisplacement- and planing-type hulls are built with round or vee bottoms and a broad, nearly flat, beam and will run on top of the water. Boats of this nature are used in racing. As the speed increases, the amount of displaced water decreases. At top speed, it will level off and skim on top of the water with only a small portion of the bottom and the lower unit of the outboard motor in the water.

Another type of planing hull is the hydroplane boat which is used only for racing. This boat usually has a break-like step across the bottom, a little aft of amidships. This deep notch creates a cushion of air behind the step at forward speed, and in this manner reduces the amount of bottom surface exposed to water friction, thus lifting the hull into a planing position on top of the water.

## BOAT HANDLING

Although boats and cars have numerous things in common, their steering action is quite different. For example, when the steering wheel of a car is turned, the front of the vehicle changes its direction. When the wheel of a boat is turned, however, it is the stern (rear) that moves to change its course or direction.

With the boat and propeller going forward, and the rudder amidships, the boat tends to move on a straightforward course. When the rudder is put over either to the right or left, the water through which the boat is moving strikes the rudder face and forces the stern in the opposite direction. At the same time, the discharge current strikes the rudder face and pushes the stern over further. Thus, when the rudder is moved to the right, the stern will be forced to the left and the bow to the right. The reverse will be true when the rudder is put to the left.

The handling of any boat is also greatly affected by the wind, whose effect varies with the design, superstructure, free-board, high bow, etc. Boats which float high in the water are generally more difficult to handle in high winds than are those of deeper draft. A boat which is heavily loaded and lying low in the water is influenced by current and tide, while a boat lightly loaded and riding high on the water is influenced by the wind.

The depth of water will also affect the response of the rudder. A boat in shallow water reacts very sluggishly, whereas in deep water, a normal rudder response is obtained. For this reason, it is necessary to proceed through shallow water with a great deal of caution. In view of the foregoing, no precise rules can be laid down as to how a boat will react under different conditions of sea, wind, tide, and currents.

Figs. 15 to 23 serve to illustrate the likely effect of propeller and rudder direction during forward and backward motion of motor-operated boats, it being assumed that the sea is calm and that there is no tide or current.

## Boat Going Astern; Propeller in Reverse

Maneuvering of the boat becomes more complicated when going astern and the propeller in reverse, because of the additional forces at work. Here, the sidewise pressure of the propeller is opposite to that of going forward and is a pressure to port. Thus, with the rudder amidships, the stern of the boat will back to port, as shown in Fig. 15.

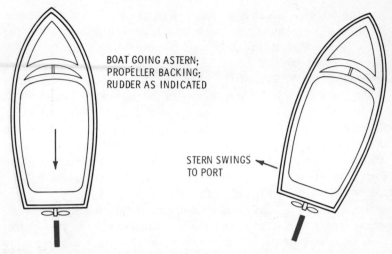

BOAT GOING ASTERN;
PROPELLER BACKING;
RUDDER AS INDICATED

STERN SWINGS
TO PORT

Fig. 15. Position most likely taken by boat when going astern, propeller in reverse, and rudder amidship.

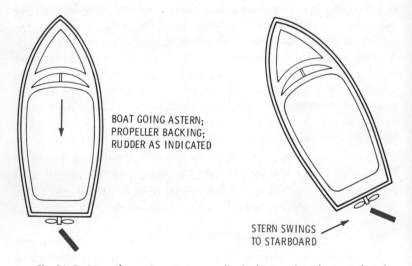

BOAT GOING ASTERN;
PROPELLER BACKING;
RUDDER AS INDICATED

STERN SWINGS
TO STARBOARD

Fig. 16. Position when going astern, propeller backing, and rudder to starboard.

If the rudder is put over to starboard, and with the propeller in reverse, the action of the suction current against the face of the rudder will tend to throw the stern to starboard. See Fig. 16. Unless

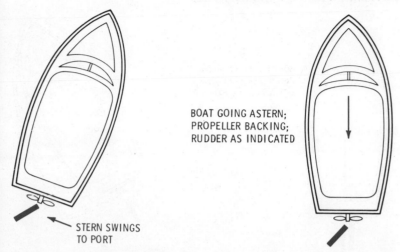

BOAT GOING ASTERN;
PROPELLER BACKING;
RUDDER AS INDICATED

STERN SWINGS
TO PORT

Fig. 17. Position taken when boat is going astern, propeller backing, and rudder to port.

the speed astern is very great, however, this force is not strong enough to overcome the effect of the sidewise pressure and the discharge current, and the stern will back to port.

If the rudder is put over to port, the effect of the suction current on the face of the rudder accumulates the effect of the sidewise pressure of the propeller and the discharge current, and will force the stern rapidly to port, as shown in Fig. 17.

## Boat Going Forward; Propeller in Reverse

With the boat forward and the propeller backing, the forces of the propeller play a large part in maneuvering. If the rudder is in an amidship position, the stern will move to port, as the only active forces are the sidewise pressure of the propeller and the discharge current. This action of the boat is shown in Fig. 18.

With the rudder to starboard, the stern goes to port rapidly, but as headway is lost and the boat begins to go astern, the effect of the suction current on the rudder face slows the motion. Since a single-propeller boat tends to back to port when moving astern, the stern will still tend to port unless the boat gathers considerable speed astern. This action of the boat is shown in Fig. 19.

355

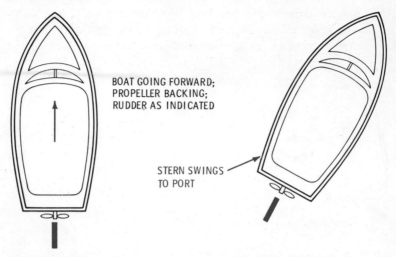

BOAT GOING FORWARD;
PROPELLER BACKING;
RUDDER AS INDICATED

STERN SWINGS
TO PORT

Fig. 18. Position taken by boat when going forward, propeller backing, and rudder amidship.

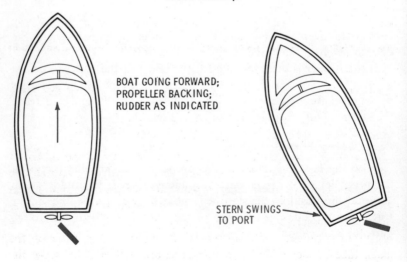

BOAT GOING FORWARD;
PROPELLER BACKING;
RUDDER AS INDICATED

STERN SWINGS
TO PORT

Fig. 19. Position taken when boat is going forward, propeller is backing, and rudder to starboard.

With the rudder to port, the normal steering tendencies of the rudder tend to throw the stern to starboard. This will happen if the boat has considerable headway. As the headway is lost, how-ever, the effect of the sidewise pressure of the propeller and the discharge current in conjunction with the increasing force of the

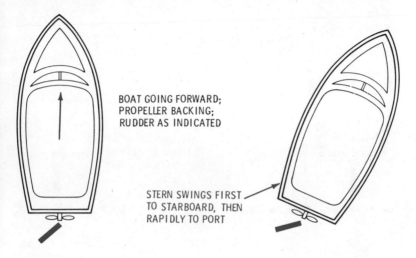

BOAT GOING FORWARD;
PROPELLER BACKING;
RUDDER AS INDICATED

STERN SWINGS FIRST
TO STARBOARD, THEN
RAPIDLY TO PORT

Fig. 20. Position taken when boat is going forward, propeller is backing, and rudder to port.

suction current against the face of the rudder swings the stern rapidly to port, as shown in Fig. 20.

## Boat Going Astern; Propeller Forward

In a situation of this sort, the sidewise pressure of the propeller and the wake current are persistent factors and may cancel one another. Hence, if the rudder is amidship with no outside forces acting upon it, the boat will tend to follow a straight course, as shown in Fig. 21.

With the rudder to the starboard, the action of the water on the back face of the rudder as it moves astern will tend to throw the stern to the starboard, while the action of the discharge current against the forward face of the rudder tends to throw the stern to port. As the boat loses sternway, however, the direct steering effect of the rudder takes over and the stern swings to port (Fig. 22).

357

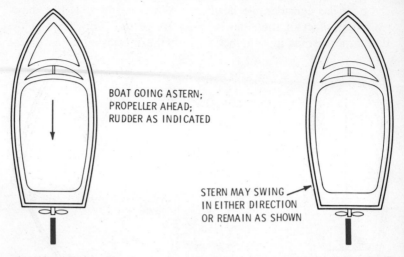

BOAT GOING ASTERN;
PROPELLER AHEAD;
RUDDER AS INDICATED

STERN MAY SWING
IN EITHER DIRECTION
OR REMAIN AS SHOWN

Fig. 21. Position taken when boat is moving astern, propeller ahead, and rudder amidship.

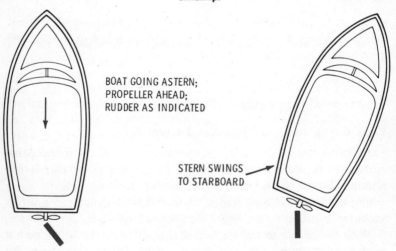

BOAT GOING ASTERN;
PROPELLER AHEAD;
RUDDER AS INDICATED

STERN SWINGS
TO STARBOARD

Fig. 22. Position taken by boat when going astern, propeller ahead, and rudder to starboard.

With the rudder towards the port (Fig. 23), the action will be the same as with the starboard rudder, and the direction is deter-

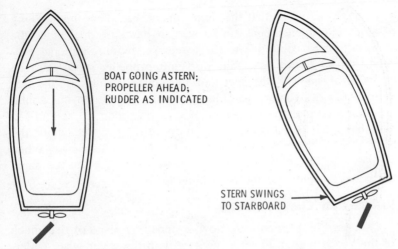

BOAT GOING ASTERN;
PROPELLER AHEAD;
RUDDER AS INDICATED

STERN SWINGS
TO STARBOARD

Fig. 23. Position taken by boat when moving astern, propeller ahead, and rudder to port.

mined by the strength of the active forces. As the boat loses stern-way, the direct steering effect of the rudder takes over, and the stern swings rapidly to starboard.

## Twin-Motor Boats

The increasing popularity of twin-motor installation, particularly on outboard cruisers, will necessitate a brief explanation on handling such installations. One advantage of dual-motor installation is the added factor of safety, since in the event of a breakdown of one motor, the remaining one will be operating. Another factor is the additional speed which will be obtained.

In this connection, it should be noted that there is no direct relationship between boat speed and horsepower. Thus, for example, if a certain boat moves at a speed of, say 14 miles per hour with a 7-horsepower motor, the speed will not be 28 miles per hour by installing a 14-horsepower motor. The same can be said of dual-motor installations: two 25-horsepower motors will not give the same cruising speed as that of one 50-horsepower motor, because of the additional water turbulence created by two propellers.

It should be noted that the same forces that affect the handling of a single-propeller boat are present in handling dual units, the main difference being due to the forces set by an additional propeller. On twin-unit boats, the port-unit propeller speed must be in synchronism with the speed of the starboard unit. If the two motors run at somewhat different rpm, very annoying sound pulsations normally result. Also, if one propeller is going ahead and the other astern, there is a sharp turning movement of the boat, turning the bow to the side of the backing propeller. When maneuvering a boat with twin-propellers running in the same direction, the rudder is the controlling factor.

## Planing on Choppy Water

Outboard motor boats are now designed to plane so that much of the boat's bottom is not in contact with the water when underway. Often, waves contact the hull bottom amidships—approximately beneath the seats. This can cause a bumpy ride. To lessen this motion, bring the boat's bow down so the point where it contacts the water is well ahead of the seats. Then the sharp vee of the prow can divide the waves effectively. If your equipment includes *Mercury's* power trim, this can be accomplished by touching the control button.

The old standard method of lowering the bow is to shift passengers and other movable weights, such as fuel tank and loose gear, forward. You have to experiment to find the most effective trim. You can experiment with motor tilt, too. Move the adjustment pin forward one hole at a time. Propeller thrust then lifts the stern more, puts the bow down, and brings the sharp vee of the hull more into play.

## BUYING A USED BOAT

When signs of spring begin to appear, many a would-be boater realizes it is time to do something about getting himself a boat and motor. If the boating desire is strong but the budget is weak, it may be worth your while to check the possibilities of a used boat. There are advantages worth considering in this idea. Do your used-boat shopping among reputable marine dealers in your area, so you know the boats and motors you are shown are well chosen and well-balanced outfits. This point alone is a big time-saver, for there's no need to study boats, motors, and accessories individually, and then put together your own boat. You get a ready-to-use package.

Another feature in getting a used boat is that, since it has been in operation, the bugs have been ironed out and the performance capabilities are known. Perhaps your dealer has a particular boat he has seen in operation and knows what it can do. Or, since it is ready to go, he may offer to put it in the water for a trial run. Perhaps you are so new to boating you are unsure what general size or type of boat would best serve your needs. The used outfit offers a chance to get onto the water in something you think will probably do, but without investing too heavily in it. Should a season of use convince you something else would better serve your needs, then you can trade it in on exactly the right boat.

## INSURANCE FOR SMALL-BOAT OWNERS

When pleasure boating took hold after World War II, it took the insurance people by surprise. About all they had to offer the small-boat owner was "yachting insurance," originally intended for large ocean-going vessels.

The out-dated provisions of the old policies gave the small-boat owner some coverage he didn't need, and he was unable to get some special protection he needed. It wasn't until recently that the insurance companies took steps to provide the type of coverage most boat owners wanted. At first, the costs were too high. The underwriters having no experience to rely on, moved cautiously, and so the first policies contained so many restrictions that they amounted to almost no protection at all.

Now the picture has changed, as companies have discovered the loss from boating policies is much lower than that of many other types of coverage they offer. Coverage on boating equipment has been broadened and refined to meet individual needs and the cost has moved steadily downward. Insurance companies are going all out to meet the needs of pleasure boaters with a full coverage policy which will give ample protection.

A boat should be insured at its current value. Since a pleasure boat depreciates like an automobile, it should be reappraised from time to time, either by the owner or by a specialist to make sure it is not overinsured.

The owner should not forget to increase his coverage to take in expensive accessories he may have installed after having purchased his boat. Some equipment, such as ship-to-shore radios, depth finders, and other electronic equipment, can add many thousands of dollars to the value of the boat.

## REGIONAL TYPES OF BOATS

Each region of the country seems to have its own specialized form of small boat. Some of these include the banks dory of New England, the pirogue of Louisiana, the west coast SK boats, and the john boat of the Ozarks.

The john boat has probably become the most widely known. It was originally made by hand of wood planks. The boats were mainly used for fishing "Flat trips" down the rivers of the lower midwest. The scowlike craft wasn't much for looks, but it was a highly efficient fishing boat. Larger boat manufacturers saw the usefulness of the john boat and soon they were being made of aluminum and fiberglass and finding their way to all parts of the country.

CHAPTER 15

# High Horsepower
# Outboards

The introduction of the V-6 (200 horsepower) outboard motors has opened up a new world of boating. The higher horsepower motors were needed to meet the need of fishermen and other pleasure boaters who would ordinarily use two outboards to get the larger boats underway. (Fig. 1.)

*Evinrude* and *Johnson* have both introduced a 200 V-6. Since both are owned by *OMC* it is only correct to assume that both motors are similar, if not the same. According to the reports released by the makers—the engine is all-new. It is not just a couple of cylinders added on to the existing four cylinder models.

The engine (200 V-6) uses cross-flow scavenging to make sure each cylinder gets the proper fuel at the right moment. In a cross-flow engine, the fuel charge enters on one side of the cylinder. It's turned upward by the deflector on the piston, and runs up the intake side of the cylinder to the combustion chamber. Here it's compressed and fired. The burn gases then move down the opposite side of the cylinder, and out the exhaust ports. The charge follows a continuous U-shaped path into, across, and out of the cylinder.

In a loop-charged engine, fuel enters at the rear and sides of the cylinder. It is actually aimed by the ports toward the top of the cylinder, Fig. 2. The charge flows up into the combustion chamber where it's compressed and fired. It continues its loop

363

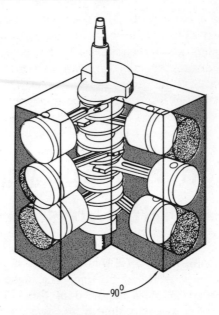

**Fig. 1. Illustrating the 90-degree V-block powerhead.**

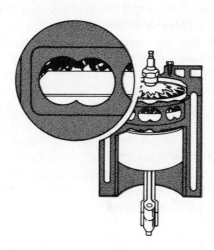

**Fig. 2. The loop-charged engine. Fuel enters at the rear and sides of the cylinder —moves up into the combustion chamber—continues its loop down and out the exhaust ports.**

down and out the exhaust ports. The piston has no deflector, and the charge is nearly the same in both cross-flow and loop engines. The engine designers make their choice by balancing the advantages of flat-top pistons against the extra size and weight of a cylinder block with cast-in, aimed ports.

The new V-6 of *Johnson's* has a unique shape for the three exhaust and three intake ports in each cylinder. These are drilled with overlapping holes to get a port that's very wide (almost flat) across the top. This shape gives more port area, faster port opening than a conventional round port. The rapid opening gives very strong tuning pulses—the key to power and fuel economy in any two-stroke engine.

There are three two-barrel carburetors, one barrel for each cylinder. The high-rise manifold has sloping passages from carburetors to reed boxes that offer the least possible resistance to the charge in its movement from the carburetor into the crankcase.

Another powerful outboard for boats is the 175 horsepower V-6 made by *Johnson*. It has the same 90-degree V, 149.4 cubic inch powerhead. It has a smaller carburetor and develops its rated horsepower, 175, at 5000 rpms instead of the 5250 of the 200.

Both V-6s have such standard features as double-drilled intake and exhaust ports, for more port area per cylinder displacement and faster port opening. They have dual fuel pumps, *MagFlash*® CD ignition and 15-amp alternators.

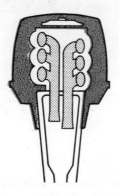

**Fig. 3. A tuned exhaust system.**

Each V-6 cylinder bank has its own tuned exhaust system, including individual megaphones feeding into a common expansion chamber, for more power and less fuel consumption. Fig. 3.

Both engines have temperature- and pressure-controlled cooling systems, one for each bank. At idle and low speeds, the temperature control provides quick engine warm-up; the pressure control takes over at higher speeds for efficient cooling.

Both the 175 and 200 are available in long (20-inch) and extra long (25-inch) shaft lengths. (Fig. 4.) A single heavy-duty shock

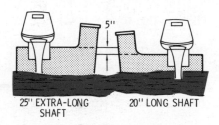

25" EXTRA-LONG SHAFT  20" LONG SHAFT

Fig. 4. Motor shaft length for various transom dimensions.

absorber takes impact forces from hidden underwater objects. Fig. 5.

The control center consists of a single lever control. It also houses the key switch electric start and hot warning horn.

Six aluminum and six stainless steel propellers are available for the 175 and 200.

## Specifications For The V-6, 200 HP

**(Johnson 200)**

| | |
|---|---|
| HP at rpm | 200 @ 5250 |
| No. cylinders | 6 |
| Engine type | 2-stroke |
| Displacement (cu. in.) | 149.4 |
| Effective compression ratio | 7.25:1 |
| Weight (lb.) | 377 |
| Ignition type | Magneto CD |
| Carburetion | 3  2-barrel |
| Choke | Automatic, Electric |
| Alternator output (amps) | 15 |
| Electric start | standard |
| Test prop (in.) | 14½ x 19, 3-blade |
| Trim adjust | 15°, stepless hyd. |

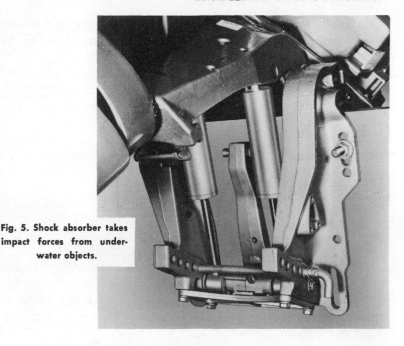

Fig. 5. Shock absorber takes impact forces from underwater objects.

*Johnson* has designed into the midsection of the 200, 175 and the extra-long 140 a power Trim 'N' Tilt. This is made of a heavy-duty shock absorber and two hydraulic trim cylinders. The trim offers 15-degree engine angle adjustment at speed and the tilt and 65 degrees for trailering, launching and beaching. The trim is actuated by a remote switch at the helm. A dial indicates the trim position. Fig. 6.

The extra-long version of the motors are now being sold since more power is available—there are more boats with more freeboard and deeper hulls to carry more people and equipment. The extra-long versions allow the manufacturers of boats to add 5 inches additional freeboard to the stern of their larger outboard craft.

The *Johnson* outboards (2 through 140 horsepower) burn regular leaded or unleaded gasoline. The 50-to-1 ratio gas to lubricant fuel mix, is correct for the 175 and 200, but they require gasoline with a minimum of 94-octane rating.

367

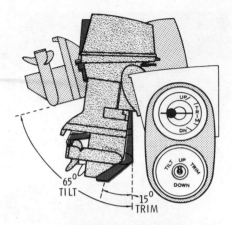

**Fig. 6. Trim 'N' Tilt control.**

Standard on all *Johnson's* 1977 models is a "Push Key" choke for easier starting. The operator pushes the key while starting for cold-motor choking. A plastic device added to the key makes it more comfortable to operate the choking mechanisms. The remote choke is built into the electric start key switch.

# CHAPTER 16

# Propellers

A propeller changes the energy or torque of the motor crank-shaft into thrust. This thrust or push against the water actually propels the boat. When a propeller turns in the water, it is something like a screw turning in a block of wood. Water is liquid, the propeller's effort draws water from in front of the propeller and pushes it out the rear against surrounding water. This creates what is called a *thrust cone*. Accelerated water generates the thrust that moves the boat. Some of the effort of the propeller is dissipated into the surrounding water in the form of slippage, turbulence and drag. A properly designed propeller may have as little at 10% slippage on a planing type of boat, or as much as 50% slippage on heavy work boats. Good propeller design and proper application does make a big difference.

## PITCH

Pitch is the twist or angle at which the propeller is set to the direction of travel. Fig. 1. It's easier to express this angle in inches, that is, the distance the propeller will theoretically travel in one full turn. A 20″ pitch means the propeller would theoretically travel 20″ on one turn. Since there is slippage and turbulence, the actual distance is somewhat less. The higher the pitch, the greater the forward travel.

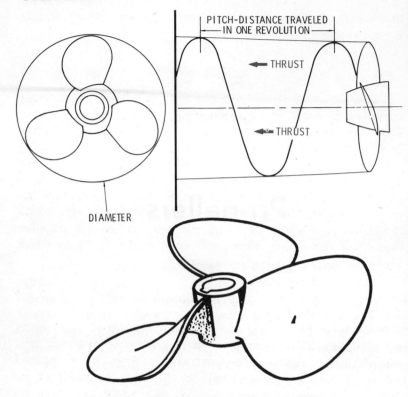

PITCH-DISTANCE TRAVELED
IN ONE REVOLUTION

◄— THRUST

◄— THRUST

DIAMETER

Fig. 1. Illustrating the pitch or angle of propeller.

## DIAMETER

The diameter of a propeller is the diameter of the circle described by the tips of the rotating propeller. The diameter of a propeller is regulated with the pitch and gear ratio to make the best combinations for each speed range.

There are two common propeller measurements. If a propeller is specified as 10 × 12 size, this indicates it is 10″ diameter by 12″ pitch. Dimensions are always given in this order. Diameter is determined by doubling the distance between blade tip and center of the hub. Pitch refers to the blade angle. In this example, the 12″ pitch indicates that with each prop revolution the boat theoretically would advance 12″. Due to slip loss, actual advance is somewhat less.

## CAVITATION

Cavitation could be the result of poor propeller design, wrong blade area or pitch for the application, bent propeller or gearcase, large boat keel and others. Usually the result of cavitation can be seen in form of paint or metal eaten or burned off the propeller surfaces or gearcase. These burned areas are the result of vapor bubbles which have been formed by the water's inability to flow over or around poorly developed areas—that is, areas which impede or obstruct the natural water flow. These bubbles attach themselves to a surface of higher pressure, such as the propeller blade face and cause minute but high pressure impacts which erode the surface where they collapse.

## VENTILATION

Ventilation is the effect of external air or exhaust gases being made available to the propellers. The propeller blades during their operation have a pressure and suction side. When air is induced into the propeller's working area, the suction or back side of the blade will accept any migrant air, thus causing loss of thrust, increase in motor rpm, and poor performance. Causes of ventilation are too high transom setting, wrong motor angle, severe turns, large keel, fouled boat bottom or lower unit, or loss of converging ring from thru-hub exhaust propeller.

## MATCHING PROPELLER TO BOAT

One of the first questions asked by the boat owner is: What prop should I use with my boat and motor? First, determine how the boat will be used—or what the normal load will be. If this boat usually operates with one specific passenger load, propeller size selection is relatively easy. If it has multiple uses ranging from light to heavy loads, it may be necessary to select one or two propellers for best results.

371

Stock propellers furnished with most outboards and stern drives are a compromise. Since they have a fixed diameter and pitch, they are limited in use and do not provide satisfactory performance under all the variations of hulls and loads.

The propeller not only moves the boat but it also regulates the engine rpm, and horsepower is directly related to rpm. The engine has a horsepower rating, but in most instances the full benefit of the horsepower is never realized. Equal emphasis should be placed on the rpm at which the horsepower is attained. This is where the propeller comes into the picture. Outboards are designed to be run at peak rpm for full efficiency. Excessive rpm with its increased friction and wear is harmful. It is equally bad to run the engine so overloaded that it cannot achieve its rated rpm. This results in excessive carbon buildup in the cylinders, poor fuel economy, preignition, frequent spark plug failure, scoring of cylinder walls, and burned pistons.

The key to proper matching of propeller to motor is not the size of the boat, but speed (revolutions per minute) of the motor. Modern outboards and stern drives develop their maximum horsepower in a rather narrow range of rpm's. Propellers should be selected and tested at full throttle and within the proper operating range of the motor.

There is no way to be completely sure if a tachometer is not used. Should one not be available, and a water speed indicator is available, the next best method is to test the propeller at full throttle and not the speed indicated. If this speed falls within the range shown in the propeller chart of your motor, then it is operating within safe rpm limits. If you are in a lower speed range, then go to a lower pitch. If the speed range is too high, go to a propeller of greater pitch.

## Prop Size

Why do outboards and stern drives of the same power sometimes take different prop sizes? This is due to differences in lower gear ratios. These are geared so that the propeller shaft turns at a slower speed than the rpm at the powerhead. This is usually expressed as a ratio such at 12:21 or 14:28, referring to the number of teeth in the drive gears. In the first example, the crankshaft gear has 12 and the propeller shaft gear has 21. This means the propeller shaft turns only 57% as fast as indicated rpm at the powerhead.

The lower the gear ratio the larger the propeller that can be used, and vice versa. In other instances, engines of different makes may develop their horsepower at different rpm levels. Everything else being equal, higher rpm engines require smaller props to achieve greater rpm.

### Fuel Consumption

To get a boat up on plane takes the full power of the motor and requires an efficient, properly matched propeller. Once on plane the power demand is greatly reduced. At this point, you can throttle back, and select your cruising speed, usually the lowest power setting which maintains the boat in a clean planing attitude. This speed will provide the maximum miles per gallon of fuel.

## PROPELLLER AND WATER SKIING

Water skiing requires a propeller of a lower pitch than cruising because of the need for greater acceleration and thrust to get a skier on top and the boat on plane. This is more necessary on lower horsepower motors, since modern middle- and high-horsepower motors have ample power to carry one or more skiers with a standard propeller. But there is a risk of overspeeding the motor if a skiing propeller is used for regular cruising. And the use of a cruising propeller for skiing tends to overload the motor. If in doubt, change the propeller and protect your investment in the motor.

In most cases the change in propeller will help in water skiing. Original equipment propellers are pitched a little on the high side. Not knowing the boat the engine will be used with, the manufacturer pitches the prop a little high so the engine does not exceed top rpm if placed on a light boat. However, on a heavier boat, or with water skiers, this propeller tends to overload the engine, resulting in poor speed, poor acceleration and sluggish performance, making it difficult to get a skier up. This is corrected by using a lower pitched prop.

## TWO AND THREE-BLADED PROPS

The amount of propeller thrust is governed by three factors: pitch, diameter, and blade area. A three-bladed propeller of a given pitch and diameter will have greater thrust than a two-bladed propeller. Three-bladed propellers are used for most runabouts and cruisers. Two-bladed propellers are generally used for high speed running with very light loads—as in racing. A four-bladed propeller is used on large, slow moving boats, where great thrust, but little speed, is needed.

## CUPPING

Most propellers can be ordered with cupping. Cupping consists of a slight, but critically accurate turning of the trailing edge of the blades. This increases the jet stream volume and reduces slipping or cavitation. Cupped propellers, most effective on light, fast hulls, can be run higher on the transom, which gives greater speed by reducing drag. When using cupped propellers, reduce pitch one inch.

## BRONZE VERSUS STAINLESS STEEL PROPELLER

Bronze propellers resist corrosion, outlast aluminum, can be easily repaired and may last as long as the motor. However, their use in salt water is not recommended because of the great increase in galvanic corrosion of the gear case. The stainless steel propeller (SST) made of stainless steel has the advantages of durability and repairability of bronze plus many advantages of its own. The SST weighs about ⅓ less than bronze. This means less drag and more horsepower available to move the boat.

The blades of the stainless steel are thinner for cleaner bite and more thrust without increased ventilation, yet the propeller is twice as strong as bronze .The SST delivers up to three more miles per hour in speed and uses less fuel at the same speed setting. The SST resists marine growth. It is twice as strong as aluminum.

Stainless steel is noted for its extreme tensile strength and yield strength. The SST is also resistant to abuse that affects other propellers. A greater demand for SST props has caused the manufacturers to produce a wide range of these physically superior props at reasonable prices. The stainless steel prop is five times as strong as aluminum.

## SELECTING AND FITTING A PROPELLER

Most motors are equipped with a propeller of a diameter and pitch considered by the manufacturer to operate satisfactorily in the majority of boat applications. This propeller allows the engine to run at its rated revolutions per minute at full throttle on the average boat with the average load. With the great variety of boat sizes, weights and types, this propeller may have to be changed before the first run. Use the propeller application chart provided by propeller manufacturers to get the correct prop.

### Transom Height

For outboard motors, proper transom height is essential for maximum forward thrust from your propeller. If the transom is too high, the propeller will ventilate (take in too much air around the propeller) and may cause damage to your motor from excessive slippage. If the transom is too low, the motor will cause excessive drag, resulting in loss of speed, loss of power and production of undesirable spray.

To achieve the ideal transom length, it may be necessary to cut out or add to the transom. This step, of course, is unnecessary when selecting a stern drive propeller.

On a family-type boat the anticavitation plate of the outboard should run level to ½″ below the boat bottom with the proper transom height. On large boats, propeller level is ½″ to 1″ below boat bottom. On light fast boats, the engine can be raised on the transom so that the anticavitation plate is level or above the bottom of the boat. Cupped propellers may be necessary if slippage of the propeller occurs.

### Angle of Tilt

Usually the best operating tilt angle is achieved when the driveshaft of the motor is perpendicular to the surface of the water

PROPELLERS

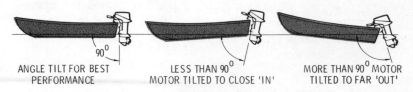

ANGLE TILT FOR BEST
PERFORMANCE

LESS THAN 90°
MOTOR TILTED TO CLOSE 'IN'

MORE THAN 90° MOTOR
TILTED TO FAR 'OUT'

**Fig. 2. Motor tilt angle.**

when the boat is at full throttle. Fig. 2. It is impossible to determine this angle without putting the boat into the water and running
with normal load and at rated full rpm. If the motor is tipped too
close to the transom, the boat will dig or plow in a bow down
position, with consequent performance loss. In addition, the boat
will tend to swerve to the right and steer hard left. If the motor is
tipped too far away from the transom, the boat will "gallop" or
"porpoise" in a bow high position, and will swerve to the left and
steer hard right. All outboard motors are equipped with tilt adjustment for achieving optimum angle. On stern drive boats the
tilt angle will be preset by proper factory installation.

If the outboard motor is not centered exactly on the transom
the unbalanced thrust will result in poor performance, hard steering and possible gearcase damage.

**Keel Interference**

A keel that is too deep or too wide will permit air bubbles to
flow back to the propeller, causing not only slippage of the propeller, but also cavitation "burn" which will erode the propeller.
To correct this condition it may be necessary to reshape the keel,
tapering it to approximately ¼" in height at the transom, begin-
ning the taper about 30" forward from the transom. An improper
keel will also cause slippage in turns.

**Boat Loading**

Distribute the weight, both passengers and gear, so that the
boat is properly trimmed and will neither dig nor porpoise. This
is especially essential for test runs in selecting the proper propeller
and tilt angle.

376

PROPELLERS

## Operating Range of the Motor

Your outboard motor develops its rated horsepower within a
given range of rpms. This is usually 4500 to 5500 rpms. All outboards and stern drives are designed to run at full throttle and
propellers should be selected at full throttle to operate within the
recommended range. A motor, outboard or stern drive, which is
run frequently at a speed higher than its rated rpm may be damaged and its life shortened. A motor which is consistently over-
loaded by being run at full throttle at less than its rated rpm will
load up with carbon, foul its plugs and overheat. Either way, poor
performance will result.

Since it is almost impossible to tell by sight or sound when a
motor is running within a proper rpm range, the use of a tachometer, or at least a speedometer, is necessary. This is a low cost
investment for insuring good motor and propeller performance.

## Test Standard Propeller

With all adjustments made and with an average load, test your
propeller at full throttle. If the motor does not reach the rated
rpm range as indicated on the tach, or the boat speed falls below
the range indicated in the propeller chart, the propeller has too
much pitch which is overloading the motor. A propeller of a
lower pitch must be tried.

If the motor overspeeds, that is the rpms go above the recommended range at full throttle, or a speed is achieved which is
higher than the speed range indicated for this propeller in the
propeller chart, then a propeller of more pitch must be tried. It
will be necessary to increase propeller pitch until the motor is
held within the safe rpm and speed range with full throttle under
average conditions.

As a rule of thumb, one inch of decrease or increase in propeller pitch will result in a change of about 300 rpm's in engine
speed, depending on the gear ratio of the particular unit.

## Clean Boat Bottom

A major cause of poor boat performance is a fouled bottom—
an accumulation of marine growth, moss and barnacles in sea

377

water; and the accumulation of dirt, slime, lime and other matter in fresh water. Cleaning the boat bottom will greatly improve boat performance. Antifouling paint will slow down the accumulation of these materials and organisms. But, in salt water, it may increase erosion on the gear case due to galvanic action.

## Corrosion and Erosion

Propeller life can be shortened by both corrosion and erosion. The most common kind of corrosion is galvanic. This is where a slight current flows from one metal part of the motor to another when the lower unit is immersed in water, especially in sea or badly polluted water. As the current flows, minute particles of metal are carried away in solution.

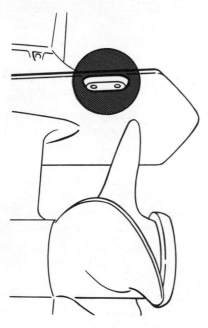

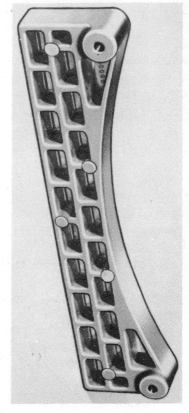

Fig. 3. Sacrificial corrosion protection.

378

The simplest type of protection against galvanic corrosion is the selfsacrificing zinc anode plate, in which the zinc of the anode is eaten away instead of the propeller or lower unit. See Fig. 3.

A difficult-to-control type of erosion is "Cavitation Burn." This is where minute particles of metal are eaten away as bubbles of air collapse on the surface of the propeller. This erosion can be seen and steps can be taken by removing obstructions on the hull and imperfections in the keel and by cleaning a dirty boat bottom.

Fig. 3 shows the mounting place of the anticorrosion anode which is wired to an electronic circuit to prevent galvanic action.

Fig. 4 shows how the electronic unit is connected to protect the boat, propeller and gearcase. The system uses two small electrodes. They are installed through the boat below the waterline. Then they are wired to the battery-powered solid-state controller. One electrode monitors the level of corrosion protection achieved on the water-immersed metal and directs the power supply to maintain the optimum protection current flow, regardless of variables in paint coating or environment. It operates by causing a reverse, regulated current flow. It is low voltage so it can't harm swimmers, fish or the ecology.

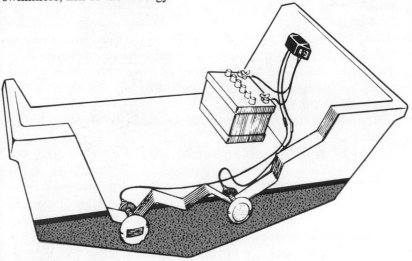

Fig. 4. An electronic unit used to control corrosion of immersed metals.

## QUESTIONS AND ANSWERS ON PROPELLERS

**Can I troll better with a different sized wheel?**

*Answer.* Low pitched propellers are always best for trolling. The lower the pitch the better. Standard propellers with relatively high pitch troll too fast and in throttling down to extremely slow speed, they tend to overload the engine. A low pitched wheel relieves overloading, permitting the engine to idle faster while moving the boat slowly.

**I have a twin engine outboard. Can I get a propeller of opposite rotation and run one motor in reverse?**

*Answer.* No. This is a frequent question, and we would caution anyone against attempting to run any engine in reverse continuously at high speed. The power units are not made to withstand the reverse thrust and this type of operation can only result in lower unit failure. Some lower units have been available with reversed gearing so counter rotating propellers can be used in a dual installation.

**What is the purpose of the rubber cushion hub in an outboard prop?**

*Answer.* It is not intended to prevent blade damage as is sometimes assumed. This device protects lower unit parts by cushioning the shock of propeller impact. Its prime purpose, however, is to prevent excessive breakage of shear or drive pins that otherwise would occur due to the jolt or shock that is experienced in the process of shifting gears.

**The rubber hub in my propeller seems to be slipping. Is this possible?**

*Answer.* It is definitely a possibility. But, it does not occur too frequently. Take a look at the propeller. If the blades are visibly bent or distorted, you very likely are experiencing cavitation—and this is often mistaken for a slipping bushing. Have it checked by the prop manufacturer or a reliable prop service station. The bushing can be replaced if it needs it or the blades can be restored to proper accuracy to eliminate the cavitation.

**Why do I shear so many pins without apparently hitting anything?**

*Answer.* The engine may be turning too fast in the shifting range. The shear pin hole or slot may be sloppy or oversized. The shear pin may be of improper strength for the amount of power involved, or the cushion hub may be frozen tight.

**My outboard seems to vibrate excessively, yet the propeller hardly shows signs of use, why?**

*Answer.* This is not unusual. Propeller blade damage very often is not discernible to the naked eye and blades can become bent or distorted without showing signs of impact or abrasion.

**What about plastic propellers?**

*Answer.* Nothing to date has been developed that has all the qualities of propellers made of metals. A good propeller must be durable, repairable and above all, it must perform well. So far the available plastics fail in these important requirements.

**Is an adjustable pitch propeller possible or satisfactory?**

*Answer.* An adjustable pitch propeller permits more flexibility of operation than the standard props supplied with the outboard. However, it is only efficient at one setting since the blade is a true helical surface only at one particular pitch angle. Two or three well designed rigid props of pitches needed for different loads will give better performance than an adjustable propeller.

**Does it make any difference where the outdrive is vertically positioned on my stern drive?**

*Answer.* Generally it is best to mount the outdrive on the transom so that the cavitation plate is located approximately 1" below the bottom of the keel or hull if there is no keel. Stern drives on houseboats are generally located deeper in the water and may have strut extensions. High performance ocean racers will position the cavitation plate even with or above the hull bottom for best performance.

**Will a propeller change help my I/O installation?**

*Answer.* Generally the boat manufacturer exhaustively tests the various models to insure that the boat performs properly. If, however, the owner increases the boat displacement by installing heavy optional equipment, a different propeller will be required. In most all cases, the propeller to be used would be comparable in diameter but have less pitch.

**Why won't my stern drive perform as well as another stern drive of comparable length, beam, weight and I/O installation?**

*Answer.* Differences in hull design, such as hull dead rise, position of center of gravity and transom angles can account for signifiicantly different performance. Transom angle is important since it govern the maximum tilt setting of the stern drive and consequently the shaft angle.

**My houseboat plows when the stern drives are tilted to the furtherest lock bar position, in an attempt to correct the bow-down attitude and the propellers cavitage. Why?**

Courtesy Michigan Wheel Co.

Fig. 5. Dyna-Quad is designed for heavy load boats with engines of 40 HP and over, it provides faster acceleration, greater maneuverability and reduced vibration over comparable 3-blade props. It is an excellent choice for houseboats and large outboards where good load-carrying performance is important.

*Answer*. The bow-down attitude results from the longitudinal position of the center of gravity being forward of midships. Merely changing shaft angle will not correct the severe plowing which would be experienced. As the lower unit is tilted toward the furtherest lockbar position, effectively changing the shaft angle, the depth of the propeller is immersed is decreased and ventilation will occur causing a breakdown of thrust. This phenomenon is sometimes mistakenly termed cavitation.

**Will a 4-blade propeller increase the performance of my houseboat?**

*Answer*. In many instances, yes. Many stern drives are limited by aperture design to the size propellers that can be swung; the diameter being smaller than that for the maximum efficiency. The 4-blade propeller of equivalent diameter can have better propeller efficiency than the compromise 3-blade under such operating conditions. A 4-blade propeller will provide better acceleration, better cruising performance, better maneuverability, and result in a smoother ride. See Fig. 5.

**What prop should I use on a 30′ boat with a 185 hp engine?**

*Answer*. Much more information on the boat, gears, and type or service is required to make a reliable prop selection. Past service is required to make a reliable prop selection. Past performance information is helpful too unless yours is a stock outfit with known performance characteristics. Your marine dealer or major propeller manufacturer can furnish a propeller analysis form which their engineers can study to advise you.

**Can one propeller give top speed plus lots of power?**

*Answer*. Generally no. To gain high speeds involves sizes or pitch ratios unsuited to load carrying or working conditions. Decide what is most important and select the prop accordingly, or change props with boating conditions.

**You suggest a 13″ diameter × 14″ pitch for my boat. Wouldn't a smaller diameter with more pitch do the same?**

*Answer*. Pitch cannot be substituted for diameter. Diameter is directly related to horsepower, rpm, and speed, which indicate your requirements. If the operating conditions call for a 13″ diameter a 12″ cannot be substituted without adversely affecting performance by decreasing efficiency.

**Will a prop change correct a disturbingly large wake?**

*Answer.* Probably not, unless the change causes a non-planing boat to plane. Wake is directly proportional to hull displacement. Fast boats in planing position throw less wake than slow displacement boats even though the planing boat goes faster than the slow, wake-throwing hull.

**In building a boat: (1) Where do I set the engine? (2) Where do I locate the prop? (3) What size rudder shall I use? (4) What shaft angle is best? (5) What size shaft do I need? (6) What shaft materials are best?**

*Answer.* Engine location is closely tied with trim calculation so it's impossible to answer without complete scientific characteristics of the boat. Engine weight and center of gravity must be

Courtesy Michigan Wheel Co.

Fig. 6. SMC bronze prop.

calculated in connection with all the other weights and centers. If it's impossible to obtain these characteristics, use a loose rule that the best location for engine weight is 55% of the load water-line length of the boat abaft the fore end of that waterline.

(2) Aft, just forward of the transom.

(3) For boats of 20 to 30 foot length, rudder blade should be about 5% of the figure found by multiplying the waterline length of the boat by the extreme draft. Boats of 40 to 50 feet need rudders of about 4%. Larger boats need an area of about 3%. Blade should extend downward, even with lower prop tip and aft far enough to get area from the above formula.

Courtesy Michigan Wheel Co.

**Fig. 7. PJ aluminum propeller.**

(4) Generally, as low as possible, never more than 15°, allowing proper clearance between blade tips and boat bottom. A modestly steep shaft angle does not have a noticeable effect on performance. Normally the difference between, say, 8° and 14° is negligible.

(5) This is related to horsepower, rpm, and type of shaft material used. See Fig. 6.

(6) Monel, stainless steel and bronze, in this order. All resist corrosion. Monel is strongest. See Fig. 7.

**I run on mile-high western lakes. Should I adjust prop size accordingly?**

*Answer.* Yes, gasoline engines lose power when operated above 3000 feet altitudes. A smaller pitch prop will compensate some by bringing rpm to correct operating point. Boats operated at high altitudes and low altitudes need a prop for each condition.

**I have a right hand prop but need a left hand. Can it be changed?**

*Answer.* No. Propeller hand cannot be changed. Turning it around won't change the hand.

**How much can you change prop pitch?**

*Answer.* Depends on the individual propeller. Average standard bronze props can be changed about 2° up and down. Remember that the metal near hubs cannot be changed. Excessive stress and strain can distort or kink blades, causing poor prop efficiency.

**What are the true pitch, variable pitch, and controllable pitch propellers?**

*Answer.* A true pitch propeller measures constant pitch at any radius . . . a section of a true helical surface. A propeller whose pitch varies radially, that is, is not constant but increases from the hub to the tip, is a variable pitch propeller. Variable pitch propellers are used on high speed craft and reduce cavitation which might result at such speeds. Many larger boats use variable pitch propellers to compensate for wake or varying inflow velocities which result from the depth of the immersed hull. With a controllable pitche propeller, the pitch angle of the blades can be mechanically adjusted when the boat is underway.

**Shall I have my propeller dynamically balanced?**

*Answer.* Most premium grade propellers are dynamically balanced at manufacture. All other propellers can be dynamically balanced but only on special order and at additional price. Such a balance is inherent proof of manufacturing perfection insofar as blade thickness, width, spacing, etc. are concerned. This inherent accuracy is not destroyed by blade damage, making it unnecessary to dynamic balance during repair. A good static balance at the repair station will suffice as the inherent accuracy of the propeller is still there.

**What is electrolysis, its cause, correction?**

*Answer.* Electrolysis is the flow of electricity caused by the difference in potential of two dissimilar metals immersed in electrolyte. It acts as a plating process and one metal is eaten up and deposited on the other. Prevent harm to underwater parts by attaching sacrificial anodes (usually zinc). Replace from time to time as they deteriorate.

**Do I use the same size wheel if I convert to a cupped-edge propeller?**

*Answer.* No. Diameter remains the same, but additional load placed on the engine by the "cupped edge" requires that pitch be reduced 1″, or 2″ in propellers above 14″ diameter. See Fig. 8.

**What benefits does a cupped-edge wheel offer?**

*Answer.* Cupped-edge props for fast boats and high rpm reduce slip, giving as much as 3 mph more speed on the average, and eliminate cavitation.

**How close to the bottom of the boat can blade tips run and what is the required aperture clearance?**

*Answer.* The clearance between the propeller tips and the hull should be at least ⅙ to ⅐ the propeller diameter. Clearance is equally important along the forward edges of the blade where they swing in line with the deadwood and should not be less than ¹⁄₁₂ of the diameter.

**Shall I use 2-, 3-, 4- or 5-blade propellers?**

*Answer.* Excessive horsepower, direct drive and high advanced speeds indicate that propellers of high pitch-diameter ratio be employed. Generally 2-blade propellers are used. At somewhat lower advanced speeds and shaft speeds, 3-blade propellers with

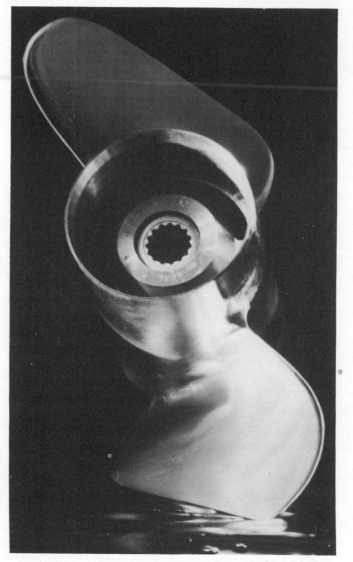

Courtesy Michigan Wheel Co.
**Fig. 8. Cupped edge 2-blade prop.**

pitch-diameter ratios of approximately 1.0 are required for best prop efficiency. It is in this category that most pleasure boats lie. See Fig. 9.

388

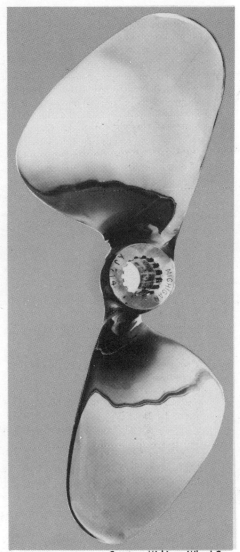

Fig. 9. OPC racing 2-blade prop.

Courtesy Michigan Wheel Co.

At even lower advanced speeds and shaft speeds, 4-blade propellers with pitch-diameter ratios of approximately .8 or less are required for optimum prop efficiency. On large cruisers and com-

389

mercial applications such as trawlers, shrimpers, tugs and work boats, 4-blade props are generally used. If excessive vibration is a problem, 5-blade props are used. See Fig. 10.

Courtesy Michigan Wheel Co.

**Fig. 10. A 3-blade OPC racing propeller.**

### What are normal slip percentages for various craft?

*Answer.* With propellers correctly selected for the operating conditions, the slip percentages would be as follows: racing hulls 10 to 15 percent, planing runabouts 15 to 25, planing cruisers 25 to 35, displacement cruisers 30 to 40, sailing auxiliaries 35 to 40 and work boats 40 to 80.

### The salesman said my boat would go "X" mph. I go about ⅔ as fast, can that be right?

*Answer.* "Claimed" boat speeds are often overestimated. Were his speed trials and yours accurate? Were test conditions similar? It's hard to answer with so many factors to be considered.

**Shall I use heat to install or remove my prop?**

*Answer.* Heat should never be used to install a propeller, and therefore, should seldom be required for removal. If a wheel puller and hammering with soft hammer on propeller and/or shaft end does not work, gentle warming with a blow torch may help. Do not use a welding torch as the quick, harsh heat will change the grain structure of the bronze, setting up internal stresses resulting in hub splitting.

**Can I put an inboard engine in my outboard hull?**

*Answer.* The big question here is whether you will throw the hull out of trim with a heavy inboard mounted midships when the hull was designed to carry an outboard in back of the transom. Normally such conversions are never successful unless the hull was designed to carry the engine weight aft, or you have a V-drive or a transom drive with the engine well aft.

**My outfit doesn't have the speed I expect, though I've tried several types of props. Why?**

*Answer.* Some boats do not have the power to "get over the hump" or attain planing speed. Other boats that achieve planing speeds may not have the power required to reach speeds desired. In such cases repowering is the only answer. Power requirements are proportional to the speed cubed.

**Will a reduction gear give me more power?**

*Answer.* Reduction gears in themselves do not provide power—they absorb it. They provide the means of using a greater propeller diameter, which may be more efficient. They are commonly used with high rpm engines in relatively large hulls, requiring greater blade area than can be used driving direct.

**To change from a standard 3-blade, what diameter or pitch modifications must be made for a 4-blade propeller (to retain comparable engine operation relative to rpm)?**

*Answer.* For the 4-blade Dyna-Quad (*Michigan Wheel Company*), usually associated with pleasure boats, maintain the diameter and reduce pitch 1″. For the 4-blade Work-Horse style, usually associated with commercial craft, reduce diameter 5% to 6% to the nearest even-inch diameter. For narrower 4-blade Trawler style, maintain same diameter and pitch.

**My motor is rated at 3200 rpm. Should I use a wheel small**

**enough to turn this rpm at full throttle, though I want to cruise at 2800?**

*Answer.* A propeller is most efficient at the maximum rpm your engine will turn it; the farther back from maximum your rpm is set by throttle, the greater the loss in efficiency. It is well to run somewhat less, say 300 rpm, than maximum. In this instance, prop should be of a size that will turn 3000 at full throttle and be the best size for cruising at 2800 rpm.

**What is propeller "slip"?**

*Answer.* Slip refers to apparent slip and is a nondimensional figure expressed in percentage. It is the difference between theoretical mph and actual mph divided by theoretical mph. Theoretical mph is calculated by multiplying propeller pitch and propeller rpm and dividing by 1056. As an example, a boat that goes 20 mph measured speed, is driven by a 12″ pitch propeller turning 2600 rpm. Theoretical mph is 12 × 2600 divided by 1056 equals 29.6 total mph. Subtracting 20 from 2916 equals 9.6 which divided by 29.6 equals 32.5%. Slip is not to be confused with propeller efficiency.

**Why do hulls of the same length, beam, weight and power vary so in performance?**

*Answer.* Here the effect of an engineered design is realized. The difference between a boat designed by a qualified naval architect and one built by backyard techniques may be many miles per hour. Boat design is both a science and a skill which has evolved over many years. The designer must be cognizant of the effect of weight, weight distribution, deadrise and other hull characteristics which can affect overall performance. Otherwise, a poor performing boat results.

**Can't I get more than "X" miles per gallon of gas?**

*Answer.* Don't think of miles per gallon—think of gallons per hour. Fuel consumption is related to the overall efficiency. Engines all use almost exactly one gallon of gas per hour for every 10 hp developed. For example you burn 15 gph, your engine puts out 150 hp.

**A prop larger than I can swing is indicated for my boat, engine, and gear. Should I use a large diameter as I can and add pitch to hold motor rpm down?**

*Answer*. Change the gear, increasing shaft rpm, reducing prop diameter requirement, or change shaft angle or prop aperture to accommodate correct size. If impossible use a 4-blade prop for diameters 18″ and up. Under 18″, a 3-blade larger in diameter than required, can be clipped to maximum usable diameter.

**Won't a step-up gear increase my speed?**

*Answer*. With an extremely fast boat (step bottom hydro or drag boat), depending on your engine, a step-up gear may let you use a prop size better suited to your needs. Gears for "class" boats are usually worked out by trial and error, so stick to what has been done sucessfully for similar boats. Step-up gears are

Courtesy Michigan Wheel Co.

**Fig. 11. Extra wide blade for stern drive.**

the opposite of reduction gears, but we still figure hp and rpm at the prop. With step-up gears, shaft rpm of 10,000 is not unusual in racing-craft.

**How can I tell if I need a left or right hand prop?**

*Answer.* Stand in back of the boat. If the shaft turns clockwise a right hand prop is needed. Most marine motors take right hand props.

**What causes squatting?**

*Answer.* Many things. A slipping or cavitating prop causes a vacuum and digs a hole which the stern settles into. Correction of prop size often corrects this. Poor hull design, or a good hull put out of trim by misplaced engine or load is a leading factor. Heavy keel, unfaired strut, scoops, or automatic bailing fixtures— or anything that disrupts smooth, free flow of water to prop, can cause cavitation and subsequent squatting.

**On a sailboat under sail, should the prop be rotating or locked?**

*Answer.* There is less drag when the prop rotates.

Fig. 12. Super-Prop is the result of advanced propeller technology. It is made of aluminum and is as fast as the fastest propellers at higher prices. It is also available in stainless steel.

**With twin screw, is opposite rotation required?**

*Answer.* Theoretically it is best. It definitely aids maneuvering, by advancing or retarding one engine as required. For steering, nonopposite rotating motors cause no steering problems.

**With twin screw, should rotation be inboard or outboard?**

*Answer.* Rotation is normally outboard looking at top of prop from stern of boat. Right-hand prop rotates to starboard, left-hand to port.

**What do the stampings on my prop mean?**

*Answer.* Most props are stamped on forward end with diameter, pitch and shaft size. Diameter is always first, pitch second. Size is likely repeated on the side of the hub with the manufacturer's name, type prop, hand, and date of manufacture. See Figs. 11 and 12.

Since 1976 is an "America's Cup" year, sailors are looking for another upsurge of interest in their favorite sport.

Courtesy Mercury Marine, Div. of Brunswick Corp.

# CHAPTER 17

# Canoeing

Canoeing has lately been rediscovered as the most versatile and natural outdoor all seasons sports. It has attracted many without even rudimentary safety and paddling techniques.

A canoe or two is your best and least expensive means of reliving with your family our Continent's heritage. First, expressly designed for our waterways by America's original inhabitants this watercraft is virtually unchanged today, one indication of its perfection, other than through the utilization of such modern maintenance free lifetime materials as aluminum.

Some canoes, or course are made of canvas and wood. There is a difference when you expect to pack a canoe for any distance and have a load inside. Canoes can also be equipped with outboard motors to make sure you arrive back safely in time to avoid the storm.

Canoes have some distinct advantages for those who love the water and the outdoors. You can paddle our rivers and streams, bayous and swamps, lakes and ponds, and the fingers of our oceans that poke inland. Local, urban, and remote wilderness can be explored. Fishing, recognizing animals, birds, trees and flowers can all be done by canoe. A canoe can be paddled, powered, poled, rowed or sailed.

## Double-End Models

The double-end model canoe continues to be the most popular for both new and experienced canoeists. Fig. 1. The aluminum model is sturdy and lightweight. *Grumman* makes one which is stretched formed, heat-treated marine aluminum alloy, which means it can be used all seasons on both fresh and salt water. The double-end canoe is the most versatile. The sheer at the ends have been compromised to reduce wind effect. They can be paddled, sailed, or powered. In order to carry the people or load you need —it is best to pick the canoe capable of operating under the conditions you expect to encounter. The double-end canoe, the one most people expect a canoe to look like, is available in 13, 15, 17, 18- and 20-foot models. There is a reason for having the various options. Table 1 shows you may need to take a few things into consideration before making a choice.

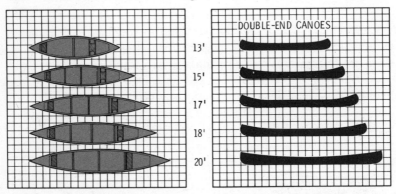

Fig. 1. Double-end canoes.

While there are many sizes and shapes of canoes, each has been designed for specific purposes. All of them can, and do, perform well under all canoeing circumstances. But the differences in sizes and shapes can make different kinds of canoeing that much easier, that much more enjoyable. To choose the canoe that will give you the greatest pleasure and satisfaction, you must give some thought to your own needs and most frequent uses.

Decide who and how many are going canoeing. If it is for yourself, to do a little solo fishing or exploring, a small canoe like

**Table 1.**
**Standard weight hulls are made from .050" 6061 marine aluminum alloy.**
**Lightweight models are constructed from .032" 6061 marine aluminum alloy.**

| LENGTH OF DOUBLE-END CANOE | 13′ | | 15′ | | 17′ | | 18′ | | 20′ | |
|---|---|---|---|---|---|---|---|---|---|---|
| MODEL | Light Wt. | Stan. Wt. | Light Wt. | Stan. Wt. | Light Wt. | Stan. Wt. | Light Wt. | Stan. Wt. | Stan. Wt. | Peace Canoe |
| WEIGHTS (Pounds) | 44 | 58 | 55 | 69 | 60 | 75 | 67 | 85 | 115 | 117 |
| LENGTH (Inches) | 157½ | | 180⁵⁄₁₆ | | 203¾ | | 216¾ | | 240 | 240 |
| BEAM (Inches) | 35⅜ | | 35⅛ | | 36⅛ | | 35⅝ | | 40⅛ | 40⅛ |
| CENTER DEPTH (Inches) | 12⅞ | | 12⅛ | | 13⅛ | | 13⅛ | | 14 | 14 |
| NO. OF RIBS | 3 | 1 | 5 | 3 | 7 | 3 | 9 | 5 | 12 | 12 |
| BIA CERTIFIED: Max. horsepower | 3 | | 5 | | 5 | | 5 | | 7.5 | 7.5 |
| Max. persons cap. (Pounds) | 555 | | 560 | | 675 | | 765 | | 970 | 970 |
| Max. weight cap. (Pounds) Persons, motor & gear | 590 | | 650 | | 755 | | 845 | | 1110 | 1110 |
| KEEL | STAN. | | STAN. | | STAN. | | STAN. | | BULB "T" | |

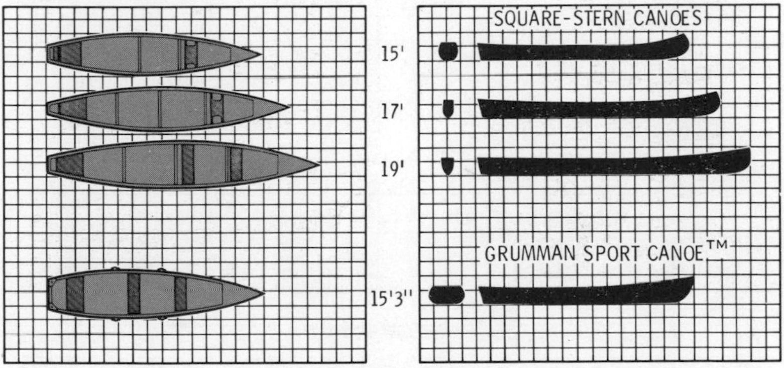


**Fig. 2. Various shapes of canoes.**

the 13-foot lightweight model might be for you. It weighs only 44 pounds in aluminum. If your canoe is for family activity, you'll need a canoe large enough to carry the load factor involved.

All of the aluminum canoes can be paddled, poled, powered, sailed and/or rowed. The different shapes and the different modifications of keel, weight and size-within-a-shape help you to get the best performance in your specific type of canoeing. That's why it is important to decide how you are going to most often use your canoe.

Three shapes of canoes are shown in Fig. 2. The double-end is the most familiar. The square stern is another shape. The *Sportcanoe®* is a trademark of *Grumman Boats* and is designed for the sportsman.

Here again, there is some basis for chosing a canoe. Take a look at Table 2 and see what the characteristics are—and decide what you'll need for your fun and pleasure.

**Table 2. Square-Sterns and Sportcanoe™**

| LENGTH OF SQUARE-STERN MODEL | 15' | 17' | 19' | Sportcanoe |
|---|---|---|---|---|
| MODEL | STANDARD WEIGHT ONLY | | | |
| WEIGHT (Pounds) | 77 | 85 | 116 | 112 |
| LENGTH (Inches) | 180 | 203½ | 228¼ | 183 |
| BEAM (Inches) | 36⅛ | 36⅝ | 40⅛ | 43 |
| CENTER DEPTH (Inches) | 13⅛ | 13⅛ | 14 | 14 |
| NO. OF RIBS | 6 | 8 | 12 | 10 |
| BIA CERTIFIED: Max horsepower | 5 | 5 | 5 | 5 |
| Max. persons cap. (Pounds) | 645 | 745 | 1020 | 360 |
| Max. weight cap. (Pounds) Persons, Motor & gear | 725 | 825 | 1100 | 440 |
| KEEL | STANDARD | | BULB "T" | |

**Shallow Draft (White Water) Models**

| LENGTH OF DOUBLE-END SHALLOW DRAFT CANOE | 15' | 17' | 18' |
|---|---|---|---|
| MODEL | STANDARD WEIGHT | | |
| WEIGHT (Pounds) | 74 | 81 | 91 |
| LENGTH (Inches) | 180 | 203¾ | 216¾ |
| BEAM (Inches) | 35⅛ | 36⅛ | 36⅝ |
| CENTER DEPTH (Inches) | 12⅛ | 13⅛ | 13⅛ |
| NO. OF RIBS | 5 | 7 | 9 |
| BIA CERTIFIED: Max. horsepower | 5 | 5 | 5 |
| Max. persons cap. (Pounds) | 560 | 675 | 765 |
| Max. weight cap. (Pounds) Persons, motor & gear | 650 | 755 | 845 |
| KEEL | SHALLOW DRAFT | | |

The double-end canoes are the most versatile—performing better than any other in fast-moving rivers or rapids (white water) and are equally at home on quiet lakes, ponds and rivers.

If you intend to use an outboard motor more than a paddle, you should give extra consideration to the square stern (a flat back) designed and engineered to accommodate the motor. All square sterns and the *Sportcanoe* feature spray rails which deflect water away from the canoe. If you are going to take your canoe to large bodies of water and carry heavier loads (such as game), look at the capacity of the 19′ square stern. It is the one usually selected by professional guides and outfitters. It has the most ribs and is strengthened and stiffened by a bulb "T" keel to handle power as well as the greater loads. The square sterns have most of the easy paddling characteristics and sailing qualities of the double-end canoes.

## KEELS

A standard keel is generally selected if it is used in "quiet water"—mill ponds, slow moving rivers, still lakes and bays.

White water or sport canoeing where the rivers are fast running and there are rapids require a shallow-draft keel. This type of keel is designed for greater strength and maneuverability. They are usually 30% heavier than the standard keels.

## WEIGHT

Both the lightweight and the standard weight have the same construction. The hull is thicker on the standard weight (.050″ as compared to .032″ on the lightweight). To reinforce the thinner hull more ribs are added to add strength.

However, the thinner skin does dent easily. After hard useage it may not appear as sleek and smooth as it did when it was new, but the canoe is still watertight. The dents and dings are strictly "cosmetic" and will in no way interfere with the canoe's performance.

Lightweight models are for the wilderness canoe camper who is faced with frequently carrying the canoe from one body of

401

water to another. Many find it ideal for general canoeing where one man or much handling (such as cartopping) is involved. This is a point worth considering.

## SIZE

The size of your canoe is related to the amount you will carry. Add the weights of the persons that you anticipate carrying in your canoe at one time. Also estimate the maximum weight of motor and other gear to be carried. Take a look at Table 2 and see what length you need for the *maximum persons capacity*. Select the length which has a maximum greater than the weight of the people you will carry, and a maximum capacity greater than the total weight of persons, motor, and gear. If your total in either category approaches the limit shown in Table 2, select the next longer canoe.

The length of the canoe trips you expect to make also relates to size. Generally speaking, the longer the trip, the longer the canoe used. For one-man fishing, a 13′ canoe is ideal. But for several-day trips and several people, a 17′ or 18′ canoe may be the best, rather than a smaller size with adequate capacity. If you intend to portage or carry the canoe often, you may still decide on a smaller canoe to minimize weight.

Families with growing children may want to consider purchasing two canoes instead of one large one. Children learn to paddle well in a remarkable short time, and the use of two canoes reduces paddling effort, increases total carrying capacity and allows for greater versatility.

## LAUNCHING

Do you have your own canoes or will you rent them? There are rental dealers along most popular waterways. It's best to get your craft from them if you must rent. Write *Grumman Boats,* Marathon, New York (13803) for a *free* "Rent-A-Canoe Directory" listing over 400 canoe liveries.

Sometimes you can launch from a dealer's location; at other times the dealer may be willing to deliver the canoes to the "put-in" point of your choice. In any case, he's your best source of information on overland transportation. You may have to pay for any damage to the canoes, so be careful!

What size canoes? Be sure to find out the canoe's weight capacity and decide on the size and number of canoes accordingly. A quick glance at the Tables provided in this chapter will tell you what to ask for in a canoe.

Whether you load the canoes on land or in water depends largely on the canoes. With the aluminum canoes, the Mariners found they could load them on land and carry them to the water without any damage to the canoes. However, extreme care should be taken with the more traditional, wood-and-canvas canoes. Each canoeist should know his or her specific seat in a specific canoe, and should be partly responsible for seeing that none of the gear carried in that craft is left behind.

One of the areas where you can use the help of experts is in portaging or carrying the canoes over distance on land. Though it might seem easier to avoid unloading the canoes by getting several people to carry them with all gear aboard, *it doesn't work*. The job goes quicker and easier by toting the empty canoes in the traditional overhead fashion, then returning for the equipment.

## CANOE SAFETY

Basic safety rules apply to all boating sports. Keep them in mind and use them when canoeing.

1. Wear a personal flotation device (PFD) . . . U.S. Coast Guard rules require carrying an approved PFD for everyone on board.
2. Keep your body low as you enter the canoe with one hand on each gunwale.
3. Don't overload. Know the safe carrying capacity of your canoe.
4. Caught in a squall? Lie flat in the bottom.
5. Stay with your canoe if it capsizes or is swamped . . . Even if full of water, an aluminum canoe will support you in the water until help arrives.

The double ended canoe can be used to get there fast with a small outboard hung over the side. It comes in handy when a storm is brewing and a safe haven is needed quickly. These aluminum canoes are now available in colors.

Courtesy Grumman

Maine is a twice-blessed boating state; its inland lakes and streams have few rivals anywhere and its coastal waters renowned for their scenery.

Courtesy Mercury Marine, Div. of Brunswick Corp.

# CHAPTER 18

# Stern Drive

There are a couple of manufacturers of stern drives. The two major manufacturers are *OMC* and *Mercury*. Both producers of stern drives are equipped with a complete line of engines.

When checking out stern drives there are a few things which should be compared before making a decision. The *turning*—more turning ability makes for easier docking and maneuvering. The *shifting*—power shift is usually required to make sure changes are made with a smoothness necessary for maneuvering in tight spots. Of course a steering system that does not have the wheel spin out of your grip is desirable too. *Tilting*—is important when it comes to beaching, trailering, or changing the prop. The noise level should be considered as well as the trim.

## TURNING

The ability to turn your boat rather quickly and through a wide range of swing makes a difference when docking, when trying to work your way through a crowded harbor or when trying to maneuver in the wind. The angle the outdrive can turn varies with the manufacturer. In the case illustrated, Fig. 1, the OMC outdrive can turn a full 90°.

Power steering is necessary for V-8 engines. It takes too much muscle to turn the outdrive. Steering effort is greatly reduced with

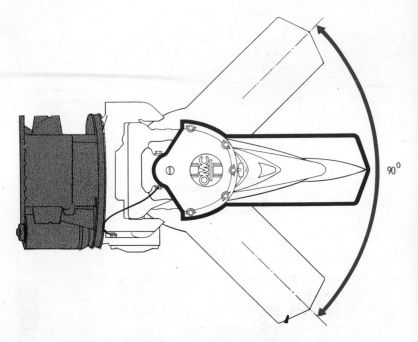

**Fig. 1. The OMC outdrive assembly can turn a full 90 degrees.**

power steering because hydraulic pressure supplies most of the muscle. This is especially true when maneuvering at high speeds. That extra steering effort normally required is no longer needed.

Feedback from the drive unit to the steering wheel is negligible in both single and two-station installations. The positive response to steering wheel movement improves controllability at all times for that extra margin of safety. Fig. 2.

Fig. 3 illustrates another innovation in steering. *OMC* calls it *"Tru-Course"*® steering. It is designed to keep you on course in a turn or straight ahead. This system uses a worm and sector gear to resist torque rather than transmitting it to the wheel. Usually the wheel must be held firmly or it may spin away from you when you make a hard turn. This *Tru-Course*® helps to eliminate the hard pull on turns—the wheel will not spin at all—it stays where you put it until you turn it.

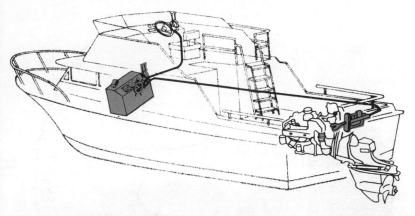

Fig. 2. Dual steering control circuit.

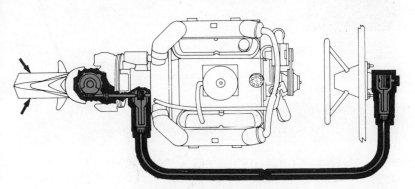

Fig. 3. OMC *Tru-Course* steering system.

## TRIM

To trim a boat, it is necessary to change the angle of the drive unit. Fig. 4. Both *Mercury* and *OMC* have their own power units to easily accomplish the trim function for you. *Mercury* calls theirs the *Power Trim*® and lets the boat driver change the angle of the drive unit while the boat is in motion at any speed. This is necessary to compensate for variations in water surface or boat load. There is also a preset manual trim for use by those who prefer.

The main advantage of the power trim unit, both manufacturers, is the snappy takeoff, smoother rides on choppy water, better fuel economy and safer shallow water running. The *Power Trim*® unit by *Mercury* can be changed by pushing a button. The control unit has three buttons, Fig. 5. The center button moves the unit up, raising the bow; the lower button moves the unit in, lowering the bow. By simultaneously pressing the upper two buttons, the unit

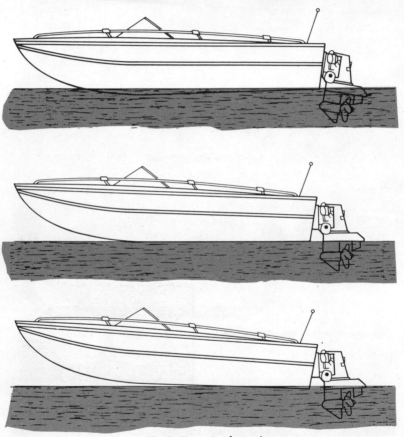

Fig. 4. Illustrating boat trim.

can be raised to "full up and out" position for safe beaching or launching. When you are underway your boat can be kept on perfect plane under varying load or water conditions. When the weight is up front, the trim acts as a load leveler and helps keep the bow up. Since you're planing more perfectly, there is a re-

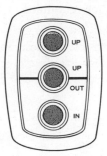

Fig. 5. Mercury push button power trim unit.

duction in the water friction against the hull and you have a savings in gasoline consumption as well as a smoother ride. In choppy water, you pull the bow down until you're slicing smoothly through the waves.

Power trim comes in handy when you are trying to get in close. Trim the drive unit out for slow speed operation in shallow water, or lift to the "up/out" position for easy beaching or launching. Another advantage is trailering. The power trim helps protect the drive unit by lifting it up and out of the way.

*Selectrim*® is *OMC's* trade name for their power trim unit. Fig. 6. It does not have to be reset if you use the tilt mechanism. The

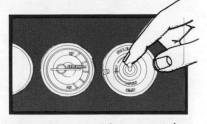

Fig. 6. OMC power trim unit controls.

*Selectrim*® unit is completely inside the boat to reduce corrosion. Since *OMC* changes the entire engine and drive mechanism angle —they are both attached to one another without flexible coupling —the angle of the transom is not considered important.

## TILT

The outdrive needs to be tilted on a number of different occasions. If you are beaching your boat or trailer launching it, there is a need to tilt the drive unit up and out of the way. The manufacturers differ on how high it should be tilted. Most of them tilt for 60° while *OMC* recommends 75°. The higher it tilts the greater the benefits. You can change the propeller without getting into the water or having to haul the boat out. Fig. 7 illustrates the tilting possibilities of stern drives.

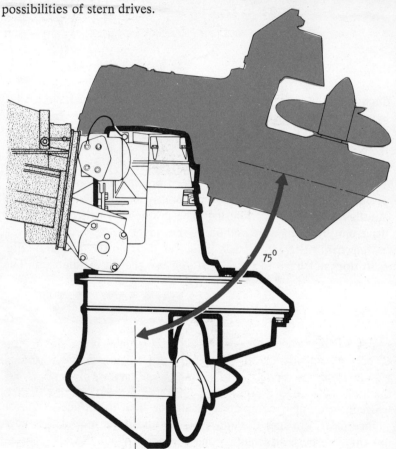

75°

Fig. 7. Outdrive tilt needed for launching or hauling boat.

## MOUNTING THE ENGINE

The *OMC* stern drive is a unitized engine and outdrive. Fig. 8. The *OMC* outdrive is not mounted to the transom. In fact, it doesn't touch the transom. It is directly mounted to the engine and the engine is mounted to the boat's stringers. This design is said to result in low level of outdrive noise and vibration.

Fig. 9 shows how the others are mounted with the engine permanently fixed and only the outdrive moving to trim the boat. There are advantages to both types of mounting. Only the boat owner can tell which is suited for his needs by taking a comparison ride.

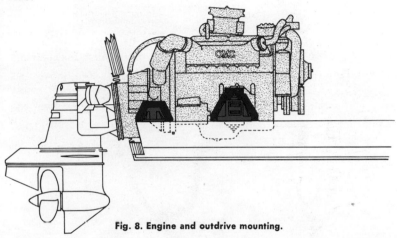

Fig. 8. Engine and outdrive mounting.

## SAFETY

One of the greatest dangers in stern drive units is the possibility of fire or explosion from the ignition of bilge vapors. Gasoline vapors are easily ignited. The manufacturers are very conscious of this and have done a number of things to prevent the accidental ignition.

*Mercury,* for instance, has a flame-screened distributor that will not ignite combustible bilge mixture. The alternator has been spark baffled. The starter motor and the starter solenoid have been designed to prevent ignition of combustible bilge mixtures. An internally sealed carburetor prevents fuel leaking outside, even if flooded.

Some of the characteristics of the boats can be improved. The manufacturers are working on them constantly. However, the

411

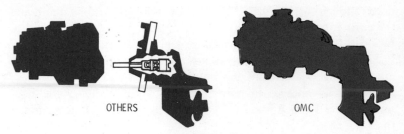

Courtesy Mercury Marine, Div. of Brunswick Corp.

**Fig. 9. Two types of engine and drive mountings.**

greatest safety hazard is people. You and your passengers have to become aware of the dangers of boating. You must take certain safety precautions and keep a cool head under all conditions. The Coast Guard conducts courses for boaters. There are many safety procedures which can be learned from the courses. Everyone can benefit from a little directed instruction.

Courtesy Mercury Marine, Div. of Brunswick Corp.

**Fig. 10. *Mercury 120* engine with stern drive.**

## Table 1.  Stern Drives—Specifications

| ENGINE | 120 | 140 | 165 | 888 | 233 | 255 | 280 |
|---|---|---|---|---|---|---|---|
| cylinders | 4, in-line | 4, in-line | 6, in-line | V-8 | V-8 | V-8 | V-8 |
| displacement | 153 cu. in. | 181 cu. in. | 250 cu. in. | 302 cu. in. | 351 cu. in. | 350 cu. in. | 350 cu. in. |
| bore & stroke | 3.875" x 3.25" | 4" x 3.6" | 3.875" x 3.53" | 4" x 3" | 4" x 3.5" | 4" x 3.48" | 4" x 3.48" |
| compression ratio | 8.5:1 | 8.5:1 | 8.0:1 | 8.0:1 | 8.0:1 | 8.5:1 | 8.8:1 |
| main bearings | 5 | 5 | 7 | 5 | 5 | 5 | 5 |
| carburetion | 2V | 2V | 2V | 2V | 2V | 4V | 4V |
| choke | thermostatic | thermostatic | thermostatic | electric | electric | thermostatic | thermostatic |
| full-throttle operating range | 3900-4300 rpm | 4200-4600 rpm | 3900-4300 rpm | 3800-4200 rpm | 3800-4200 rpm | 3800-4200 rpm | 4600-5000 rpm |
| **STERN DRIVE** | | | | | | | |
| shift | mechanical | mechanical | mechanical | mechanical | mechanical | electro-hydraulic | electro-hydraulic |
| gear ratio | 1.98:1 | 1.98:1 | 1.65:1 | 1.50:1 | 1.32:1 | 2:1 | 1.50:1 |
| maximum prop diameter | 16" cupped | 16" cupped | 16" cupped | 16" cupped | 16" cupped | 20" left-or right-hand rotation | 16" left-or right-hand rotation |

Every MerCruiser stern drive has a valve-in-head engine with hydraulic valve lifters; 12-volt-42 amp marine alternator; 40 amp circuit breaker; adjustable rubber engine mounts; Jet Prop exhaust; shock-absorbing propeller hub; runs on regular gas.

Courtesy Mercury Marine, Div. of Brunswick Corp.

**Fig. 11. Mercury 255 engine with stern drive and hydraulic transmission.**

## STERN DRIVES

*Mercury* makes a complete line of stern drives. The engines may be 4, 6 or 8 cylinders. The cubic inch displacement runs from 153 to 351. Some special features are available depending upon your needs. Take a look at Table 1 and see what a wide variety of

Courtesy Mercury Marine, Div. of Brunswick Corp.

**Fig. 12. MerCruise Tempest 350-cubic inch engine.**

power is available for house boats, cruisers, offshore runabouts, and racers.

The four-cylinder *Mercury* 120 is a stern drive engine with hydraulic valve lifters and five main bearings to support the crankshaft. The stern drive unit has a mechanical shift and a 1.98:1 gear ratio. This model can have power steering installed if desired. Electric tilt or manual tilt can be chosen by the owner. Fig. 10.

The 350 cubic inch V-8 drives this *Mercury* 255. It is rated at 255 horsepower. A hydraulic transmission is designed for marine use and attached to the power package. A 2:1 gear ratio swings a 20-inch diameter propeller sufficient to power large houseboats, offshore runabouts and cruisers. Fig. 11.

This *MerCruiser* Tempest stern drive package consists of a 350-cubic inch V-8 marine engine coupled to a stern drive unit. The stern drive is available in right or left-hand rotation for dual-engine installations. The engine includes dual four-barrel carburetors and is equipped with capacitor discharge ignition. Fig. 12.

415

Courtesy Mercury Marine, Div. of Brunswick Corp.

**Fig. 13. A 350-cubic inch V-8 with universal joint drive train.**

The Typhoon has been designed especially for inboard tunnel hulls competition. The 350-cubic inch V-8 engine is complemented by a stern drive unit with a high-performance gearcase. Cleaver-type stainless propellers are available up to 28-inch pitch. Fig. 13.

The Tornado offshore stern drive package includes a 1:1 or 1.33:1 ratio drive. It can be had in either left or hight hand rotation. Of course other things must be added to get it into the water. It will need a transom plate assembly, drive line assembly, tailstock assembly, engine plate mounts, transom-mounted water pickup and a competition oil filter to complete the package.

Fig. 14. *MerCruise* Tornado model engine.

# Glossary

**Abaft**—Toward the stern; behind.

**Abeam**—A term used in reference to the position of an object outside the boat, and at right angles to the fore and aft centerline of the boat.

**Aboard**—On board; a person is aboard when on the boat.

**Above**—The nautical equivalent of upstairs.

**Abreast**—Side by side; also, opposite, over against, or in line with, the vessel's beam.

**Accelerate**—To increase the speed of movement, such as increasing the speed of an engine.

**Adrift**—Floating, unmoored and unanchored at the mercy of wind and waves.

**Afloat**—Resting on the water surface.

**Afoul**—In collision; in a tangle, or snarled up in some way.

**Aft**—A nautical term, meaning the stern or rear of a vessel; opposite to fore.

**Aground**—Boat resting on or touching the bottom.

**Ahead**—In or toward an advanced position; as full speed ahead; also forward of the bow.

**Air-fuel ratio**—The ratio by weight of a fuel as compared to the air of the carburetor mixture. The commonly accepted ratio of air to fuel for combustion in a gasoline engine is approximately 15 to 1. Thus, for every pound of gasoline used, 15 pounds of air must be supplied. Since gasoline weighs approximately 600 times as much as air, it follows that $600 \times 15$ or 9000 times as much air must be supplied if a volumetric comparison be made.

**Air gap**—The space between electrodes of a spark plug, and between field poles and armatures in motors and generators.

**Alongside**—Side by side, as alongside a pier, a jetty or another boat.

**Alternating current**—A periodic electric current which reverses its direction at regular recurring intervals.

**Amidships**—In or toward the middle, or center section of a boat.

**Ammeter**—An instrument for measuring the flow of an electric current.

**Ampere**—The unit of measurement of an electric current. It is the practical equivalent of the unvarying current which when passed through a standard solution of nitrate of silver in water deposits silver at the rate of 1.118 milligram per second.

**Ampere-hour capacity**—A term used to indicate the capacity of a storage battery. The amount of electricity which a battery will deliver within a certain time limit is known as its capacity, or ampere-hour capacity. Thus, for example, a battery that will deliver 3.5 amperes for 20 hours is said to have a capacity of 70 ampere-hours.

**Anchor**—A device that is attached to a boat by a rope or cable, and that when being cast overboard fastens itself to the bottom, thus keeping the boat in a particular position or place. Also any weight secured to the boat by a rope or chain and thrown overboard to prevent drifting.

**Anchorage**—The act of anchoring, or condition of laying at anchor; a place suitable for anchoring.

**Anchor aweigh**—An anchor when it is just clear of the bottom.

**Anchor buoy**—A buoy attached to or marking the position of an anchor.

**Anchored**—Held in position by an anchor.

**Anchor light**—A white light displayed by a ship at anchor.

**Anchor watch**—A watchman on deck duty particularly at night while the ship is at anchor.

**Anticlockwise rotation**—When the shaft of an engine or machine rotates in opposite direction to the hands of a clock it is said to have an anticlockwise or counterclockwise rotation.

**Aquaplane**—A platform attached by rope astern of a power boat on which a person may ride while towed rapidly over water.

**Armature**—In an electric motor or generator, a core of soft metal stampings upon which is a wire winding, constructed to rotate near the poles of the field magnets.

**Astern**—Behind a boat; in the rear, or after part. Also going backward, as to drift astern; the opposite to ahead or forward.

**Athwart**—Across, or from side, the length, direction or course of, or in that direction.

**Athwartship**—Across the ship from side to side; at right angles to fore and aft.

**Atmospheric pressure**—The pressure exerted by the atmosphere. At sea level atmospheric pressure is about 14.7 lbs. per square inch, decreasing as altitude increases.

**Atomize**—To reduce to extremely fine particles as in the air-fuel mixture supplied to an engine by carburetor action.

**Auxiliary**—An engine used to supplement the power derived from sails on a sail boat.

**Aweigh**—Refers to the anchor being just off the bottom.

**Backfire**—A premature explosion in the cylinder of a gas engine during the exhaust or the compression stroke tending to drive the piston in a direction opposite to its normal way of travel; also an explosion in either the admission or the exhaust passages of such an engine.

**Backwash**—Water thrown aft by the turning of the propeller.

**Bail**—Any small container used in bailing water out of a boat.

**Ballast**—Any relatively heavy substance used to maintain a boat at its proper draft or trim, or to improve the stability of a boat.

**Ball bearing**—A bearing in which the journal or revolving part turns upon loose hardened steel balls which rolls easily in a race, thus converting sliding friction into rolling friction.

**Barnacle**—Any of a number of marine crustaceans which attach themselves to the ship's bottom.

**Batten down**—To close or make watertight, in reference to hatches and cargo; to make seaworthy.

**Battens**—A strip of wood nailed or clamped around the edges of the covering of a hatchway to hold it in place.

**Battery**—A group of two or more cells connected together for furnishing electric current.

**Beam**—The extreme breadth of a boat at its widest part. Thus, for example, a boat is said to have an eight-foot beam, when it measures eight feet at its widest part.

**Beam sea**—A sea at right angles to a vessel's course.

**Bearing**—The direction of an object as observed aboard ship. The direction is usually expressed in terms of nautical degrees and parts thereof as noted by the compass points.

**Belay**—To make a turn or turns with a running rope around a pin or other object to hold or secure a boat; to make fast, etc.

**Below**—On or to a lower floor or deck, downstairs, below deck, etc.

**Bend**—To make fast, such as bending a cable to an anchor; a knot used in joining two lines.

**Bending shackle**—A device used to secure the anchor chain to the anchor.

**Berth**—The mooring place for a boat; also a place on a boat to sleep.

**Bight**—The middle part of a rope, a loop or double part, or a bent rope.

**Bilge**—The curved or angular part of the hull where bottom and sides meet; also the space under the cabin floor, or floor boards.

**Bilge pump**—A pump for removing bilge water.

**Bilge water**—Water accumulated in the bilge by leakage or seepage.

**Binnacle**—A case box or stand containing the compass, usually located near the helm.

**Bitter end**—The last extremity or end of a rope.

**Bitts**—A pair of vertical wooden or iron heads on board a vessel to which mooring or towing lines are made fast.

**Block**—A grooved pulley or sheave incased in a frame or shell which is provided with a hook, eye or strap, by which it may be attached to an object. Blocks are used extensively on shipboard to raise sails and other heavy objects. They are classed as single, double, threefold, etc., according to the number of sheaves contained in them.

**Blow-by**—A term used to indicate leakage or loss of pressure as leakage of compression between pistons and cylinder in a gas engine.

**Boat hook**—A wooden staff with a metal hook on one end, used for fending off, holding on, or picking up small objects from the water.

**Bollards**—Upright wooden or metal posts, as on a dock to tie up boats.

**Boom**—A spar with a special use, such as a cargo boom, the boom for a sail, etc.

**Bore**—The interior diameter of an engine cylinder, a hold made by boring, etc.

**Bow line**—A mooring line leading from the bow of the boat.

**Bow**—The forward or front end of boat.

**Brackish**—Said about water containing salt in a moderate degree, hence distasteful, nauseous; not fit for consumption.

**Brake horsepower**—The useful horsepower developed by an engine as ascertained by the application of a brake or absorption dynamometer.

**Breaker arm**—A movable arm of a pair of contact points as employed on distributors or magnetos in gas engines.

**Breakers**—Said of waves of the sea that break on the beach, or because of obstructions to their free passage.

**Breast off**—To shove off from a pier or from another boat.

**Bridge**—The raised platform in the forward part of a vessel from which the vessel is navigated and controlled.

**Broach**—To veer suddenly into the wind and expose the boat to the danger of capsizing.

**Broaching to**—To turn up into the wind suddenly and unintentionally; to be thrown broadside into the surf.

**Broadside**—The side of a boat above the waterline, or the exposed side of the boat between bow and stern.

**Btu (British Thermal Unit)**—The quantity of heat required to raise the temperature of one pound of water one degree Fahrenheit at or near its maximum point of density.

**B.T.D.C.**—An abbreviation for "Before Top Dead Center," used in reference to piston location in relationship to a stroke or cycle.

**Bulkhead**—A partition or wall whose purpose it is to increase the safety of the ship.

**Bunks**—Beds or cots used for sleeping aboard ship.

**Buoy**—A floating object moored to the bottom, to mark the channel or to point out the position of something beneath the water, as an anchor, shoal, rock, etc. Buoys are of different shapes and colors with reference to their position or the nature of the object marked.

**Cable**—A chain or wire rope of great strength, used with an anchor or for towing.

**Cable length**—One hundred fathoms or 600 feet.

**Calorie**—In the *cgs* units of measurements, a calorie is the quantity of heat necessary to raise the temperature of one gram of water one degree Centigrade at or near its highest point of density. Also called gram-calorie or small calorie. One BTU equals 252 gram calories.

**Calorific value**—The heat produced by the combustion of a unit weight of fuel.

**Cam**—A wheel-like disk of irregular shape attached to the camshaft of an engine for imparting exactly timed movements to the valve gear of an engine.

**Can buoy**—A cylindrical metal buoy.

**Canoe**—A long narrow boat sharp at both ends and usually propelled by one or more paddles, with no rudder or sail.

**Carbon**—A common element which when properly combined with oxygen will burn. It usually forms in the combustion chamber of an engine during the burning of the fuel mixture and lubricating oil.

**Carbon monoxide**—A colorless and odorless gas, which is a product of incomplete combustion of carbon. It is very poisonous to all animal life, since it combines with the hemoglobin of the blood, expelling oxygen. Its presence in the exhaust gases from internal combustion engines has caused many fatalities.

**Carburetor**—A device for automatically mixing fuel with air. It acts by passing air through or over a liquid fuel and carrying off a portion of its vapor in combination, forming an explosive mixture.

**Cast-off**—To depart, or to untie, as when leaving a dock or a pier.

**Caulk**—A method employed to make boat seams watertight by filling them with cotton, oakum or similar material.

**Cavitation**—Propeller slippage due to the formation of a vacuum around it. It causes a loss of efficiency.

**Ceiling**—The inner lining of a boat.

**Centerboard**—A device consisting of a broad board or slab of wood or metal that is lowered through the keel of a boat to prevent it from being shoved off course by wind pressure.

**Centerline**—A straight line either real or imaginary passing longitudinally from bow to stern.

**Chafe**—To wear a surface of a rope or spar by rubbing.

**Chafing gear**—A guard of canvas, rope, or similar material around spars, lines, or rigging to prevent wear.

**Chain plates**—Plates of iron fastened to the side of a vessel to which the chains of the lower rigging are connected.

**Channel**—The deeper part of a river, harbor, strait, etc., where the main current flows, or which affords the best passage. Depending upon its size and frequency of water traffic, a channel may or may not be marked by buoys.

**Chart**—A hydrographic or marine map on which is projected a portion of water and, usually, adjacent or included land intended for the use of navigators.

**Chine**—A longitudinal member of a flat or Vee-bottomed vessel, laying along the bilge between the bottom and top sides.

**Chock**—A heavy wooden or metal fitting secured on a deck or pier and having jaws through which lines or cables may be passed; also, a block or wedge of wood or other material used to secure cargo in the holds so that it will not work loose.

**Circuit**—The path of current flow in an electric wiring system. Also the path taken by liquids or gases under various conditions of guidance or pressure.

**Class**—A term used to designate a group of boats built to identical design and specifications.

**Cleats**—Items of hardware to which lines are fastened.

**Clerk cycle**—A term used with reference to a two-stroke cycle engine.

**Clinker**—A form of boat building in which the external planks or steel plates are put on so that one edge of each overlaps the edge of the plank or steel plate next adjacent. Also termed "lapstreak."

**Clockwise rotation**—Rotation in the same direction as the hands of a clock.

**Coaming**—Raised pieces of wood or iron around a hatchway or cockpit to prevent water from running below.

**Cockpit**—A space lower than the rest of the deck which affords easy access to the cabin and forms a sheltered place.

**Coil**—A series of rings laid down by a rope or cable to facilitate instant usage.

**Compass**—An instrument for determining bearings and courses by indicating the true north. The circular card attached to the mariners compass are marked by the thirty-two points and the 360 degrees of a circle.

**Compression**—Act of compressing the working fluid within the cylinder as the piston moves from bottom to top with all valves closed.

**Compression ratio**—A ratio expressing the extent to which a fuel or air charge is compressed. It is the ratio of the total volume of the piston displacement plus the clearance space to the volume of the clearance space and is found as follows:

$$\frac{\text{Piston displacement} + \text{Clearance space}}{\text{Clearance space}} = \text{Compression ratio}$$

**Connecting rod**—That part which connects the piston to the crankshaft of a gas engine. It changes the reciprocating motion of the piston into rotary motion at the crankshaft.

**Connecting-rod bearing**—The bearing in the lower end of the connecting rod by means of which it is connected to the crankshaft.

**Contact points**—Interrupting contacts in a distributor or magneto whose function it is to induce a high tension current in the ignition system.

**Course**—The direction steered by a boat, usually expressed in degrees.

**Cowling**—A removable metal covering employed for protective purposes.

**Craft**—A general term referring to small or medium-sized boats.

**Crankcase**—The lower part of an engine structure surrounding the working parts.

**Crankshaft**—The main shaft of an engine forming the cranks for converting the reciprocating motion of the piston into rotary motion of the shaft.

**Crankshaft counterbalance**—A series of counterweights, forged as a unit with the crankshaft section or manufactured separately, whose function it is to offset the reciprocating weight of the piston and rod assembly and thus to provide a dampening effect on the engine impulses.

**Cruiser**—A power boat equipped with cabin, permanent berths, fixed plumbing, and cooking arrangements, etc., necessary for living aboard.

**Cycle**—The complete series of events which occur when the original position of all moving parts are restored and recurrence begins. In a four-stroke cycle engine this requires four strokes of the piston. In a two-stroke cycle engine only two strokes are required to complete the cycle.

**Cylinder**—A circular bore in the engine block in which the piston moves, and in which combustion takes place. The volume of the cylinder may be found by multiplying its cross-sectional area by its depth.

**Cylinder block**—The single casting containing the cylinders of an internal-combustion engine.

**Cylinder bore**—The part of the cylinder in which the piston moves.

**Cylinder head**—That part which covers and seals the end of the cylinder.

**Cylinder liner**—A cylindrical sleeve that is pressed into the cylinder block and in which the piston moves. This liner or sleeve provides a readily renewable wearing surface for the cylinder.

**Dagger board**—A form of centerboard in small boats.

**Dead ahead**—Directly ahead, as in a straight line with the keel.

**Dead center**—The extreme upper or lower position of the crankshaft throw at which point the piston is not moving in any direction. The dead center is commonly abbreviated "D.C."

**Deck**—The floorlike platform of a horizontal section or compartment of a vessel.

**Degree**—A unit for measurement of angularity of a circle; one degree equals 1/360 part of a circle.

**Dinghy**—An open boat; a rowboat carried on a ship.

**Direct current**—A term employed to designate a non-ripple or continuous electric current flow, such as that emanating from a storage battery.

**Displacement**—The volume or weight of water displaced by a floating body as by a boat, the weight of the displaced water being equal to that of the displacing body.

**Dock**—A landing pier for boats, suitable for handling of freight and passengers.

**Dogs**—Small, bent metal fittings used to secure watertight doors, hatch covers, etc.

**Draft**—The depth of hull from water line to lowest point of keel.

**Drift**—The deviation of a boat from its set course, caused by the currents.

**Dry rot**—Decay in wood caused by fungus infection.

**Ease off**—To slack up or to pay out line.

**Ease the rudder**—An order to decrease the rudder angle.

**Eddy**—Water running contrary to the main current, especially water having a circulatory direction. Eddies occur especially on the lee side of an object, as a boulder, a cliff, or a building.

**Electrolyte**—A mixture of distilled water and sulphuric acid used in storage batteries.

**Electromagnet**—A core of magnetic material, such as soft iron, surrounded wholly or in part by a coil of wire through which an electric current is passed to magnetize the core. An example of this is the solenoid magnet used in certain starting motor circuits.

**Engine**—A form of power-producing machine, such as an internal or external-combustion engine. An example of an internal-combustion engine is the gas and Diesel types, whereas a steam engine is of the external-combustion type.

**Even keel**—Position of a boat when in perfect balance.

**Expansion period**—That portion of the engine cycle during which the combustion gasses expand and exert pressure on the piston; also called power stroke.

**Fake down**—To coil down a rope so that each coil of rope overlaps the next one underneath in such a way that the rope is clear for running.

**Fall**—Commonly the entire length of rope used with blocks to comprise a tackle; strictly speaking, the end to which the power is applied.

**False keel**—An additional keel attached to the main keel to increase the boat's stability.

**Fantail**—The overhanging stern section of a vessel, from the sternport aft.

**Fast**—A mooring rope, hawser or chain; called according to its position, a bow, head, quarter, breast or stern fast; also a post on a pier or on shore around which hawsers are passed in mooring.

**Fathom**—A measure of length containing six feet, or the space to which a man can extend his arms. It is used chiefly in measuring depth of water by soundings, length of cables, cordage, etc.

**Fender**—A guard or device of wood, rubber, canvas or rope laid over the side to protect a boat from damage when landing, or when tied up at pier.

**Flat boat**—A boat with flat bottom and square ends, used for transportation of bulky freight, especially in shallow waters.

**Float level**—In carburetors a pre-determined height of fuel in the fuel bowl.

**Floors**—Short timbers bolted across keel to which frames are attached.

**Flywheel**—A heavy wheel fitted to the crankshaft by means of which speed fluctuation of an engine is absorbed or moderated.

**Foot-pound**—A unit of work being equal to the work done in raising one pound against the force of gravity the height of one foot.

**Fore**—Opposite to aft or after referring to the forward part of the boat.

**Fore and aft**—General direction of the keel or parallel to the boat's center line.

**Forward**—Toward the bow.

**Foul**—To become entangled, to come into collision; as, one boat fouled another.

**Foul anchor**—The anchor when it hooks, or is entangled with another anchor, or with a cable, or wreck, or when the slack cable is entangled.

**Four-stroke cycle engine**—An engine wherein an explosion takes place for every other revolution of the crankshaft, there being four piston strokes to the cycle. The various strokes are termed: (1) Admission (intake); (2) Compression; (3) Power, and (4) Exhaust.

**Frame**—The skeleton structure forming the ribs or framework of a vessel.

**Freeboard**—The distance between the water line and deck of a vessel.

**Fuel**—A general expression for the oil-gasoline mixture used in outboard motors.

**Fuel pump**—A pump to feed the fuel from the gas tank to the carburetor of an engine.

**Fuse**—A circuit interrupting device designed to prevent damage in case of short circuit and overload in a wiring system.

**Galley**—The kitchen or cooking compartment of a vessel.

**Gasket**—Any ring or washer providing a packing or seal between two metal surfaces.

**Gear**—A general term for accessories used aboard a vessel, such as ropes, chains, pulleys, etc.

**Gear case**—A case enclosing gearing to exclude water and foreign particles. In an outboard motor the gear case is the lower unit.

**Gram**—A unit of weight in the cgs system equal to 1/1000 of a kilogram or 1/454 of a pound.

**Grapnel**—A small anchor with several arms used for dragging.

**Ground tackle**—All gear used in anchoring.

**Gudgeon**—A metallic eye bolted to the sternpost on which the rudder is hung.

**Gunwale**—The side of a boat; the upper edge or railing.

**Guy**—A line used to steady and support a spar in a horizontal or inclined position.

**Gypsy**—The drum or windlass on which line or cable is turned.

**Hand lead**—A lead weighing from 7 to 14 pounds secured to a lead line and used for measuring the depth of water and taking a sample of the bottom.

**Hard over**—An order to put the rudder as far over to the side designated as possible.

**Hatch**—A framed opening through the deck or cabin top leading to the area below.

**Hawser**—A large rope for towing, mooring, securing ship at a dock, etc.

**Headway**—The forward motion of a boat.

**Heave**—To draw or pull, to throw a line, to cause the boat to come into position, as when docking.

**Heave the lead**—To take soundings with a line or lead.

**Heave ho**—To pull hard, a cry of sailors when hauling up anchor.

**Heave to**—To bring the vessel's head or stern into the wind or sea and hold her there by the use of rudder and engines.

**Heaving line**—A light line weighted at one end, to heave ashore, where a heavy cable or hawser is attached as an assist when docking a vessel.

**Helm**—The apparatus by means of which a ship is steered, comprising rudder, tiller, wheel, etc. commonly the tiller or wheel alone.

**Helmsman**—The person who steers.

**High tension**—A term used to indicate high voltage such as that induced in the secondary winding of an ignition coil.

**Hitch**—A temporary knot or noose by which one rope is fastened around another rope, spar, or post, so as to be readily undone.

**Hold**—The interior of a vessel in which cargo is stored.

**Horsepower**—Doing work at the rate of 33,000 foot pounds per minute or 550 foot pounds per second.

**Hull**—The frame or body of a vessel exclusive of masts, sails and rigging.

**Hydrometer**—A device used to measure the specific gravity of a liquid, commonly used for determination of the state or charge in a battery.

**Hydroplane**—A fast lightweight boat with a flat bottom designed primarily for racing.

**Idling**—An engine is said to be idling when it is running without load.

**Ignition distributor**—An engine motivated switching device timed to conduct electrical impulses in the proper order to the spark plugs of ignition of the fuel charge.

**Ignition system**—The means of igniting the fuel in the engine cylinders; this includes the battery, the ammeter (when used), the ignition switch, coil, cam and breaker points. There are two types of ignition systems used to provide ignition in a gas engine as: (1) Battery ignition and (2) Magneto ignition.

**Ignition timing**—The crank angle relative to top dead-center at which the spark occurs in a gas engine.

**Indicated horsepower**—Abbreviated IHP. The horsepower developed within the cylinders of an engine as ascertained by the pressure recorded on an indicator diagram.

**Induction coil**—Also termed ignition coil. A device forming a part of an ignition system necessary to produce a spark to ignite the fuel charge.

**Inertia**—The property of a body to resist changes in its condition from rest to motion.

**Inland rules of the road**—The rules enacted by Congress governing the navigation of the inland waters of the United States.

**Intake manifold**—The pipe or tube which conducts the fuel mixture from the carburetor to the engine cylinder.

**Internal-combustion engine**—A heat engine in which the pressure necessary to produce motion of the mechanism results from the ignition or burning of a fuel-air mixture within the cylinder; thus a gas engine is an internal-combustion machine.

**Jacket**—An outer casing forming a space around the engine cylinders to permit the circulation of water for cooling purposes.

**Journal**—That part of the crankshaft which is supported by the main-bearing shell.

**Kedge**—A small anchor used to move a vessel. It is placed ahead or astern, and the vessel is hauled up to it.

**Keel**—A longitudinal member of the boat's hull, along its extreme bottom to which its ribs are secured.

**Keelson**—A longitudinal structure incorporated with the framing of a boat to contribute stiffness and prevent local deformations.

**Kilowatt**—A unit of electrical power equal to 1000 watts or 1.34 horsepower. Its electrical symbol is kw.

**Kilowatt-hour**—A unit measurement of electrical energy equal to 1000 watt-hours. Its electrical symbol is kwh.

**Kit boat**—A boat to be assembled from carefully designed parts. Complete instructions accompanied by sealed drawings are usually furnished with each kit.

**Knot**—A unit of speed equivalent to one nautical mile or 6080.20 feet per hour. A land mile is 5280 feet. If a vessel runs with a speed of eight nautical miles per hour her speed is said to to eight knots (speed per hour being understood). Also an interlacement of the parts of one or more ropes.

**Land**—The raised concentric sections of a piston on either side of the ring grooves.

**Landfall**—Sighting or making land when at sea. When the point of land is sighted where the navigator had calculated, he is said to make a good landfall.

**Lands**—The portion of a piston between the grooves carrying the piston rings.

**Lanyard**—A short piece of rope or line for fastening articles in boats.

**Lap**—A racing term meaning a complete circuit of a prescribed course.

**Lapping**—The method of producing exceedingly smooth and highly accurate surfaces by rubbing with oil and a fine abrasive powder.

**Lash**—To bind with a rope, cord or chain so as to fasten; to lash something to a spar.

**Launch**—The movement of a vessel from land into the water, especially the sliding into the water on ways in which it is built.

**Lead line**—A line secured to the lead and marked to be used in soundings.

**Lean**—Pertaining to a motor fuel containing too large a percentage of air, opposite to rich.

**Lee**—The side opposite to that against which the wind blows; a sheltered location.

**Leeboard**—A board fitted to the side of a flat-bottomed craft to prevent its drifting leeward.

**Leeward**—The part or side of the boat opposite to the direction from which the wind is blowing.

**Lighter**—A small vessel used for loading and discharging vessels lying at anchor.

**Line**—A rope used in towing, or hauling something aboard, or in mooring to a dock or wharf, as bow line, stern line, etc. Also, a hose or a pipe, as an air line.

**Liner**—The inner bore or sleeve of a cylinder in which the piston moves; and which is replaceable.

**Linkage**—A system of links or bars joined together to transmit power.

**List**—To incline, or lean to one side. Said of a ship as she lists to port.

**Liter**—A measurement of volume in the cgs system. One liter contains one cubic decimeter or .264 gallon. The weight of one liter of water at its greatest density is approximately one kilogram.

**Log**—An apparatus for measuring the speed of a boat, hence, the record of the rate of speed, or of the daily progress.

**Log book**—A book containing the record of hour-to-hour happenings when afloat.

**Log line**—A line to which the log apparatus is attached.

**Loran**—An electronic navigational system by means of which the location of various land stations are obtained.

**Lower unit**—That part of an outboard motor located below the powerhead.

**Magneto**—An electrical device used to generate electricity for ignition of gas engines. A magneto-ignition system differs from that of battery ignition mainly in that the magneto is operated by the engine itself.

**Marina**—A dock or basin providing secure moorings for power boats, yachts and launches. Marinas are usually equipped for servicing and repairs of boats and machinery.

**Mechanical equivalent of heat**—The relation between the values of the unit of heat and the unit of mechanical work. It has been found experimentally that one British Thermal Unit (BTU) equals approximately 778 foot-pounds of work.

**Metacenter**—If a vertical line is drawn through the center of gravity of a body floating in equilibrium in a liquid, and a second vertical line is drawn through the center of buoyancy (center of gravity of the displaced liquid) when the body is slightly displaced from its equilibrium position, the two lines meet at a point called the metacenter.

**Midships**—The center or broadest part of a boat.

**Misfiring**—Said of an internal-combustion engine when its explosive charge fails to ignite at the proper time.

**Mooring**—The place or position of a moored vessel.

**Mooring buoy**—An anchored buoy fitted to receive a boat's mooring line or hawser.

**Mushroom anchor**—A mushroom-shaped anchor with the shank extending from the concave side.

**Navigable**—A term applied to a waterway permitting the passage of boats.

**Navigation**—The science or art of conducting ships or other vessels from one place to another, including more especially, the method of determining a ship's position, course, distance covered, etc., on the surface of any body of water by applying the principle of geometry and astronomy.

**Navigator**—One who navigates or sails; especially one who directs the course of a ship; or one skillful in the art of navigation.

**Nose heavy**—Said of a boat with a tendency of the bow to submerge, or dig in to the water an excessive amount.

**Oar**—A device for propelling or steering a boat, being a slender piece of wood made with a handle at one end, and a broad blade at the other, working as a lever. In rowing the fulcrum is at rest and is called the oarlock or rowlock.

**Oarsman**—One who uses oars for propelling a boat; a rower.

**Offshore wind**—Wind blowing off or away from the land.

**Outboard**—Outside of the boat's hull; situated outboard, as an outboard rigging, or an outboard motor.

**Outboard motor**—A small or medium-size internal-combustion engine, with the propeller integrally attached, and designed to be temporarily attached to the stern of a boat.

**Outcarry**—To carry more sail than designated, also, to outsail.

**Painter**—A line by which a small boat is towed or made fast.

**Pawl**—A pivoted tongue or hinged bolt, adapted to fall into notches, or interdental spaces, on another part so as to permit motion in one direction only, as in a capstan or windlass.

**Pay out**—To let out cable or cast off on the line.

**Pennant**—A long, narrow piece of bunting carried at the masthead.

**Pier**—A structure extending into navigable water for use as a landing place for boats; a promenade or to protect or form a harbor.

**Ping**—Usually referring to engine noises of uncommon class, and caused by improper operation.

**Plank**—Individual board used in covering side, section or side of boat deck.

**Plowing**—A condition caused by improper design or loading of boat resulting in bow digging.

**Port**—The left side of a boat looking from the stern towards the bow.

**Piston**—A cylindrical part of an engine fitted into the cylinder bore, and which transmits the force of explosion to the connecting rod and crank.

**Piston clearance**—The distance between the piston and its cylinder cover at either end of the stroke.

**Piston deflector**—A bar or convex obstruction cast into the piston head of a two-stroke cycle engine to prevent escape of the fresh fuel mixture into the exhaust.

**Piston displacement**—The volume of air or gas displaced by the piston in a single stroke.

**Piston head**—The closed part of the piston above the rings.

**Piston lands**—The parts of the piston between the rings.

**Piston pin**—A stud or pin which forms a journal to which the piston rod is connected; also called wrist pin.

**Piston rings**—Split packing rings placed in the upper part of the piston to prevent leakage between the piston and cylinder wall.

**Piston skirt**—The part of a piston below the piston-ring groove.

**Piston stroke**—The movement of the piston from one end of the cylinder to the other. The piston stroke is equal to twice the throw of the crankshaft.

**Porthole**—An opening in a ship's side; a port.

**Pre-ignition**—Ignition of the fuel charge before the compression part of the engine cycle is completed.

**Primary winding**—That winding of an ignition coil having the smaller number of turns, and which conducts the low-tension current.

**Propeller**—Any device for propelling a craft through a fluid, such as water or air; especially a device having blades, which when mounted on a power driven shaft, produce a thrust by their action on the fluid.

**Protractor**—An instrument for measuring angles, commonly used in solution of navigational problems.

**Purchase**—Any rigging consisting of two or more blocks used to hoist heavy weights.

**Quarter**—Part of a vessel's side near the stern.

**Quay**—A cargo discharging wharf which is parallel with the basin or harbor edge, and has water on one side.

**Radio compass**—A direction finder used for navigational purposes.

**Radio compass station**—A station on land in which a radio compass is used to determine the direction of ship stations. By such determinations using two or more stations, and triangulation, the position of the ship may be found.

**Rake**—The angle of the bow or stern of a boat in relation to the water.

**Reciprocating**—A back-and-forth movement, such as the action of the piston in an engine cylinder.

**Relay**—A relay is a device that is operative by a variation in the conditions of one electric circuit to effect the operation of other devices in the same or another electric circuit. In automotive type gas engines, voltage and current regulation is normally obtained by relay action.

**Remote control**—Operation of boat from a central remote location, by means of mechanical and/or electrical devices.

**Ribs**—The frame around which a boat is built.

**Rich**—Pertaining to a motor fuel containing too small a percentage of air. Opposite to lean.

**Ride**—To lie at anchor; to ride out a storm.

**Rigging**—A general term for tackle and gears, as well as ropes, cables and blocks, etc.

**Rips**—A term used for short steep waves caused by cross currents, tidal effects, etc.

**Round bottom**—A boat designed with a round bottom, partly or through its entire length.

**RPM**—Abbreviation for revolutions per minute of a shaft or rotating machine part.

**Rowboat**—A small boat designed for the use of oars as a propellant.

**Rudder**—A flat piece of wood or metal attached upright to the sternpost by hinges or gudgeons so that it can be turned, as by a tiller, causing the vessel's head to turn in the same direction, because of the resistance offered to the water by the rudder.

**Rudder indicator**—An electrical or mechanical device located at a steering station to indicate the angle of the rudder with relation to the keel line of the vessel.

**Rudderpost**—The vertical post in the stern of a vessel upon which the rudder is supported.

**Rules of the road**—Regulations enacted to prevent collisions between vessels.

**Runabout**—A small outboard boat designed for sport and pleasure.

**Scale**—A hard incrustation deposited on the inside of a vessel in which water is heated, such as in an engine cooling system.

**Screw**—The propeller.

**Sea buoy**—A large buoy marking the seaward approach to a channel.

**Seal**—Any device to prevent the passage or return of oil, gas or air. Also used to describe a method of packing around a crankshaft of an engine to prevent oil from leaking out of the crankcase.

**Seam**—The space between adjacent planks in wooden vessels.

**Seaworthy**—Capable of putting to sea and meeting usual sea conditions; refers to a vessel that can stand heavy seas.

**Secure**—To make fast; order given on completion of operation.

**Sheer**—The curve or sweep of a vessel's deck.

**Shaft**—A round section having one or more journals on which it rests and revolves, as the shaft of a gas engine.

**Shim**—A thin piece of metal to take up wear as between two parts of a journal or bearing.

**Ship**—A vessel capable of carrying boats and having space for cargo and passengers.

**Skiff**—A boat with centerboard and light enough to be rowed.

**Sound**—To measure the depth of water with a lead line or sounding machine.

**Spark**—A small arc of short duration produced by an electric current.

**Spark gap**—The air space between two metallic points in a spark plug through which the spark jumps.

**Spark ignition**—The operation or method of firing the explosive charge by means of a spark in an internal-combustion engine.

**Spark plug**—A cylindrical device fitting into the cylinder head of an internal-combustion engine, carrying two electrodes separated by an air gap across which the high tension current from the ignition system discharges, forming the spark for combustion.

**Standby**—To be near on hand to help; an order to be prepared to execute; an order or maneuver.

**Starboard**—The right side of a boat looking forward, indicated at night by a green light.

**Stern**—The after part of a boat.

**Stern line**—A mooring line leading from the stern of a vessel.

**Stern post**—A vertical bar of timber joined to and erected on the after part of the keel.

**Stow**—To fill or load a vessel with cargo; also to pack or put in place aboard ship.

**Strake**—Any plank running fore and aft on the sides or outside the bottom of a boat.

**Strand**—To run aground; a number of yarns twisted together, which in turn may be twisted into a rope.

**Stroke**—The linear distance traveled by one motion of an engine piston.

**Swamp**—To cause a boat to be filled with water; to sink, by being filled with water.

**Swell**—Undulations of the sea having greater length than ordinary waves, usually caused by the wind of a distant storm.

**Tarpaulin**—A heavy, treated canvas used as a protective covering.

**Taut**—Tightly drawn; not slack.

**Thermostat**—An automatic device for regulating temperature by opening or closing a valve to regulate the flow of cooling water in an engine. Also used in numerous household appliances and for protection of electric motors. All thermostats utilize either the differential expansion of solids, liquids or gases subjected to heat or the principle of the thermocouple.

**Third brush**—As applied to the electrical system of an engine, this refers to an auxiliary brush used for the purpose of field excitation. It is so placed on the commutator in relation to the main brushes that it serves to regulate or govern the current output of the generator.

**Throw**—In a gas engine, it is the distance between the center of the crankshaft main bearing and the center of the connecting-rod journal.

**Thwarts**—Cross-seats in small boats.

**Tide**—The inflow and outflow of water caused by the gravitational influence of the moon.

**Tiller**—The stick or lever attached to the rudder by which the boat is steered.

**Timing chain**—A chain connecting the crankshaft and camshaft of an engine.

**Timing gears**—The gear train through which the crankshaft drives the camshaft and accompanying accessories necessary for the correct valve timing of engine.

**Topsides**—Sides of hull above water.

**Torque**—The twisting or rotary effect produced by an outboard motor. That which produces rotary motion.

**Tow**—To pull a vessel, barge or other craft through the water by means of line or cable.

**Transom**—The board or boards forming the after end of a more or less square-sterned boat. In outboard boats, it is that part of the boat from which the motor is hung.

**Trim**—The way a boat floats in the water; the difference in draft at the bow of a boat from that of the stern.

**Trough**—The hollow between two waves; opposite of crest.

**Tug**—A small sturdily built, powerful boat fitted for towing purposes.

**Turnbuckle**—A metal device consisting of thread and screw capable of being set up or slacked back, used for setting up rigging.

**Two-stroke cycle engine**—An engine wherein an explosion takes place for every revolution of the crank shaft; there being two piston strokes to the cycle. The strokes are termed: (1) Compression and (2) Expansion.

**Underway**—A boat is underway when it is moving through the water, not made fast and not aground.

**Veer**—To pay out cable or line; to change direction of a boat in reference to wind.

**Wake**—A boat's track or trailer left astern.

**Water line**—The line painted on the side of a vessel at the water's edge to indicate the proper trim.

**Wharf**—An installation for loading or discharging vessels; particularly a platform of timber, stone or concrete against which vessels may be secured to load or discharge.

**Winch**—A hoisting device secured to the deck used to haul lines when docking, loading or unloading. Also a device used on boat trailer to facilitate loading.

**Windward**—The direction from which the wind is blowing. The windward, or weather side of a boat is that toward the wind.

**Yacht**—Any one of various types of relatively small vessels, characteristically with sharp prow and graceful lines, and ordinarily privately owned and used for pleasure.

**Yaw**—To steer badly, zigzagging back and forth across an intended course.

This fiberglass fisherman's boat is powered by an 85 horsepower outboard by *Johnson*. It gets you to your fishing location in a hurry.

Courtesy Johnson Motors, Div. of Outboard Marine Corp.

Courtesy Mercury Marine, Div. of Brunswick Corp.

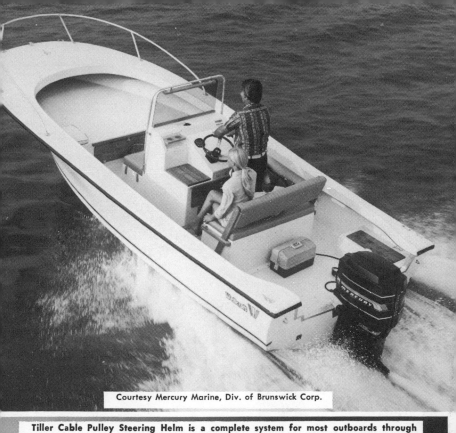

Courtesy Mercury Marine, Div. of Brunswick Corp.

Tiller Cable Pulley Steering Helm is a complete system for most outboards through 40 HP (single engine) and 25 HP dual engine installations.

Courtesy OMC.

The sportcanoe is everything-for-everybody. It is very versatile for family fun, fishermen, and duck hunters as well as friends. It can be put on the car top carrier and use up to a 5 HP motor. If necessary it can be rowed easily.

Courtesy Grumman

This beauty is powered with a six-cylinder *Kiekhaefer Mercury* engine rated at 125 HP and develops 4800-5200 RPM at full throttle. This engine features the new *Thunderbolt* ignition system.

Courtesy Mercury Marine, Div. of Brunswick Corp.

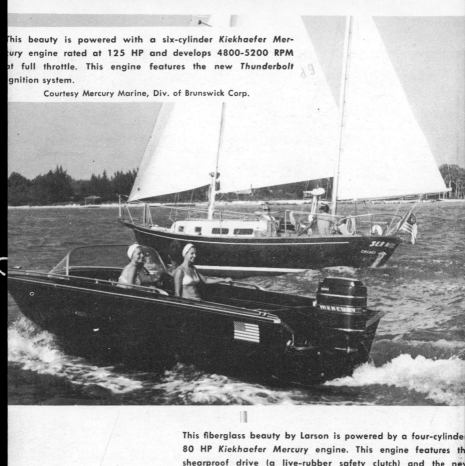

This fiberglass beauty by Larson is powered by a four-cylinder 80 HP *Kiekhaefer Mercury* engine. This engine features the shearproof drive (a live-rubber safety clutch) and the new pointless *Thunderbolt* ignition system.

Courtesy Mercury Marine, Div. of Brunswick Corp.

**Two fiberglass boat designs.**
Courtesy Mercury Marine, Div. of Brunswick Corp.

# Index

# Audel BOOKS *practical reading for profit*

## APPLIANCES

### Air Conditioning    (23159)

Domestic, commercial, and automobile air conditioning fully explained in easily-understood language. Troubleshooting charts aid in making diagnosis and repair of system troubles.

### Commercial Refrigeration    (23195)

**Installation, operation, and repair of commercial refrigeration systems.** Included are ice-making plants, locker plants, grocery and supermarket refrigerated display cases, etc. Trouble charts aid in the diagnosis and repair of defective systems.

### Air Conditioning and Refrigeration Library—2 Vols.    (23196)

### Home Appliance Servicing—3rd Edition    (23214)

**A practical "How-To-Do-It" book for electric & gas servicemen, mechanics & dealers.** Covers principles, servicing and repairing of home appliances. Tells how to locate troubles, make repairs, reassemble and connect, wiring diagrams and testing methods. Tells how to fix electric refrigerators, washers, ranges, toasters, ironers, broilers, dryers, vacuum sweepers, fans, and other appliances.

### Home Refrigeration and Air Conditioning (23133)

Covers basic principles, servicing, operation, and repair of modern household refrigerators and air conditioners. Automotive air conditioners are also included. Troubleshooting charts aid in trouble diagnosis. **A gold mine of essential facts for engineers, servicemen, and users.**

## AUTOMOTIVE

### Automobile Guide    (23192)

**New revised edition.** Practical reference for auto mechanics, servicemen, trainees, and owners. Explains theory, construction, and servicing of modern domestic motorcars. FEATURES: All parts of an automobile—engines—pistons—rings—connecting rods—crankshafts—valves—cams—timing—cooling systems—Fuel-feed systems—carbureators — automatic choke — transmissions — clutches — universals — propeller shafts—dierentials—rear axles—running gear—brakes—wheel alignment—steering gear—tires—lubrication—ignition systems—generators and alternators—starters—lighting systems—batteries—air conditioning—cruise controls—emission control systems.

### Auto Engine Tune-up    (23181)

**New revised edition.** This popular how-to-do-it guide shows exactly how to tune your car engine for extra power, gas economy, and fewer costly repairs. New emission-control systems are explained along with the proper methods for correcting faults and making adjustments to keep these systems in top operating condition.

### Automotive Library—2 Vols.    (23198)

### Diesel Engine Manual    (23199)

**A practical treatise on the theory, operation and maintenance of modern Diesel engines.** Explains Diesel principles—valves—timing—fuel pumps—pistons and rings—cylinders—lubrication—cooling system—fuel oil—engine indicator—governors—engine reversing—answers on operation—calculations. AN IMPORTANT GUIDE FOR ENGINEERS, OPERATORS, STUDENTS.

## Gas Engine Manual    (23061)

A completely practical book covering the construction, operation and repair of all types of modern gas engines. Part I covers gas-engine principles; engine parts; auxiliaries; timing methods; ignition systems. Part II covers troubleshootng, adjustment and repairs.

## Auto Body Repair for the Do-it-yourselfer (23238)

Another popular Audel paper back book covering auto body repair and body maintenance. This book shows the do-it-yourself car owner how to save money by following the easy detailed step-by-step procedure of how to use touch-up paint; how to prevent rust from spreading; how to repair rust spots and dents by using various body fillers. It also covers in great detail the repair of vinyl tops, cleaning upholstery and removing scratches from window glass.

## BUILDING AND MAINTENANCE

### Answers on Blueprint Reading    (23041)

Covers all types of blueprint reading for mechanics and builders. The man who can read blueprints is in line for a better job. This book gives you the secret language, step by step in easy stages. NO OTHER TRADE BOOK LIKE IT.

### Building Construction and Design    (23180)

A completely revised and rewritten version of Audel's **Architects and Builders Guide.** New illustrations and extended coverage of material makes this treatment of the subject more valuable than ever. Anyone connected in any way with the building industry will profit from the information contained in this book.

### Building Maintenance    (23140)

A comprehensive book on the practical aspects of building maintenance. Chapters are included on: painting and decorating; plumbing and pipe fitting; carpentry; calking and glazing; concrete and masonry; roofing; sheet metal; electrical maintenance; air conditioning and refrigeration; insect and rodent control; heating maintenance management; cutodial practices: A BOOK FOR BUILDING OWNERS, MANAGERS, AND MAINTENANCE PERSONNEL.

### Gardening & Landscaping (23229)

A comprehensive guide for the homeowner, industrial, municipal, and estate grounds-keepers. Information on proper care of annual and perennial flowers; various house plants; greenhouse design and construction; insect and rodent control; complete lawn care; shrubs and trees; and maintenance of walks, roads, and traffic areas. Various types of maintenance equipment are also discussed.

### Carpenters & Builders Library—4 Vols.    (23244)

A practical illustrated trade assistant on modern construction for carpenters, builders, and all woodworkers. Explains in practical, concise language and illustrations all the principles, advances and short cuts based on modern practice. How to calculate various jobs.

Vol. 1—(23240)—Tools, steel square, saw filing, joinery, cabinets.
Vol. 2—(23241)—Mathematics, plans, specifications, estimates.
Vol. 3—(23242)—House and roof framing, laying out, foundations.
Vol. 4—(23243)—Doors, windows, stairs, millwork, painting.

### Carpentry and Building    (23142)

Answers to the problems encountered in today's building trades. The actual questions asked of an architect by carpenters and builders are answered in this book. No apprentice or journeyman carpenter should be without the help this book can offer.

### Do-It-Yourself Encyclopedia    (23207)

An all-in-one home repair and project guide for all do-it-yourselfers. Packed with step-by-step plans, thousands of photos, helpful charts. A really authentic, truly monumental, home-repair and home-project guide.